CALGARY PUBLIC LIBRARY

SEP ⁻ 2013

from
scratch

from scratch

INSIDE THE
FOOD NETWORK

ALLEN SALKIN

G. P. PUTNAM'S SONS

New York

G. P. PUTNAM'S SONS
Publishers Since 1838
Published by the Penguin Group
Penguin Group (USA) LLC
375 Hudson Street
New York, New York 10014

USA · Canada · UK · Ireland · Australia
New Zealand · India · South Africa · China

penguin.com
A Penguin Random House Company

Copyright © 2013 by Allen Salkin
Penguin supports copyright. Copyright fuels creativity, encourages diverse voices, promotes free speech, and creates a vibrant culture. Thank you for buying an authorized edition of this book and for complying with copyright laws by not reproducing, scanning, or distributing any part of it in any form without permission. You are supporting writers and allowing Penguin to continue to publish books for every reader.

Library of Congress Cataloging-in-Publication Data

Salkin, Allen.
From scratch : inside the Food Network / Allen Salkin.
p.   cm.
ISBN 978-0-399-15932-9
1. Food Network (Firm)—History.   2. Food Network (Firm)—Biography.
3. Television cooking shows—United States—History.   4. Cooking, American—History.
5. Food—Social aspects—United States—History.   6. Food habits—United States—History.   I. Title.
PN1992.92.F66S25   2013   2013025095
384.55'22—dc23

Printed in the United States of America
1   3   5   7   9   10   8   6   4   2

BOOK DESIGN BY NICOLE LAROCHE

While the author has made every effort to provide accurate telephone numbers, Internet addresses, and other contact information at the time of publication, neither the publisher nor the author assumes any responsibility for errors, or for changes that occur after publication. Further, the publisher does not have any control over and does not assume any responsibility for author or third-party websites or their content.

Dedicated to Jay Salkin.
He enjoyed a good meal.

CONTENTS

Roll Over

Before there was a Food Network, there was no Food Network, or even a world in which it was obvious that there ought to be a Food Network.

In the early 1980s, a handful of "celebrity chefs"—many of them connected to a miraculous restaurant in Berkeley, California, called Chez Panisse—rose to prominence with a revolutionary new philosophy of local, high-quality ingredients, prepared inventively. Like-minded chefs—Jeremiah Tower, Charlie Trotter, Wolfgang Puck—established themselves in gourmet pockets of Southern California, Boston, Chicago, and Manhattan, with mind-tickling innovations and fusion cuisine, such as gourmet pizza topped with duck sausage and chicken sun-dried tomato spring rolls. But by the end of the decade, many trend-watchers were pronouncing the celebrity chef fad as over as neon shoelaces and big hair. These brilliant chefs may have been appreciated by a smart set of food lovers, but it was unclear if the wider culture would continue to care.

Well-known TV chefs were few, among them Julia Child, Martin Yan of *Yan Can Cook*, and Jeff Smith of *The Frugal Gourmet*, all of whom appeared on PBS stations. Some of them sold a lot of cookbooks, but the fact that they were on not-for-profit television conveyed the impression that there was no profit and little impact to be had. For the most part, they were relegated to stirring and tasting in spartan kitchen sets on weekends, except on those occasions when they were invited for six-minute cooking segments on *Good Morning America*. Even PBS wasn't much interested in adding more cooking to its lineup.

Few TV producers toiled in the ghetto of food shows, and by all practical measures, no food television industry existed. There were no talent agents focused on food talent, scant studio spaces fit for cooking, few product endorsements, and no massive food festivals attracting tens of thousands of fans.

It is past cliché these days to refer to chefs as "the new rock stars." The idea was born, as you will see, at the same time Food Network was. But the comparison runs deeper than the phrase implies. It took mid-century improvements in radio technology, recording, and television, plus a baby boom and a burgeoning middle class, to create the rock star. When the blues were electrified into rock 'n' roll, a new generation heard something amazing, exciting, and true just as the entertainment industry was able to deliver it. So, too, appetites were awakened in the 1990s, when the expansion of cable TV and the Internet met a food subculture that was ready to find a hungry audience. When I was growing up in the 1970s and '80s, I had no idea that it was possible to make cookies at home except by opening a box of cookie mix or slicing a frozen roll of Pillsbury dough. Then one day I was on a high school trip with a friend whose mother had made him chocolate chip cookies "from scratch."

"What do you mean?" I asked.

"She used flour and sugar and butter."

My brain exploded. Of course, it shouldn't have. Nestlé had been printing a recipe for Toll House cookies on bags of chocolate chips since the 1930s. But this knowledge had been lost in my house and in a lot of others. I don't think we had flour. We had Bisquick. Those from-scratch cookies were the best thing I had ever tasted. Thank you, Mrs. Merriman.

There was no Food Network to overcome the lack of food knowledge in my house. On TV, I watched cartoons after school or, when we got cable, old movies. I certainly would have watched Food Network, though I can't tell you why I was starved for such knowledge. A yearning for something authentic and true in an era when the noisy ideals of a previous g-g-generation were hitting a wall? A world where the government proposed ketchup as a vegetable for school lunches? I don't know why I was hungry, but I was. We all were, it turned out. When I went to UC Berkeley and was surrounded by the flourishing food culture of the late 1980s, within a year I was perfecting my guacamole and baking my own bread.

By 1996, around 31,000 people over the age of eighteen were watching Food Network (the term used by those who work there; outsiders call it The Food Network) at any given time, and about a third of those viewers were from households with children. In New Hyde Park, New York, a shy teenager named Todd Mitgang was watching. His mother never used any green but iceberg lettuce and every meat was prepared the same way—a shake of salt, a shake of garlic powder, and under the broiler. The best restaurant he had ever been to was a Benihana; he ordered Rocky's Choice. The stir-fry was a revolution to him—it combined steak and chicken. Over the next few years, he watched Food Network after school, and was spellbound as Sara Moulton demonstrated knife skills on *Cooking Live*, Mario Batali cooked with fresh garlic, and Emeril threw something spicy on meat and exclaimed, "Bam!"

Fast-forward to 2012, when Todd opened Crave Fishbar, a seafood restaurant in Manhattan. A reviewer wrote, "Mitgang slices scallops thin and douses them in enough curry oil to heat up Manitoba. He adds sliced heirloom cherry tomatoes to black bass sashimi for the right amount of zing. Then he ups the ante with king salmon that's cut as thick as a corn-fed rib-eye."

Roll over, Benihana, tell McDonald's the news.

Somehow Food Network captured an audience that did not know that it wanted twenty-four hours a day of food television. Then, having roped in the early adopters, the network figured out how to create an even bigger audience. Food Network is not single-handedly responsible for the "food revolution," but it took what was happening in some food-forward pockets of the world—including, fortuitously, those within a three-mile radius of its Manhattan headquarters—and delivered it to everybody. It made converts and, yes, sometimes in its greed and ambition, it perverted the message along the way. Then, it kept pulling out a divining rod to learn what fresh pockets had formed, and honed the message to fit the new reality it had helped create.

For this book, I interviewed nearly everyone you will meet here and many you won't: stars, executives, makeup artists, drivers, agents, producers, Web developers, prep cooks, and many others. I read original documents, strategic plans, research reports, old marketing pamphlets, press releases, and news articles. Among the on-screen talent I interviewed were Curtis Aikens, Sunny Anderson, Mario Batali, Mark Beckloff, Sissy Biggers, Bill Boggs, Anthony Bourdain, Anne Burrell, Tom Colicchio, Scott Conant, Cat Cora, Jane Curtin, Melissa d'Arabian, Mark Dacascos, Paula Deen, Dan Dye, Nora Ephron, Susan Feniger, Guy Fieri, Bobby Flay, Tyler Florence, Marc Forgione, Nadia Giosia, Duff Goldman, Nina Griscom, Donna Hanover, Chuck Hughes, Emeril Lagasse, Robin Leach, Lisa Lillien, Lisa Loeb, Jeff Mauro, Mary Sue Milliken, Masaharu Morimoto, Sara Moulton, Marc Murphy, Pat and Gina Neely, Jamie Oliver, Wolfgang Puck, Rachael Ray, Claire Robinson, David Rosengarten, Marc Summers, Michael Symon, Ming Tsai, Justin Warner, Geoffrey Zakarian, and Andrew Zimmern. Almost every star I asked agreed to be interviewed at length, except for Robert Irvine, Sandra Lee, and Giada De Laurentiis, although I did speak to each briefly at times and spent time in their presences observing and taking notes. Ina Garten and Alton Brown declined. In both cases, I found unpublished or little-known interviews they had done with other reporters, and I interviewed numerous associates. If a conversation is quoted, someone who was in the room at the time told me what was said. Thanks to help from Food Network employees past and present, I dug up recordings of old programs, photos, and promotional reels once thought lost.

This is not an officially authorized Food Network book. The network generously made its executives available to me for long interviews, allowed me to attend tapings, to access some of its programming archive, and to sit in on some internal planning meetings. But no one at Food Network had any right of approval over the content, nor did I show them anything I had written, other than a two-page sample of the prologue when we were discussing how much access they would allow as the project went forward. Likewise, I am represented by the William Morris Endeavor agency, which also represents many Food Network stars. While my literary agent, Eric Lupfer, helped shape my original book proposal, no one at the agency, including agents who appear as characters in this book, was shown any material for approval, nor given any other special consideration,

One other thing before you read on. There are a lot of characters, a lot of names in this story. I refer to most people, even executives, by their first names, because that's how it's generally done at Food Network—Bobby, Emeril, Rachael—unless it made sense because of duplicate names or common usage to use his or her last name. I know it would be easier to digest if I could have boiled the story down to two or three essential characters. But one of the facts of the story of Food Network is that a rich array of people had their entrances and exits, playing central parts along the way. The main character of this story does not change, and that is the network itself, which has had quite an interesting life so far.

A Final Toast to *Emeril Live*

have never met another guy who could walk into a room with, like, two hundred people and somehow find the one person that needed the hug the most," says a tearful Susie Fogelson as she raises a champagne glass to Emeril Lagasse.

The head of marketing for Food Network, Susie pauses to avoid choking up in front of thirty executives and staffers gathered in the network's central kitchen in New York City. "He would be able to find the person, like a magician. 'Someone told me it's your birthday. How old are you, twenty-seven?' And she's like ninety-two."

Emeril could have used a hug himself. After a ten-year run, Food Network had just killed *Emeril Live*, his cooking show that had debuted in 1997 with a band and a live audience. It was a genre-bending formula that quickly made Emeril a household name and his kitchen catchphrases "Bam!" and "Let's kick it up a notch!" a part of pop culture.

But now, a few weeks before Christmas 2007, the cameras have been switched off in the sixth-floor studio and the last burner extinguished. The executives are trying to honor his accomplishments, but Emeril's shock is setting in, his mind wheeling between disjointed thoughts: "Why are they doing this? Budget? Ken's not here? He didn't even call me? How can this be real?"

Ken Lowe, the chief executive of Scripps, the parent company of

Food Network, has been a dinner guest at Emeril's home. But today Ken has not made the trip to New York from corporate headquarters in Cincinnati.

The network president, Brooke Johnson, stands near Susie amid the orange cabinets and cutting boards. Brooke takes a small sip of champagne, and her calm feline eyes betray little.

Susie, tall with curly chestnut hair, is having a hard time. By tradition, each on-air talent at Food Network has one executive he or she is closest to, the person they call for inside information. For Emeril it is Susie. When the head of marketing, who'd hired Susie, left three years ago, Emeril had phoned Brooke and insisted that Susie take his place.

As she sees the famous chef's heavy bulldog face, she flashes back to seven years earlier, when she moved to Food Network from Nickelodeon. Back then, most viewers thought Food was the Emeril Network. His show was on every weeknight at 8 p.m. and he overshadowed all the other stars. When the network, marginally profitable in 2000, wanted to raise its profile, it didn't trot out Bobby Flay or Mario Batali. Emeril was its million-dollar man in chef's whites, the first food TV star to be signed to a seven-figure contract. It was actually only around $333,334 a year for three years, but the network wanted to impress affiliates with its financial health and commitment to its ratings star, and trumpeted it as a million-dollar deal.

Susie had gone on a forty-day promotional tour with him doing dinners and cooking demonstrations—Emeril Salutes L.A., Emeril Salutes San Francisco, Boston, etc. He would rush out to a kitchen station in a ballroom or convention center and the gathered advertisers, local cable company executives, and fans who had either bought or won tickets would stand and whoop with glee. He'd give a quick talk about what he loved about the city's food, demonstrate one of his recipes, and then pose for photos with admirers.

Emeril had friends everywhere. After each event, he would take Susie and his entourage to dinner. She had known his bombastic TV personality from watching him for years at home, but at the dinners,

Emeril showed a sweetness and gentleness she had not imagined, his big soft hands gesturing slowly as he spoke, his Antaeus cologne radiating a warm, embracing scent. He had a sly twinkle in his eye and radiated the deep confidence of someone who knew who he was in the world. On *Emeril Live*, all he had to say was "let's add some more gahlic," and the audience—his audience, the people who lined up week after week to fill his bleachers—would burst into applause and cheers. Before commercial breaks, Emeril would set down his spatula, rush over to the band, and grab a pair of drumsticks, showing skills on the skins he'd learned as a musical prodigy on the high school drum team. Everything had come together and he was on top.

But now, as he is toasted in the Food Network kitchens in 2007, Emeril acknowledges the good wishes as his heart grows heavier and his anger percolates. How did this day come? he asks himself.

Keeping Emeril happy had been the network's priority from the moment it first saw the ratings for *Emeril Live*. When Brooke came to the network as head of programming in 2003, Ken Lowe told Emeril that her main focus was keeping his show at the top of its game. And from the day she started, she recognized that Emeril was king and she rarely made a decision about hiring new talent or green-lighting a series without consulting him. Brooke, a veteran TV executive who had helped the A&E network jettison its original arts programming in favor of dramatic series and crime dramas, was known for making aggressive changes that worked. She spent money on audience research to figure out the truth about what was and wasn't working and how to fix it, and then she fixed it. Gut instincts mattered, but when the gut is fed facts, its instincts tend to improve. So when she took over as president in 2004, one of her first acts was to commission a study to find out how the viewing public perceived Food Network.

The outside consultants found that to many television viewers, the network delivered little besides unexciting "dump and stir" cooking shows where a chef stood behind a counter demonstrating how to make a meal. Other networks were starting to offer more exciting food programming. They presented Brooke with a graphic, the Food Network logo as a pie. It showed that Travel Channel, TLC, and the broadcast networks had bitten off portions of her market with shows shot on the road, real-life wedding tales, and other "reality" programming. The consultants titled the graphic "Nibbled to Death."

The authors of the study might as well have put Emeril's face in the conclusions, a big red X marked over it. When you looked past the live band and the quick opening monologue, his two shows, *Emeril Live* and his lower-key half-hour weekend show, *Essence of Emeril*, were basic cooking shows. If Food Network wanted to grow, it was going to have to become less of the Emeril Network.

But, Brooke, Susie, and other executives were not ready to let go yet. This was Emeril—surely something could be done. Brooke assigned the *Emeril Live* production team hundreds of thousands of dollars to update the set. They moved it to a new studio, added a Viking range, and cut out his monologue, which allowed him to head straight to the kitchen, where he was most comfortable and his energy was highest.

Susie and her marketing team came up with a new overall network slogan that began appearing at commercial breaks: "Food Network: Way More Than Cooking."

For three years, as the *Emeril Live* audience continued to age, programs such as Alton Brown's half-hour on the science of food, *Good Eats*; the breakthrough competition show *Iron Chef America*; and *The Next Food Network Star* started to thrive and attract younger viewers. Susie, like other Food Network executives, noticed the change.

Then in 2007, a "Brand Lens Study" used focus groups inside and outside the network to distill the direction Food Network would have to take if it wanted to keep up with the more exciting programming emerging on other networks, especially *Top Chef* on Bravo. The report's conclusions found many ways to say "Get out of the studio."

Brooke talked to Emeril that year, speaking with her characteristic directness.

"I don't know if the show can go on," she told him in her gravelly voice. "I don't know if we can afford the show anymore. The direction of the network may be changing."

"You're full of it," he'd responded in a half-joking tone. She might be engaging in some kind of negotiating ploy for when his contract came up. "C'mon, the audience is getting a little older. The show will bounce back. This show is the network still. You're not canceling it."

He wasn't getting it, Brooke realized. The network was spending hundreds of thousands of dollars a week on *Emeril Live*. Other shows typically cost $40,000 an episode, including the star's salary. So a whole thirteen-show season of a new series would cost what a week of Emeril cost. His price gave Brooke little room to make the rest of her talent roster happy. Ten years was a hell of a winning streak on television. Couldn't Emeril see that? Bobby Flay had evolved. His good-natured new competition show, *Throwdown*, was easily beating *Emeril Live* in the ratings. Just as she had challenged Emeril, she challenged Bobby to come up with something new, and he had dreamed up the concept for *Throwdown* himself.

But Bobby was a consistent star, not the center of the network's universe. How could Emeril be expected to believe she was serious?

In the last couple years, the show had booked younger musical acts and invited younger chefs to cook with him. It was a fertile gambit, but telling. A local deejay named Sunny Anderson, from New York's Hot 97 FM, demonstrated a fried chicken recipe. She was charming and pretty and African-American, a group that was not well represented in the network talent. The producers and Susie gaped at her ease on camera. Soon Sunny had her own show, *Cooking for Real*.

Not long before the end of *Emeril Live*, Susie phoned Emeril's talent agent Jim Griffin, a legend who represented Regis Philbin, Joe Namath, and Geraldo Rivera. It was a last-ditch effort to keep Emeril secure in the network stable and, perhaps, save *Emeril Live*. Susie wanted Emeril to become a regular competitor on *Iron Chef America*, the competition show that pitted two chefs against each other in an hourlong cooking battle in the center of a mini-stadium. *Iron Chef America* had a cult following and strong ratings among the viewers advertisers craved, eighteen to forty-nine years old.

Susie laid out the case to Jim. It would expose Emeril to a new generation, she told him. His original audience was getting old and he wasn't attracting a new one. *Iron Chef* would lend Emeril an edginess. "I don't want to lose him from prime time," she said.

Jim wasn't having it. "We don't want Emeril in an aggressive situation like that," Jim told her. He wanted Emeril to stay soft and safe, retaining his authentic cuddliness. Instead of pitting him in a battle royale against established *Iron Chef* competitors like the tattooed Clevelander Michael Symon and the kimono-wearing, histrionic Masaharu Morimoto, Jim wanted Food Network to invite new family-friendly guests to *Emeril Live*. He suggested Elmo, the Muppet from *Sesame Street*. Emeril had appeared with Elmo in 2001 in a home video called *Elmo's Magic Cookbook*, which was, as the advertising noted, "an enchanting mix of whimsical songs and fun food facts" in which Emeril showed kids how to "take it up a notch" by shouting "Bam!" as they added toppings like broccoli to homemade pizza.

Susie hung up, exasperated. Elmo!

A few weeks before the end, Brooke brought Emeril in and told him straight up that the *Emeril Live* episodes he was taping were his last. The decision had been made. Ken had signed off on it.

He nodded and left her office, but to those around the network, he seemed to be acting as if it wasn't going to happen, as if he believed something was going to change.

Ever since high school, working 11 p.m.–to–7 a.m. shifts in a Portuguese bakery in Fall River, Massachusetts, and sleeping in the afternoons between the end of classes and the start of his shift, Emeril had had a plan—what his next step would be, which chefs he would train under, what neighborhood he wanted as a location for his first restaurant, then his second and third. But on the day of his final episode he finds himself with no plan.

Over the next few weeks, he is racked by self-doubt. In addition to

asking him to do *Iron Chef*, Brooke and Susie had tried to coax him
to travel around the country for more out-of-the-kitchen segments on
Emeril Live. They wanted him to connect with his audience, bring air
and natural light to the show. Had he made a mistake, he asked himself,
when he and Jim bucked those demands? They had protested that
Emeril was a real restaurateur, not merely a TV personality like so many
of the newer Food Network stars. It was crucial for his self-identity and
his brand identity that he never stray too far from a working kitchen. He
no longer had time to barnstorm around the country in a van with a TV
crew, they argued. *Emeril Live* was like *The Tonight Show*, Jim had
insisted to Brooke, a formula that was safe and working and did not need
to fundamentally change.

Now Emeril thinks maybe he should have listened to Brooke and
fought Jim. But a few weeks after the last day of taping for *Emeril Live*,
Brooke calls him into her office again. The network has decided to end
production on his other cooking show, *Essence of Emeril*, which had run
off and on for twelve years.

This is too much. He stares at her, his eyes flaring, but he says
nothing. So that's how they are playing it, he thinks. They have hundreds of *Essence* and *Emeril Live* in the can. What do they need the real
Emeril for when they have those hours of old Emeril to exploit?

He retreats to his restaurant in New Orleans and cooks on the
line. Obviously the network is evolving, he thinks. Okay. But I don't
understand why it's evolving without me being a part of it. I don't know
why I'm getting the door shut on me. I've given a lot of time and a lot
of my life to build the network and paved the way for a lot of people.

When he is next back in New York, he sits in Susie's office. They are
talking about how he might fit into the future of the network.

"Maybe you should try doing something on *Next Food Network Star*,
or maybe *Iron Chef*?" Susie asks him hopefully, not letting the idea go.
She hates seeing this man she idolized unable to come to terms with
this change, like an aging quarterback who cannot accept he was being
benched. "How about that, *Iron Chef*?"

Emeril had built this network, had given it fifteen years of his life.

When he started on his first show in 1993, *How to Boil Water*, Food Network was in 6.8 million homes. Now they are in more than 90 million. He had been here long before Susie arrived. Before Brooke. Rachael Ray had been barely removed from her job as a shopgirl selling candy apples at a counter in the basement of Macy's when he'd been cooking for Leno and yelling "Bam!" on *The Tonight Show*, bringing in men, young women, and millions of viewers who had never dreamed they'd ever tune in to a cooking show.

He helped people. He raised money for charity. All the hosts who came after him had sought out his advice on how to build their careers, how to be the best versions of themselves on camera. He'd seen their hunger, increasingly desperate in recent years as the stakes for success had risen: fame-grappling starlets who couldn't make a piecrust from scratch and men with hair gel in their knife kits, all willing to fight like subway rats for a toehold in the fickle Food Network family.

Iron Chef. He is not going to kowtow to these people. He is not some novice cooking graduate grasping for a show before he'd worked a single shift in a professional kitchen.

"How about *Platinum Chef*?" he barks at Susie, walking out of her office, his rage, embarrassment, and fear bubbling over. "Have you thought of that?"

This was not the Food Network it used to be.

Starting
from Scratch

Perhaps it should have been obvious that food would be a good subject for a television channel. The raw ingredients were all in place. In the early 1990s, cable television was typically delivering twenty-five or thirty channels, but the industry knew fiber-optic and satellite technology would soon allow it to deliver hundreds. There was an opening for new TV content, an American culture rife with niche interests to fill it, and an emerging class of experienced cable executives ready to experiment.

The thirty-channel universe had already proven it could be done: ESPN, MTV, and CNN had started in the early 1980s, and HBO in the 1970s. New, narrower proposals, were surfacing, hoping to land slots in the 500-channel universe: a 24-hour therapy and self-help network, an all-anthropology network, a history channel.

But the killer ingredient, a food-fascinated subculture, seemed to lie hidden. It took one of those special people, the kind of creative creature who is often a bit odd in any environment but can exist quirkily in the middle rungs of a corporate culture, great at ideas, less adept at company politics, to unearth what appeared to be, even to him at first, a crazy concept.

In 1975, when Joe Langhan started working as a cameraman at Colony Cablevision in his hometown of Woburn, Massachusetts, cable television was in its infancy. He'd recently graduated from the University of Massachusetts, and was selling rare coins and stamps for a dealer in Boston, and taking production classes at the Orson Welles Cinema in Cambridge. One day he wandered past the local cable TV office on Main Street in Woburn, and saw a sign: *TV Studio*. "What is a TV studio doing in the middle of Woburn?" Joe asked himself.

It certainly sounded more interesting than selling old stamps. On pure impulse, Joe went in and asked the manager if there were any jobs; he even offered to start working for free. He was hired, for pay, and his first assignment was to videotape a high school football game. Joe, the son of a wholesale meat cutter, couldn't believe his luck. He got to work in the open air with a camera and make something that would be broadcast on television! A year later, he became a production assistant, helping to cut the promotional videos that showed potential customers how easy it was to have cable installed: Look, folks, we don't have to drill giant holes in your house!

In those days, cable TV subscribers did not expect much. They heard cable would improve the quality of their TV picture, and for a subscription fee of around $15 a month, they'd no longer have to climb onto their roofs to adjust balky antennas. Later, Colony sought to attract new customers and curry favor with the municipalities that had granted it exclusive licenses, by offering programming of local interest, such as sports and news. For some New Englanders, being able to watch a live minor-league hockey game at home on a cold winter night was a significant life improvement.

Over time, Joe made a name for himself as a guy who could get things done no matter what he was assigned. One day, he got a call from a Colony executive, who told him the company was considering developing a targeted local channel for its cable system in New Bedford.

"There are a lot of Portuguese people there," the executive said. "Do you know a lot about the Portuguese?"

"I know Prince Henry the Navigator was Portuguese," Joe said, answering honestly. "I learned that in high school."

"Good, good," the executive said. Any affirmative answer was good enough. "Do you think you can start some Portuguese programming down there and get Portuguese people to buy cable TV?"

"Sure, why not?"

In the new role, he bought foreign rights to soccer games and negotiated with Portugal's national TV network to air its soap operas.

Then in 1984 came the Big Dan's trial: six ethnically Portuguese men were going to be tried for the gang rape of a twenty-one-year-old woman in a New Bedford bar called Big Dan's Tavern. The case had become a national news story because other patrons were said to have cheered as the woman was attacked on a pool table. The Portuguese immigrant population protested that the woman had acted lewdly and the treatment of the accused was motivated by bigotry. (The case would later become the basis for the 1988 movie *The Accused*, for which Jodie Foster would win an Oscar.)

Joe, by then the head of programming for all of Colony's cable stations, suggested to the general manager of the New Bedford cable station, Paul Silva, that Colony should broadcast parts of the trial. Massachusetts had recently passed a law allowing cameras in courtrooms, and this was a big, controversial local story that would not be covered properly by the broadcast channels in Boston.

Colony was owned by the Providence Journal Company, and Paul contacted his superiors with Joe's suggestion. "ProJo" was most closely identified with its excellent newspaper, which had been published daily since 1829, and it was a conservative company, more comfortable with its cable stations running local sports and dispatches from Boy Scout picnics than running reports on a rape trial. The company vetoed the idea, reasoning that if it showed a minute more of courtroom testimony from one side or the other, it could be accused of bias.

Paul gave Joe the bad news. But Joe knew he was right. "You've got to convince the guys at the Journal," he beseeched Paul. The case was the only thing people were talking about. "We are the only people with local news in New Bedford and Fall River. People are interested in trials, they will watch trials. We have to cover this. You've got to convince them, Paul. You've got to convince them."

Paul came up with what he thought might be a solution. With Joe's help, he wrote a letter to the trial judge, Superior Court Judge William Young, asking if Colony could broadcast the entire trial, gavel to gavel. This would solve the problem of bias because the cable company would make no editing decisions. Judge Young would have full control and could decide to turn off the camera at any time. The judge agreed and so did ProJo—but not without sending the question all the way to the CEO, Michael Metcalf, who gave the final okay.

Soon CNN was showing parts of the trial taken from the Colony feed, and CNN liked it so much that a year later they ran seventy hours of the second murder trial of Claus von Bülow, who had been accused of poisoning his rich wife, Sunny. (Von Bülow's acquittal was itself the basis of a movie, 1990's *Reversal of Fortune*, for which Jeremy Irons would win an Oscar.) That, too, was such a success that in November 1990, a new cable network was announced that promised live and taped coverage of controversial trials. It would eventually be named Court TV. As far as Paul Silva and the executives at Colony headquarters were concerned, Joe Langhan had basically invented Court TV—not that anyone ever sent him a check for it.

By the early 1990s, Colony had grown into a midsize cable television provider operating systems throughout the country for 600,000 subscribers. Joe started a Spanish-language channel tailored for Cuban immigrants in Florida, developed local news shows in the Pacific Northwest, and researched Laotian programming for a proposed channel in Lowell, Massachussetts.

He looked every bit the bland middle-aged businessman from a small American city, wearing unflattering suits he bought at a discount store with dull ties and white shirts. Joe lived alone in a run-down, two-bedroom ranch house in Westport, Connecticut, that he had bought after his divorce four years earlier. He had a state-of-the-art Proton television with a Sony picture tube and high-end electronics inside. With his wide brown eyes and a head of sandy, graying hair, which he combed down over his pale forehead, he could blend into the background almost anywhere. He did so in his own living room, where his skin and hair tones matched his beige hand-me-down couch.

On those nights when he wasn't traveling, he typically went to a bar with a buddy to drink Budweiser and watch a Red Sox game. Dinner was usually pizza—Joe loved pizza and, from his years of traveling for the cable company, he knew nearly every pizza joint in the Northeast.

Pizza, really, was his only food interest.

One morning in the spring of 1991, Joe put on one of his sturdy two-piece suits and drove the ninety minutes from his ranch house to the annual gathering of the New England Cable Television Association at a Sheraton hotel on Goat Island, a half-mile-long bar of scrub and sand in Narragansett Bay connected to the mainland by a short causeway. It was there that Joe saw a narrow-faced man coming toward him, wearing a colorful abstract tie and a sharp blue suit. A few months earlier Trygve ("Tryg") Myrhen (pronounced "Maron") had been named CEO of the Providence Journal Company, the parent of Colony.

Tryg, a cable TV pioneer, had landed in Providence after resigning as the head of Time Inc.'s cable division. He had proved himself an adept businessman—he'd taken the cable division public in a $300 million IPO in 1986, and been involved in some of cable TV's most significant launches, with MTV and E!—but he'd left two years after the IPO because of differences with Nick Nicholas, the parent company's CEO. Both men understood what was happening in the media landscape, but had different ideas about how to exploit the expansion. Nick wanted to grow the cable operation by building pay television networks on the HBO model, and Tryg wanted to develop new advertising-supported channels in the mold of MTV and ESPN.

Tryg was not being allowed to set the priorities he wanted, so he left.

Despite Colony's successes, ProJo had foundered ever since Michael Metcalf had been killed in a bicycle accident in 1987. Enticed by Tryg's availability, ProJo's board had interviewed him for the CEO job in early

1990. Tryg told ProJo he only wanted to come aboard if they were willing to invest in creating new national basic cable channels. Newspapers are fun, he argued—his mother had been an editorial writer for the *Cleveland Plain Dealer*—but they were not the future.

Most ProJo stock was owned by descendants of the newspaper's founders, a gaggle of stodgy New England Brahmins, and no matter how successful Tryg might turn out to be at wringing profits from cable operations, they were not thrilled to hear their beloved business dismissed. One board member told Trygve that starting a new national cable channel was as risky as investing in Hollywood movies, and the century-and-a-half-old newspaper company was not going to get involved in that sort of shady business. They turned him down.

But after a rough year of recession, with classified newspaper advertising dropping off and little sign that the city's dwindling shipbuilding and manufacturing jobs were coming back, the board was more willing to take risks. If there was some sort of sea change happening in the media business, they needed someone adept to navigate it. They called Tryg back in 1991 and agreed to his terms.

In ProJo's cable division, Colony, Tryg was not handed a dream team of young media executives. None had worked at television powerhouses like Viacom or arrived with media degrees from newly wired schools like NYU or MIT. Nevertheless, Tryg decided to work with what he had in Providence, to see if he could lay out a vision, set a priority, and have the men—they were pretty much all men—he'd inherited execute it. Tryg believed that if he made it clear that Colony was now a fertile place for new ideas, the ideas would come.

When Tryg arrived, he was encouraged to meet Joe. The head of programming might not have launched MTV, but he had started the Portuguese and Spanish channels, and had suggested that court channel.

Joe had barely been around the Colony headquarters, so that morning at the Sheraton was the first time he had seen Tryg in the flesh. Joe stopped his new CEO in the hall and introduced himself. "Hello, sir," he said, extending his hand. "I'm Joe Langhan, head of programming for Colony."

Trygve's pale blue eyes flashed recognition, and he quickly got down to business. "Great," Trygve said, shaking hands. "I've been meaning to talk to you." With a CEO's skill for boiling an idea quickly down to its essence, he gave Joe a mission:

"Joe, we have the opportunity to participate in an extremely promising new business at the company. That business is basic cable programming. I have already received approval from my other board members and the executive committee to participate carefully in this business."

Joe nodded. This guy is straightforward, he thought.

"The profit potential here is enormous in a way that is understood by very few people. But it can also be exciting to work on—and if done right can make a real contribution to society."

He told Joe there were three rules to consider in developing a new channel:

"First, it has to cover a category not yet served by television but for which there is demonstrable public interest." Americans spent billions of dollars annually on pop music and music magazines—thus, MTV.

"Second, the channel has to be able to deliver twenty-four hours a day of programming related to that category for a reasonable cost." Record companies paid to produce music videos. Putting them on the air interspersed with in-studio news segments and clever comments from young "VJs" was a very economical proposition.

"Third, the channel has to have the potential of being entirely advertising-supported." Record companies wanted to advertise on it, as did anyone interested in reaching the youth market. Although most cable channels were collecting per-subscriber fees—ESPN was fetching the most, about 25 cents a household, and even MTV charged a small fee—Tryg believed free was key. "The right channel," he said to Joe, as he had said to others at Colony, "offered for free, will be so attractive to viewers and so easy to pick up that other cable companies will clamor to carry it, and we can sell advertising nationally."

If it all comes together, Trygve explained, Colony could rival Ted Turner's CNN and TBS Superstation.

The spiel lasted less than ten minutes. Joe asked him one question: "How do we figure out what kinds of subject areas might be worth looking at?"

Trygve told him just to look at the culture: come up with a number of potential subject areas, then research advertising dollars, the numbers of magazines sold, and the media coverage for each subject. "I am determined to work with you to get us into this business and to do it right," he said. He nodded and headed into the main conference room for the next presentation.

It was a revolution in priorities. Suddenly, thanks to Tryg, Joe was being encouraged from the top to think big and according to an exact set of criteria. Everything was in place except the mystery ingredient itself—the subject. Joe felt stirrings of the same excitement he'd had when he held a video camera at that first football game in Woburn. "I'm going to come up with something new," he thought.

> "We weren't going to have a smut channel. We weren't going to have anything that we saw as detracting from society. But on the other hand, I saw any societal benefit as a secondary benefit of being in the business. The first thing we had to concern ourselves with was whether or not we could make any money."
>
> —TRYGVE MYHREN

During the next half year, Joe tried to dream up ideas. He thought of a 24-hour pet channel. Although Joe traveled far too much to own even a goldfish, he knew a lot of people loved their animals. Unfortunately, research showed that pets and related products—carpet cleaner, collars, air fresheners, chow—were not a big enough industry with enough major brands. A pet channel would never sell enough advertising to cover seven days a week of programming. In fact it was difficult to consistently sell even the eight minutes of ads around a weekly half-hour pet show.

He pondered an all-talk-show channel. Phil Donahue's syndicated daytime show was still wildly popular, as was the five-year-old *Oprah*

Winfrey Show, along with a range of others, from low to high. But after some quick research, Joe concluded that talk shows were too talent-based and therefore risky. Viewers tuned in for the personality of the host. If you didn't find the right person, you had nothing, and if you tried to poach established hosts, you'd need a dozen of them to fill the day, and it would cost a fortune.

Tryg's method of winnowing down ideas was working, but so far Joe had nothing to show for it.

Then, in early 1992, a superior at Colony asked Joe to take a meeting with Ken Levy, the director of new business for Johnson & Wales University, whose main campus was a block away from Joe's office in downtown Providence. J&W had students studying accounting, fashion industry marketing, cooking, and other trades, and it was in the midst of investing $50 million in buying and renovating run-down buildings. One of them, the abandoned home of local Channel 10, WJAR-TV, had an entire floor still outfitted as a television studio, with high ceilings and overhead lights. Ken had been toying with ideas about what to do with it. He had little experience with television, but Colony was nearby, and he discovered that Joe was involved in developing new programming, so . . .

They met in Joe's office. "One idea we're thinking of is adding a degree program for TV production," Ken said. "The students could make some shows and you guys could put them up on your channel."

Joe sighed. He'd heard such ideas before and thought they were useless. A degree was not a necessary qualification for the few TV jobs there were, even in an expanding industry. Joe, for one, hadn't gone to TV school. He typically told young people interested in the business, "Look, if you want to do this, it's like saying 'I want to be an actor.' It's a business where ten percent of the people make ninety percent of the money. Unless you are willing to work really hard to get into that ten percent, you aren't going to make much. Besides, you should choose a real major in school. Study something like history or English. You don't want to come out of college and all you know is television, because there's not really a hell of a lot to know about it."

He looked at Ken and told him so.

Ken chuckled. "Hear me out," he said. "I've got another idea that'll make this more attractive for you. If we start this, the TV production students could film classes taught in our cooking school."

"What would you do that for?" Joe asked.

"You may not know this, but we're the largest culinary school in the world." J&W had about 2,000 culinary students, and Ken had helped expand the program to an extension campus in South Carolina.

To Joe, this seemed like a career with even less likelihood of leading to prosperity than TV production.

"You could take the tapes of the cooking classes and put them on one of the channels you have," Ken said. "You know, those Interconnect channels?"

Interconnect were two public service channels that were part of Colony's license agreement with the state—they displayed slides containing local ads and public service announcements such as upcoming junior hockey sign-ups. Unfortunately, cooking shows would not fulfill the purpose of Interconnect. Colony had to deliver those PSAs.

"It may create opportunities for you, but it doesn't sound like that great an idea for me," Joe said.

Ken persevered. For the past few years, J&W chef-instructors had been making regular three-minute appearances on local broadcast news, whipping up quick recipes for a feature called "The Dean of Cuisine." Maybe, Ken suggested, J&W could use the old studio space to produce longer "Dean of Cuisine" segments or even whole cooking shows, the way WGBH, the PBS-affiliate in Boston, was doing. Colony could be a partner somehow, running them on Interconnect.

"You know," Ken said. "The trouble with these cooking shows on PBS, my wife and I love to watch them, but we don't want to watch them on the weekends. After cooking dinner on weeknights, we sit down for like an hour or two to watch television. We'd love to watch a cooking show then."

Cooking shows at night? Joe was trying to be open-minded, but this seemed an extremely unlikely idea to him. Nevertheless, he knew he would be expected to type up a memo for the guy who had insisted he take this meeting, so Joe decided to stop arguing.

Over the next few days, however, the meeting stuck with Joe. Ken had said he and his wife really wanted to watch cooking shows at night. Joe certainly didn't, especially during baseball season, but Ken did not seem like a guy who would tell you a lie in order to sell you something. If Ken said he and his wife yearned for cooking shows, it was proba- bly true.

Might this somehow fit into what Tryg had been asking for?

At his barbershop not long afterward, Joe asked the woman cutting his hair if she watched cooking shows. "Oh, I like Martha Stewart," she said. Stewart's lifestyle magazine *Martha Stewart Living* had debuted a year earlier, and she was a frequent guest on morning TV shows.

Joe had never heard of her.

One night soon after, Joe was out at a Fall River townie bar, drinking beer with his friend Bill Walsh, a thick-chested probation officer and former high school basketball star. Offhandedly, Joe mentioned that he was thinking about an idea, Colony starting a channel with cooking shows.

"Oooo-weee!" the big man said, adopting a Louisiana accent.

"What the hell is that?" Joe asked, looking sideways at him along the bar.

"You never watch Justin Wilson?" Bill responded.

Wilson, a Cajun, had a cooking show on PBS on which he prepared down-home food and, in a heavy Bayou accent, told corny jokes, among them his boast that he always wore both a belt and suspenders because, "Theah some tings you don' wanna leave to chance."

"I've never heard of him," Joe said, gaping at Bill.

"He's great," Bill said. "He tells you how to cook jambalaya and pineapple upside-down cake and he's funny as hell. He's got all these catchphrases."

"You watch a cooking show?" Joe was stunned. As far as Joe knew, Bill's main hobbies were lifting weights and drinking Budweiser.

"I gar-on-tee!" Bill said, quoting Wilson's most famous catch-phrase.

Jesus, Joe thought, eyeballing his friend. It's one thing if the ladies at the barbershop watch cooking shows, but if even Bill watches this stuff, this could be something.

Over the next few days, Joe read that the most popular television cooking show hosts ever had been Graham Kerr, known as the Galloping Gourmet, and Julia Child. The most successful new hosts were Jeff Smith, known as the Frugal Gourmet, and Martin Yan, whose joke-a-minute wok-fest, *Yan Can Cook*, ran on PBS on Sundays after Smith's show.

Joe started spending some of his weekend hours sitting on his hand-me-down couch and watching these programs on the Proton. Back in his early days with Colony, he'd helped produce some cooking segments for the local news. He remembered a chef in Woburn had once demonstrated how to make frog legs.

"You've got to try these," the fellow had said, lifting a plate toward Joe when the shoot was done.

"I don't think so," Joe said. If the legs had been served as a pizza topping, then maybe he might have considered it. He did remember that shooting the segment had been fairly easy, though. The chef showed up with a few ingredients, and it was shot live on two cameras.

At a local newsstand, he saw that many big national food and food-related magazines were stuffed with ads: *Bon Appétit*, *Gourmet*, *Good Housekeeping*, *Ladies' Home Journal*. So there was a potential audience—which included a probation officer and a hairdresser. The programming was cheap. Advertisers were interested.

Not long after the meeting with Ken, Joe had lunch with Paul Silva, who was now his boss at Colony. Joe mentioned he had been kicking around an idea that came out of a meeting with an administrator from Johnson & Wales.

To Paul, the birth of Court TV earlier that year had been a direct result of Joe's insistence on showing the Big Dan's trial. Joe might behave like an absentminded professor sometimes, his personal life unattended and his house a mess, but he saw things before other people did. He was an idea man through and through.

"Levy is suggesting a daily cooking show on Interconnect," Joe said. "But this thing might actually be worthwhile to take up the ladder as a cable network." He told Paul what he'd found in his roundabout research, especially that there was a bigger potential audience than one might think.

Paul admitted he was part of that audience. "I watch cooking shows," he said, mentioning *The Frugal Gourmet*. Paul said that as soon as Joe finished his sandwich, he was to go to his office and put together his case for a network about food on a one-page document they could pass around.

Many of the men at Colony had worked together since the 1970s. They trusted and liked each other, and they had all been given the same talk by Tryg that Joe had gotten on Goat Island. They understood what was wanted.

Bruce Clark, the president of Colony, had driven around the Northeast on business trips with Joe many times over the years. On one of them, Bruce had said he was hungry. Joe had gestured to the backseat, strewn with magazines, boxes, spools of cable, and random electronics.

> "If I hadn't had the meeting with Paul, if Paul hadn't told me to go down and write the goddamn thing out, I mean who knows, I may have dragged it out for months, or weeks, and may have gotten distracted with another idea."
>
> **—JOE LANGHAN**

"There's a great pizza back there that's only been there a day and a half," Joe said.

Bruce had started his TV career at age seventeen installing cable in his hometown of Elmira, New York, and then served as a Marine in Vietnam. He had a military man's ability to make quick decisions: he turned down the pizza that day, but when Joe and Paul came to his office with the one-page idea for a food channel, describing the popularity of PBS food shows and the number of magazine titles, Bruce approved it, suggesting only that Joe add a few lines about potential advertisers before taking it across the street to the parent company.

"If you two guys think it's a good idea," Bruce said, "that's good enough for me. Let's get it to Jack."

Jack Clifford, the executive vice president of ProJo, oversaw all of the company's TV properties, broadcast and cable. Jack had been in the TV business since the 1950s, and shaved his head in emulation of actor Yul Brynner. He was jealous of the profits Ted Turner was making and, even before Tryg arrived, had begun to look into how ProJo could get into the cable channel business. On his own, he had noticed that PBS was getting its best ratings on weekends with its cooking shows. Jack was also a serious amateur cook. He taught bread-making classes on the weekends and hosted chili-cooking competitions sponsored by Colony. He proudly showed off his own "killer chili"—so named because a coworker had once nearly asphyxiated from an allergic reaction to cumin.

As soon as he heard Joe, Bruce, and Paul tell him something about a guy from Johnson & Wales who had proposed a half-hour cooking show, Jack interjected.

"Hell to that!" he said, convinced that a great idea had just occurred to him. "Let's do a network! Nobody's doing it!"

Joe knew that the best way to get Jack to act on something was for Jack to think it was a product of his own brilliance.

"Not a bad idea!" Joe replied.

Jack, on a roll, continued. "It's not just cooking shows. This is a network about food in all its aspects."

Soon the whole troupe—Joe, Bruce, Paul, and Jack, along with Andrew Thacher, the director of electronic initiatives for ProJo, and Paul McTear, the head of finance for Colony—was sitting around a conference table in the corner of Tryg's office on the top floor of ProJo headquarters.

They were aware that the arrival of the 500-channel universe had stalled a bit. Congress was considering rate regulations on the cable industry, which had been using regional monopolies to squeeze consumers, and the nervous industry was reluctant to invest in new wires and technology. But Tryg did not want to wait. He wanted to have networks up and running for the day when the expanded universe arrived. He liked the idea of a cooking channel. As Jack effused, Tryg looked over Joe's one-pager, thinking of ways to make additional money from the concept other than by collecting subscriber fees.

Boy, he thought, there may be other ways to make money from this: cookbooks, a food brand, maybe?

"This could be really big," Trygve said to the men. "This does sound like what I'm looking for." He could see them stir with excitement. He liked their enthusiasm. But he also knew that no one in that room had started a national network from scratch before.

Tryg knew that even channels that seemed like a good idea might not work out. CBS had famously tried to start a cable channel devoted to fine-arts programming, which had tanked after a year, costing CBS millions. "Okay, it's not going to be that easy to execute," Tryg said. "Food is a big area. How do you develop shows? But it has all kinds of potential. We've got to move with this thing. We're going to have to go out and find some people that have experience in starting up networks, because none of us have it."

Outside the office, Jack told Joe, Paul, and Andrew to do as Tryg said and come up with some recommendations about who they could bring in to help launch a food channel. Joe was thrilled. Tryg was giving them permission to find someone who could actually do this thing. That meant it might get done.

Cable TV was beyond its infancy as an industry, but only just entering its turbulent adolescence. It was old enough to have developed some expert hands, but young enough that those hands could still be wild. One of them was Reese Schonfeld, who was itching to run a network again. In 1980, it was Reese who had brought Ted Turner's vision of an all-news cable network to life. Ted had come up with the idea, but Reese had hired the talent, bought the desks, gotten the signal to the satellite. He had run CNN from its birth and served with seat-of-the-pants aplomb as its president for its first three years. In an era when the big broadcast networks were spending hundreds of millions annually to make a half hour of nightly news, CNN under Reese spent $25 million for an entire year of 24-hour-a-day programming.

Tall and prone to impulsive decisions, Reese had gotten into the TV business after being expelled from Harvard Law School for not attending classes, and then making it through Columbia Law School, but never taking the bar exam. All that time, he'd also worked at UP Movietone News and had fallen in love with the work. When the wire service had offered him a chance to cover a Democratic National convention, he'd never looked back. Reese stayed with United Press for seventeen years, until the company was sold. He had become famous for knowing how to get things done in the TV business for far less money than anyone else. In turn, he was also known for holding grudges, impatience, and temper tantrums during which he would turn purple from the bottom of his sharp chin to the top of his oval, thinly covered scalp. He would bellow at whoever was not doing what he wanted done until he got his way, and then quickly calm down and return to a normal color.

Ted Turner had removed him as the president of CNN in 1982 after complaints that Reese was running the network chaotically—failing to delegate, and hiring and firing anchors and hosts unilaterally, upsetting egos big and small.

Reese spent the next eight years involved in a series of start-ups that never quite got started, including an international news network in partnership with the Soviet Union's state-controlled news channel, TASS, which faltered when the USSR collapsed. He produced a television show for *People* magazine, and in 1991, put together the International Business Channel, partnering with networks in Germany, Japan, and around the world. He wanted to be the controlling owner this time. Tryg's former nemesis, Nick Nicholas, had pledged tens of millions toward IBC, but in February 1992, Jerry Levin ousted Nicholas in a corporate coup at Time Warner and killed Reese's project.

So Reese was at loose ends when he got a call from Stephen Cunningham, one of his consultants on the business channel project. Joe had been given Steve's name as a TV start-up expert who might be able to move the cooking channel concept forward. Now Steve was heading to Providence to meet with the Colony team. Steve wondered if Reese might be interested in a cable channel about food.

The idea of cooking programming was not completely foreign to Reese. A year earlier, two old colleagues from New York, Allen Reid and Mady Land, had come to see him. A married couple, they had moved to Nashville, where they'd been making cooking shows for local channels. "They are so easy to produce," Allen told Reese. "We could build a big business making these shows, but we need some way to syndicate them. How do we bring these shows to market? You're the expert on that."

Reese knew cheap programming was useful in the cable business. But cooking shows? "It's not the business I'm in," he told them. "I'm a news guy. I know where to sell news. But who do you sell cooking shows to? I can't do it without a platform in the cable industry. Listen, if I hear of something, I will let you know."

Now he was hearing something. "Why not?" Reese said to Steve.

Steve, who had helped start the shopping channel that became QVC, was one of a few consultants the Colony men were interviewing, but he was the only one who could offer Reese Schonfeld, cable legend. He and Reese would charge $20,000 a month to study a launch strategy.

Tryg knew Reese from his days on the board of CNN. He was aware of drawbacks with Reese's temper, but recognized that there were few men with Reese's track record for getting things started. He asked Steve to arrange for Reese to come to Providence for a follow-up meeting, which he did in the spring of 1992. Tryg, friendly and businesslike, and Jack, energetic and aggressive, both led the meeting and asked

Reese what he might want to be paid to stick with a cooking network all the way through start-up.

Reese flashed a toothy smile. This was his chance to prove he could do it again, but better. "I want to be the president of the network and to own a piece of it," he said.

The Providence men said they would consider it.

After Reese left, Tryg said to Jack, "Well, Reese knows what he's doing." Jack nodded. They decided to agree to his terms if he confirmed that he wanted to come aboard.

A few hours later, Reese arrived back at his apartment on Manhattan's Upper West Side. He and his wife, Pat O'Gorman, a TV producer, had removed the kitchen from their apartment because they did not like to cook. They had a coffeemaker and a place to stow dog food. "Delivery," Pat often said to friends, "is one of the blessings of living in Manhattan."

After the long round-trip to Providence, Reese settled down into bed and asked Pat what she thought of a 24-hour cable channel devoted to food.

Like Reese, Pat had spent most of her career in news. She was a no-nonsense lady, gruff and direct. All she knew about food on television was all most people knew: Julia Child, *The Galloping Gourmet*, and that new one, *The Frugal Gourmet*: three odd ducks. "I think it's the stupidest thing I've ever heard," she answered. "Why would anybody watch people cooking on television?"

But she could see that her husband was stirred up by the idea. Reese was at his best when he was busy. He was the type who did not move out to the beach in the summer, preferring to hole up in his Manhattan office and create deals. He studied TV ratings charts, placed calls to potential overseas investors, and took whatever meetings he could while other men lazed away in the Hamptons.

The Colony people seemed to have done their homework, he thought. Their research showed there was a broad audience for the existing cooking shows on PBS. People they'd interviewed wanted more.

"Well," he told Pat, "I think if they really offer it, I'm going to take it anyway."

———

By the late spring of 1992, Joe had become a nuisance around the Johnson & Wales cooking school. He kept showing up with a small video camera and asking to stand in the back of classrooms filming. After students filed out, there would be Joe, a forty-two-year-old man with an awkward demeanor peppering instructors with questions about culinary terms and methods. Ken Levy thought it was getting stranger and stranger. He wanted to make sure Joe was not unhinged, and asked a J&W colleague to check up on him by quietly calling a friend at Colony. Was Colony seriously looking into doing something on TV involving cooking?

"Yes, don't worry," came the response. "We're serious. Joe is okay."

Meanwhile, Reese was well aware of the need for quick action. When he and Ted Turner had launched CNN, other entities were also thinking of cable news programming. To beat the competition, Reese and Ted had taken their plan to an annual cable convention in 1979, announced it at a press conference, and to prove how far along they were, presented a list of shows CNN would carry. In fact, they had hired their first anchor only twenty-four hours earlier, had not purchased a camera or found a studio. As Reese later told Joe, "The list of shows scared everyone else off. Everyone who was there said, 'Wow, these guys are so far advanced, so far ahead of us,' that they just dropped out."

On July 2, 1992, Reese and Steve, working with Joe and others at the Providence Journal, delivered a report. Reese had already teased it earlier with a memo to the principals:

Gentlemen:
Permit me to cut to the chase:

I. After thirty days I am absolutely convinced that the Food Channel is a business that will be worth between $250,000,000 and $500,000,000 on the day that it is carried in 40,000,000 cable homes.

II. Therefore the most difficult part of our task is to convince the
cable industry that it should grant this extremely valuable
franchise to the Providence Journal/Johnson & Wales.

III. Our report will explain why we think the cooking franchise is
so valuable and it will present and discuss various plans for
gaining cable acceptance.

Now, the authors expressed a "major concern" that a competitor, especially Discovery Channel, which carried cooking shows already, could announce a spin-off food channel first. They suggested that "we announce first."

The report included a list of thirty programming ideas. Among the talent mentioned were Larry King, the talk show host Reese had originally hired at CNN; Alistair Cooke, an Englishman known as host of *Masterpiece Theatre* on PBS; Paul Prudhomme, a noted New Orleans chef; and Julia Child. None of them had been approached. Among the show ideas:

- Haute Cuisine: Fancy meals for fancy occasions.
- Talking About Food: Larry King–type call-in show where callers and the host dissect the menus at White House dinners, the specials at the fanciest restaurants in the world, and the pros and cons of fast food.
- Cooking for Babies: What should mothers be serving their babies, and what should they be eating while they are breast-feeding?
- Eating While Pregnant: What should expectant mothers be eating, along with pickles and ice cream at 3 a.m.?
- Cooking Game Shows: The winner gets a grocery cart full of coupons or a year's free shopping or twenty pounds of beef or a year's supply of Campbell's soups.
- Cooking by Dad: The show that focuses on easy-to-prepare meals for those times when the kitchen is controlled by an

ignoramus, along with his screaming children who are sick of
hot dogs, pizza, and peanut butter.

- Cookbook Reviews: This could be a Siskel and Ebert kind
  of show with a beefman and a healthmark fanatic . . .
- Great Hotel Dining Rooms: An ongoing tour of the finest
  hotel dining rooms in the world.
- So You Want to Own a Restaurant?: A regular feature that
  would serve as an ongoing exercise in entrepreneurialism.
- Great Meals from History: An Alistair Cooke–hosted discussion of the gastrointestinal tendencies of the world's leading
  historic figures.
- Letting Go: Curing bad kitchen habits picked up from your
  mother.
- Edited Cooking Shows: We would have a host who critiques
  the old cooking shows and teases Julia Child about the equipment she used, highlighting those recipes that still make the
  mouth water.

Another section of the report noted: "Cooking shows are among the
least expensive programs produced on television . . . between $8,000
per hour (Reid/Land Productions) . . . $12,500 . . . if produced in a
union situation . . ." Costs would be even lower in a company-owned
studio.

"Moreover, the programming is timeless and will retain value far
into the future. Second . . . there are a number of ancillary revenue
streams that could generate substantial revenues, including database
applications, cookbook sales, couponing revenues, and potential magazine applications."

"Couponing revenues"? That was a concept from Andrew Thacher.
Andrew found new technologies for ProJo to invest in—everything
from cellular phone ideas to ways of delivering news via computer—and
he had been asked to help with the Food Channel plan. He found a
small company in Beaverton, Oregon, with the means to transmit cou-

pons via television. If a commercial for frozen green beans was shown, a viewer could push a button on a detachable calculator-size reader. At supermarket checkout, he or she would present the reader and receive the discount.

The Food Channel business model leaned heavily on "Couponix." Reese accepted Tryg's approach that to make the channel irresistible, they'd have to give it away for free. But no other start-up cable channel was forgoing subscriber fees. It was not considered economically possible to survive only on advertising. On average, cable providers were paying 12 cents per subscriber to each channel in 1992. Even Court TV was receiving 9 cents per subscriber. The free approach would set Food apart, and Couponix, it was thought, would compensate. The plan projected that advertisers would pay 5 cents per subscriber for Couponix's power to reach consumers directly and collect data on who clicked what when. In total, the plan calculated, Couponix would deliver $420,000 to the bottom line the first year and nearly $5 million in year five.

The plan calculated that including programming and other expenses, the network would need to raise roughly $43 million to start, even with projected advertising and Couponix revenues of $32 million over the first three years. And it projected that to attract sufficient advertising revenue to turn a profit by year four, the channel would need to be available in 3.5 million cable homes in its first year, 10 million the second, 20 the third, and 40 million in year five.

Colony could put the Food Channel in its 600,000 homes, but how would you get to 3.5 million in the first year if being free was not attraction enough for cable providers? The proposed solution was to approach cable companies as investors. Each company would be asked to contribute $6 million cash and to commit to putting the Food Channel into as many homes as possible. For the $6 million, each would own ten percent of the network, and for every 666,000 subscribers provided, an investor would gain an additional one percent ownership. If seven cable companies each gave $6 million, that would yield the start-up money necessary, plus however many homes they pledged. The plan included an end date on the free ride. If the Food Channel still existed after ten years, it would begin charging per-subscriber fees.

Thus the task was set: find seven cable providers willing to put up both cash and subscribers. And do it as fast as possible. Reese wrote that to preempt competition, the network had to be on the air by June 1993, less than a year away.

Find investors, hire staff, acquire programming, and get a network broadcasting into more than three million homes in less than a year? It would take iron stomachs to endure the sudden ups and downs and, worse, the dispiriting lulls.

To start at least, there was good news on the advertising front. Jack, Andrew, and Reese had traveled to Cincinnati to meet with the top ad buyer for the consumer products giant Procter & Gamble. Without P&G it would be a rough go.

Jack Clifford gave the pitch in his carnival barker's voice: "It's good, clean fare, safe for families . . ." Reese chimed in with comments about what a viable business plan they had and how economical the programming would be. Julia Child, he was sure, would be persuaded to appear now and then. Plus, there was his own experience with start-ups. Finally, the ad buyer broke in: "That's enough."

Oh shit, Jack thought, anxiety rising. Here we go, they're going to tell me to go blow it out my ears.

Everyone looked at the buyer.

"We're in. We're in," he said. "We'll give you a three-hundred-thousand-dollar buy the first year."

Jack, Reese, and Andrew tried not to gasp.

"That's twice as much as we usually offer to new networks. If there's going to be a food network, we've got to be on it," the buyer said. "And we think your company, your research, it's pretty solid, and I think you're going to make it. We'll raise it the second year."

Confidence mounted in Providence, but they still needed at least seven investors. The Food Channel team started making the rounds to media companies—and suddenly the progress slowed.

The cable company TCI—whose leader, John Malone, had coined the phrase "500-channel universe"—turned them down flat.

Robert Stengel, an executive at Continental Cablevision, argued that not charging cable operators even one cent a subscriber was foolish and keeping the channel free for ten years, as promised, crazier. It was accepted industry wisdom that cable networks needed two streams of income: subscriber fees and advertising. If you charged at least a penny to start, it would be easier to raise it to a nickel later.

"You'll run out of money in a couple years and you'll be asking us to pitch in more," Stengel said. He thought the plan was the kind of cheap, provincial thinking he would expect from a small-time cable operator like Colony. He knew it and every other operator hated having to pay Ted Turner for his channels every month when the smug bastard from Atlanta was also collecting advertising money without having to cover the expense of dispatching trucks to make sure every old lady's cable was screwed into the back of her Trinitron properly. But that didn't mean it made sense to start a network based on a fantasy of free channels for everyone! He was surprised that Tryg had signed off on this mess. Having sat on the first board of CNN, Stengel knew how chaotic Reese could be, and how nasty he could get when anyone questioned him. As far as Stengel was concerned, Reese was not an asset to this project. Two strikes against it. But he respected Tryg and Jack too much to say no outright.

Comcast did turn them down outright.

So did Teymour Boutros-Ghali, vice president of Time Inc. Ventures. He agreed that the crucial component in the channel's success was securing carriage across many cable systems. He understood why the plan was structured as it was; giving ownership to a group of cable providers would indeed ensure carriage. But Time Inc. did not want to own small pieces of companies. It created too much confusion. For instance, if Time was interested in the "synergy" of having shows named after its own food magazines, how would it deal with the other partners? Who would control the valuable brands? It was too messy. Time was in the midst of starting a syndicated TV show based on *People* magazine, called *Extra*, a project the company would own 100 percent.

"We're in this business to get big pieces, to start new franchises," Boutros-Ghali told Jack.

What he did not tell them was that he also knew Reese, and had heard that Reese was as volcanic as ever.

Yet another rejection came from Charles Dolan, the CEO of Cablevision on Long Island. Dolan alarmed Jack and Andrew when he told them that he had been looking into the idea of a food channel himself. "It's a great idea and we're doing it," he said. They were further jolted when Dolan introduced them to the executive in his programming group who was in charge of investigating its feasibility. But months after their initial meeting, no one from the ProJo Food Channel team had heard anything, so Tryg called Dolan to ask if he was in or out. Dolan was dismissive. He told Tryg a food channel "doesn't make any sense. It's way too big a category." And, he added, even if someone could figure it out, "I don't think you guys really have the talent over there to get it done."

Meanwhile, there was a problem with the name. "Food Channel" was trademarked. "Food Network" was also trademarked, although not for the purpose of a television channel. In any case, the problems with clearing the names legally increased the ProJo team's anxiety that someone else would beat them to the punch. If those names were gone, surely someone else was up to something.

Jack suggested Television Food Network; TVFN for short. No one had that. It stuck.

But so far, all they had was a name and a pledge from P&G. No investors were aboard. As the months wore on, some of Joe's colleagues started to rib him. One day Jeff Wayne, Colony's head of marketing, saw Joe hunched over the business plan. Jeff, like many others, had been skeptical all along that the channel could be viable without collecting per-subscriber fees.

"You still kicking around that food idea with Johnson & Wales?" Jeff laughed. "You haven't got real work to do?"

Joe nodded. His ideas had been mocked before. He was used to it. "There still may be something there," he said quietly. "We'll see."

But the cascade of bad news continued. Johnson & Wales dropped out. J&W had first been asked to contribute $10 million to be part owners, then, when the school administration balked, $2 million for a smaller stake, but they had been edgy all along. The school was in the midst of massive spending on expansion. The more Ken Levy and others at J&W considered the TVFN plan, the more they realized the channel was about entertainment and not their core mission, education.

Then, Steve Cunningham dropped out. He'd been tapped to run a new shopping network. After legal wrangling, Steve retained a small ownership stake in whatever became of the project. Reese would be left with a roughly 5 percent share. So far these were shares of nothing.

Then there was Couponix. The Oregon company had not actually developed a working prototype. All it had was a cartoon that when broadcast could make a toy dog bark. No one knew if advertisers would even want an electric coupon machine or if supermarkets would add technology to accept it. Joe and Reese had to face reality and remove it from the business plan, leaving a big financial hole.

At this nadir, Reese and Joe kept fighting to keep TVFN inching forward. Like a veteran superhero gathering his old Justice League comrades to fight a new battle, Reese made the rounds, asking for help from those who had stood with him before and made TV miracles.

One of them was Robin Leach, the nasal-voiced host and producer of the loved and ridiculed syndicated show *Lifestyles of the Rich and Famous*—"Champagne wishes and caviar dreams." Reese had hired Robin in 1980 as a reporter on a celebrity-focused CNN news program called *People Tonight*. It became one of the new network's most popular shows and helped Robin develop the idea for *Lifestyles*.

When Reese came to see him at his office in the Lipstick Building on Third Avenue in Manhattan, Robin was wrapping up the fourteenth season of *Lifestyles*. Ratings were down and the show was nearing its end. Robin might have played his host role with wacky bombast, but he was also a shrewd businessman, up early to meet with stations carrying his show, videotaping customized promotions for their regions, and haggling with satellite operators for better prices. Reese explained that he wanted him aboard a new project. He flattered Robin, telling him his fame and his understanding of start-ups would be essential. Perhaps Robin could leverage his celebrity connections to attract notable guests for a new talk show he could host himself, just like *People Tonight* on CNN.

"Right now you'd be the biggest star we have," Reese said. "Your name will impress people."

Robin was certainly one to bask in such praise, especially when his show was dying.

"What's the project, Reese?"

"A twenty-four-hour-a-day food network."

Robin was silent for a moment. It occurred to him that Reese had gone out of his mind. Poor guy. Started CNN, got booted, and now he was grasping at whatever he could in order to get back in the game. Then he paused and reconsidered. Reese had proven he was no joke.

"Well, Reese," he said, "every time I've been told I was mad, it turned out to be the best thing since sliced bread."

"That's right," Reese said. "Sliced bread."

"But how on earth do you do twenty-four hours of food?"

"That's the challenge we both have. Can you help me?"

The two struck a deal. Robin would be paid based on the number of subscribers the network attracted. He had good relationships throughout the country because of his travels to syndicate *Lifestyles*. In addition to appearing on the air for TVFN, he could use those relationships and his famous name to get meetings and cajole smaller cable providers to add it to their lineups.

Robin liked having skin in the game. The arrangement Robin agreed to was that once the network got up to sixty million subscribers—if it ever did—he would be paid something more than a million dollars.

Robin Leach coming aboard was not likely to make the difference between TVFN living or dying. What did make a difference, however, was a landmark new law governing cable television, passed by Congress in October 1992. Part of the complicated legislation was called "retransmission consent." It forced cable providers to compensate broadcast channels for carrying them. For example, if Comcast wanted to include local channel 3 on its cable lineup in Philadelphia, it had to pay the owner of channel 3 in some way.

What kind of payment? It took months for the cable and broadcast industry to figure it out. The cable providers needed to spend their money on laying better transmission wires, so instead of compensating local broadcasters with cash payments, they settled on offering space on their expanding dials as barter. What the owner of a broadcast channel gained was the right to a second slot on the cable dial. This is how Fox started FX, NBC launched what became MSNBC, and ABC got cable providers to carry ESPN2.

Once Reese recognized what this might mean for TVFN, he leapt. First, it meant that ProJo could use its leverage from the broadcast channels it owned in Kentucky, Texas, and elsewhere. If each ProJo station used retransmission consent to win an extra slot on a local cable system, TVFN could be wedged into those slots, adding hundreds of thousands of homes.

Second, Reese recognized that retransmission consent meant that owners of other broadcast channels had also gained the power to demand second channel slots—and not all of those owners were prepared for the opportunity. Reese called George Babick, an executive at the Tribune Company. He had been CNN's first advertising sales manager. Tribune owned eight TV stations around the country in big urban areas, Los Angeles and New York among them.

"Listen," Reese said to his old colleague, "do you think Tribune would be interested in getting involved with this TV Food Network? You guys have big markets, ten million homes, and you're getting basically nothing for it from the cable companies." If Tribune gave TVFN its retransmission consent rights, it would receive a large ownership percentage of the new network.

George's office was on the nineteenth floor of the Tribune Tower, ten feet away from the president of Tribune Broadcasting, Jim Dowdle. George had presented many ideas to Dowdle over the decade he'd been there, but inevitably, Dowdle would get a team of underlings to spend months generating charts, spreadsheets, and research reports, and then the decision was almost always "no." Slow death. George missed the fast-breaking excitement of working on a start-up with Reese.

Perhaps it was because Dowdle had passed on the opportunity to make Tribune an original investor in the SciFi channel, a decision he regretted bitterly. Perhaps it was because cable was growing like mad, and Tribune did not have a solid piece of it. But it took Dowdle a stunning and uncharacteristic two days to approve the deal. Tribune kicked in around $10 million cash and got 30 percent ownership of TVFN, and in return, the upstart network got Tribune's retransmission consent rights for ten million homes across the country. George would soon quit the Tribune gig and, promised his own small ownership share in TVFN, go to work for Reese in New York.

Because cable providers did not have space immediately available to add more channels, TVFN would not have all of Tribune's ten million homes at launch, but the agreement signaled that the channel was well on its way. With the Tribune commitment, the team began to make the rounds again, and this time the results were different.

E.W. Scripps, a media company based in Cincinnati, was considering starting its own cable channel. Lawrence Leser, the Scripps chief executive, brought the TVFN proposal to Ken Lowe, a rising executive in the company, who was painstakingly trying to cobble together a winning plan for Scripps to start what he aimed to name Home, Lawn and Garden Channel. Ken had recognized that women were an underserved cable audience and that "lifestyle" programming could be a way to reach them.

Ken liked the food idea—it fit in with the research he had done. But

he disliked the approach and the show ideas. It was all too informational and instructive, boring. What's more—the old bugaboo—giving
it away free for ten years went against the wisdom of every revenue
projection he had done on his channel. Advertising would not be enough
to cover expenses. The plan looked like chaos and pure bravado to him.
Although it was infringing a bit on the territory he envisioned for
Home, Lawn and Garden, for which he aimed to produce a few cheerful cooking shows, the food plan made him feel more confident about
his own, better-thought-out, proposal.

He went back to Leser. Ken praised the concept, but concluded, "I
don't think I'd invest in it."

"We already have," the CEO said. Pressed by TVFN to make a decision fast, they had not waited for Ken's input. As it had for Tribune, it
seemed a way to acquire something without committing much cash.
Ken shrugged and handed back the plan. Not his problem. Scripps
ended up kicking in $9 million and pledging to deliver the network to
630,000 of its cable subscribers, in return for a 13 percent ownership
stake.

With Scripps and the Tribune Company on board, Tryg went back
to Continental. He called the company's founder, Amos Hostetter Jr.,
and made a personal appeal. Amos decided the company could risk
$9 million on a plan Tryg endorsed so wholeheartedly. Robert Stengel
still wasn't sure about Reese, but Tryg had proved himself enough to
convince Hostetter to take a gamble.

On August 16, 1993, more than two years after Goat Island and a
year after ProJo had hired Reese, the investors were in place and an
agreement was finally signed. The original ownership of TVFN is easiest to understand as three pies—Management, Class B, and Class A—
and a grasp of this ownership structure helps make sense of what
happened later, when a lot of decisions were made based on financial
necessity. The money and power that the numbers represented would

come to influence which personalities held sway in shaping the channel's growth: who got rich, who got famous, and who didn't.

"Management" was the smallest pie—10 percent, held by the founding companies behind TVFN, ProJo, and Reese's company, Pacesetter Communications—and it would earn profits after everyone else had recouped their investments. It was cut into two unequal slices, three-quarters for ProJo and one-quarter for Pacesetter.

"Class A" was the largest—60 percent, divided into five roughly equal slices owned by Tribune Cable Ventures, Scripps Howard Inc., Landmark Programming (a cable operator), Continental Programming, and ProJo. Each had invested around $9 million in TVFN, and were on the hook to pay for losses, but they would also be the first to enjoy profits, should there ever be any.

"Class B" owned 30 percent of TVFN, and had given FN carriage, but not cash: C-TEC Cable Systems, Times-Mirror Cable Television, Adelphia Communications, and a subsidiary of Cablevision Industries (unrelated to Charles Dolan's Cablevision). Every Class B partner received 2 percent for every 1 million households it delivered. Some of the Class A owners also had pieces of Class B, depending on how many households they delivered. After four years, the size of the shares froze.

Reese had proven his worth in this essential early phase, sticking with the project through ups and downs that might have made a less adventure-tolerant chief queasy. For his part, Joe was tapped to move to New York as the first employee of the new network. His creativity and persistence had started the thing, and Colony figured he was entitled to stick with it. When that was decided, Joe tried asking Reese for a small ownership share of the network, but Reese explained that he had already promised stakes to a few of those he was eager to bring in. If he gave away more equity to Joe, he would be diluting the shares and lose the leverage he needed to attract top talent.

Strangely, a few days before Joe moved to New York, he came home from a business trip and realized his Proton television had been stolen.

There was no sign of forced entry, and Joe was too busy with every-thing to ever file a police report.

Reese had set the start date as somewhere around Thanksgiving 1993, which gave them only a few months to get a national network on the air.

More trying tests lay ahead. The network they were starting was un-like any that had come before. Only one on-air personality was com-mitted, there were zero fully-thought-out show ideas, and they had no network headquarters—no network at all really, except the hypothetical one agreed to on paper.

CNN with Stoves

Reese established the TVFN start-up headquarters in a tiny three-room apartment on Seventh Avenue and West Fifty-third Street. The walls were quickly covered in yellow Post-it notes, each darkened with heavy scribbles as Reese issued his staff an ever-evolving to-do list. He had hired a few employees, including Susannah Eaton-Ryan, the former manager of the punk rock club CBGB, who also had experience overseeing TV production facilities; Ricki Stofsky, a news producer from local channel 5; and Rochelle Brown, a recent college graduate hungry for a break in the TV business.

Susannah had worked with Reese on a short-lived syndicated TV show he'd produced in 1989 called *Crimewatch Tonight*. Those few who had not known him prior to the TVFN project began referring to all of the hires who had known him, such as Robin Leach and George Babick, as F.O.R.s—Friends of Reese. Others were Robin Connelly, an aspiring talk show host who had been romantically involved with a relative of Reese's, and Jonathan Lynne, the son of Reese's former lawyer, Michael Lynne, a co-founder of New Line Cinema.

It was, basically, insanity in that office. When Rochelle had applied for the job of production assistant, she sent a cake with her résumé. One food-world snob Reese had hired stuck her finger in to taste it, wrinkled her nose, and said, "It's from a mix." On Rochelle's first day, Ricki shoved aside a pile of videotapes and assigned her an upturned box to use as a desk.

For Reese and everyone else on the business side, the project was a business play made possible by the changing realities of cable TV—not a way to spread the gospel of a food revolution. He had a rough list of what needed to get done to pull the network together. Some of the items were obvious essentials, like finding a real broadcast home. Others were wishes, such as figuring a way to bring Julia Child aboard in some capacity because she was the biggest name you could get in the TV food industry. And a few items on Reese's list were thought through only in general terms: they needed something to put on the network, but exactly what shows with what talent was not clear. The original list of show ideas included in the business plan had been hastily composed, and although it had been improved over the next year to attract investors, it still was unspecific. Who exactly would host what?

In those days a bumper crop of fully formed food celebrities did not exist, so Reese, Joe, and the others simply went casting about for chefs with presentation skills and looks that might work on television. The hires might seem random, as if anyone who could flip an omelette would do, but even in rough form the team was exactly how Reese had envisioned it: a few TV professionals who could get the job done no matter what was burning around them, combined with enough food experts to fulfill the mission conferred in the network's name—not just "television network," but "television FOOD network." If Reese knew next to nothing about food, he knew enough to know to ask for help.

In March 1993, Sue Huffman, the former food editor of *Ladies' Home Journal* and then the director of consumer affairs for the packaged food giant Best Foods, attended a party thrown by the International Association of Culinary Professionals (IACP) in New York. There, she was introduced to Pat O'Gorman and her husband, Reese. He was a month away from signing the key papers with investors, and the conversation quickly turned to his TV project. Sue had been intrigued about the network since reading about the proposal in a recent *Wall Street Journal* article, "They're Playing a Game of Chicken to Decide Who Rules the Roost":

> The architect of the food network is no epicurean. "I'm a meat-and-potatoes guy," says Mr. Schonfeld, who, at 215 pounds, says he is satisfied with his waistline. He envisions live call-in shows, "something with food and celebrities," he says, as well as programs on food and health and a weekly half-hour show, *How to Feed Your Family on $75 a Week.*

The day after the party, Sue received a call from her old boss, Myrna Blyth, the editor of *Ladies' Home Journal.* "I just found your next job," Myrna said.

"I wasn't aware I was looking," Sue replied.

Reese had been meeting with every person in the food world he could find. Myrna had just had a meal with Reese and he'd told her he needed someone to develop a schedule of programming for TVFN, someone who knew food, because he didn't.

"Well, it's Sue Huffman," Myrna told him.

"That's interesting." Reese said. "I just met her last night."

An hour later, Sue's phone rang again, and Reese asked if she'd be a paid consultant and draw up an improved version of the programming scheme. She knew magazines, and he wanted the programming day at the network to unfold like the sections of a magazine: news, how-to, health, and entertainment.

She agreed, and soon dropped off the schedule at Reese's apartment on a Sunday on her way to LaGuardia Airport. It had deeper descriptions of the basic show ideas. As Sue and her husband drove through traffic, she thought, "Okay, I earned a couple of shekels out of this and I'll never hear from him again, so that's that."

She was wrong. The schedule was good enough for Reese to show to the cable system operators he and Colony were still trying to bring to the closing table, and he touted Sue's pedigree in the food world and her affiliation with Best Foods to advertisers. But most important to Reese, Sue knew Julia Child.

Reese wanted to have the undisputed queen of TV cooking associated with TVFN in whatever way he could. In the late spring of 1993, Sue and Reese flew up to Cambridge, Massachusetts, for a dinner meeting with Julia, her boyfriend John McJennett (Paul Child had been in a nursing home since 1989 and died in 1994), and Nancy Barr, Julia's friend and producer—who had introduced Sue to Reese at the IACP party.

Julia's television contracts with PBS and *Good Morning America*, where she was a regular contributor, forbade her from cooking on any other networks, but Reese and Sue suggested they could offer her a contract to appear sporadically on TVFN delivering commentaries on the food world and sitting as an interview subject: no sautéing, stuffing, or trussing required. Julia agreed in principle, especially motivated by the idea that TVFN was going to figure out a way to secure the rights to her old shows and broadcast them, a task Reese said he was working on.

Although there was an agreement in principle, it took some negotiating to hammer out details. Reese was so desperate to tell cable providers at a June 8 sales meeting that Julia was aboard that TVFN's lawyers exchanged a flurry of faxes with Julia's lawyer, William Truslow, negotiating the language Reese could use to describe her relationship with the network. Truslow warned her not to commit to too much, noting that even if she agreed to contribute some kind of television essay only once a week, that would mean fifty-two essays a year—some of which would appear at the same time her new PBS series *Cooking with Master Chefs* was debuting. He also warned her that if she entered a contract to do fifty-two essays and then couldn't deliver, she was opening herself up to being sued. "If they have obtained advertisers on the basis that you are going to appear every week—and you may be sure that is how they are going to obtain advertisers—then the damages could be more than nominal," Truslow wrote. A day before the affiliates meeting, Reese was able to announce:

> We are pleased to say that we have been talking with Julia Child about her appearing from time to time on the Food Channel to contribute occasional short television essays and commentary on various subjects relating to food and gastronomy. . . . While Mrs. Child has agreed to the general concept of occasional contributions, we are still in the process of working out the arrangement with her, which hopefully will be completed in the near future.

By summer 1993, Sue was officially the director of programming at TVFN. Reese gave her a small ownership stake in the network, carved out of his own share. He had done the same to entice George Babick to come aboard as the head of advertising sales.

He turned his attention to the news show that he saw as the most important piece of the programming puzzle. The first day Rochelle Brown showed up for work, Reese issued a command to her: "Help me find a way to get Donna Hanover on the phone!"

Donna was a veteran local news anchor who had been working at various New York stations for years. Her husband, former federal prosecutor Rudolph Giuliani, was running for mayor, aiming to unseat the incumbent, David Dinkins.

When Reese called and asked Donna to come in for a meeting, she did not know what it was about, but she respected him and agreed. Donna, with short, blond anchorwoman's hair, dressed in a sensible skirt suit, showed up at Reese's cramped headquarters, and Reese explained he was working on launching a food channel.

"Why are you thinking of me?" she asked, taking in the cramped office. "I'm honored, but I am the queen of order-in."

"I want somebody that understands a tally light," Reese said, referring to the red light on top of a television camera that indicates it is live. "Someone who can teach all the food experts television."

He explained to Donna that the heart of the network would be a newsroom from which other programs radiated like spokes around a hub. Reese was doing what had worked before. At start-up, CNN had had that structure, a focus on the anchor desk with various softer shows arrayed at the edges of the schedule, such as *People Tonight* and *Larry King Live*. This would be CNN with stoves.

Reese wanted Donna to co-anchor the hard news program, to be called *Food News and Views*. He remembered how, in its early days, CNN had reported on the independent 1980 presidential candidate John Anderson. The major networks had been ignoring Anderson, focusing on the race between Jimmy Carter and Ronald Reagan, so CNN had made Anderson its story, covering his rallies with serious attention. Carter's refusal to allow Anderson to participate in televised presidential debates became major news, and CNN attracted historic ratings by taping Anderson answering debate questions in real time and cobbling together a tape-delayed version of the debate with his responses inserted in proper sequence.

Reese aimed for *Food News and Views* to find the food world equivalent of John Anderson, a story the world would take notice of. It needed a seasoned TV news anchor. Reese pledged to pair Donna with a food expert. It didn't matter who. Donna was key.

What he didn't tell Donna was that having her aboard also made sense for the same reason he had signed Robin Leach: she was somebody. Donna could be depended on to talk about the network at cocktail parties amongst the New York political and media elite. And if her husband happened to win the mayoral election, all the better—not only for the network's stature, but for its chances of being picked up by Manhattan's primary cable provider, Time Warner.

Donna wasn't sure. Reese seemed confident and his track record was amazing, but a 24-hour food network? No one had invented smell-o-vision, she reasoned. It's one thing to talk a chef through a six-minute cooking segment on a local morning show, an exercise she had presided over many times, but an entire network focused on something that was all about taste and smell, except viewers couldn't taste or smell it?

She agreed to think about it and do a screen test. Maybe Reese knows more than me, she thought as she squeezed out of the office. She did not have a full-time television gig at the time, so she was open.

Finding a food expert to cohost *Food News & Views*, whether or not Donna took the job, was a matter of less thought for Reese. Anyone who knew a little bit would do.

David Rosengarten, as it turned out, knew more than a little. David had made a career switch in the mid-1980s when he was teaching theater courses at Skidmore College and had walked into a gourmet food shop in downtown Saratoga Springs advertising cooking classes. He was fascinated with food; his father, Lenny, had had a restaurant, Seafood City, which had failed when David was a geeky eleven-year-old; he remembered the pale lifelessness of the zipper showroom where his father returned to work. There were no steaming clams there, no sizzling swordfish. Lenny had channeled his kitchen wisdom into his son, patiently explaining how each kind of seafood required its own type of batter for frying; scallops, for instance, needed the heaviest batter, lest it slide off.

Inside that gourmet shop in Saratoga Springs in 1983, David had an irrepressible urge to see his name on the list of cooking instructors. He asked the woman running the shop if teachers were paid. They were, and she agreed to give him a tryout. The following Saturday he taught a class on how to cook Szechuan Shrimp. His students, a small group of local women, were charmed. He was invited back, and eventually his students started taking him out to dinner and toasting his skills and his cleverness. His undergrads in Introduction to Directing at Skidmore never gave him this kind of love.

Instead of risking everything on one food venture like his father had,

David decided to try to make it as a food writer. He moved to Manhattan and became friends with a charismatic young sommelier named Josh Wesson he'd met at a "New American" restaurant called Hubert's. Soon, with the help of a literary agent, they sold a book to Simon & Schuster called *Red Wine with Fish: The New Art of Matching Wine with Food*, published in 1989.

During the period when David was trying to catch on as a writer, Tony Hendra, a British-born comic actor most famous for playing the manager of the fictitious heavy metal band in the mockumentary *This Is Spinal Tap*, had begun writing food and beverage—mostly beverage—columns for the *New York Observer*. At one point, the beery Hendra embarked on a nostalgic tour of all the bars named Blarney Stone in New York City—there were six in 1991—finding that "they all have that great porridgey fug and that dear old rodent-colored meat on the steam table." Josh Wesson knew Hendra, and soon they were fantasizing with David about an idea for a TV show that would feature their diverse talents. Most food shows since the start of television had been instructional: a chef facing a stove and demonstrating a recipe in what came to be known as a "dump and stir" format. The show the three men planned, full of skits and gags, would be a departure. The conceit was that Tony would play a food ignoramus being taught the basics of wine by Josh and of food by David. Called *Your Basic Food Group*, it would be infused with a pop culture attitude.

They could imagine only one venue for it, because there was almost only one venue for a food show—PBS. WGBH in Boston was the producer of most PBS food programs, having launched *The French Chef* in 1963 and carried on from there, and David, Tony, and Josh found a WGBH producer, Laurie Donnelly, who pitched the idea to PBS. When the station agreed to finance a pilot, David thought he was on the verge of everything he had ever dreamed about.

Not that there weren't bumps. When the pilot was done, WGBH executives liked it, but asked for changes. They wanted a theme to carry through each episode. A second pilot was made, then a third was ordered, all of which added up to more than $200,000 spent. That was the way things were done at the center of the food TV business prior to Food Network. At the executives' request, the show was renamed *Three Men in a Kitchen*, echoing the title of a recent hit movie, *Three Men and a Baby*. Eager to make a third pilot that would really knock their socks off, Hendra convinced his friends, the magicians Penn and Teller, to appear. They demonstrated how to make a Valentine's Day blancmange, a sweet gelatin dish shaped into a heart. When cut into with a sharp knife, it spurted blood made of corn syrup and food coloring.

David knew Julia Child because he and Josh had started a newsletter called *The Wine & Food Companion*. When he had gone to Julia's home with his wife and newborn daughter to collect information for an article on omelettes, Julia, generous but always straightforward, had opened the front door, gazed at the child, and asked, "Is she going to need milk or is she on the home dairy?" David's wife blushed.

David convinced Julia to do a turn for the third pilot. She strapped on her apron and demonstrated how to make a "strawberry fool," a mixture of berries and whipped cream. As she beat it vigorously, the fool became so aerated that it rose fluffily over the side of her mixing bowl. "I was at the White House once, cooking for them," Julia told the camera, "and I made this. And it always slops over the top of the bowl, so this is what I did," she said, bending over and giving a hearty blow— *Pthhhht!*—which shot the dessert off the edge and back into the bowl. She burst into laughter.

By early 1992, WGBH seemed poised to order a whole season of *Three Men in a Kitchen* for broadcast. But one day that winter, David received a phone call from the producer.

"David, it's Laurie," she said. "I've got some bad news."

"After they spent all that money?" he responded.

"It doesn't make any sense, but I'm afraid so."

A new head of programming had come in at PBS and axed *Three Men in a Kitchen*. "Diversity" was the word of the day. "PBS," Laurie quoted the executive explaining the decision, "does not need a show with three white men in a kitchen." In fact, the public network seemed uninterested in adding new cooking shows of any hue. Geoffrey Drummond, who produced Julia Child's later series for PBS, as well as *The Frugal Gourmet*, had been suggesting they expand cooking shows out of weekend hours, and been told, "This is the network of *Nova* and *The News Hour. Sesame Street*. We are not interested in spending any more time in the kitchen than we already do."

David was devastated.

Not far removed from his theater studies days, David decided to try to view the setback as if he were a veteran of the Great White Way: "Yesterday they told you you would not go far," he sang to himself, quoting the song "There's No Business Like Show Business." "Next day on your dressing room they've hung a star."

But the next day did not seem to be coming. It took three years for *Gourmet* to run an article David had written on balsamic vinegar, which paid $1,500. His book agent, David Chalfant, had been nagging him for months to reach out to a TV producer named Charlie Pinsky who produced a number of high-quality PBS food shows. "Get to Charlie!" Chalfant would repeat to Rosengarten whenever the writer complained that his career was stalled. Charlie produced Pierre Franey, a renowned French chef who had a successful series on PBS in which he traveled through America cooking in gorgeous locations.

David had been reluctant. He was full of ego, but not sure what he had to back it up. Charlie Pinsky produced slick shows. Perhaps he'd be allergic to the schmaltz of *Three Men in a Kitchen*. But one Sunday afternoon in the summer of 1993, sitting in his apartment sweating, David was feeling just desperate enough to place the call.

The producer picked up.

"Charlie, my name is David Rosengarten."

David's newsletter had made enough of a mark among serious food people that Pinsky had heard of him. "Yeah, I know who you are."

Emboldened, David dove in: "Well, I'd really love to meet with you sometime and talk with you about a possible TV project."

"The timing is bad, I'm packing right now, I'm leaving tomorrow for France for six months to shoot with Pierre Franey."

That's that, David thought. Time to back out gracefully: "All right, well, when you come back. . . ."

"Well, wait a second," Charlie said, remembering something. "Where do you live?"

It turned out they lived only a few blocks apart.

"You know, I've got to take a break from packing. I'll tell you what, I'll walk over and say hi."

Ten minutes after Charlie arrived, he was studying David's videotape of *Three Men in a Kitchen.*

"Okay, you're good on TV," Charlie said, after watching for a while. "Listen, before I go to France tomorrow, I'm having lunch with a guy named Reese Schonfeld. Do you know Reese?"

"No."

"Well, he's starting this thing called the Television Food Network. Have you heard about that?"

"Honestly, no."

"Okay, well, Reese is probably gonna ask me for some names of people for, you know, talent. Do you mind if I mention your name?"

David was thrilled. "No, mention my name. Yes."

David was correct that he was not Charlie's *tasse de thé.* But Joe Langhan, when he set up the meeting between Charlie and Reese, had told Charlie that TVFN was going to be "like a factory. We have to mass-produce shows and knock them out fast." What Charlie took from the conversation was that TVFN was not going to pay him well to produce the kind of high-end shows he liked, but he wanted to be helpful while gracefully steering TVFN away from himself. David might be just what Reese and Joe were looking for: a guy who knew something about food and would not soon get tired of being on camera. Anyway, David was all Charlie had to offer Reese the next day at lunch.

The next day, David's phone rang and an unfamiliar voice greeted him.

"Dave Rosengarten?"

"Yes."

"Did you have a meeting with Charlie Pinsky and you showed him a tape?"

"Yeah."

"Could you possibly messenger that tape to us?"

"Sure."

Two days later, another brusque phone call: "David Rosengarten?"

"Yes."

"Would you be so kind as to come to a studio on West Fifty-seventh Street? We'd like to do a little test."

David had no knowledge of what they wanted from him. Would he be asked to demonstrate Szechuan Shrimp? But, like anyone looking for a break, he went. Outside he saw a professionally dressed woman with short blond hair. He did not watch much local news, or follow local politics closely. He did know a lot about stinky French cheeses. "Do you know if the Television Food Network is here?" he asked her.

"Well, the network is not here," she said. "But I am supposed to show up to do something for the Television Food Network, too, and this is where we're supposed to be."

"All right, well, great! My name's David Rosengarten."

"Hi," the woman replied. "My name is Donna Hanover."

They went in together and were shown to a stage with spotlights trained on a table in the center. It was dark all around. They each took a chair.

A voice from the darkness barked, "Start talking!"

"What do you want us to talk about?" David asked, peering into the darkness.

"What did you have for lunch!" the voice barked again.

"Well, er, Donna, I had a tuna salad sandwich for lunch, it was pretty good. How about you? What did you have for lunch?"

David was good at banter and Donna started enjoying herself. She felt like she would enjoy working with him.

Reese had seen enough. David could talk. The talent he really cared about, Donna, had taken to him. The food person, Charlie, had said David knew his stuff. He'd do.

Four minutes into the test, David saw a six-foot-three figure come hulking out of the darkness. Reese walked up to the table and, ignoring David, extended his hand to Donna.

"I think we found our co-anchor!" he said to her.

"Co-anchor for what?" David thought. "Me? Her? When? Who is this tall man?"

Reese strode away from the table without so much as a glance at Rosengarten. David saw his agent walk off after the tall man.

David said good-bye to Donna and went home. A few hours later, he heard from his agent: "Well, I hope this is okay with you, Dave," David Chalfant said. "You have a contract for two years at a hundred thousand dollars a year, being the co-anchor of a nightly news kind of magazine show about food." Donna had also agreed to come aboard.

Rosengarten, uncharacteristically, was too stunned to speak.

With that pillar of the schedule in place, Reese turned his attention to the softer shows on the schedule, contacting his old friends Allen Reid and Mady Land. Since the late 1980s, the couple

> "It was instant simpatico. He is like a nuclear physicist of food."
>
> **—DONNA HANOVER**

had been producing *Cookin' USA* for the Nashville Network (which eventually became TNN and then Spike), starring Merle Ellis, a butcher. Knowing Reese might soon be looking for new talent, whenever Allen and Mady saw a guest they liked, they asked the chef to tape five extra solo minutes. They now had a stockpile of sample tapes.

In August 1993, the producing couple went to New York to see Reese, tapes in tow. They began suggesting shows he might want, but Reese didn't care that a certain chef might be famous for his expertise with seafood or Italian cuisine. There was no seafood or Italian show planned for launch. Reese wanted to plug in talent to do the shows in the schedule Sue had helped draw up. One show concept Reese was particularly fixated on was *How to Boil Water*. It was the idea of Reese's friend Jim Gaines, a *Time* magazine editor who had recently gotten divorced and did not know how to cook for himself. Gaines suggested that single men needed a program to teach them the basics. Reese told Allen and Mady he wanted them to produce it. The only question was who would host it.

Some food world experts he'd met were pushing Reese to find a place on TVFN for Jasper White, a chef who had been a central figure in a renaissance of Boston cuisine, winning the 1990 James Beard award as Best Chef in the Northeast. Jasper, thirty-nine, had a fleshy face, bushy hair, and a thick salt-and-pepper beard; he wasn't particularly telegenic but was well known on the East Coast.

Allen began making the case for a different chef who had made numerous appearances on *Cookin' USA* and who had just published a well-received cookbook. Emeril Lagasse had been named Best Chef in the Southeast by the James Beard Foundation in 1991 and *Esquire* magazine had just named NOLA, his second restaurant, Best New Restaurant. Allen had hoped to do a show featuring Emeril's groundbreaking interpretations of Creole cuisine. His cookbook was full of fascinating recipes like Stir-Fry of Sesame Ginger Crawfish over Fried Pasta. But Reese was not offering a Creole show.

"Reese, I'm telling you, this guy Emeril Lagasse is terrific," Allen argued, trying to get Emeril onto the network any way he could. "He has a twinkle in his eye. And this guy Jasper doesn't."

This was an argument among friends. Allen and Mady already knew they were going to produce the show no matter what—no one could make a food show as cheaply as they knew they could, so they stood by their guns. Reese dug in. "I'm not interested in Emeril. He's okay, but he's not good enough." Reese did not think Emeril was appealing as a television personality, nor was he being chattered about in the New York media world. With a working-class Massachusetts accent seeming to turn every vowel into an "awww" sound, Emeril was not someone Reese would have hired to host a news program.

"He's terrific!" Allen pushed.

"I don't think so."

Robin Connelly, the F.O.R., was sitting on the floor sorting videotapes as the dispute played out. Robin had watched the five-minute Emeril tape Allen and Mady had screened for Reese. Emeril, thirty-three, had a thick head of dark hair, a trim waist for a chef, expressive eyebrows, and his working-class Fall River accent, rather than being unappealing, could also be described as a sweet growl—manly, inviting, and shy at the same time.

Reese shouted over his desk to Robin, "Well, what do you think of this guy?"

"He's a hunk," she said. Robin was young and, more important, Robin was female and not a jaded television veteran. Reese thought the main audience for TVFN was going to be females aged twenty-five to fifty-four. Females will tune in to watch hunks. Even a newsman knows that.

Reese turned his attention back to Allen. "Okay, we'll choose Emeril."

Many of those who would be drawn to cook on television could trace their motivational fires to family dramas in childhood—wanting to put things right by producing something perfect in the kitchen. But a rare few seemed to have been born with the pilot light lit. Emeril was one of those. Born in Fall River, Massachusetts, Emeril began helping his mother, Hilda, put vegetables into her homemade soup when he was five years old. As he grew, she gave Emeril the daily job of going to the local Portuguese bakery for bread. At ten, entranced by the aromas, he talked them into giving him a job. He was paid a dollar an hour and worked four hours after school every day washing pans and being taught how to make muffins and bread. Even when he followed another passion and became an accomplished drummer in his teens, cooking won out over music. Offered a full scholarship to the New England Conservatory of Music, he turned it down, opting to pay his own way through the two-year culinary program at Johnson & Wales. His mother was upset, but his father, a security guard at a local mill and a garment dyer, said, "Emeril, if you think that this is something you love, which obviously you do, and if you think this is a way you can get a ticket out of here, then you go for it."

He graduated, and spent years improving his craft at restaurants in France and then in the States, before being hired in 1982 to replace the renowned Chef Paul Prudhomme at Commander's Palace in New Orleans. There Emeril made his mark, becoming identified more with the Louisiana city than with his New England birthplace. He had not done it simply to win a ticket out, as his father had said. For Emeril, his decisions were a matter of ruthlessly following his gut. He would act impulsively because he trusted his instincts. And neither they nor the people he hired to help execute his plans had yet failed him.

In 1990, he opened his own restaurant, Emeril's, in a derelict warehouse district in New Orleans. On a night in February 1991, his intuitive genius was on display when he learned that Julia Child was coming to dinner. His week had already been tough because the annual national conference of the IACP was being held in New Orleans, and Emeril's was the hottest dining spot in town, a must-visit for food world dignitaries. Rumor had reached Emeril that Julia was seeking talent to appear on a new series she was planning for PBS called *Cooking with Master Chefs*. He thought that if he could earn a turn on Julia's show, it would help promote his restaurant and New Orleans cuisine. But, as he prepared to address his staff during the nightly pre-dinner meeting, he saw tired faces looking back at him. This was not the spirit a visit from Julia Child deserved.

He stopped talking about the menu. "Guys, this level of energy isn't going to do it! You're not tuned in. I think what we need to do right now"—he waved a beckoning arm as he starting to walk toward the front door—"Follow me."

Improvising, he led the waiters outside the restaurant, a former pharmacy warehouse, as dusk was descending on Tchoupitoulas Street. He began to jog. Uneasy laughter broke out, but the staff followed him, giggling, and picked up the pace to a full-on run as they circumnavigated the block.

"All right," Emeril said, as his laughing employees streamed back into the restaurant. "Now we're ready for service. Let's do it!"

Julia was won over by the bustling restaurant and the charismatic chef. In March 1993, just as Emeril's first cookbook, *Emeril's New New Orleans Cooking*, was coming out, a crew came to New Orleans to tape the premiere episode of *Cooking with Master Chefs*. Julia and Emeril prepared Shrimp Étouffée and boiled crawfish, pinching the cooked crustaceans at their ends to remove the meat. In later years, Emeril would boast, "I taught Julia Child how to suck head and pinch tail!"

A few days after Allen and Mady's meeting with Reese in August 1993, Emeril was in his cluttered restaurant kitchen, having just finished a three-month tour promoting his first book. His instincts, and his willingness to trust those close to him, would be tested again. Marti Dalton, his business manager poked her head in.

"Em, there's a call for you," Marti said, "that TV producer."

Emeril was tired from the book tour, but when he had shot an extra five minutes after his appearance on the Nashville Network, Allen had assured him he was working to get Emeril his own TV cooking series.

"Emeril," Allen said, "this TV Food Network thing is actually going to happen and we've got the go-ahead to make a show with you."

"Do I have to leave New Orleans?" Emeril asked.

"Well, you'd have to come to Nashville once in a while." Allen explained the show, *How to Boil Water*. Emeril would teach everything from making sandwiches to how to slice a cucumber. "Easy," Allen said.

"Gee, I don't know," Emeril said. "I'm going to teach people how to boil water? I'm going to show them how to make grilled cheese sandwiches?"

Allen agreed it was a strange fit, but encouraged Emeril, saying, "Hey, it's a start. You're going to be on television. It's better than not. If you don't do this, it will be Jasper White."

"Let me think about it and get back to you," Emeril said.

The episode of *Cooking with Master Chefs* in which he cooked with Julia was slated to run on PBS in October. Emeril talked over Allen's offer with Marti. There was no guarantee that the appearance with Julia would lead to offers to do something more culinarily complex on television. *How to Boil Water* was a bird in the hand.

"You should do it," Marti said. "It will help bring people to the restaurants."

He followed the advice. "Okay, all right. I'll give it a shot."

He called Allen and accepted the offer. Over the next few days, Emeril and Marti spent what free time they had drawing up recipes and script ideas for the TVFN series.

Down in Nashville, Allen and Mady began working on three shows Reese had assigned them: *How to Boil Water* with Emeril, *Food in a Flash* starring Curtis Aikens, an expert on fruits and vegetables, and *The Dessert Show* with Debbi Fields, the founder of Mrs. Fields cookies.

Emeril would come to town for eight days and shoot sixty-five episodes of *How to Boil Water*, about eight a day and enough for TVFN to run a new episode every weekday for three months. Reese, following the model of a news channel, did not want reruns. On one episode, Emeril literally explained how to fill a pot with water, turn on the stove, and boil it.

On the day Emeril left town, Allen would take down the facings of the cabinets, move a few pieces around, put up different cabinet facings, and the next day start an eight-day cycle of shooting sixty-five episodes of *The Dessert Show*. Out Debbi went and, after a one-day changeover, Curtis Aikens arrived for his sixty-five episodes. Reid/Land was producing what must have been a record: 195 half-hour television episodes every thirty days.

Emeril had tried to tell himself it would be good for his personal development, almost meditative, to get back in touch with the basics like making egg salad and tuna fish. But he felt ridiculous doing it. When the first few episodes trickled up to New York, the TVFN staff were concerned. Emeril mumbled and was hunched over. He had a hard time remembering to look at the camera. But for the time being, they needed programming desperately, so the show went on.

> "It was $50 a show or some crazy nonsense . . . I had to bring my own coffee, it was like—I remember staying at this place in Nashville, a really cheap hotel. It was ridiculous. That's what it was."
>
> —EMERIL LAGASSE

There was less planning than reacting. Now a few shows were in production, and they were to be ready around the planned network debut, Thanksgiving week of 1993. But in late August, a big problem arose. November might be too late. After various court challenges and an evolving understanding of the new cable law, it became clear that if TVFN was not "a channel" putting out a signal by October 6, 1993, the retransmission consent agreements could be in legal jeopardy and everything might fall apart.

This time, Joe's well of experience joined with Reese's to save the day. Joe recalled when Colony Cablevision had applied for a license to become the cable operator for Fall River, Massachusetts, back in the 1970s. The man in charge of the effort, George Sisson, had promised local officials that the cable system would offer more than twenty-five channels. "George, what are we going to have on these channels?" Joe had asked him.

"We'll have to make some stuff up," Sisson replied. Once the license was granted, they put up The Television Tuning Channel, which showed nothing but wide bars of color with an unwavering sound tone, and The Barker Channel, which ran a loop of promotional tapes from HBO and other fledgling pay services: "You must see *Standing Room Only: Neil Sedaka!*"

Joe suggested that TVFN could meet the October 6 deadline by starting out as a barker channel. Reese worried they would permanently lose the allegiance of anyone who happened to tune in, along with the allegiance of the cable providers who would have to put the dreck on their systems, but agreed there was little choice.

But could they be said to be officially broadcasting "a channel," as their agreements called for, if all they were running was a short loop? They called Colony Cablevision's lawyer in Washington, D.C. He'd never seen a legal definition of what a channel had to carry to be considered "a channel." He told them he'd go over to the FCC and nose around quietly. "They'll draw up a definition right away if they know what you're up to," he explained.

A few tense days passed and the lawyer called Joe and Reese. "There is none," he said, giving them the good news. "Nothing says how many hours of original programming you have to have to be 'a channel.'"

Reese knew a guy in Canton, Massachusetts, Barry Rosenthal, who had made a marketing video for *Crimewatch Tonight*. He immediately called him and asked if he could pull together a promotional video for a 24-hour network about food.

Barry idolized Reese as a cable pioneer. "Reese, if you're launching the twenty-four-hour Poop Network, I'm in." Despite Reese's occasional tantrum, many of those who worked with him loved him and were fiercely loyal. His extreme personality gave him a depth of character those near him could tell stories about and bond over. Plus, he always remembered his friends. "When Reese works, we all work," an F.O.R. said.

Barry cobbled together a loop of strung-together food show pilots and one original thirty-second spot.

"It's another day in America," that thirty-second segment of the loop began, a cheerful narrator echoing Ronald Reagan's 1984 campaign commercial, "It's morning again in America." The segment opened with a shot of a schoolhouse topped with a rooster weather vane, dissolved to generic shots of a woman putting a sprig of lettuce into her mouth, a boy eating pizza, and a man biting into an ear of corn. "And before it's over," the narrator cooed, "two hundred and fifty million people will eat nearly a billion meals, each in their own way. Whether it's a hearty country breakfast, lunch on the go, an afternoon snack or a quiet dinner at home, there's a place you can turn to help you make it a little easier, a little healthier, and a lot more fun. The TV Food Network: It's all you need to know about food."

The loop, put out on a satellite signal before the deadline, would only hold space for so long. They vowed to beam original content to cable providers as soon as they had it. Reese, Joe, and Jack discussed announcing an official start date when a regular programming slate would go out. They agreed that the Monday of Thanksgiving week would be best because it would provide a theme for shows to follow in the buildup to the biggest food day of the American year. Jack took out a calendar. "Only problem," he said, "is the Monday of that week is November 22." The three men were all old enough to well know that November 22 was the day John F. Kennedy was assassinated. This would be the thirtieth anniversary, not an auspicious date to start a network, especially if you wanted media attention. They decided on Tuesday, November 23, 1993.

Reese gave his wife, Pat, the job of finding a permanent home for TVFN. There was no way to get a lease signed and a studio built in time for the launch date, so Reese set about establishing a temporary home for the first few months. F.O.R. Susannah Eaton-Ryan found Unitel Studio, at 503 West Thirty-third Street near Eleventh Avenue, in the grungy blocks near the Lincoln Tunnel. A squat, beige brick building darkened with car exhaust, it had a tiny bit of office space and a small stage to shoot rudimentary talk shows, but no proper kitchen.

The area was a well-known hive of street prostitutes. When Sue Huffman phoned her husband, Jim, with directions to pick her up one night, she warned him, "I just want to tell you, there's a hooker right out in front of the door, and when you pull up, she's gonna think you're pulling up for her. So just a heads-up." Ricki Stofsky, the producer, took to referring to one pimp as Jiffy Pop because his hat looked like the expanding foil cover on stovetop popcorn. Some of the young staff grew used to nodding hello to the prostitutes they'd see at the

McDonald's on the corner, one of the only places nearby to eat. Jiffy Pop sometimes greeted them with a suggestive, "Hi, how are you doing?" as if he were looking for recruits.

Reese, starving for content, made deals for vintage episodes of Dione Lucas's 1950s cooking show and *The Galloping Gourmet*. Graham Kerr owned his own rights, so the negotiation was easy. Dione's rights were owned by Art Modell, the farsighted owner of the Cleveland Browns, who had helped create *Monday Night Football*. Modell couldn't believe his luck that someone wanted to broadcast black-and-white cooking shows, but he was not going to give them away. TVFN paid $180,000 for two years of broadcast rights for Dione Lucas, $75,000 for *The Galloping Gourmet*, and $125,000 for episodes of James Beard's old cooking show, which had been thought gone but were unearthed. To freshen these "classics," *Saturday Night Live* veteran Jane Curtin was hired to come to the new headquarters and tape introductions. Susannah, who oversaw the shoot, was astonished at how much white wine and how many cigarettes Jane managed to consume during the day. Explaining for cameras that viewers were about to watch Dione roast a chicken and then, after a pause, that viewers had just watched Dione roast a chicken was clearly not Jane's favorite gig ever. Even if it was not Reese's intention, the inclusion of these shows managed to establish a genetic link between revered names in the world of food and television and the new channel, as if TVFN was setting itself up as the keeper of a gourmet flame.

> "I had Peter Kaminsky and Sean Kelly as writers. We decided that every chance we got, we were going to insert a potato joke. . . . For one show, I had to talk about a dish that was larded liver. It was so disgusting to me. I thought this was horrible—people shouldn't be eating this. It got to the point where I didn't want to talk about food anymore. It was like joining a cult, all the focus on food, the discussions about food."
>
> —JANE CURTIN

As November 23 approached, when 6.5 million homes would be set to receive it, TVFN broadcast practice episodes of *Food News and Views* and a talk show, *Get-*

ting Healthy, shot on the news set on West Thirty-third Street. Also on the schedule was another show Reese believed crucial to the network's success, TVFN's version of *Larry King Live*, a 10 p.m. showcase where celebrities and newsmakers would stop by the studio to chat live about anything food-related, called *Robin Leach: Talking Food*. Robin had seen rats outside the building. But he was so appalled to see rodents inside the studio the day he made his very first show that he asked the main cameraman to pan on the vermin. To Robin's recollection, one of the first shots that went out on the Television Food Network was of rats scurrying across a black floor.

As large a personality as Robin was, no one mistook him for a food person. It was pretty much blind luck that TVFN had brought David Rosengarten aboard. What it had landed in him was someone with a deep and geeky affection for food arcana along with a thespian's hammy tendency to turn everything into a show. In many ways, David's marriage of fine cuisine, ego, and vaudevillian showbiz schmaltz would set the tone for what viewers experienced of the network in its early years. Unmistakably, David knew his stuff. Viewers could see that, and he was helped by the addition of food-obsessed people like Doris Weisberg, who once led eating tours of Greenwich Village, and Dorie Greenspan, a respected cookbook author. Both produced some of the earliest shows and delivered the idea that the channel might be a bit schlocky, but it was serious about food.

On November 22, the night before the network's official debut, some of the talent indulged in dark humor and off-color gags as they taped their last practice episodes—which went out for broadcast that night to an untold number of cable homes across the country that were receiving the signal in advance of the announced start date. On *Food News and Views*, Donna smoothly delivered the information that the average cost of a Thanksgiving dinner was up by a dollar. The camera switched to her co-anchor. "In a related story," David read, allowing a slight smirk, "since a rabies epidemic has crippled the raccoon population on the East Coast"—bad news it would seem—"turkeys have flourished. And that's good news for the holidays! Wildlife experts in upstate New York say they are seeing more wild turkeys this year than ever before. . . . About eighty to ninety percent of the raccoons have died."

Later, a story about thieves raiding a Thanksgiving food pantry in St. Louis was followed by the item that Pepsi had signed a five-year agreement with an airline. And so the day's food news unfolded until David started a segment on the popularity of different brands of frozen waffles. "Well, it may not be long before Kellogg is saying, 'Leggo my Eggo . . . '" David paused for comedic effect. "Market share, that is."

Robin Leach was worse on *Talking Food*. Much worse.

Reese had installed Robin Connelly, who had called Emeril "a hunk," on Robin Leach's show as his sidekick. To avoid the on-air name repetition, she adopted the stage name Kate. Some excerpts:

ROBIN: We are getting so close to Thanksgiving here. I wanted to deal with one of the major problems that I have at Thanksgiving which is, how do you really give it to old Tom Turkey.

[Kate laughs politely, Robin whistles and makes a pop noise with his mouth.]

KATE: I would never have thought you would've had a problem with stuffing, Robin. But, anyway, I'm gonna show you a very neat trick.

ROBIN: I do, because it's a big bird.

KATE: Uh-huh. Yes . . . ?

ROBIN: I'm just a regular guy.

KATE: [laughing] Regular guy. Faced with a big bird.

ROBIN: Yes.

KATE: Yes. Well I can see why you might be nervous about that. So I've got here, our friend . . .

ROBIN: Tom!

KATE: Tom.

ROBIN: Tom!

KATE: Ooh! Tom's a little damp.

ROBIN: Tom's a little wet. . . .

KATE: Yep. Stuff it, go ahead. Go ahead, put some in there. Give it a try.

> *[Robin takes a huge fistful of stuffing from bowl, even though there's a big spoon in the bowl.]*

KATE: Oh, Robin!

> *[Robin puts some in the bird, removes his hand, shows he is making a fist, and then pounds it in. Rhythmically.]*

On November 23, there was a celebratory party at the Rainbow Room above Rockefeller Center. Mayor-elect Giuliani was there with his wife. Curtis Aikens, who had taped his shows in Nashville and not met his comrades, was intimidated by being around a big celebrity like Robin Leach, and tried avoiding him until Robin recognized the star of *Food in a Flash*, cornered him, and boisterously declared, "Curtis! The pay's not well, but the party's fantastic, so let's go for a ride!"

Reese was fuming because TVs at the Rainbow Room weren't tuned to the network. Later he gave a speech and thanked Joe, but said that Joe could not be at the party because "as usual, he is back at the studio making sure everything is going okay."

Joe, who was at the party, heard that and thought, I really should be at the studio in case something goes wrong, and dashed back.

It is a testament to how seat-of-the-pants it was that the tapes from the first day's shows have gone missing. According to the best recollections of those who were working that night, the first show officially broadcast on the channel was the hourlong *Food News and Views*. In it, Donna mispronounced "ragout." Instead of saying "ragu," she gave it two words, "rag" and "out." The producers had to do a second take or risk losing credibility. "We can't put that out on the air as the first episode," someone declared.

On the cover of that week's *TV Guide* was a shot of the actors starring in a reunion of *The Waltons*, and the magazine did not mention the upstart food channel, nor include its offerings in the listings section. A TVFN press release touted the network's new stars, including "the

Engagin' Cajun," Emeril Lagasse, and Gayle Gardner, host of a live call-in show about health.

During the following days, the content on the network settled down—slightly. *Food News and Views* featured a phone interview with someone from Butterball discussing how a turkey should be cooked. An on-set guest was Abe Lebewohl, the owner of 2nd Avenue Deli, who brought a huge platter of sandwiches and discussed the finer points of corned beef. For the first few weeks, the big food news story that Reese wanted David and Donna to own was recombinant bovine growth hormone (rBGH), a controversial chemical used in the cattle industry. Experts on cow biology were interviewed daily on the air. As time went on and the mainstream media did not take note of the important journalistic work *Food News and Views* was doing, Reese turned off bovines and onto credit card fees charged to restaurants. He argued that restaurateurs would find it essential viewing. Bursting into the greenroom one night where the anchors were prepping, Reese bellowed, "Did you see the news about MasterCard? MasterCard lowered their restaurant fees by an eighth of a percent! This is big. We've got to really play this up. Give it emphasis!"

To break up the hard news during broadcasts, there were light features like an illustration speculating what the cast of the network sitcom *Friends* would look like fat, and a recurring humorous debate segment, based on the CNN show *Crossfire*. It pitted David's old *Three Men in a Kitchen* sidekick Tony Hendra, a food conservative, against author Barbara Kafka, a food liberal. It was called *Rhubarb*. Typical topic: bison as food. Kafka was pro, Hendra con: "Why not eat roadkill?" he asked.

Robin Leach was a central character in these wild proceedings as the first weeks unfolded, often rushing beerily onto the set seconds before air, straight from Madison Square Garden a few blocks east, where he'd been watching the Knicks.

> "Going on the air that first night and knowing that everybody had said, 'You can never pull it off,' we stuck a chicken bone in their throats. We went on the air and did it."
>
> —ROBIN LEACH

Once when the actor B. D. Wong was a guest, Robin insisted on referring to him as "a Chinaman," as in "How does it feel to be a Chinaman in Hollywood?"

B.D. was livid, but tried to act with class, asking, "Well, if you mean what is it like as an actor in my culture. . . ."

Robin dug in. "No no no, I mean, as a Chinaman."

Whatever preposterousness Robin brought, he hit his marks. Reese's affection for him was unflagging, and he consistently brought in celebrities. Author Paul Theroux came in to discuss his book *Millroy the Magician*. Singer Judy Collins stopped by, as did Francis Ford Coppola.

Despite the uneven content, Reese and his ragtag troops were thrilled that they had gotten a television network on the air in a matter of months. Now that TVFN was broadcasting, there would be a brief chance to take a breath. It was far from profitable, faced deep skepticism from investors, and was chaotic, but word of its existence was slowly spreading.

Less than three weeks after the debut, the staff, after working nearly around the clock, held their own low-key TVFN Christmas party at Landmark Tavern, a bar fifteen blocks uptown.

Reese and Joe were still trying to secure rights to broadcast old episodes of Julia's original WGBH series *The French Chef*, and they still didn't have a deal for Julia to contribute essays to the news show. *The French Chef* rights were half-owned by WGBH, and Julia was entitled to 50 percent of the rights fees.

The TVFN team thought they had an advantage because Henry Beckton Jr., the president of WGBH, was on the board of the Providence Journal. But Beckton recused himself, and turned over the negotiations to his assistant at the station. The ProJo board authorized Reese and Joe to offer a million dollars to WGBH for the rights. Unfortunately, Beckton's underling had a boyfriend who was a chef, and he told her that Julia Child was worth more than a million dollars, and WGBH turned down the million-dollar offer without asking Julia whether or not she would like half a million dollars for her old shows. Soon after the network launch in November, Julia asked Reese why her programs weren't on. TVFN now offered WGBH half a million, and Julia urged WGBH to take it. The deal earned Julia $250,000, and led to her agreeing to appear occasionally on the network, generally on *Food News and Views* segments, as Sue and Reese had suggested over dinner in Cambridge.

Reese needed ideas for shows to produce in-house once they moved to their permanent headquarters, where they would have kitchen facilities and could make real cooking shows. That January, David managed to get Reese's attention for a few minutes.

"I have an idea for a new kind of cooking show," David began.

David had been useful on *Food News and Views*, Reese thought, keeping Donna happily in harness. David was not terrible.

"Okay. The typical cooking show," David continued, gushing forth before he lost the famously impatient Reese. "The first third is appetizers, second third the main course, and the last third dessert. It's a menu. But listen. How many people do you think watch that thirty minutes and then reproduce the menu? Very few, you know. Five percent or less. So you are wasting the structure of thirty minutes. Why should the menu govern your structure? Why don't we find another way to take advantage of thirty minutes? Okay. So my show will take either a dish or an ingredient and spend the whole thirty minutes on that ingredient. Or dish."

There was one second of silence. Reese told David, "That sounds good. When do you want to start?"

David couldn't believe what he was hearing. How could this be so easy?

"I don't know. March?"

"Okay. We'll have Josh White produce you. Go talk to him."

David floated out of Reese's office. Wow. He had a cooking show. A show of his own! He could have an entire episode on how to properly batter seafood for frying!

Three months later David was preparing to tape his first episode of the show named *Taste*. He was setting things up on the counter in the studio, nervously going over his lines in his head, the beats of the show.

Suddenly, a door opened and silhouetted in the light was a six-foot-tall female figure.

David glanced up, but at first did not recognize who it was.

Then he realized. Dear God, he thought. Today?

It was Julia, visiting the network for one of her segments. David was nearly paralyzed as she strode up to his set.

"Oh, what are we cooking today?" she asked.

"Well, er, uh, Julia, we're, I'm, ah, doing a show about bruschetta."

"Oh, very good. Show me what you're going to doooo."

David began demonstrating how he was going to chop some tomatoes and other toppings for toasted bread. Then he showed her his choreography, moving to the oven and saying, "And then through the magic of TV . . ."

Julia's eyes widened. "I HATE that stupid expression! The magic of TV. It's bullshit!"

"All right. Sorry. I'm sorry," David stammered, trying not to drop the tray of finished bruschetta. "I won't. I won't use it again."

"I'm sure you'll do fine." Julia turned and walked out of the light.

Haphazard as the assemblage of the talent had been, most shared a belief in the importance of good food for a good life. Robin and other stars were flying around the country trying to sell small cable operators on carrying TVFN. In Dallas, Curtis, who had learned to read and write at the age of twenty-six, met with the owner of Marcus Cable, Jeff Marcus, and pledged that people like himself and Emeril really cared about the transformative power of a family meal. "This is about trying to use television to make people's lives better," Curtis said.

Sold, Marcus replied, "We're going to get this network on the air."

"Chefs Are the New Rock Stars"

A television channel, no matter how small-time, creates opportunities. Even a new local public access channel means that some frustrated artist may find an outlet—and perhaps an audience.

TVFN was far more than a local public access channel. At launch it reached communities dotted throughout the nation: White Plains, New York; New Bedford, Massachusetts; Costa Mesa, California; Knoxville, Tennessee. A variety of talents started showing up, some of them faded local celebrities just wanting to see themselves back on television again, others with stunningly farsighted visions of what might be made with this squalid little start-up.

For now, there was a thrown-together team tasked with meeting an unrelenting daily deadline amid balky equipment, general chaos, and the forceful insistence of the man in charge that everything would get done, damn the disbelievers. TVFN was running a few hours of original programming a day, repeating it up to six times. Many of the advertisements were of the low-rent variety: Ginsu Knives, Flowbee haircutting products, and other items available by ordering from a toll-free number.

Reese had long planned to add a restaurant review show to the schedule. To cohost this, he tapped one of those who were looking for a way back in front of the cameras. Bill Boggs was a veteran TV host with a locomotive jaw and dark blue eyes. Back in the 1980s, Boggs was doing daily television news in Philadelphia when he realized one afternoon that the Chippendales exotic dancer in a bow tie whom he was interviewing for a light midday news feature was probably the eighth Chippendales exotic dancer in a bow tie he had interviewed over his long years doing light features. Looking across at the shiny shaved chest, Boggs said to himself, "I've got to change what I'm doing." He went on to help produce Morton Downey Jr.'s shock-mongering syndicated talk show in New York. After Downey was canceled in 1990, Bill, burned out, met a radio producer for a station in Greenwich, Connecticut, and on a lark, asked if he could do a talk show about food on Saturday afternoons. The producer agreed, and Boggs, unpaid, was soon doing phone interviews with celebrities like Dizzy Gillespie, Dick Clark, and Ed McMahon, asking each a question he had honed to get them talking: "What was your dinner table like when you were ten years old?"

Boggs, who loved to tell stories about himself, would refer to his practice of asking every interviewee the same thing as using his "signature questions." Radio was a taste of the attention he needed, but television was what he craved. Without it, he felt like nobody special. Boggs managed to land a meeting with Reese and, with his news background and celebrity connections, he won a recurring slot on *Food News and Views*, delivering food-related gossip for a segment called "The Daily Dish." Boggs would scan the tabloid newspapers, pluck out items, and then rewrite them to read on TV. A great day for him was when he revealed that Bill Clinton on the campaign trail had shaken hundreds of hands and then was so hungry that he'd eaten pie with his unwashed fingers.

When Reese was ready to add the restaurant review show to the schedule, he cast Boggs. It was originally called *Eating Out*, until Reese realized that the phrase's double entendre made people giggle. After a few months, the name was changed to *Dining Out* and then to *TV Dinners*.

Boggs's cohost was another at-sea talent drawn to TVFN. Nina

Griscom was a thirty-something Manhattan socialite, tall, blond, thin, and married to her third husband, a Park Avenue plastic surgeon. She had finished a stint on a little-remembered HBO entertainment news show and her lawyer, a friend of Reese (F.O.R.), connected Nina with TVFN. She told Reese she was qualified for a restaurant review show because she had a knowledge of cuisine won from a lifetime of cooking and eating. That plus her good looks, on-camera experience, and social connections was enough for him.

Nina would arrive at the network for a day of taping that started at 6 a.m., and she would always take note of the seedy dressing room, the sofa split with cigarette burns, and the makeup table scattered with powders and creams that Nina's practiced eye recognized as cheap crap. But she persevered. They taped five shows a day, a week's worth, and reviewed three restaurants from around the country in each. There was little actual eating out. The network could not afford to send Bill and Nina to every restaurant they were reviewing, especially not to the Western states. Restaurants would ship their best dishes to TVFN by overnight mail, where they would be refrigerated and warmed up in time for the cohosts to sample on camera. A chef's signature charred veal chop might arrive from its cross-country journey and wait in the refrigerator for up to a week. Fifteen plates of food would be set out in the morning in the kitchen, and if the week-old veal chop was on an episode being taped in the afternoon, it might sit for six hours in the open—by then one of the most well-worn veal chops ever to appear on national television. The hosts tried to prepare and speak knowledgeably about a dish by reading local reviews of each restaurant, but it could be tough to focus as they sat across from each other at a rickety-looking table with a tired piece of meat between them. As Boggs remembered: "I would say—we're looking at this veal chop—'Nina, what, what do you think of this, it's a special of the house, Joe's veal chop.' 'Well, I don't know, Bill, why don't you describe it?' 'No, you do it.' 'You.' 'Well, Nina, you know, I've never really seen a veal chop that looks exactly like that.' And the reason being, there are spores like growing from the bottom of the veal chop. 'And the wasabi mayonnaise, I've never seen one quite so green.'"

No matter how few people were watching, TVFN was show business, and Nina and Bill felt like stars. To the best of their abilities, and despite the unappealing format, they were spreading the word about the world of fine food to the cable customers receiving the channel in 1994.

David Rosengarten was managing to get a food-forward message across on *Taste*. A young *New York Times* reporter, Sarah Jay, singled out the show for praise, noting that "Mr. Rosengarten has reconceived the idea of what a cooking show can be." On one episode, David prepared oysters, making sure to discuss their aphrodisiacal qualities. He had suggested to his producer, Josh White, that they backlight the scene with swirling purple light. As David ate, jazz music began to play and the lighting changed, his feathered blond hair silhouetted against an orgiastically dark violet hue, which pulsed like a giant amoeba in mitosis.

The day after it aired, Reese called Josh and David to his office. "What the fuck!" he screamed at them. "How did you put a purple fucking blob on my network?" This network was aimed at housewives, the audience he and George Babick had been promising they'd deliver to advertisers, and Reese didn't believe that housewives wanted gyrating purple blobs and cheap titillation.

Cowed, Josh and David promised to play it straighter in the future. David also had run-ins with Sue Huffman. To him, the head of programming was a legend in her own mind, prattling on about her days interviewing chefs for the newspaper in St. Louis and reminiscing about editing the food coverage of *Ladies' Home Journal*, which David considered a bible for philistines interested in preparing Jell-O molds with canned fruit and marshmallows. But Sue had power. She had helped deliver Julia Child to Reese. Not long after the oyster episode, David was making final preparations for a show about how to tell a good chocolate mousse from a bad one, and was getting ready to demonstrate the best way to achieve the proper light, airy texture: well-whipped egg whites.

Sue sidled up to the counter and asked him, "Are you going to use raw egg whites in this mousse?"

"Yes, we are!" David replied, as brightly as he could through his teeth. "It's what gives it its lightness and its airiness."

"Well," she said, avoiding looking any of the production staff in the eye, "you're going to have to change that, because we've decided that there'll be no more raw egg on this network." Sue, who eventually became president of the IACP, was not the ignoramus David believed and well knew that egg whites were necessary, but she was following dictates from above.

"Ah . . . why?" David asked gently, as if he were speaking to an infant. The episode had been on the slate for a month, and she was weighing in now?

"Well, we just, you know, we're afraid of the liability. Raw eggs, there was a report on *Dateline*. Salmonella. We don't want anyone to get sick and sue us."

"But . . ." Josh tried to protest.

"So take out the raw egg."

Sue had the force of Reese behind her. As she left the set, the backstage kitchen staff decided that the only choice was to make the mousse out of whipped cream. During the short segment break, David spooned the unmousselike mousse into its glass, then eight people rushed forward and punched holes in the brown mass with toothpicks, hoping to create the illusion that there was air in it.

Sue, in turn, was intimidated by Reese. When the new kitchens were being designed, Reese had walked in on her showing architectural plans for the whole floor to a designer, far more information than he wanted exposed to a non-employee. "I don't want him to see the plans," Reese yelled, then ripped the papers out of the designer's hands, threw them on the floor, and jumped up and down on them until his point was made.

Despite the fuddy-duddies, there was fun to be had on the air and behind the scenes. The producers of *Food News and Views* had managed to entice Jeff Smith to sit for an interview and oversee a cooking demonstration by his assistant Craig. Smith was drinking a lot of clear liquid from a water glass. "Jeff, you know, it seems that you and Craig get along extremely well," David began. "That's how it always appears on camera, but there must be times when you disagree about things?"

The Frugal Gourmet said, "Oh, no, no, no. That never happens. Craig has a very talented tongue."

David looked right into the camera and held the glance for a beat, a classic TV comedian take.

For all David's vamping, *Food News and Views* brought the region's important chefs and food thinkers through the studios, a daily reminder to both viewers and visitors that this network really did see food as something that could be serious, funny, beautiful, and culturally and economically important.

Also helping the network establish that it was treating food as a subject both important and enjoyable was the inimitable Julia, with her every-month-or-so appearances on *Food News and Views*. She arrived like a fairy godmother, spreading her credibility like pixie dust. Of course she was by this time no longer a pixie. Sometimes getting the septuagenarian ready for her appearances could be a challenge. One time, as makeup artist Keira Karlin was smoothing foundation onto her face, Julia began nodding out, while holding on to a bag of McDonald's french fries.

"Ms. Child," Keira said, trying to keep her awake.

"Oh yes, yes, I'm sorry," Julia said, recovering briefly.

But after a few moments, the pull of a pre-show siesta overwhelmed the great star and she began slumping farther and farther over in the chair. Keira gamely soldiered on, getting the makeup in place with pads and Q-tips as Julia drifted off. Even while she slept, Julia never released her grip on the fries.

Julia was the queen of TV food personalities, but one of the biggest new stars of this first period of the network was Debbi Fields. Her series, *The Dessert Show*, had been brought to Reese by Allen Reid and Mady Land. The founder of Mrs. Fields cookies was an impressive businesswoman, who had also authored a number of cookbooks, and who came with built-in name recognition. She was certainly smarter than her on-screen persona as a kind of dazed blond housewife. At her company, Debbi had pioneered the use of computers to streamline production across a national food chain.

But among the young backstage staff in New York, it became sport to ridicule Debbi for her long fire-engine-red fingernails, gigantically blown-out hair, and relentless good cheer. On one episode, she didn't even try to pronounce her recipe for Bananas l'Orange correctly: "Bananas LUH Orange—and I know I may not say Luh Orange properly, but it really does taste good!" Justin Morris, a staff editor, created a Debbi blooper reel, highlighted by an episode in which she had chocolate all over her fingers and uttered, "I loooove chocolate." Justin slowed it down to quarter speed so it came out as "luuuurvvvve chooooooooo cccccolate" and dissolved into a slow shot of Debbi licking her fingers. The young staff laughed over it for a half hour.

The more seasoned minds at the network recognized an opportunity when mail started arriving in which viewers asked, "How does she cook with those fingernails?" They were distracted by her talons, which skewered and ruined rolled-out piecrusts, and trapped dough underneath. Instead of defending her, the network developed one of its first promotional campaigns around it. Print ads showed a photo of her and her hands and asked underneath, "How does Mrs. Fields cook with those fingernails?"

Emeril was attracting far less attention. He certainly could have correctly pronounced *l'orange*, but French was not required of him, and he was awful on *How to Boil Water*. This was not Allen and Mady's fault. The Nashville producers had tried to talk Reese into using Emeril on a more complex cooking show. After a few months, Reese decided he did see TV potential in Emeril, but thought the chef still lacked the on-air strength of personality to hold an audience on his own. Reese called Emeril from New York and said, "We've got good news and we've got bad news."

"Okay, give me the good news," Emeril said from New Orleans.

"Good news is, Emeril, we think you've got potential to be on television."

"Cool."

"Bad news is you're fired. You're overqualified for *How to Boil Water*."

"Oh," Emeril replied. "Uh, great."

They tried a second show, *Emeril and Friends*, where he cooked with guest chefs, making their recipes and being asked to closely follow a script. But the Creole specialist not cooking Creole food was still strait-jacketed and stiff.

Reese's wife, Pat, had found a suitable home for TVFN. The network signed a lease for the vacant thirty-first floor at 1177 Sixth Avenue, a building on the edge of Rockefeller Center, and set about remodeling. Pat's lack of familiarity with what cooks actually required quickly became evident after the network moved in the spring of 1994. Chefs and the kitchen staff complained that the stoves were electric, which chefs hate because the heat can't be controlled as precisely as gas, and the on-set sinks did not have proper plumbing. For running water, they illegally tapped into the sprinkler system. Under the counter, the sinks emptied directly into slop buckets, which production assistants toted out between takes.

The studio had a main set with steel lettering over it that read: *Kitchen Central*. Smaller sets around it were so flimsily assembled that the production assistants had to stand behind them and hold them up during taping. But at least there was now a studio equipped to produce some real cooking shows, complete with a somewhat more proper backstage kitchen where food could be prepped. Also, mornings and late nights around Rockefeller Center were generally free of prostitutes.

Reese made most of his decisions on the fly, walking through the halls, quickly issuing orders to whoever was standing closest to him. But he took his time figuring out what to do with Emeril. He had come to see Emeril as worth keeping because Sue Huffman had joined the chorus insisting Emeril had too much culinary talent to be squandered. Reese finally accepted that asking the chef to plod through prepared scripts and other chefs' recipes was folly. He came up with a name for a new program, *Essence of Emeril*—like any fan of newspapers, Reese loved alliteration. He flew down to New Orleans and explained that the chef would be allowed to cook his own recipes and not be scripted. In August 1994, *Essence of Emeril* began taping at the new studios in New York. "The whole network smells like a giant shrimp cocktail!" Emeril improvised enthusiastically on an early episode, turning the studio's lack of ventilation into a good thing. Measured by the number of recipe requests the network was receiving, *Essence* soon became one of the network's most popular shows. At the end of every show was a mailing address to which viewers could write requests for recipes.

But the bizarre combination of worlds Reese had forged generated unusual friction. One day on the set, Susan Stockton, a trained chef who helped run the backstage kitchen, put out a beautiful fresh snapper. Emeril said, "I love it." But Pat, filling in as producer, barked into Susan's headset, "No food with faces!" Pat was squeamish. Susan was forced to chop lemons and place them over the fish's eyes. One time, a guest chef wanted to make a quail dish with pine nuts and grape relish, but Pat told her tartly, "We're not doing little birds right now."

There were also sweet little moments. Marion Cunningham, the author of the influential revision of *The Fannie Farmer Cookbook*, made around sixty-five episodes of a homey show called *Cunningham & Company*. She invited prominent guests like legendary cookbook editor Judith Jones and restaurant consultant Clark Wolf to chat at a kitchen counter about their favorite dishes, cook a bit, and, in the final segment, sit around a table eating and chatting more. When restaurant critic Ruth Reichl did not want to blow her anonymity on the show, Reese bought her a red wig, which she wore to go undercover for years after. Trying to put Marion at ease on camera, the production staff taped a photo of her dog, Rover, onto the main camera. Instead of saying "Action!" the director barked "Woof!" when it was time to start.

It was haphazard. Hosts were cast based on who happened to show up in Reese's office on a certain day, who could recognize a tally light, and who came recommended by an F.O.R. In some ways it was not so different from a public access channel. And yet when Shep Gordon, a Hollywood agent and movie producer who was obsessed with the artistry of chefs, read an article about what was happening at the dingy TVFN studios in New York, he instantly recognized a chance to make a rewarding marriage he had long envisioned.

Shep was not one of the marginal television personalities who came knocking on Reese's door for a crack at TVFN. This was an entertainment industry veteran who believed that TVFN could become a launching pad for a new kind of celebrity. The network fit in with everything he had been building toward since a warm May night on the French Riviera in 1983.

On that night, Shep had been sitting in a bustling restaurant with Timothy Leary, one of the fathers of LSD, and G. Gordon Liddy, the infamous Watergate coconspirator. They, along with opera star Luciano Pavarotti, Clint Eastwood, and Jack Valenti, the head of the Motion Picture Association of America, had made the short drive from the Cannes Film Festival to Moulin de Mougins, a renowned three-star restaurant built into the stone foundation of a sixteenth-century mill. Shep had coproduced the documentary *Return Engagement*, which was debuting at Cannes. It followed Leary and Liddy as they toured the United States debating the state of American culture.

Leary and Liddy went way back. In 1966, when Liddy was an assistant district attorney in New York, he'd prosecuted Leary twice on drug charges. On this night at the restaurant, Leary had tapped out lines of table salt onto the white tablecloth, pretending they were cocaine. Liddy came out from the men's room, and saw him hunched over the lines with a franc note tightly rolled up under one nostril, pretending to snort them. "Timothy, what are you fucking doing?" the ex-military man shouted. His voice boomed through the Moulin de

Mougins and a tense hush descended over the dining room. Into the pause strolled the restaurant's head chef, Roger Vergé. Shep was hypnotized by him as he approached the table; Vergé's chef's whites gleamed with an internal brightness; he had an aura, as if he had been plugged into a socket, and yet he also seemed as serene and detached as an enlightened monk.

Vergé was well-known among foodies for his Cuisine de Soleil, which focused on the fresh flavors of the Mediterranean. Shep had come to Moulin de Mougins for the scene, not the cuisine, and had never heard of him. Vergé arrived at the table, his combed-back silver hair and brush-style mustache immaculate, and spoke in a calm, measured tone, English clear under a French accent. "Is everything okay?" the great chef asked, looking unblinkingly at Shep, the one who seemed less inebriated than anyone else.

"Yes, yes, fine. Er. Just a little joke," Shep said.

"Very well," Vergé said, nodding at the party, then striding back through the hushed dining room. Leary brushed the salt aside, Liddy picked up a scotch, the situation calmed. Shep's attention stayed focused on Vergé. What a beautiful man, so happy, Shep thought, watching the chef chat with patrons on the other side of the room. "The way he talked to us was so calm and beautiful and purposeful. Right now in this room, all of Hollywood is here, but he is *the* guy. All the attention is on him, and yet he is so peaceful."

Shep was a fan of the *Kung Fu* television show. The main character, played by David Carradine, was a devoted student of a blind martial arts master. The master called the student Grasshopper, and schooled him in the ways of staying centered and strong, no matter what was happening around him. The Hollywood crowd at Moulin de Mougins was sweating, their knees jumping under their tables with cocaine energy. For years Shep had been more interested in what he was putting in his nose than what he put into his mouth. Now he felt his own heart pounding, and in that moment, he realized he was becoming a member of a club that he did not want to join. Bewitched by Chef Vergé, he made a decision: I need to learn how to get to that joyful, peaceful state amidst this chaos. I have to be this guy's Grasshopper.

There had never been anything comforting to Shep about food. His father was a quiet accountant and his domineering mother had focused her love on his more promising brother. The meals served in his emotionally cold home triggered no warm associations, and as an adult, a meal of macaroni with ketchup and Sara Lee pound cake for dessert suited him fine.

Shep had started his working career with a series of odd jobs, at one point toiling in the shipping department of a company that made clothing for corpses. After losing his job as a probation officer in Los Angeles in the late 1960s, he was lounging with a college friend in the pool at the Hollywood Landmark hotel, a famous hangout for rock bands. Jimi Hendrix was also in the pool. The guitarist spied Shep, whose hair was nearly as kinky as his own, and, according to the story Shep has entertained people with for years, he said, "Are you Jewish?"

"Yes."

"You should be a manager."

Jimi beckoned over a couple of members of the soul group The Chambers Brothers, who were also living at the hotel and who had just had a hit with the eleven-minute psychedelic song "Time Has Come Today." The group in turn introduced Shep to Alice Cooper. Shep became Alice Cooper's manager and helped the lead singer develop his Prince of Darkness act. Shep had him make public appearances with a boa constrictor wrapped around his shoulders and packaged one of his albums in paper panties. And it was Shep who threw a live chicken onstage at a 1969 Alice Cooper show in Toronto, an infamous incident that cost the bird its life.

For the next eight years after Shep's encounter with Vergé, Shep co-hosted an annual party during Cannes at Moulin de Mougins, with his friend, actor Michael Douglas. He became friendly with Vergé, and each year after the film festival, Shep would host a ten-day trip with the chef and a group of friends to a region of France that the chef selected; Cognac one year, Burgundy the next. Vergé was part of a posse of French chefs loosely represented by a French agent who would bring them to the United States to help promote their cookbooks and restaurants, and every time Vergé came to the States, Shep traveled with him. Whenever Vergé would offer a cooking class or do a demo on TV, Shep was there, eventually learning enough to assist in the kitchen.

Shep became such an epicure that, wherever he traveled, he would find the best restaurants. In 1986 came a crucial meeting that seven years later would help Shep become a key figure in the evolution of the Food Network. He was in New Orleans, where he had heard about a new chef cooking at Commander's Palace. At the front desk his party was told the wait would be forty-five minutes, and they were led out toward the bar past the kitchen.

As he would the night Julia came to dinner, Chef Emeril Lagasse demonstrated amazing instincts about when to rise to an occasion, spotting Shep's group and coming out of the kitchen.

"Ayyyy! Brother!" Emeril, twenty-seven, bellowed to Shep.

Shep had never met the chef, but he had enough savvy to go along with it when Emeril said, "You're having trouble getting a table? I got it covered." He led Shep and his group to a prime table on the balcony and carried their plates of food to the party personally.

As the meal wound down and Emeril sat down with them, Shep asked him, "Who do you think I am? Because I've never been here before."

Shep was underestimating Emeril's instincts. Emeril knew a group of big spenders when he saw them. Emeril admitted he didn't know Shep. "You know," he said, "once a month or so I pick somebody who's coming through the kitchen, and I give 'em a ride. And you're the guy I picked. What do you want to do after dinner?"

"Well, we're going to go see the Neville Brothers."

"You like Cognac?" Emeril asked.

"Yeah."

Emeril took out a bottle of 1952 Cognac, emptied it into paper cups, and they all piled in a cab to see the Neville Brothers at Tipitina's.

Shep began earning a reputation for bringing together the culinary world with Hollywood. Most of America still viewed anyone who worked in a kitchen as someone with about as much status as a lawn care professional. Even Wolfgang Puck, one of the first to be labeled a celebrity chef, could find himself treated as "the help" in certain circles. In 1990 Shep ran into Wolfgang at a charity event in Hawaii. The chef told Shep that he had flown in alone, coach class, although the promoters had promised him first class, with two hundred pounds of food. No one was at the airport to meet him, and when he arrived at the hotel where the dinner was to be held, there was no room in the refrigerator for the food he'd loaded into two taxis at the airport, and no prep cooks to help him. Wolfgang was given a dolly and told he could use it to wheel the food over to the hotel next door, which would hold it. The next day before dawn, one of the most famous chefs in America was alone chopping food, for which he was not being paid, and was fantasizing that it would be better to be a famous French chef: Maybe someday if I am as big a chef as Roger Vergé, Wolfgang thought, I will be treated like a human.

Shep knew the Frenchman did not have it much better. He had accompanied Vergé to a hotel in Arizona where the chef was to cook for a charity gala. The night before the event, the two friends tried to have dinner in the dining room. The maître d' sent them away, informing Vergé, "The help is not allowed to eat here."

Shep started scheming. Since meeting Vergé, he saw chefs as great popular artists who were not getting their due, just as African-American musicians once were forced to follow the so-called Chitlin' Circuit to promote their music, playing for free in clubs across the country. Shep, whose roster of clients included Teddy Pendergrass and Luther Vandross, was part of a generation of promoters who got musical artists of all colors paid handsomely for gigs. Shep decided he was going to break up the Chitlin' Circuit for chefs. He began arranging for chefs to cook backstage at concerts. When Sammy Hagar, a Shep client, was

Van Halen's lead singer, Shep arranged for the Southwestern cuisine pioneer Dean Fearing to cook for the band backstage before a performance in Dallas. Shep invited a local disc jockey to the dinner, knowing the DJ would brag about the meal on the air the next day, injecting Fearing with rock-and-roll chic. By providing the still-lowly profession of chef with Hollywood-style marketing expertise, he blazed a trail that many would follow to vast profit in years to come.

In August 1991, Shep, back in Hawaii, arranged for a dozen local chefs who had gathered for an informal conference at the Maui Prince Hotel to come to his house to meet Vergé and Fearing. Until that time, restaurant and hotel menus in Hawaii had been ruled by gummy French-influenced dishes such as Steak Diane and Lobster Thermidor—a dish made from a crustacean caught in cold waters six thousand miles away. Vergé and Fearing pushed the Hawaiian chefs, who included Roy Yamaguchi and Alan Wong, to align themselves with the new culinary movements on the mainland started by restaurateurs who bought from local farmers and celebrated local specialties. The chefs listened raptly, and from this meeting, the Hawaii Regional Cuisine movement was born. The next year Shep invited journalists and celebrities to a launch party for the movement at Schatzi on Main, Arnold Schwarzenegger's Santa Monica restaurant, and hired a former Miss Hawaii to dance the hula.

A month later, a group of chefs, including Jonathan Waxman, formerly of Chez Panisse, Larry Forgione, whose An American Place pioneered New American Cuisine on the East Coast, and the Cajun genius Paul Prudhomme, attended the annual American Wine and Food Festival in Los Angeles, a modest annual event hosted by Wolfgang to benefit Meals On Wheels. The chefs spent an extra night or two at the Four Seasons Santa Barbara Biltmore for an informal confab of culinary stars. Forgione, Waxman, Fearing, Prudhomme, Jeremiah Tower, Alice Waters, Robert Del Grande, Jimmy Schmidt, Bradley Ogden, Mark Miller, and others agreed that their generation of American chefs had achieved fame never before known. But not a one of them was getting rich. Wolfgang was doing the best. He had just opened a Spago in Las

Vegas, but he was hardly on easy street, and even a chef-businessman like him was expected to push his own dolly into banquet kitchens. Did Bruce Springsteen have to lug his own tower of amps into a stadium?

As the group lounged on the Biltmore's famous patio overlooking the Pacific Ocean, an idea began to take shape that they ought to band together in some way, form an association of culinary stars that could push for higher fees, decent hotel rooms, and better overall treatment. Shep was suggested as someone who would be perfect to represent such a group.

It took until the next year's L.A. festival in September 1992 for much to happen. Shep was at his office when he received a phone call from Wolfgang. "Shep, will you come to lunch tomorrow at Spago? I want to discuss some things with you." When he arrived, he saw more than twenty of the most famous chefs in the country. The restaurant was closed and they sat in chairs facing him as if he were a teacher in a class-room. The chefs told him they wanted what big-time musicians had, killer representation. Would he do it?

Shep understood them immediately. This, he thought, was what he owed his master, Vergé. Grasshopper's powers had grown and were now being called upon. He told them he'd do it, and started discussing how: endorsement deals, appearance fees, licensing food products that carried their names and were sold in supermarkets. Shep told them his favorite line about the beauty of life once the checks from licensing deals start flowing in: "You don't get rich from working. You get rich from going to your mailbox." He had done this with Alice Cooper albums, lunch boxes, and T-shirts, some of which he owned a percentage of himself.

He suggested that the chefs read a book by the sports marketing pioneer Mark McCormack, *What They Don't Teach You at Harvard Business School: Notes From a Street-Smart Executive*. In it, McCormack discussed how he and his company, International Management Group, trans-formed professional golfers like Arnold Palmer and Jack Nicklaus from small-time earners who won big trophies into national brands who earned millions annually through endorsements, product lines, and ap-pearance fees. The key, McCormack wrote, was the rise of sports on television. Starting in the early 1960s, the national TV networks began bringing golf tournaments into millions of homes every weekend, and it was McCormack who recognized the opportunities that opened up. He leveraged them into riches for a roster that included Joe Montana, Björn Borg, and many others. Crucially, the value of these athletes' brands was not affected by how little the networks were paying for broadcast rights. What mattered was that Palmer, Nicklaus, Player, and the rest were blasted into living rooms every Sunday, burning their images into the minds of millions of viewers. Thanks to TV, Palmer earned far more money off the course than prize money on it.

"Our interest and expertise had always been in developing income opportunities for our clients off the playing field, in establishing licensing and promotional relationships, and in managing them in a way that would provide those athletes with a steady income long after their playing days were over," McCormack had written in his book.

Chefs had not entirely missed out on the endorsement game. In 1976, Nouvelle Cuisine pioneer Michel Guérard was a consultant for a line of Nestlé frozen foods. James Beard did ads for Mouton Cadet wine and Omaha Steaks. In the early 1970s, Julia Child endorsed Cuisinart, and in the mid-1980s appeared in an ad for the California Winegrowers, for which she was paid $100,000. More typical fees for the time were the $10,000 Alice Waters and Wolfgang were paid for doing a phone company commercial. Nice, but not appreciably more than the rate a C-level actor would fetch for an advertising shoot.

Shep acted fast. In November 1992, he formed a company, Alive Culinary Resources, and told reporters that he was moving into promoting chefs.

On November 29, the *Los Angeles Times* wrote about the founding of the agency under the headline "When the Road Is Rough for Celeb Chefs: Celebrity chefs supposedly went out with the '80s. Not according to Shep Gordon." Four months later, in March 1993, Florence Fabricant in *The New York Times* filed "The Man Who Would Turn Chefs Into Household Names": "Shep Gordon, an agent in California, thinks chefs and restaurateurs should be treated more like rock stars and hopes to put their names in lights. . . ."

Among the ideas Shep described to Fabricant were for chefs to sew patches with product logos on their coats, just like racing-car drivers, food festivals where the entertainment value of watching chefs cook would be "hyped," chefs featured in *People* magazine, and what the reporter termed "a stretch-limousine lifestyle for chefs." (Fabricant would soon have her own occasional segment on TVFN, appearing on *Food News and Views* on Wednesdays to recap her buy of the week. This never did lead to the production of FloFab posters or T-shirts. Then again, Shep never represented her.) He started delivering fast for the thirty-seven men and women in white in his stable. Dean Fearing was tapped to prepare the 1993 Rock and Roll Hall of Fame dinner in Los Angeles, where Springsteen, Jackson Browne, and Eric Clapton were served tortilla soup. Shep arranged for Wolfgang to make the Grammy Awards dinner in 1993. (Puck became the chef for the Academy Awards Governor's Ball in 1995.) Then Shep made a deal with Time-Life Home Video for Emeril, Fearing, Pino Luongo, Daniel Boulud, Michel Richard, and Vergé to appear in an instructional cooking series. The chefs were paid about $5,000 each for three days' work. With Sony Records, Shep produced a series of song compilations packaged with recipes. One, called *Cocktail Hour*, paired tunes by Dean Martin, Peggy Lee, and others with a recipe for spiced cashews with citrus-marinated chicken morsels by Mary Sue Milliken and Susan Feniger, the photogenic young owners of the hot L.A. restaurant Border Grill.

Shep was happy to flex his kung fu–dealmaker muscles on behalf of such noble men and women. In 1993, he used connections at Radio City Productions to help Forgione land a gig cooking for President Bill Clinton at a fund-raiser for the Democratic National Committee. The event's printed program devoted almost as much space to Forgione as it did to the musical talent, Whitney Houston and Kenny G. The three-paragraph bio on the New York chef concluded, "A champion and re-inventor of our national cuisine, Larry Forgione is a great American artist. His creations represent our culture's past, present and future." Such language may seem rote to a reader now, but in 1993, few of those who dined on the Roast Breast of Chicken with Monticello Style Soft Corn Pudding (summer compote of morels, leeks, Vidalia onions, and a Midwest caramelized chicken sauce) would have conceived of bestowing such a high-falutin' description on a cook. An "artist"? many of them were likely wondering, and what the hell is a "Midwest" sauce?

The part of Shep's plan aimed at raising the consciousness of taste-makers, so they would consider chefs as great artists, was in high gear. But he had to reach the masses who would make the cash registers sing. To rope them in, as McCormack had advised, television was the key.

> "I had an event with Kenny Loggins, who I was managing, and Wolfgang was cooking. And Kenny got a couple of hundred thousand dollars while Wolfgang got nothing. Kenny got twenty-five rooms. He got one little dinky room. Kenny got first class, Wolf got coach. And when the night was over and the performance and the meal were over and there was a meet and greet, Kenny's line was twenty people and Wolfgang's was three hundred. It was pretty obvious. Anybody could buy a ticket to a Kenny Loggins show, I don't give a shit who you are, you couldn't get in to Spago."
>
> —SHEP GORDON

Shep's timing was as good as it had been that day he decided to go swimming at the Landmark Hotel. Reading about Food Network in entertainment-industry trade publications, he realized that this was what Grasshopper had been waiting for. When Emeril was brought to New York, Shep pounced and set up a meeting with Reese. At the new TVFN offices, Shep explained his approach, modeled on Mc-Cormack's, that chefs needed what golfers had, more television exposure. Even if the TV work didn't pay very well—this made Reese nod—it would open up possibilities for endorsements.

Shep commanded a ready-made roster of celebrity chefs, mostly from the West Coast, a pool Reese had barely touched.

Reese had randomly grabbed whomever Sue or another expert suggested, but Shep was talking about a gold mine of talent from the region that had led the reinvention of American cuisine.

Shep mentioned a few chefs from his orbit—Wolfgang Puck, Roger Vergé, and Milliken and Feniger. When Reese made the faux pas of referring to them as "cooks," Shep noted the offhand insult, but held his tongue, focusing on the goal. Shep knew that if some of the chefs could get on TV, more commercial opportunities would come.

He focused on his old friend Emeril. Shep suggested an experiment that would cost the network little but could earn it a lot. Chefs, at this time, were not likely to sell golf balls or T-shirts. But they could, Shep figured, sell spices. Why not, he proposed, give Emeril advertising time on his show during which he could sell his own line of spices?

Reese agreed to the plan. He could make Emeril a happier employee without having to increase his paycheck directly, and if the spices started selling well, Shep promised, he would work out a revenue-sharing plan with the network.

Shep met with Emeril and his business manager, Tony Cruz, selling them on the idea of trying to use the chef's growing stardom to sell a branded line of spices. "Let's try this out," Shep told the men. "Let's see if we can make this happen and capitalize on it." Tony and Emeril agreed to let him give it a shot. Shep would be a 50/50 partner. Shep pushed Emeril to develop a few spice blends, found a company in Arizona to make them, and produced short TV spots. He flattered Reese by naming one of the spice blends Essence of Emeril.

Emeril, meanwhile, was doing his part to connect with the audience. First, he managed his image, by asking for a little help in the makeup chair. He was sensitive about a camera that shot down on the countertop from above. It was designed to offer views directly into mixing bowls and pans, but sometimes caught views of the back of a chef's head as he or she leaned over. "I don't like that camera," Emeril told Ricki Stofsky, the regular producer of *Essence*. It showed his bald spot. Abandoning the overhead camera was not possible—viewers needed to see the food sizzle—so Emeril's makeup person came up with a solution, applying black cosmetic powder to his scalp where his hair was thinning.

More important, he stuck to his guns when he sensed he had come up with something audiences would connect to.

Reese had dictated that none of the crew would receive on-screen credits. The network had many camera and sound people who worked nights at news jobs and "moonlighted" during the day at TVFN below their normal union rates, so it was better to allow everyone to work in anonymity. This annoyed some of the younger TVFN staffers, who yearned to see their names on the screen, but Reese would not budge. The cameramen could get awfully tired during the day shift. Emeril, flying from his unholy number of espressos, could see them nodding off as he cooked on the kitchen set. One in particular used to go slack-jawed as he passed out.

Inspired first by the need to keep the cameramen awake, Emeril started yelling as he added ingredients to dishes—"Bam!"

Emeril liked the sound of it. It seemed to add an extra something to any recipe. Since he no longer had to follow a script, he began improvising more exclamations—"Let's take it up a notch!" "Yeah, baby!" and an occasional "Hey, now!"

Emeril had only been using "Bam" for a few months when he started hearing an occasional fan in his restaurant yell it back to him. One day Jonathan Lynne came striding down to the studio area where Ricki was overseeing an *Essence* shoot. His official title at the network was Special Assistant for Creative Affairs, but Jonathan considered his real title to be Head of Development, and he reported directly to Reese, offering what he considered a more youth-oriented and savvy take on everything. Jonathan, showing his connection to the "MTV generation," had come up with an advertising slogan used in print ads for TVFN: "I want my Mmm-mm TV!"

Many of the TV veterans like Ricki did not like Jonathan. He was fancy. He showed up to work in Brooks Brothers suits and Hermès bow ties. Everyone knew his father was the head of New Line Cinema, and it was widely believed that he'd gotten his job because his father had made a call to Reese.

Jonathan came up to Ricki.

"Lose the 'Bam,'" he said.

"What?" she asked.

"Lose the 'Bam.' Emeril can't say 'Bam' anymore. It's a rip-off of Larry Sanders." Jonathan was referring to *The Larry Sanders Show* on HBO in which one of the characters used the expression, "Hey, now!" Jonathan felt Bam! was part of the whole kit of Emeril's expressions that were not original. It would reflect badly on TVFN if people noticed.

"We're not going to," Ricki said.

He walked away. Later, Ricki told Emeril about the request. He said simply, "Nah." She told him she'd said the same to Jonathan.

Whatever success *Essence of Emeril* was having was only relative. By mid-1994, TVFN was still available in less than ten million homes. In Manhattan it was on only part-time. Although Tribune owned an important channel in New York, WOR, Channel 9, Time Warner was resisting adding TVFN in the city because channel space was at a premium. The cable provider made a retransmission consent deal with Tribune and TVFN, agreeing to swap the one million homes it would have provided in Manhattan for two million homes in other parts of the country. This was a good result for the overall amount of homes TVFN was reaching, but it was awful for advertising sales. If the advertising community centered in Manhattan could not watch the food channel in its offices and its apartments, it was less likely to encourage clients to buy time on it. The problem grated on Reese and his head of advertising, George Babick.

> "The 'bam' thing was a serious red flag because it wasn't original. I absolutely acknowledge that I was wrong. I was coming at it from the point of view of someone who was embedded in television. If I saw something I knew could be looked at like a cheap rip-off, I was going to try to get rid of it."
>
> **—JONATHAN LYNNE**

For those who could see it, the weekday schedule for fall 1994 included the following shows:

- *How to Boil Water*
- *7 Day Workout*
- *Food News and Views*
- *Getting Healthy*
- *Meals without Meat*
- *Feeding Your Family on $99 a Week*
- *The Dessert Show*
- *Café Olé*
- *Taste*
- *Essence of Emeril*
- *TV Dinners*
- *Robin Leach Talking Food*
- *Cooking Classics*

Most were now only repeated three times a day. Critics were savage. In *Newsday*, Wayne Robins compared watching TVFN to watching laundry, unfavorably. Walter Goodman sat through a six-hour shift of programming, and in *The New York Times* drolly described Emeril as "a New Orleans chef in a shiny shirt who poppled with enthusiasm." The critic craved an antacid after the six hours, noting that, "I caught a few commercials, too, but nothing yet for Maalox." Writing in the *New York Observer*, in an article headlined "Foodies' CNN: A Bit Undercooked," Phoebe Hoban wrote, "One thing that's missing from this low-tech, hi-cal network is a real sense of the joy of cooking." She noted that for one thing, "Jane Curtin looks in need of Prozac as she sits in a dreary kitchen and drones the introductions to the Cooking Classics series." Reese seemed to take it all in stride, embracing the technical problems and uneven programming as endemic to a start-up network. "We'll gradually get better," he told Hoban. "We welcome people with food intelligence, who come in with their own ideas."

One day in the summer of 1994, an idea came with help from Shep's assistant at Alive Culinary Resources. Lionel Wigram (who would later produce the Harry Potter films) told his boss that he was concerned that the Television Food Network was not doing well and, more important, that it was not yet using many of Alive's chefs. Was there anything Shep could come up with to give the network a boost?

The answer came to Shep immediately. What had made rock stars gigantic was festivals. Woodstock, Monterey Pop, the Isle of Wight had launched careers, led to recording contracts, made it possible for acts to tour solo and rake in big bucks, selling merchandise. Shep added his own twist: if you could get Emeril onstage at a festival cooking with Michael Douglas, people would think the chef the equal of the movie star—not a cook and an artist, but two artists.

Shep started planning a festival and pitching his celebrity friends. "Hey," he would tell an actor or a music star, "not that many years ago, none of you got paid. These are great artists, they're no different than you. You've got to help these guys out. What does it mean to you to give up a day?"

The Big Feast on the Beach in November 1994 was Shep all over. There were the key chefs from Alive—Vergé, Forgione, Fearing, Emeril, Mary Sue, and Susan. Sam Choy and Mark Ellman came from Hawaii and cooked a traditional luau. Sharon Stone was to present a program called "Cook for Peace" during which Tibetan monks would construct a sand mandala, but she did not show. The monks did. Sammy Hagar, Michael Douglas, and Fab Five Freddy came to cook, and Alice Cooper prepared Rattlesnake Chili. The Village People played their hits.

Like the guitar and the dove in the original logo of the Woodstock Music and Art Fair in 1969, the festival logo contained a guitar, a fish, a bottle of wine, a wedge of citrus, and a swirly treble clef symbol, representing the melding of worlds that Shep had been working to achieve since the night with Leary and Liddy when he'd only had eyes for Vergé: the means by which a puff of grill smoke and a power chord could transform chefs into pop stars.

Chefs were flown in first class and given hotel rooms. The whole thing was shown on TVFN as a special, providing the kick Shep thought the network needed. Reese was excited because the cost was covered by sponsors, mostly American Express, sold on the value of being associated with celebrity chefs by a deal-making friend of Shep's named Herb Karlitz. Plus, broadcasting a big event was something a news channel would do. Inexpensive and newsy: Schonfeld heaven.

The Feast on the Beach was a rough-and-ready attempt at marrying pop culture with fine food, but even without Shep's onetime girlfriend Sharon Stone, it certainly had more pizazz than some of the flim-flam food entertainment being shown on TVFN: a rotting veal chop, crazy-long fingernails, and concrete mousse.

It did not all go smoothly. Pat O'Gorman was dispatched to Miami to be the lead television producer of the festival, which took place just a few weeks before the one-year anniversary of the network. At one point, Shep was watching Michael Douglas onstage with a chef, and he dashed into the production truck to see how they were handling the broadcast. Shep was appalled when he saw that TVFN had sent its cameras to cover the luau. Going out on the television feed was a squat group of Hawaiians digging a steaming pig from a hole in the ground. Shep went nuts and tried to get Pat's team to run the cameras back to cover the movie star instead of the smoldering swine. "This is my event, I'm producing it!" he cried. "This is what we're here for! The guy came down on his own dime! He's doing it for free, it's Michael Douglas, and you've got to show him!" No one in the truck took any action. A television decision had been made for reasons no one knew. When the festival was over, Shep had such bad blisters from running around in the Miami heat that he could barely walk. He canceled his flight to New York and hired a car to pick him up from the curb of his Miami hotel and drive him up to the curb of his New York home.

While the Big Feast did not propel TVFN into the ratings strato-sphere or perfectly please Shep, it did help bind him closer to the net-work and set the model for the modern food festival. A decade later, a festival in Miami would become a key annual event in the food televi-sion universe.

It also demonstrated what Shep could pull off. At first, sales of Emeril's spices had been slow. Shep did not understand the grocery store business the way he knew record stores. Then one day he was on a plane sitting next to an executive for a chain of supermarkets. The executive explained that if you want a brand to pop, you have to sponsor special displays at the end of aisles and pay for good shelf space. Shep thought it over. He arranged for supermarkets to put a special display near the chicken. Within a few years, Essence of Emeril, Bayou Blast, and his other spices were selling roughly a million dollars a year nation-wide, and Shep, a 50/50 partner, was receiving six-figure checks in his mailbox.

The network never managed to secure its cut of the profits, despite Emeril's and Shep's willingness to keep their end of the bargain. As a TV broadcasting operation, it was improving slowly. But as a business enterprise, something that would make enough money to keep the elec-tric stoves on and the slop buckets rotating, the network was a novice.

Bobby, Sara, Mario, and the Too Hot Tamales

R attlesnake chili on the beach was not the complete solution for what was still wrong with the network. No matter how relentlessly Reese tried to keep costs contained, losses were going beyond projections. According to the original business plan, the network was projected to lose $18 million in its first year, $16 million in its second, and much less in its third. In reality, it lost $6.6 million in its first frantic months in late 1993, $19.2 million in 1994, and was on track to lose more in 1995.

That year, the five Class A partners received a capital call requiring that each kick in $3.65 million. Those who had been believers were starting to lose faith in the business model, and those who had never liked giving a cable channel away without subscriber fees were even less hopeful.

Jack Clifford, ProJo's top liaison to the cable system operators, was hearing complaints about the quality of the network's programming. It looked awfully cheap—because it was. Some of the providers' customers were writing letters asking them to dump TVFN. Cable operators who were investors, such as Scripps and Adelphia, were contractually bound to keep it on. Advertising sales, virtually the only revenues, were lagging.

Reese stayed positive. In mid-1994, he was predicting the network could break even and earn back its start-up costs of roughly $50 million within three years, when it would reach 20 million homes and be able to extract more from advertisers. But by July 1995, he just as confidently told reporters they'd break even in four years, when their $70 million in start-up costs were recouped and 25 million homes were receiving TVFN. The goal line was receding.

Jack had begun grousing to Tryg Myhren about Reese, saying he refused to listen to anyone. Jack liked being listened to. But Tryg still believed Reese was the right man for a start-up that was bound to be chaotic and require a strong hand on top. For Tryg, there was no better evidence of the strength of Reese's guiding hand than the extremely satisfying day, a year and a half into TVFN's broadcast life, when Charles Dolan of Cablevision called. "It's time for you guys to sell to me," Dolan told Tryg. "I didn't think you guys would get this far, but now that you are this far, you understand how expensive this is. I know you're losing money. I'm going to be doing some other niche channels. We can spread the costs, sell ads across all the channels. We can do this in a more efficient way and cut the costs dramatically. You know I know how to run channels."

Tryg had to smile. If Dolan was calling, something was working. "That's nice, Chuck," Tryg replied. "We're not going to do that. If you want to invest in the channel as a minority investor, you're welcome."

Spurned, Dolan never did invest, but his backhanded faith in the network helped keep Tryg and ProJo behind TVFN and Reese despite the losses.

At one of Reese's informal hallway meetings, Joe heard someone mention the idea of TVFN starting a website. ESPN had one, as did other channels. In 1995, however, the cost of launching a website was around $100,000. For that kind of money, TVFN could produce a whole season of a television show, maybe two. The idea was dismissed, but Joe was fascinated. Joe told Reese that he and Don, the IT guy at the network, wanted to look into starting a website because it might help reduce the cost of delivering recipes.

"All right," Reese said, "but don't let it screw up everything else you're doing." He wasn't sure he wanted the recipe problem solved so fast, especially if it was going to cost a lot.

Joe and Don hoped to find a company that might build a website for less than $100,000, or tell them how it could be done. One of the companies they met with told them it had already "gone to the trouble" of registering "TVFN.com" for them and quoted the price of $100,000. Joe asked for the domain name back, please, but the company's reps explained that if TVFN was not interested in their services, they were not interested in relinquishing the name. The bastards kept it. Once they experienced this Wild West domain name claim-staking, Joe and Don researched potential names and registered foodtv.com on August 19, 1995.

Shortly afterward, they went up to Boston and bought lunch for some former MIT Media Lab researchers who had started a business making websites. Generously, the MIT expats explained the basics of how to do it and said there was software that would help. It would cost, Don figured, around $15,000. Reese gave the nod, and within a few weeks, Don had created a primitive website with four sections: a list of shows, chef biographies, a contact form, and a terribly confusing catalog of recipes. It only cost $12,750. Don and Joe began watching their Web traffic. "Okay, thirty-five people this week," Joe remarked to Don, after it had been up a few months. "We only got seventeen last week, didn't we?"

Meanwhile, the network's home city was enduring its own financial troubles, but these would turn out to present an opportunity. In 1991, after New York City had endured the Wall Street plunge of the late 1980s, the collapse of real estate prices, years of recession, and rising crime—2,262 murders in 1990—*Newsday* asked in the headline of an essay by futurist Alvin Toffler, "Is the Apple as Obsolete as De-troit?" Toffler declared, "New York had finance. It had media. It had culture. But those structures are now in serious trouble."

The economy had not improved much over the next few years, but something culturally nutritious was germinating in certain precincts, perhaps as a result of the city's troubles. Many of the old French-influenced restaurants of Midtown and the Upper East Side had be-come as tired as congealed béarnaise, but in neighborhoods farther south with lowered recession rents, young chefs influenced by what was happening in California, Asia, and Europe were inviting the adventur-ous in for a taste.

One of the first of the new New York chefs to break through was a native New Yorker who had grown up playing basketball and front-stoop blackjack with street toughs in East Harlem. Ask Bobby Flay where he went to college, and he'll say UCLA—"University of the Cor-ner of Lexington Avenue."

His parents split when he was five, and Bobby lived with his mother on East Seventy-eighth Street between Second and Third avenues, gravitating to the rough kids in his neighborhood. They often got into fights with rivals, setting up meetings with kids from across town on neutral territory—the skating rink in Central Park—where they'd use their fists, chains, and even knives to settle scores over girls, money, slights of all kinds. Bobby, although somewhat shy, was a natural leader. He always seemed to have something up his sleeve, his tight blue eyes and shock of curly dark red hair projecting a cross of boyish carelessness with calculating coldness. When playing pickup basketball, Bobby was the point guard. When playing blackjack, he was the dealer and banker.

Bobby attended St. Francis Xavier High School, not far from where his restaurant Mesa Grill would one day stand. He briefly played on the Xavier basketball team, but he did not take well to a high school coach telling him what to do. He quit after three days of practice, began cutting classes to go to the horse track, and eventually left the school entirely.

His father, Bill Flay, managed the Theater District restaurant Joe

Allen, a hangout for Broadway producers. Bill set him up first as a bus-
boy, then a dishwasher, then a prep cook, chopping vegetables in the
kitchen. At first, Bobby was not an ideal employee. He showed up late
and left early, convinced that he could skate by because he was the boss's
son. Bill had a talk with him. Bobby didn't want to continue high school,
fine, Bill could deal with that, but he wasn't going to watch Bobby flunk
out of his first job and land aimless on the street. He knew Bobby was
basically a good kid and wanted him to stay out of trouble.

"Look, let me explain a couple things to you," Bobby's father told
him, and then he repeated the wisdom he had given him since he was a
boy: "Just do the right thing, Bobby."

"But what does that mean?"

"You know. Just do the right thing," Bill replied. "Don't do the wrong
thing, do the right thing. If you keep doing the right thing, it will all
work out for you in the end. It's a gut feeling."

That was enough. Bill's words became the son's mantra. After Bobby
earned his high school equivalency degree, Joe Allen himself, seeing
promise, paid his $6,800 tuition to the French Culinary Institute in
New York. Bobby did well and liked working in kitchens, but by the
time he graduated at twenty-one he had been working in them for four
years, which seemed like forever to him, a fifth of his life. It was the
mid-1980s and a lot of the friends he'd grown up with were making serious money down on Wall Street. Kitchen work paid $240 for seven-day,
ninety-hour weeks. So, attempting to ride the winds of his native city,
Bobby decided to try his hand at being a stockbroker. A friend found
him a job as a clerk at the American Stock Exchange. His first paycheck
there was $200, less than at his kitchen job, but he persevered, work-
ingthe wire room, answering four phone lines at once, and following
orders. He believed that if he paid his dues on the Street, he'd be a rich
man in his twenties.

After six months, Bobby had had enough. This wasn't the right thing.
As far as he could tell, Wall Street was basically guys in suits receiving
orders, fulfilling orders, giving orders, having drinks, and riding trains
home. Numbers moving around inside computers and phone lines. It

was boring and small. No spice. You couldn't even really see the dice, or whatever they were playing with. Even horse-racing was a deeper art. "There is no creativity in this," he concluded. "Just money."

Bobby quit and went back to where, in his gut, he felt comfortable— the kitchen. He landed a job with Jonathan Waxman, the chef and eventual Shep client, who introduced New Yorkers to California cuisine at a series of restaurants in the 1980s. Next, Bobby left to explore the Southwest, and upon his return—around the time his friends on Wall Street were taking a financial beating from the 1987 crash—he took a job as the head chef at Miracle Grill, a hopping spot with an outdoor patio in the East Village, where he tried offering spicier fare and gained a reputation for it. During Bobby's run there, his mother met the talk-show host Regis Philbin at a party and bragged about her son. Bobby soon got a call from a television producer and was summoned to make "a perfect summer potato salad" on *Live with Regis and Kathie Lee*. He aced his first TV appearance.

The city's financial troubles would work in his favor. Jerry Kretchmer, a real estate developer looking for alternative investments, decided to deepen his foray into the restaurant business. He and Bobby opened Mesa Grill on a slowly gentrifying stretch of Broadway in the old Toy District near the Flatiron building. It was dark and quiet at night, spooky. The menu would be full of Southwestern cuisine, spicy stuff that could easily frighten chili-averse East Coast diners, but it was unique, the block was unique, and Bobby had studied both.

He and Kretchmer built a high-ceilinged space with banquettes upholstered in fabric printed with cowboys and bucking broncos—they looked like boys' pajamas from the 1950s. At a time when most Americans had never heard of jicama, the menu featured tostadas topped with grilled tuna, jicama shreds, and black bean salsa; and cornmeal-stuffed tamale husks with garlic cream and cilantro. The first thing customers saw when they entered was a six-foot-tall photo of a pair of dice that had come to rest on a three and a two. Five is a decent, hardworking number for the first roll in craps, a potential winner offering many chances for side bets during a shooter's turn.

On January 17, 1991, the official opening night of Mesa Grill, Bobby, twenty-five, was working in the kitchen and keeping his eye on the dining room through a long window. As he looked out, Jerry sidled up beside the chef. "Congratulations, Bobby," Jerry said. "We just went to war." He meant it literally. Earlier that day, the first bombing raids had begun in Operation Desert Storm.

The first plates of food went out around 7 p.m. As Bobby and Jerry watched, customers started asking for their orders to be packed to go. There was a war on CNN and they wanted to sit on their couches at home and watch. Bobby eyed the scene with the calm he'd learned on the streets. Don't blink. Know who you are and who has your back and stay rooted to that, no matter what chaos erupts.

This is the only thing I know how to do, he thought, gazing at the now empty dining room. So I'm gonna come back tomorrow and do it again and hopefully people will show up. I can't stop the war. I can't predict the war.

In 1991, few restaurants of note opened; two that survived included JoJo, run by a then-little-known Frenchman named Jean-Georges Vongerichten who was experimenting with Asian cuisine, and Mesa Grill. In an unsigned editorial headlined "The Day the Eating Stopped," *The New York Times* noted that restaurant industry employment was down 7,000 jobs, but praised the development, saying dining out had become boring and overblown in the 1980s and that the real reason the industry was suffering was that patrons were tired of paying $25 for a "small plop of risotto with baby shrimp."

> "I only operate in a place that I feel that I have skill in. So I don't make it up. I'm willing to take the challenge of saying, 'I'm not afraid of this, because I know I can do this.' I don't put myself in that position when I don't have that skill set."
>
> —BOBBY FLAY

This dearth meant that when a restaurant did open, it got noticed. *New York* magazine critic Gael Greene touted Bobby's place as a must-try in her 1991 restaurant preview a week before the opening: ". . . the foodniks' imperative is now Mesa Grill." By the time the hostilities in the Middle East were over a couple of months later, Bobby earned a review from Bryan Miller in the *Times*, who praised Mesa's food as "sassy" and noted "the sizzling social scene characterized by loose-fitting Italian suits, ubiquitous ponytails and more exposed legs than at Churchill Downs."

The first time Bobby heard from restaurant-world friends about the existence of a television network about food, he ran through a quick set of calculations: Food network? A 24-hour network? Who the fuck's gonna watch that? But when a producer called from *Talking Food*, Robin Leach's show, in early 1994, Bobby recalculated. Why not go on TV and let whoever is watching know the address of Mesa Grill?

And so, in January 1995, four years into his success at Mesa Grill, and having opened a sister restaurant, Bolo, a block away in 1993, Bobby took the subway up to the studio for his first appearance on TVFN. It was not the big-budget production of *Live with Regis and Kathie Lee*, which taped at a luxurious space near Central Park. Then again, Robin's sidekick, Robin "Kate" Connelly, was younger and prettier than Kathie Lee.

Bobby had married a fellow chef in 1991 after knowing her for only five weeks, but the marriage was ending. The last twenty minutes of *Talking Food* was often a cooking demonstration in which Kate assisted. She and Bobby hit it off and soon they had a first date. Bobby took her to Monkey Bar, a society dining spot in Midtown. Kate, who had a young son, told the babysitter she'd be gone two hours, "tops."

The couple's daughter, Sophie, was

"I got home four and a half hours later. I've never had such a good time in my life on a date, ever, ever, ever. I don't remember what I ate. There was always something to talk about. He was funny. It was the easiest thing in the world" [the bride said]. . . . During the ceremony, the bridegroom was surrounded by several male buddies, including the pony-tailed chef Mario Batali of Pó restaurant in Greenwich Village and Tom Valenti of Cascabel Taqueria in SoHo. "We didn't do the bachelor party thing for Bobby," Mr. Batali said afterward. "We feel we've had a long bachelor party already."

—*NEW YORK TIMES* WEDDING ANNOUNCEMENT, OCTOBER 15, 1995

born in the spring. Bobby was literally a member of the TVFN family now.

The young chefs experimenting at downtown restaurants provided a minor league system for TVFN. Once the network moved to 1177 Sixth Avenue, it created a new show, *Chef du Jour*, to try out potential talent. A guest chef would come in and shoot five shows in two days. Most had no TV training and little on-camera experience. They were thrown onto the air and did their shows live to tape, no stopping allowed for any reason, even small fires or bleeding. Reese and others would watch the proceedings from television monitors in their offices or would lurk behind the cameras, weighing each chef's worth like a shopper thumping melons.

For Jonathan Lynne, who still had Reese's ear, young downtown chefs like Mario Batali, Bobby, and Tom Colicchio shared some of the alt-culture cred of grunge musicians like Kurt Cobain. In fact, many of the chefs mixed with the music crowd who frequented clubs like Tramps and Irving Plaza. Young people who managed to land jobs in the city spent their evenings out in a high-low cultural mash-up where food was suddenly part of the alternative and the artsy downtown: dinner in the lower-priced front room of Gramercy Tavern or at the Meatpacking District bistro pioneer Florent, followed by moshing at a no-name club on the Lower East Side. Jonathan and some of the other young employees at TVFN were among these adventurers. They would dine at the Union Square Cafe, which had opened in 1985, and then catch a show by Superchunk.

> "In those days, the main requirement to be on Food Network was being able to get there by subway."
>
> —BOBBY FLAY

Mario was a red-bearded, ponytailed Italian-American whose uniform was shorts and orange clogs. He was not only unconventional-looking, but he hailed from Seattle, the mother ship of grunge. And he had steered off a traditional culinary track that had him marking time as head chef at a hotel in Santa Barbara. He quit and headed to Italy, where he toiled for years in tiny trattorias, learning native Italian dishes that were unheard of in the United States, where spaghetti and giant meatballs with Parmesan was generally as authentic as Italian cuisine got. (Watch the influential 1996 movie *Big Night* for a historical refresher on the soul-sapping quality of red-sauce joints.) When he wasn't in the kitchen at his West Village restaurant, Pó, Batali could frequently be found charming listeners at wine-sodden after-hours roundtables at various downtown spots, especially a front table at Blue Ribbon in SoHo. After seeing an article in the *New York Observer* about Mario's roundtable at Blue Ribbon, Jonathan arranged to meet Mario for lunch at his restaurant. The chef put him in a window table and served a spectacular ravioli with radicchio reduction. "I'd like to pursue doing a television show with you," Jonathan said, as Mario moved between kitchen and table.

Back at the TVFN office, Jonathan passed Mario's name to Pat O'Gorman, one of the *Chef du Jour* talent scouts. She and Reese had a meal at Pó and watched the charismatic chef come out of the kitchen and work the room, charming everyone. They thought his orange Crocs were funny.

What the hell, Pat thought. We'll give him a shot.

When the cameras started on his first shoot day, he made some flubs, but he was strong-willed at the core.

"I'm Mario Batali," he began, "chef and co-owner of Pó restaurant, an Italian village." His brow wrinkled slightly, "an Italian restaurant in Greenwich Village." Though hardly perfect, Batali was better than many of the city's celebrated French chefs, who forgot 90 percent of their English the moment the cameras

> "The night he signed his deal . . . I was at Gramercy Tavern at the table in the front window, and he was walking by with his wife and, I was like, 'Come on in,' so he came in and we had some drinks to celebrate. . . . But I never thought about it in terms of what I could do on the Food Network. . . . I was a little cautious. Let's see if this, you know, pans out. And quite frankly the production value was so bad on some of those shows I didn't want to have anything to do with it."
>
> **—TOM COLICCHIO**

started. Even these nearly silent Gallic segments were put on the air. Everything was. The French chefs were not invited back. Mario was offered a series.

Molto Mario debuted on January 8, 1996. In one of the first episodes, Batali was demonstrating how to make a basic red sauce and began by grating a carrot. He was so focused on talking that he kept pushing the carrot into the cheese grater until he shredded the knuckles of his thumb and forefinger into the mix. He had been told about the "no do-over" rule at TVFN, but when he looked up, his hand throbbing, blood trickling, he was surprised that the producer did not give any signal to stop.

Okay, he thought. Bleeding. What do I do? Tomatoes are red like blood. He plunged his hand into a bowl of tomatoes.

The acid burned his shredded knuckles, but he managed to keep demonstrating how to crush tomatoes with your hand until there was a break for a commercial. When the show came back on, Mario held his hand behind a bowl on the cutting board, wrapped in a big towel, and leaned on it, applying pressure to stop the bleeding. He continued to cook, which was just what the producers wanted him to do. Never stop.

Mario learned and adapted. He often demonstrated baked dishes, but there was no oven on his original set. After he finished assembling ingredients in a baking dish, he lowered it under the counter in front of him, where he pretended there was an oven. As he'd finish sliding a lasagna or whole fish onto a hidden shelf, he simulated the sound of an oven door slamming shut by stamping his foot on the floor.

The network prep kitchens, which did, at least, have ovens, would have the finished dish ready to swap in and pull out of the fake under-cabinet oven—another foot stamp—when the time was right. Mario seemed to understand naturally how to make something fake look real.

And, as time went on, he started using on camera the erudition he exhibited around the 2 a.m. table at Blue Ribbon restaurant, explaining that Italian cooking had little to do with meatballs. He would salt in

European history lessons, climatology, and linguistics. *Molto Mario* became a thinking woman's, and, unusually, man's cooking show with food that inspired wanderlust.

Rinky-dink as it was, *Molto Mario* was groundbreaking stuff, but there was a big problem: almost no one in the city where Bobby and Mario lived and worked could dependably see TVFN. And if the advertising community on Madison Avenue couldn't see what they were buying, the chances of the network's thriving were slim. That Reese was deeply engaged in trying to solve this problem, calling everyone he knew in government and media looking for a way to leverage Time Warner Cable, was another reason Tryg and, to a lesser extent, Jack continued to support him.

Time Warner Cable, which owned franchises in Manhattan and northern New Jersey, was not entirely ignoring TVFN. It was legally required to carry a New Jersey public broadcasting channel, WNJN, which it put on Channel 50. WNJN was rarely on twenty-four hours a day—it usually broadcasted from about 3 p.m. until midnight—so, at launch, Time Warner put TVFN on its unused hours.

"Pat didn't give me a lot of direction, but she kind of let me do whatever I wanted. When I'd get up in the morning and look at the recipes that I had already submitted to make, I said, 'What am I gonna talk about besides the actual technique?' Here I am slicing garlic, here I am roasting onions, here I am baking potatoes. I realized that what was important at that point was discussing the regional variations. Because there's twenty great regions in Italy and each one of them is different, there's really no Italian cuisine. And that's what happened. So I decided, every time I made a dish as opposed to just merely talking about the slice, the dice, and the actual dump and stir, I really needed to talk about why Basilicata was different from Calabria."

—MARIO BATALI

Then in February 1994, Time Warner yanked the little-watched Nostalgia Channel and opened up Channel 54 to TVFN. This blissful state was only to last five months. NBC was launching a cable channel and using all of its must-carry leverage to pry open space. On July 4, the

NBC cable channel America's Talking (eventually to become MSNBC) debuted and took over 54.

"Channel 54, where are you?" became a bitter joke around the TVFN headquarters.

Until the network could get on more solid financial footing, the programming budget would continue at starvation levels. To Reese, this was the plan: get the network to the point where it was earning a few pennies more in advertising than it was spending in operating costs, use those pennies to slowly pay off the original investment and start funneling profits to principals (like him), and only then direct significantly more money into programming. Meager losses on the way to that goal were sufferable, but big losses had to be avoided, lest they goad investors to pull the plug.

Under those circumstances, relying on talent like Mario and David Rosengarten to pull off the miracle of making decent television in nearly impossible circumstances was the main programming strategy. Trying to create a full-time food network in a skyscraper on a tiny budget continued to be a constant process of adaptive invention.

Michele Urvater hosted *Feeding Your Family on $99 A Week*. It was originally to be called "Feeding Your Family on $75 A Week," but after it became apparent that that budget was too tight, Reese allowed for an extra $24. This was one budget he could raise without risking the survival of the network. Emily Rieger was a food producer for the show.

On March 12, 1996, an office e-mail was sent out:

> To: All
> From: Dinny Fitzpatrick
> RE: Hanging Duck
>
> There is a duck hanging from the ceiling on the $99 a
> Week set. The kitchen has placed it there in order to dry
> it out. Please do not touch, poke, or otherwise interfere

with the duck, as it is appearing on a program this week. The duck will be removed from the studio tomorrow morning by Emily Rieger.

Thank you in advance for your cooperation.

—Dinny

Nothing had the unrelenting momentum and low budget of a live call-in show. But the network lacked a digital delay system, so the shows were truly live. One day on *Recipe for Health*, a chef was discussing the benefits of eating tuna.

HOST: "Let's talk to Rudy. He's been waiting to ask us a question about your dish. Hi, Rudy!"

RUDY: "I wanted to ask a question. Why the fat content—funny you should bring it up—why the fat content of canned tuna versus fresh tuna is so vastly different, and I notice when cooking tuna that you can usually compare the smell of tuna to pussy. What . . ."

Later in the same show, there was another caller, perhaps a friend of Rudy's.

HOST: "Let's get back to the phone now because we have Frank from New York waiting. Hi, Frank!"

FRANK: "Hi, how are you?"

HOST: "Great."

FRANK: "I'm calling in relation to fat intake in the diet. I've been eating as fat-free as possible for about eight or nine years now, but lately I've been hearing things about the fact, the alleged fact, that you should have fat in your diet and that eating fat-free is really not a good thing and Bellllllllllllcccccch! Buh-elllll-cccchuhhhhhh." [An impressively long burp with a slight delay in the center of it, the delay not long enough to intake breath, just a kind of quick hitch as if to flip a release and switch lungs to find booster capacity for the burp. The long release of gas did not end Frank's call. He continued:] "Why are you cupping your . . ."

At that point, the control room cut Frank off.

"I think," the host soldiered on, "I think we lost Frank."

A bit much, but even those callers with their schtick and their blue jokes were very New York, embodying the city in its last days of public sleaze, just before Times Square and its old triple-X movie houses were Disneyfied.

The chefs in the prep kitchen on the thirty-first floor had to cook from 5 a.m. to midnight to keep up with the network's unrelenting shooting schedule. Trying to save money, the network had not purchased commercial-grade ovens. On a regular basis, the oven doors would shatter from the heat, sending a cascade of broken safety glass to the floor, where it rested like a spray of black gravel.

One day Susan Stockton, helping run the kitchen, was preparing for an appearance by Julia Child on Robin Leach's show. Susan was paddling a rough pastry dough in a very hot pan, precisely following the recipe so that the éclairs Julia was to pipe from a pastry bag would turn out properly.

But the vents above the stove did not ventilate. They simply sucked hot air from one place and pushed it into another. As she paddled, Susan noticed that hot air was blowing directly on the top of her head. She looked up. It wasn't the vent. It was Julia, towering over her from behind, looking intently into the pan to make sure it was being prepared properly and breathing on the top of her head.

Robin's floor producer rushed in to summon Julia.

"You have to get to the studio!" he said.

"Not until she's done," Julia replied, swatting him away and resuming her vigil at Susan's back, breathing on her head until the dough was just so.

If Julia was the TVFN's occasional fairy godmother, Robin was its dirty uncle. One night, a producer awaiting Robin's arrival for a voice-over session was surprised to see him stroll in with a guest, a tall African-American woman, who was leaning on Robin's arm, her body barely contained in a few swaths of black spandex. Robin, impatient to get back out on the town with his date, was swearing and complaining at the five-minute delay between his arrival and the start of taping.

"What a fucking joke this place is," he slurred. "If you don't get me set up, I'm fucking leaving."

Understandably, not everyone wanted a show on TVFN. Script-writer Nora Ephron appeared on *Talking Food* with Donna Hanover and cooked her favorite tomato sauce. After the taping, Reese asked the writer of *When Harry Met Sally* and *Sleepless in Seattle* if she'd be interested in hosting her own regular cooking show.

"Absolutely not," she said.

But others, enticed by what the network could be, were willing to try. In many cases, it took someone with food at the center of his or her life to give TVFN their all, someone like Sara Moulton. Her journey to the network had started many years before TVFN existed. One day in 1979, Sara, a year out of culinary school, found herself peeling a massive pile of hard-boiled eggs for a catering company in Boston. Her coworker mentioned that she had been volunteering as an assistant on Julia Child's newest PBS cooking show. Sara, a small woman with a blond bob who grew up on a farm in western Massachusetts watching and worshipping Julia, asked if more volunteers were needed. The next day her colleague said she'd talked to Julia and that Sara should call her at home.

Julia, as always, answered the phone herself. "Oh, dearie," Julia said. "I've heard sooo much about yoooo. Do you food style?" Julia's longtime food stylist was away, she explained. And shooting was set to begin soon. Sara, who had little such experience, lied. "Yes, I'm really good," she answered eagerly.

After a meeting the next day in Julia's famous home kitchen in Cambridge, the stunned Sara was hired as the food stylist for *Julia Child and More Company*. Eventually, Sara moved to New York and was hired to assist Julia, off camera, for her frequent *Good Morning America* appearances. That led her to a job running *Gourmet* magazine's kitchen. Along the way, she taught classes at a culinary school, but she always thought of herself as a behind-the-scenes person. She saw many celebrities backstage at *Good Morning America* with their entourages, private makeup people, agents, and egos. They blew through the set with noise, hair spray, and drama, all charm when the cameras were pointed at them, all dragons when they weren't. People who craved the lights and the attention were nonsense. That wasn't her, she thought. Then in 1994, a *Good Morning America* producer had the idea to do an on-air segment featuring Sara as the show's "secret weapon." She resisted at first, but it was just a one-off thing, and the hosts, Charlie Gibson and Joan Lunden, would talk her through it. Secret weapon Sara cooked as instructed and, with some surprise, thought, Well, that wasn't too bad.

Coincidentally, a few weeks later Sara received a call from Sue Huffman, whom she knew from food-journalism circles, inviting her to lunch with Reese. At Larry Forgione's restaurant, Reese and Sue told Sara they could use someone with her experience, but they were not sure what job was the best fit. Would she be willing to run the Food Network backstage kitchen? They could only offer her the gig on a freelance basis without benefits. That wouldn't work. She was the main breadwinner in her family and *Gourmet* was giving her benefits.

"Well, would you like to be food editor?" Sue asked. Sara would oversee all recipes. Sue was desperate for a more rational approach to food prep and recipe testing at TVFN, but Reese had been resisting spending money on any such improvements. "Is that a desk job?" Sara asked. "Yes," Sue responded.

"Then, no. I'm a chef. I work in the kitchen."

Sara was the kind of person Reese wanted on board, a food expert with television experience and without an established television star's salary expectations. Plus she had worked with the gold standard, Julia. Emeril had moved on from *How to Boil Water*, but Reese did not want to give up on the idea of a super-basic cooking show—America's bachelors were desperate, he believed. If Emeril was the wrong fit, perhaps blond Sara would do as the host.

"Well," Reese said. "How would you like to do some on-air?"

Until the *Good Morning America* segment a few days earlier, she would have laughed at them. But she'd liked it enough, and her friends had praised her for it, more than one telling her she looked "perky." So she agreed to give it a shot. It was only a pilot. She showed up at the studio a few weeks later and, for the cameras, made an asparagus vinaigrette and *sole meunière*—the buttery dish that had famously turned Julia Child on to French cuisine.

But Sara was the opposite of perky this time. She was an unsmiling, leaden-faced wreck. For her *Good Morning America* segment, Charlie and Joan had coaxed her along, and the cameramen, all friends, were rooting for her. In the rickety TVFN studio, she was in front of strangers, and she panicked. When she held up a bunch of asparagus, her hands were shaking so badly, the tips looked like the head of an electric toothbrush. When it was finally over, she walked out thinking, Okay, I didn't really want to do this anyway.

A year passed, during which Sara's name was tossed around the network. She had been awful in her test for *How to Boil Water*, but so had Emeril. When *Chef du Jour* started up, Pat decided to give her another shot. Sara knew this was no disappearing pilot. The five episodes would go out on the air a week after she shot them. She decided to demonstrate recipes out of *Gourmet*, and convinced the magazine to foot the bill for a few days of television training.

A couple up in Montague, Massachusetts, Lou and Lisa Ekus, had become the go-to experts for training TV chefs. New York City expats, they left the city in 1982. Lisa, who worked in public relations for publishers, realized that many authors had no idea how to answer interview questions in a way that would make audiences fall in love with them and buy their books. Lou, a researcher in prosthetics and orthotics, who often spoke about his research at seminars, began giving Lisa's clients tips on how to work around cameras, stay on message, smile, and connect with people. These informal phone calls grew into two-day workshops, tailored specifically to clients in the food world.

The Ekuses' main message was, "You're always selling the same thing. It's not the book or the product. It's yourself. Get people to fall in love with you." Just how the Ekuses made their clients lovable depended on the client. Lou tried a few techniques to loosen her up: "Pretend you're in front of the camera at *Good Morning America* rehearsing one of your guests"; "Pretend you're just talking to the control room."

She remained as unbending and humorless as dry spaghetti when he pointed a camera at her. This wasn't going to work. Why would she want to tell the control room anything about food?

Lou clapped his hands. "Okay, this is ridiculous. There has to be a reason why you should be the next Julia Child."

Sara, who believed Child to be a goddess, was livid: "There. Will. NEVER. Be. Another. Julia Child!"

Lou had trained Emeril and cookbook authors like Mollie Katzen and Lynne Rosetto Kasper. He wasn't going to fail with this five-foot-nothing farm girl. "Well, okay," he said, relenting. "Maybe you're not going to be the next Julia Child. But there's got to be a reason why you should be on TV."

"That's just it," she said. "I shouldn't be on TV."

Lou was starting to break her down. Here was the kernel: Sara saw herself as a behind-the-scenes type, a quiet WASP, the same role she played in her marriage to a man in the music business. She earned the money and kept things on track. He got to play. This whole idea of being on TV was vulgar to her.

"I'm representing *Gourmet*, and *Gourmet* should be doing this," she said. In her mind the ideas deserved attention, not the person pitching them.

"No," Lou replied. "I'm not sure about that." He stewed for a moment. "Come on!" He clapped again.

She thought hard. "Well, I'm a really good teacher," she mused, thinking of the students she taught at Peter Kump's culinary school in New York. An image formed in her mind. She was Saint Sara, the evangelist of food. She told Lou. He nodded. She gathered herself. Yes. She could play that.

Sara did her turn on *Chef du Jour* and was chipper enough that Joe Langhan asked her to substitute for Michele Urvater on *$99 A Week*. Since Reese demanded there be no reruns from one day to the next, guest hosts were often needed. Sara did three episodes, two of them taped and one a live call-in show. Sara didn't screw it up, and a few days after the taping, Joe, with his usual lack of flourish, called her and said, "We'd like you to do a show, a call-in show. Um, and it's going to be nightly, Monday through Friday, an hour long, and it's going to be live."

Although she had reservations about spending less time with her family, Sara signed on. She could keep her day job and rush over to TVFN to shoot at night. Saint Sara's mission would be done. The show, *Cooking Live*, debuted on April 2, 1996, and was shot on the *In Food Today* set. She was so short, they had to pull in a narrow riser behind the counter every night. Because both *In Food Today* and her show were live and ran back-to-back, there was only three to five minutes to turn over the set. Suddenly air time would arrive, and Sara would take live phone calls while cooking, listening to a producer in her earpiece giving commands, and worrying nearly every second about accidentally falling backward off the riser while holding a pot of boiling water.

She had to learn fast. As with *Getting Healthy*, there was no digital delay with which to censor the callers. Sara would demonstrate a meal and the calls would come piping in throughout the show. Most questions were blandly informational—the ever-popular "How do you keep the skin crisp on a roast chicken?" among them. But there were profane ones, too, most of them failing to reach even the low bar set by Rudy and Frank—but, in their own sick way, revealing that some male viewers found Saint Sara's no-nonsense kitchen attitude kind of sexy. She was approachable in a way Debbi Fields was not. On a show in her first week, Sara was making eggplant rollatini and a man named Ralph called and asked, "How do you make eggplant à la penis?"

Saint Sara handled it: "Oh, Ralph, get a life."

Sara herself was not encouraged by TVFN to have a life. Four months into her nightly stint, she informed Joe that she'd be taking two weeks off in August to visit her parents' farmhouse in Massachusetts.

"You can't go," Joe told her. "You're doing a live show."

"Do repeats," she said.

"We don't do repeats," he insisted. "It's a live show."

"I'm going on vacation." Sara was enjoying her new role, but did not take it terribly seriously. Who knew if the network would survive? This was a lark. She doubted her show would last six months even if the network did survive.

Joe brought in chef Michael Lomonaco as a substitute. Sara returned and reclaimed her show, but by January, Michael had his own show, his own set, his own graphics, and his own knives with *Michael's Place* written on them. She was still on the set of *In Food Today* with no oven. The next year her August replacement was the Boston chef Ming Tsai, an expert in Asian fusion. By January, he had his own show and set. Two men, two new sets. Sara began to think there was a bias against women chefs at the network. The men got their own music and signature knives while she had canned tunes and dull hardware.

As tight as the network was with budgets, it lacked the proper infrastructure to manage some of its cash and other resources. Reese had hired a former stripper, Betty Harris, as the chief financial officer. Betty had attended accounting school once her dancing days were done and tried her best to maintain rational books, but keeping tabs on production costs, license fees, and food bills at a start-up network where inexperienced staff were lax about paperwork was a sometimes overwhelming task. Susannah Eaton-Ryan, the head of operations, kept a safe under her desk with thousands of dollars in petty cash. So many different producers had been given the combination that almost anybody could get into it. There was an honor system, but little honor. Producers would leave a note: "I took two hundred dollars to buy bok choi in Chinatown," "Five hundred to pay for taxis for camera crew on *Dining Around*," and the like. But the notes rarely reconciled with the cash. Thousands of dollars were stolen. Other items, like chef's knives, routinely went missing from the kitchen.

Cooks complained to Joe about the ongoing thefts. One night he groused to George Babick, "It's like we're all in this situation of simultaneously producing programs, hustling advertising, and worrying about getting heavy cream and Irish butter delivered."

George, a veteran of the CNN start-up, laughed and told Joe to let the bitching bounce off him. In the intervening years, George had worked at Tribune, where the hierarchy was rigid, but now as a top-level ad man, he was having a ball trying to land $50 for two-minute daytime spots from HairDini. A wild ride was to be expected. "There are start-up people and not start-up people," he said. He suggested that non-start-up people "find jobs at Xerox."

Joe couldn't resist trying to solve the crimes. He installed a wall clock with a hidden video camera near the safe. The first thing the tape showed was time being stolen: footage of Jonathan Lynne reclining at a desk with his feet up in the middle of the day, perhaps following a late night at Tramps.

When some of the young production assistants became suspicious of the new clock's positioning, they discovered the camera and cut the wire. The staff demanded an emergency meeting with executives, claiming their privacy was being violated and that the network was stifling creativity. A lot of the anger was directed at Joe, whom many of the young staff saw as a lackey for the moneymen in Providence, their invisible and tight-fisted corporate overlords. It was not common knowledge that without Joe there would be no TVFN, and he rarely mentioned it.

Reese called the staff into his office and let each one have his say.

"I feel like I was part of something, and all of a sudden I realize you just think of me as an employee," said one.

"I'm putting everything I have into this and now you're spying on me like Big Brother?" said another.

Reese apologized. Joe, never one to spend time fighting over his reputation, remained silent. The clock disappeared.

Joe, now forty-seven, was living in an apartment on the Upper West Side, which he had sublet from Julia Child's assistant, Nancy Barr. He rarely got home until after 11 p.m. and lived on takeout pizza, takeout Brazilian from a restaurant near the network, or takeout Peruvian from a chicken place around the corner from the apartment. The young staff might not have appreciated him, but he was less concerned about making friends than lending a hand backstage or tinkering with ideas in his cluttered office. His would become some of the most pivotal work done at TVFN.

For Reese, meanwhile, the most important thing was to hold fast to his plan no matter what crises developed. His inflexibility could be maddening, especially when he erupted in rage at someone who was defying him, but more often Reese's steadfastness kept the network churning slowly forward. As the network operation became more complicated, Reese sometimes tried to exert extra control over the areas he knew best. Food wasn't it. News still was.

For instance, the staff of *Food News and Views* grew bone-weary of Reese's renewed insistence that they keep coming up with fresh news about recombinant bovine growth hormone. He remained sure that TVFN could build an audience by becoming must-see TV for anyone interested in rBGH if only the network would stick with the story long enough and consistently deliver scoops. "No one cares," the staff protested, after months of calling every rBGH activist, industry source, and regulator. "There is no new news."

Then, one day Reese's nose for news paid off. Before noon on October 3, 1995, Reese rushed to the newsroom, where he found John

McGarvie, the news director, doling out assignments for the evening show. "What the fuck is everybody still doing here!" Reese yelled.

John shot Reese a glowering look, as if to say, "What are you talking about now, Reese?"

The president of the network bellowed, "It's the fucking OJ case! Why are we not out!"

The staff looked gape-mouthed at him, wondering what OJ Simpson had to do with food. Like most everyone else in the country, they knew that the verdict in the infamous murder trial was due to be read at 9 a.m. Pacific time, but what did that have to do with them?

Reese narrowed his eyes at John. "You're making a mistake. Get these people out, get them in bars." He nodded at Rochelle Brown and another producer. "Rochelle, get to Times Square. You go downtown to the Village."

As Rochelle walked to Times Square with a cameraman, she thought Reese was crazy. It was one thing for him to tell her to use a cardboard box for a desk, but this was ridiculous.

But at a few minutes before noon New York time, she saw that drivers had pulled their cars to the curb to watch the verdict read on the jumbo television mounted at the southern end of Times Square. Rochelle watched as a pizza deliveryman slid a pie through the window of one of the parked cars, and then another. It was as if people had been sitting on their couches nervously watching a football play-off and compulsively ordered pizza. She told the cameraman to start shooting. Reese was right: The OJ verdict had a food angle. Rochelle and the other producer rushed back to the studio with their tapes. The downtown tape showed patrons at an Irish bar in Greenwich Village guzzling beer in the aftermath of the not-guilty verdict, some expressing anguish and some jubilation, everyone drinking. It was the lead story on *Food News and Views*—the emotions of the day expressed in food.

A less brilliant ploy to bring the news to the network was TVFN's Election Night coverage in November 1996. Hosted by Michael Lomonaco and Sissy Biggers, a former NBC programming executive, the special featured demonstrations of recipes like Jimmy Carter's Cheese Ring (sharp cheddar, mayonnaise, chopped pecans, and strawberry preserves), Dolly Madison's Potato Rolls, and Kennedy Chocolate Chiffon Mousse. The famed baker Sylvia Weinstock made a sheet cake of the United States. She frosted each state as returns came in during the two-hour show, red for Republican states, blue for Democratic. At the end of the night, Clinton had retained the presidency, but TVFN did not win many viewers.

Some less-news-based programming stabs were proving more fruitful. When Los Angeles chefs Mary Sue Milliken and Susan Feniger appeared on *Food News and Views* in 1994 to promote their book *Mesa Mexicana*, Reese called and asked them if they would take a turn on *Chef du Jour*. After apprenticing at prestigious restaurants in France, the pair had turned a tiny café attached to an eyeglass shop into an L.A. dining destination, using little more than a cutting board and a hot plate. They put out dishes like pickled veal tongue with lobster sauce and pear. It was still unusual for women chefs to rise to the top of any culinary scene, but since Alice Waters had blazed a trail with Chez Panisse, the climate for women had improved. After opening a bigger restaurant in 1985, they followed it up with the Mexican-focused Border Grill. In 1992, they appeared on Julia Child's *Cooking with Master Chefs*, where Emeril had also made his debut. The show was shot in Mary Sue's home, and Julia introduced them as "a lively pair of teachers." Shep's CD project pairing their recipes with music also helped boost their national profile.

In New York, Mary Sue and Susan aced *Chef du Jour*. Reese called them a week later. "Do you want to do a show on Mexican food?" he asked. "We think you could do something called *Two Girls from South of the Border*." Mary Sue and Susan, being Midwesterners originally, thought the name was inappropriate. But they agreed to the general idea. A friend of Susan's came up with the name *Cooking with Too Hot Tamales*.

Reese flew out to California to meet with Mary Sue at the restaurant of the Beverly Hills Hotel. "We want you to do sixty shows to start," he said.

It sounded like a lot to Mary Sue. "You don't want to rerun shows," Reese explained. "It has to be fresh like, um, fresh produce. You present it once and it's over."

Reese agreed on the name *Too Hot Tamales* and insisted on keeping the rights to it. You never knew when you were going to have to swap out hosts.

Mary Sue and Susan were as close as two friends could be. Susan had long ago divorced her husband and come out as a lesbian. For the first five years they knew each other, Susan watched Mary Sue endure boyfriend trouble, suggesting with each breakup that she might like to meet her ex-husband, Josh. Finally, Mary Sue agreed to hire Josh, sight unseen, as an architect for their second restaurant. Three weeks after they met, he moved in and they were soon married. For the debut of *Too Hot Tamales*, Josh dyed two chef's coats different shades of red, matching the colors he'd chosen for the Border Grill. They shot the first run of shows in about two weeks at 1177 Sixth Avenue, using Mario's set, but with more colorful backdrops. No one Mary Sue or Susan knew in L.A. subscribed to a cable provider that carried TVFN. But when they came back to New York to shoot another run of shows, the pair was amazed when a squad of firemen came running out of a building on Sixth Avenue and recognized them. "Oh, my God! It's the Too Hot Tamales!" one cried.

"What are you doing in there?" Mary Sue asked the firemen. "Is there a fire?"

"No, don't worry," the smiling men in uniform replied, watching from behind as the shapely Tamales walked up the street.

One early episode of *Too Hot Tamales*, to which the firemen might have paid particular attention, showed the women preparing a geoduck clam chowder. The geoduck clam has a unusually long, thick, fleshy neck muscle that has to be dipped in boiling water before the skin can be peeled off its meaty shaft. As Mary Sue flopped a particularly long, steaming geoduck down on a cutting board, the male cameramen began giggling. Mary Sue knew about the no-stopping rule, but as she pulled back the flesh on the neck with her long feminine fingers, this off-stage noise was so loud, she expected Pat, who was producing the show, to yell "Cut! Cut!" She glanced over at Susan, who was caught in a fit of hysterical laughter. No one yelled "Cut!" so Mary Sue soldiered on, describing the recipe. As she raised a heavy knife and brought the blade down through the meat, hacking it into bits, the cameramen grew silent.

A year later, Mary Sue was at a book signing and a male fan remarked on the geoduck episode. "I had a lot of explaining to do to my son," he said.

They were being noticed everywhere. In the gay and lesbian–focused magazine *The Advocate*, the controversial academic Camille Paglia (who had herself been a guest on *Talking Food* where she prepared a "quick and easy bouillabaisse") published an essay in April 1996, showering the Tamales with praise:

> With their energy, ingenuity, adventurousness, practicality, and cordial warmth, Milliken and Feniger are wonderful contemporary role models for American women. Feniger in particular has broken the mold of TV hosts and proved that lesbians aren't all tempeh-, tofu-, and granola-eating puritans.

As the Tamales' star rose, Shep rushed in to make a merchandising deal with Reese. Shep's promise to Mary Sue and Susan was the same one he'd made to the other chefs: "I will make sure that wherever you appear, your name will be on the marquee with the other stars." Shep told Reese he wanted it mentioned in the show credits that the Tamales had a line of chilies. Shep argued this would help the network get more exposure in supermarkets. Reese agreed and the brand was launched.

Meanwhile, Bobby, who had no agent, just his wits, continued to make frequent appearances on *Talking Food* and was given a turn on

Chef du Jour. Amongst his chef friends, he had started hearing disdain for TVFN: "I'm a chef," they would say haughtily, "not some TV clown." They would never sell out. They'd never deign to be on some channel with the *Lifestyles of the Rich and Famous* guy.

Bobby was more coldly calculating. The other chefs could posture, but he could not see a downside to this gamble. "I don't mind going on TV and letting people know where my restaurant is," he thought. He saw that Mario was getting on the air poking pasta and chatting with increasing ease on camera, his restaurant name flashing in the credits. Mary Sue and Susan had done *Chef du Jour* and had their own show cooking spicy stuff.

Bobby wanted in. What? he thought. Am I going to be left behind? Not this bronco.

As Bobby's hands were busy at Mesa Grill, he tried to come up with an idea for a show of his own. Southwestern? What would it be called? Did he need to figure that out? Something about grilling. Something he knew. The next time he showed up for an appearance at the network, in the fall of 1995, he brought a folder containing a list of dishes he might make on a show. Handing it to Joe, he said, "This could be a show."

Two months later, Bobby got a call from the network, but there was no mention of the folder. "We want to talk to you about a show. You know this guy Jack McDavid, who's a friend of yours?"

Bobby did not know how they knew he knew McDavid. The two had met at a Super Bowl weekend charity event in Minneapolis where chefs from every NFL city were invited to cook. McDavid had a barbecue restaurant in Philadelphia but hailed from the mountains of Virginia. Every other chef was dutifully wearing a chef's jacket, toque, and checked pants, but Jack wore a hat that read "Save the Farm," and overalls over his whites. Jack pulled out a six-pack of beer and in his deep country voice asked Bobby, "You want some?"

"Yeah," Bobby said.

Jack cracked open a bottle and handed it to Bobby. He took a sip— "ACCCKKK!" and spit it out. It burned his tongue and throat like boiling gasoline. "What the fuck is that?"

"Son, that's moonshine." Jack had poured the stuff into beer bottles so he could carry it on the airplane without arousing suspicion. The country boy had cojones. Bobby's second sip went down easier. They became friends.

"Yes, I know him," Bobby told the TVFN exec.

"We'd like to do a grilling show about the two of you. Like, a city guy and a country guy, grilling. We know that you have a house in the Hamptons. We could shoot it there."

Bobby did not own a house in the Hamptons. He rented a cheap summer house there with a bunch of other restaurant people. Flip-flops, a few mattresses, and a deck with a kettle grill. "That's my share house," he said. "I can't shoot there."

"Okay, but anyway, could you call Jack McDavid? See if he wants to do a show with you?"

He called Jack. "You want to do it?"

"Sure!"

Bobby came in for a meeting with Reese, Pat, and Joe. "We want to do, like, hot dogs," Reese began. To Reese and most other Americans, grilling was hot dogs and hamburgers, nothing else. "Hold on," Bobby protested. "I have different ideas. I want to raise the profile of what grilling is."

There was a moment of silence, and then Joe pulled out a folder absentmindedly from the pile on his lap and withdrew a sheet of paper with recipe ideas for a grilling show. "Uh, here's some ideas," he said.

Bobby couldn't believe it. "Wait a minute," he said, "that's the paper I gave you."

Joe did not acknowledge that they were Bobby's recipes. Bobby took this to mean Joe was trying to take credit for them. But Joe just wanted to get things moving. He knew it would be better if Reese thought the idea came from the programming side. Reese didn't trust chefs much when it came to programming.

"Dude," Bobby continued. "That's mine. Those are my recipes!"

Joe handed Bobby back his recipe folder. "Fine. Here. Just do it," he said. Reese nodded.

Reese swung a deal to use space on the back lot of the Home Shopping Network in Florida, where it was warm enough to shoot outside in winter. The locale would be an improvement over David Rosengarten's grilling episode of *Taste*. David's show was full of terrific tips about brands of charcoal and the advantages of an adjustable-height rack, but it required an apology from the host at the outset: "Despite the fact that I'd like to be outside with a bottle of beer," David told viewers as effervescently as possible, "I'm actually in a studio here and the fire department might not look too kindly upon open flames on the thirty-first floor of this building, so I am not going to be able to show you any live coals, but there are lots of things I can tell you and show you about cooking over live coals, so let's use our imaginations, shall we?" At the end, David displayed a nicely grilled steak, but did not actually grill one.

The production team for Bobby and Jack's show came up with a name: *Grillin' and Chillin'*. TVFN made forty-two episodes in seven days with a budget of about $1,800 an episode. Jack and Bobby took home $200 each per show. After the week of shooting down in Florida, the grills, tables, and everything else on the set was auctioned off to the local crew. In March 1996, *Grillin' and Chillin'*, amateurish but cheerful and full of tips about rubs and recipes for grilling lobster, grouper, and lamb, went into heavy rotation on TVFN. Soon after its debut, a trickle of previously non-foodnik customers who'd seen Bobby on TV began showing up at Mesa Grill.

By the time *Grillin' and Chillin'* was on, TVFN was finally being shown full-time in Manhattan on Time Warner Cable. It had happened because Reese had recognized an opportunity in channel 50, the original slot TVFN had shared with the New Jersey public affairs station. Why did New Jersey need Manhattan distribution? Reese began working every New Jersey political connection he could muster, managing to get an offer in to the bureaucrats who oversaw WNJN. He offered to pay the state, an entity always strapped for cash, $4.3 million for doing nothing other than giving up rights to reach a bunch of homes outside its jurisdiction. WNJN would stay on channel 50 in New Jersey, but in New York it would carry TVFN.

New Jersey went for the deal, as did Time Warner, since it gained the right to sell a few minutes per hour of advertising space on TVFN in New York. From then on, TVFN ad salesmen would have meetings on Madison Avenue with people likely to have the network at home, a major relief to the sales team.

It was one of Reese's best deals, showcasing his strengths—high-level connections, big thinking, and decisiveness. But it was not enough to overcome the weaknesses—temper, short attention span, occasionally irrational frugality, and overcontrol—that were fraying his relationship with ProJo and, particularly, Jack Clifford.

Among his gripes, Jack did not like some of Reese's staff, especially George Babick, the head of advertising. At one TVFN end-of-year executive meeting, Jack berated George over what Jack saw as a lack of recent sales productivity that no carriage problems could excuse. "Are your salesmen making calls?" Jack asked him. "No orders for the last couple weeks?"

George thought Jack was a bumpkin who understood only how ad sales worked at local channels where sales people could call used car dealers and pawnshops anytime with some hope of a buy. Big national buyers like Procter & Gamble placed the bulk of their ad buys only once or twice a year. "The national buys are in," George replied stiffly to Jack's query. "These guys have spent their money, and we have a lot of it. They're not buying in December. They don't buy at our convenience."

On the programming side, Jack, far more of a foodie than Reese, heard from Sue Huffman that Reese wouldn't allow recipe testing, leading to numerous on-air mishaps. Others argued that a few more reruns would bring down production costs.

Throughout Reese's second year running the network in 1995, Tryg withstood Jack's carping. Jack wanted someone in control of the network who would listen to him and obey.

Tryg also endured grumblings from the ProJo board. He had to go back more than once to ask for millions to keep TVFN going. Tryg told them he had seen a lot of network start-ups, including ESPN, MTV, and E! "They all went through hell at first," he said. "What you are seeing with Television Food Network is exactly what happens when you have the right idea."

A member of the ProJo board, Nick Thorndike, pointed out that CBS Cable went broke. "Why is this different?" he asked.

"Our run rate is dramatically smaller than CBS Cable," Tryg replied. It was normal to miss cost projections, but Reese was doing his utmost to stem spending. As long as the network could stay alive, Tryg argued, even if it was slowly burning a bit of ProJo's ample cash reserves, it stood a chance of catching on and picking up speed. Tryg could point to signs of Reese's effectiveness. TVFN was available in 12 million households in 1995, roughly double what it had at launch. More people were writing in for recipes: in the fourth quarter of 1994, the network was getting 2,500 requests a week; by the first quarter of 1995, it was up to 10,000 requests a week. When the first Nielsen ratings had come in May 1995, they showed the network was averaging 36,000 viewers at any given time—a 0.3 rating in Nielsen terms—77 percent of them women. Reese had boasted about the numbers in the press as good news for a network so young, especially the fact that 51 percent of viewers were working women, a good demographic to sell advertisers.

The ProJo board approved the infusions, but Tryg knew the company named after its newspaper remained skeptical of all cable investments. The board had never completely given itself over to Tryg's vision of turning ProJo into an industry-leading communications giant, gobbling up other companies and generating its own programming. In 1992, as TVFN was being fitfully born, ProJo had had the chance to buy a competitor, King Broadcasting, a cable operator and owner of five broadcast stations, at the recession price of $550 million. ProJo had had enough cash, but the board had insisted on finding a partner to share the risk, a leveraged buyout firm with a short-term view that clashed with Tryg's.

Tryg had steadfastly continued to explore the market for cable systems, eager to expand Colony to compete with other growing operators like Comcast and his former company, Time Warner Cable. But there were few opportunities to buy systems easily combined with Colony's existing regional holdings. As prices for cable systems increased, he finally accepted that Colony was never going to grow big enough to thrive. The best strategy for ProJo shareholders was to sell. And so, a year after the launch of TVFN, ProJo sold its Colony cable operations to Continental Cablevision in Boston, one of the TVFN investors, in a $1.4 billion deal. ProJo kept its controlling share of TVFN and a cable health network and was able to buy out the leveraged buyout firm and take full control of the broadcast stations.

With Colony gone, Jack, who oversaw all of ProJo's television properties, became more intensely focused on TVFN. For Tryg, the year following the Colony sale deepened his longing for his beloved Colorado. His wife hated Providence. The board's resistance to deeper investments in cable programming made the job increasingly uninteresting to him. East Coast skiing could not compare to the Rockies, and by the fall of 1995 he knew he was soon to announce his resignation. To keep Jack happily in harness through the coming transition, Tryg decided he had no choice but to give in and let Reese go.

They waited until the deal to deliver TVFN in Manhattan was done. Reese's contract with ProJo allowed him to spend 20 percent of his week on other projects. He had begun working a few hours a week with the BBC to bring a 24-hour-a-day news channel to American cable to compete with CNN. Jack let him know ProJo had decided that TVFN could not have a part-time boss, no matter what the contract said. Tryg and he would stand together on this. Tribune executives claimed they were unaware of the 20 percent stipulation and, never fully trusting Reese, threw their support behind Jack, too.

Reese was furious. He respected Jack as a salesman and understood that Jack had played a key role in convincing investors and cable providers to come aboard TVFN at the outset. But this was an obvious ruse. TVFN was commanding Reese's attention with or without the BBC deal. It was clear that Jack was doing whatever he had to do to get his hands on the network. What's more, in Jack's eagerness to usher Reese out as quickly as possible without scotching the New York cable distribution deal, ProJo authorized TVFN to spend hundreds of thousands of dollars to print and mail Manhattan cable customers statutorily required notices that they would no longer receive New Jersey public affairs. If the mailings had waited a few weeks, the notice could have been included for negligible cost in the regular monthly bills. The waste grated on Reese.

On the other hand, the deal ProJo was offering him to leave was good. They would allow him to retain his 5 percent ownership stake in TVFN and keep a seat on the network board. Reese allowed himself some time to think it through. He figured that the network was on its feet. He could keep his eye on things by serving on the board. If ProJo wanted him gone, it would be a nasty fight to try to stay. Ultimately, it sounded like a better idea to relent, keeping his chips, but free to work on new projects.

He stepped aside at the end of November 1995, having lasted at TVFN a few days longer than two years from the launch date. At CNN he had lasted a few days short of two years. At both networks, he had gotten an amazing job done, transforming a few rough ideas put on paper into very real desks, satellite dishes, talent, producers, distribution, marketing, and eyeballs. Reese, an enormous and forceful character, was justifiably a legend for what he had accomplished. But, like many mavericks, his explosive skills were best used in getting things going, not in running an existing operation in a stable fashion, especially not one in a subject area he cared little about. In both cases, his tempestuousness alienated some colleagues and led to blurry chains of command.

> "They said, 'Look, we'll give you everything you want. You get all your money. You get everything else. Just stop doing it.' And I said, 'Well, that sounds like a good deal to me.' And I went back trying to get into the news business again."
>
> **—REESE SCHONFELD**

What he did still care about was seeing a profit from this start-up. Although Reese was leaving as president, his role on the board assured that he was not yet done as a factor in the Food Network story.

In January 1996, Tryg announced his own resignation from ProJo, although he stayed many more months. During his five-year tenure, the value of ProJo's privately held stock tripled.

With Reese out of the way, Jack was in control of the young cable network. The TVFN team in New York could only hope he didn't stir in too much cumin.

BAM!

When Reese agreed to step down, Jack Clifford asked Jeff Wayne, a ProJo executive, if he could devote perhaps two months to overseeing the operation in New York and report back to him. Jeff had been answering up the command chain to Jack for about seventeen years—he'd eaten the killer chili countless times and survived—so he was a trusted, steady lieutenant, the opposite of the freewheeling rival that Jack had had to contend with in Reese.

Jeff had been head of marketing for Colony Cablevision and then was plucked from its ashes and installed as vice president of programming at the Providence Journal. When Jack approached him, Jeff, wearing his clunky gold wire-rim glasses and sporting an unfashionable brush mustache, was still envisioning a comfortable future in which he lived happily in Providence, coaching his twin sons' Little League team and enjoying the kind of quiet existence possible when well employed in a small city.

So he told Jack, fine, but only with the understanding that this was a temporary assignment of no more than a month, with the condition that he could spend his weekends in Rhode Island.

———

At Colony, Jeff had been skeptical of TVFN from the start, questioning the strategy of giving the network away for free to cable providers. He used to rib Joe Langhan about how unlikely it was that a food channel would ever get going, especially when Johnson & Wales kept failing to commit. Now, after two years of operation, the network was hardly living up to the investors' financial expectations. It was millions of dollars behind the projections in the original business plan. It had lost $20.8 million in 1995, and was on track to lose $18 million in 1996. Many backers wanted out.

Jeff's primary assignment was to answer two questions: How awful was the operation Reese had set up? And is this a viable business at all?

Joe showed Jeff around the network in New York, and after only a week, Jeff was more impressed than he thought he'd be at how TVFN churned out cooking shows on a pea-sized budget. There was an energy and enthusiasm to the place, despite obvious disorganization. When he called Jack with his initial reactions, Jeff raved: "Holy cow! This is going to be huge."

Jeff's reports on the state of the network were so positive that ProJo began taking every opportunity to buy out TVFN partners. It paid Landmark Programming approximately $12.6 million and E.W. Scripps $11.4 million for their roughly 12 percent stakes in May 1996, thereby valuing the network at around $100 million.

Ken Lowe, who had launched Scripps's HGTV a year after TVFN, was busy overseeing HGTV in Knoxville, and had not been consulted by the corporate higher-ups in Cincinnati about the sale. HGTV was collecting about 3 cents a month per subscriber. Even with as few as 12 million subscribers, that added up to more than $4 million in revenue a year, money HGTV got and TVFN did not. Scripps had been able to extract the fees from cable operators partly because it effectively tied them to retransmission rights from its own powerful broadcast stations and partly because it made the case that HGTV's shows were of a higher quality than most start-ups. When Scripps's sale of its TVFN stake was mentioned to Ken in passing, he understood the business reasons, yet couldn't help but think how he could bring what he was learning from HGTV to bear on a food channel. Not privy to what Jeff Wayne was actually seeing in New York, Ken continued to believe the concept of a food-centric channel was good, even if Reese's execution was not. "If we could just get our hands on it," Ken thought.

But he couldn't. In January 1997, ProJo continued to consolidate, paying an undisclosed amount for Continental Programming's 14 percent stake, leaving the Rhode Island company with 55.5 percent ownership of TVFN. The only other large stakeholder was Tribune, with around 30 percent. Each time one of the original investors sold out its Class A shares, Jack gave their seat on the board to Jeff, whose vote he could count on.

The organization certainly wasn't perfect. The ad sales department, marketing, affiliate sales, and programming never met together to plan overall strategy. Reese had kept it all in his head, conducting meetings one-on-one, barking orders as he roamed the halls. Jeff organized regular meetings between all the departments. He went over the books line by line with Betty Harris, the CFO. He pointed to a number in the budget for 1996, the coming year, an amount around $350,000.

"Uh, what is this for?" Jeff asked.

"Oh, that's for the recipes," Betty replied, looking at him expressionlessly through thick round glasses.

"What?"

"At the end of every show we put this screen up that basically says, if you want the recipe you just saw, please send a postage-paid envelope, and we'll send it." Betty explained that Reese—in the absence of Nielsen ratings—had been using recipe requests to gauge the number of viewers. If he paid the postage, more people would request recipes; if more people requested recipes, it would look like more people were watching the network. Even though the network had finally started receiving Nielsens in mid-1995, no one had called off the recipe giveaway.

It struck Jeff as lunacy. "So you're telling me that here we are at thirteen million subscribers, and you're spending hundreds of thousands of
dollars on fulfilling recipe requests?"

It was all being outsourced, she said, noncommittally.

"So, Betty, you mean when we're at like, thirty million subscribers,
this is gonna be like a million dollars?"

"Well, that's ri-ii-ight!" she said, breaking into a smile, as if to praise
Jeff's mathematical perspicacity along with the madness of the scheme
when you looked at it that way. "That's ri-ii-ight!"

After hearing this, Jeff asked Joe if the website could be improved to
deliver all the network's recipes and make them searchable. The head of
marketing put together an on-air promotion to improve traffic to the
site and tapped Curtis Aikens, the host of *Food in a Flash*, to star in it.
Aikens had gained recognition beyond the food world for learning how
to read only as an adult.

"Two years ago, I couldn't even read," Curtis told the camera, sitting
in front of a computer, typing. "And now I'm on the computer getting
the recipes for my show and all of the other shows on the Television
Food Network. And you can do it, too. Just log on to foodtv.com."

Traffic barely budged. Don found that less than 20 percent of Internet users were female. But 71 percent of TVFN's audience was. So
they came up with an ad to reach women, one that told viewers that
even if they personally were not on the Internet, they probably had a
male friend or relative who was, and who could log on and get the recipe. Traffic started improving. TVFN had a head start on the rest of
the industry. *Food & Wine* magazine did not put its first recipe online
until January 1997. By May 1997, the foodtv.com site was receiving
500,000 visits a month.

Once Jeff gave Jack his appraisal of the network, his tasks were to
trim any financial excesses he could, bring his skills as a trained mar-
keter to bear, and keep the network piloted forward until a permanent
president could be hired. Jeff axed live coverage of the James Beard
Awards show, saving the network around $250,000 a year. Coverage of
the "Oscars of Food" might have helped TVFN gain credibility in its

early years, but the business could no longer afford it. Jeff also ended the network's involvement in the TVFN charity telethons, *Let's Make Sure Everybody Eats*, which Tryg's wife had advocated, using her involvement in them as an excuse to trade Providence for New York. These raised needed funds for the poor, and memorably featured boxers Joe Frazier and George Foreman participating in one of Jack's chili cook-offs, but they cost the network $555,000 in 1994 and $825,000 in 1995.

Jeff changed the name of *Food News and Views* to the sleeker *In Food Today*, and pushed the show to be more entertaining.

He defended some territory. George Babick's team had been trying to sell advertisers on the network's audience of women twenty-five to fifty-four years old. Ratings were showing that more than half of the audience were working women—except for one show, *Molto Mario*. Its audience was predominantly male. George would argue at every meeting: "Let's not renew Mario. He's not bringing the audience that we wanted."

Jeff refused to cancel the show because he saw Mario as a larger-than-life media personality essential to the network's brand. Regular people knew who Mario was. "Yeah, we're not hitting the exact audience, but we're getting a lot of buzz, and the guy's got star potential," he countered. He doubled down, approving the production of a commercial to improve Mario's ratings. In it, Mario, still the head chef at Pó, was shown from behind stirring pots and then waving his arms as if he were a symphony conductor while an operatic song rang out, ending with:

Mario Batali
Is cooking now for youuuuu!

Reese had hired Steven Jon Whritner as head of marketing with the promise of a top-notch marketing team and a healthy budget, neither of which had ever materialized. On Whritner's first day in August 1995,

Reese had asked, "Okay, Mister Head of Marketing, what's the first thing you are going to tackle?"

"I'm going to redesign that God-awful logo," Whritner replied.

Reese flushed a bright shade of purple and managed to spit out, "I designed that logo." He forbade his new hire from touching it.

But Jeff understood the importance of logos and brand names. The right logo can burrow into a customer's brain and lodge itself there forever. "TVFN" did not exactly roll off the tongue, and the logo, designed to look like a cloche, a domed French serving platter, could easily be mistaken for a thin black rainbow with a fungus sprouting from the top. He allowed Whritner to ask the TVFN board for $250,000 to hire a West Coast design firm, Pittard Sullivan, to remake the logo. Reese—still a board member—fulminated that redesigning a perfectly serviceable logo was nonsense that wouldn't help the bottom line, but he did not have enough sway to vote it down.

Whritner came back with several options for Jeff, all of which dropped "Television" from the network's name. (The legal name remains Television Food Network.)

One weekend Jeff laid out the final choices on his dining room table and asked his wife, Beverly, to take a look. She was artsy and more the network's target audience than he. She pointed to one in which the word "food" appeared in a slightly italicized, all lowercase font and "NET-WORK" in tight caps stacked underneath it, the first two letters of each word set inside a circle. Beverly thought the design was feminine, classy, and simple. "I like that one the best," she said. It remained the basic Food Network logo until 2013. It also came with a new slogan, suggested by Pittard Sullivan, "We're Really Cooking," replacing the original, rarely used "Everybody Eats."

Next, in what was a key addition to the broadcast schedule, Jeff approved the network's purchase of the rights to the British show *Ready, Steady, Cook*. Two chefs were paired with two amateurs, supplied with a grocery bag of food, and given twenty minutes to cook something. The finished dishes were shown to the studio audience, who then voted on the winning team based only on which plate looked more delicious.

It was an early foray into cooking as a competition sport and bridged the gap between home cooks and chefs, the underlying message being, see, you can be inventive at home with little time and cheap ingredients. Food Network Americanized the name to *Ready . . . Set . . . Cook!* and rented a studio large enough for an audience. Rounding up the crowd was not easy. Popular shows that taped in New York, such as *The Ricki Lake Show* and *Late Night with David Letterman*, had no trouble, but getting bodies in seats for a game show on a network few people watched was a challenge. Even after hiring audience-wrangling companies, they regularly came up short. One Food Network staffer often had to hit the sidewalks around the studio rounding up homeless people by promising them they could eat the food when shooting was done.

Robin Young hosted *Ready . . . Set . . . Cook!* during the first season. She would stand hip to hip with the competitors and engage them in banter while they tried to cook: "What's your plan with that chicken?" "Is it tough cooking under this time pressure?" In a restaurant kitchen, the chef would have had a difficult time resisting the urge to prick Young's carotid artery with a paring knife to stop her infernal banter. Still, seeing how precisely and safely real chefs could work under pressure was instructive and entertaining.

The show's success marked a cultural breakthrough. On the 1996 Thanksgiving episode of *Friends*, then the top-rated NBC comedy, Chandler, who was feeling particularly attractive, bragged to Joey, "From now on I get the dates and you have to stay home on Saturday nights watching *Ready . . . Set . . . Cook!*"

The day after the episode aired, the Food Network staff greeted each other with three words: "Oh, my God!" followed by four more: "Can you believe it?" They'd been noticed by Hollywood!—even if their show was being used as a symbol of a pathetic life.

As the channel now known as Food Network passed its second birthday, its roster of enthusiastic chefs, writers, and academics who had devoted their lives to food was offering TVFN households throughout the country a peek into a special world they could join: Just follow Mario Batali's advice and drizzle a little vinegar tableside on each portion of the guinea hen you'd just seared—don't know what guinea hen is? Watch and learn. Adopt Jack McDavid's you-can-do-it attitude and try Grilled Day Boat Scallops over Elderberry Wood with Peas and Apples in Grilled Red Pepper Sauce. Or wow your buddies by doing like Emeril and making fried pickles with spicy dipping sauce to munch while watching football. Beats Ruffles.

Because Food Network had hours to fill, it could take viewers into formerly obscure pockets of high and low cuisine no other channel had had the time, nor the brief, to mine. On an episode of the restaurant review show, *Dining Around*, the hosts, now the respected critic Alan Richman with Nina Griscom, passionately discussed the change of chefs at Manhattan's legendary four-star French restaurant Lutèce. "When renowned chef André Soltner sold Lutèce in October 1994, everybody was worried . . ." Alan began. "And while the world held its breath waiting to see what would happen to one of the world's most prestigious French restaurants, award-winning chef Eberhard Müller stepped right in. . . . It was like starting in center field after Mickey Mantle retired."

Video from the restaurant showed the new chef and his staff preparing an appetizer of crabmeat over potatoes with black truffles and vinaigrette. In the studio, Nina and Alan dug into servings of the appetizer that had been carried across town from Lutèce. Nina weighed in on how Müller was stepping into Soltner's shoes. "He is bringing this restaurant into contemporary days and putting his own name on it, and I think he can be the new Soltner," she pronounced.

"There is no question about it," concurred Alan. On a recent visit to Lutèce, he had sampled the guinea hen with cabbage. "He has all the skill. . . . If you do classic food perfectly, there is nothing better."

In most of the towns and cities the network was reaching in 1996, very few viewers would have known the names of the chefs at their local restaurants, let alone the name of a foreigner who toiled with a boning knife in a cramped kitchen on the Upper East Side. But Food Network opened a window into a world where such things mattered. Everybody in the world of fine dining cared about Lutèce, and for the first time, you—anyone—could become one of those somebodies simply by tuning in.

Some viewers were clearly entranced by it. One night while Jeff was having dinner with Curtis Aikens at a Times Square hotel, a cab driver rushed into the restaurant and came up to the table.

"Curtis! Curtis!" he yelled. "Hey, man, I just wanted to meet you! I just, I watch you all the time on the Food Network."

"Who are you?" Jeff asked.

"I'm driving a cab! I was just driving by and I saw you two in the window!"

David Rosengarten had a similar experience in upstate New York when his six-year-old daughter insisted on stopping at McDonald's. He pulled into a gas station in Monticello, a city with a cable company carrying Food Network, to ask where he could find one, and someone there, stunned, exclaimed: "David Rosengarten wants to go to McDonald's!?"

By 1996, two New York restaurant publicists, Steven Hall and Karine Bakhoum, had become accustomed to receiving calls at 10 a.m. from TVFN producers such as Rochelle Brown and Lauren Bright asking if they had someone, anyone, they could send over to do a demo later that day on *In Food Today* or *Talking Food*. Steven realized he could attract new chefs as clients by promising them television. The owner of Cibo, a Tuscan-New American restaurant, hired Steven's company and introduced him to their head chef, Tyler Florence. At twenty-five, Tyler was five years out of culinary school, having attended Johnson & Wales's Charleston, South Carolina, campus. When Steven met Tyler, saw his wide shoulders, big hands, and farm-boy good looks, and heard the way he spoke with a clear but comfortable drawl, Steven knew he would be sending the hunk over to the TV channel soon.

Tyler was familiar with the TV business. Following his parents' divorce, his mom had been the business manager of the NBC station in Greenville, South Carolina. Tyler and his older brother spent many after-school hours wandering the studio while the local news was done live. As a boy, he had helped his mother out at home by learning to cook. Nevertheless, after Steven had sent him to compose a salad with morel mushrooms for David Rosengarten and Donna Hanover's daily food news show, Tyler walked off the set thinking he had botched it by sweating and mumbling the whole way through. But the show's producer rushed up to him offstage, gushing, "That was really great! Can you come back again?"

Tyler was shocked. "Absolutely." That night he was sitting at a desk in the basement of Cibo, barely able to move because the electricity inside him was so intense. As preparations for dinner were going on around him, Tyler thought that as uncomfortable as he'd been, he'd also felt at home in that tiny studio full of cameras and soundmen and cooking equipment.

> "I knew that my life after that moment would be different somehow. It manifested in wanting it really, really bad. Wanting it really bad."
>
> —TYLER FLORENCE

Tyler had never realized before that he could be on TV cooking. It was gratifying to be cast as a teacher on TV and to be given an opportunity to propound a philosophy of cooking—his was that gathering around the table with friends or family to eat a homemade meal is important. Exposed to the possibility of such a career, Tyler did what thousands would do in the coming years—devoted everything he had to getting his own cooking show. He vowed to stay in touch with everyone he could at Food Network. He would invite the TV people to his restaurant, treat them like royalty, and always be ready and willing if producers needed a last-minute replacement for anything. He would know his lines and prep his own food and make it easy for them to have him back.

It's a game, he told himself, and at this point it's my game to win or lose.

_____

While David, Curtis, and the Tamales were occasionally recognized on the street, Emeril had become the network's most identifiable personality thanks to the popularity of *Essence of Emeril*. Keeping him happy was important. Shortly before Reese left in November 1995, he told Joe he had promised Emeril that the network would produce a special to promote his second cookbook, *Louisiana Real and Rustic*, due to be published the following fall.

But Joe, whose job title was head of production, had let months go by without doing anything. As the book's publication date approached, he realized that he had received far more requests from friends and acquaintances to watch *Essence of Emeril* tapings than any other show. There was no room for a studio audience, so on the occasions when Joe let one or two people come to watch, they had to stand against a back wall. Joe would ask Emeril if it was okay and the chef would always say, "Oh, yeah, don't worry about it."

Emeril was still trying to shoot six or more episodes a day. By the fourth day, no amount of espresso could keep his energy level up. But Joe noticed that when there was a guest in the studio, especially a child, Emeril came alive. Once a twelve-year-old named Ross was a guest and Emeril kept asking him, "Ross, what do you think of that?" Joe realized that Emeril thrived when he had someone to talk to besides the regular crew.

"What if we did a show where we had a bunch of his fans in the studio?" Joe asked himself.

Bam!

He called Emeril and described the idea: an hourlong cooking show in front of a live audience.

"That sounds interesting," Emeril said. "Let me call you back." Emeril had been increasing his schedule of public appearances, including live cooking demos to promote his first restaurant in Las Vegas, Emeril's New Orleans Fish House. His restaurant team, including his business manager, Tony Cruz, and his right-hand woman, Marti Dalton, noticed a side of Emeril they had not seen before. Emeril could be taciturn in private, gazing down at the ground or quietly working the sauté station at one of his restaurants. But with three years of television under his belt, he was starting to ham it up as a public performer, clearly enjoying the crowd's loud responses.

Fifteen minutes after Joe had proposed the live special, Emeril called him back. "Let's do it," he said.

Joe knew he needed a good pitch in place before he asked Jeff for permission to do Emeril's special. He had decided to shoot two of them, hoping at least one would turn out good enough to use as a pilot if it made sense to do a regular series. Once the *Ready . . . Set . . . Cook!* production delivered the necessary studio space, Joe presented the idea in money-saving terms. "Hey, Jeff," Joe said. "We're spending all this money to get the live audiences for *Ready . . . Set . . . Cook!* What do you think of trying a special show with Emeril over there?"

Jeff was game. "Shit, what the hell, might as well," he said. "Emeril is such a ham."

Joe, through a crucial barrier, wasted little time mobilizing. He told audience wranglers for *Ready . . . Set . . . Cook!* to put in extra effort finding an Emeril-friendly crowd to fill the bleachers on launch day. No homeless people! He rallied the kitchen staff, telling them it would be raucous, like a rock-and-roll gig. "Why can't a food show," he asked, "be concert-like?"

Before shoot day on the Emeril special, there was another change at the top. Jeff had agreed to work at the network for two months, and it had now been more than six. In that time, he had been working with Jack Clifford and others at ProJo to find a permanent president for Food Network. Jack stipulated two requirements: that it be a woman, who would better understand the target audience, and that she come from the advertising industry, since selling ads was the key to turning a profit.

One name that emerged was Erica Gruen, whom Jack, George, and Reese had known for years. As an executive at Saatchi & Saatchi, Erica

had started the agency's fledgling online advertising division and prepared a widely read annual report on the state of the cable industry, in
which she reviewed every network, explained its programming, and
noted its ratings and household penetration.

Her experience with the Internet made her an early Web guru. In
February 1996, she had been hired away from Saatchi by Merkley
Newman Harty, but George Babick had been pushing hard for her at
Food Network. Within days of her move to Merkley, Jack contacted
Erica to gauge her interest in becoming CEO. Running a television
network was too tantalizing a challenge to pass up, and Erica leapt.

Jeff's tenure had been brief but effective. He had streamlined the
operation, brought sense to its marketing efforts, calmed nerves in
Providence, and approved some crucial new programming. As he returned to Rhode Island, cable trade magazines reported the new hire
and praised ProJo for choosing a woman to run a network. But before
Erica showed up for her first official day of work, she upset those who
had advocated for her. When she studied the network's financials, she
saw a rescue mission: Others disagreed but to her eyes, Reese had left a
mess, Jeff had stoked it, and it was her job to clean it up. She thought
Reese's business plan was preposterous and that many of his hires had
been F.O.R.s. Pat O'Gorman, his wife, was still working hard as a
producer (and would continue to do so for years). Erica was particularly
dismayed by a deal Jeff and others had put together for distribution of
Food Network in Scandinavian countries. Projections showed it would
make a bit of money, but she thought the projections underestimated
how much it would cost to translate the programs into various lan-
guages. She considered the whole thing a boondoggle meant to assure
ProJo executives all-expenses-paid business trips to the land of tall
blond women. She told Jack the deal stank and should be killed. Jack
insisted that as CEO she do it herself, which she did, instantly alienating her predecessor, Jeff.

There was also a cultural difference between the moneyed world of
advertising and the gritty start-up culture at Food Network. Erica reported for work wearing formal, neutral-colored pantsuits, and after

she took a look at the tiny office Reese and Jeff had worked out of, she decided it would not do. She took George's bigger, more isolated, office, displacing the man who had been her strongest advocate, hired a decorator, and ordered a renovation complete with a feng shui consultant. With a new leather sofa, designer furniture, and drapes, it totaled around $80,000.

Betty, the CFO, tried to talk Erica out of the office redo, saying, "Look, we don't really have a budget for redecorating. I mean, we're fighting for survival and you're going to start buying all this expensive furniture for your office?"

Erica resisted all entreaties, even from Jack, who came down from Providence. But he did not oust her, and the office decoration went ahead as planned.

Jack heard the grumbling, but ProJo was preparing to go public with an IPO, and he did not need turmoil at the top of Food Network.

By the time Erica arrived at the network, shoot day was near for the Emeril specials. She was worried and cautioned Joe: "You're spending a lot of money on this. It better be worth it."

"I don't know if it's worth it," Joe replied, "but we're obligated to Emeril to do it."

The day before Emeril was due in New York for the live *Real and Rustic* show, he was in Hawaii making a promotional appearance and visiting Shep. After the long flight to New York, he was driven to the studio. As he stepped out of the car, he was shocked to see a long line of adults and children waiting on the sidewalk. A cheer went up for him and he felt his jet lag drain away.

Susan Stockton, heading the kitchen crew on the show, was among those worried that the children would yell and cry during the taping. She went up to the line outside the theater and asked people, "What possessed you to bring your kids with you?"

"They brought us," one woman responded. Channel-surfing children, whose parents saw cooking as menial labor, had found the larger-than-life character on TV. The barrel-chested star of *Essence of Emeril* worked over fire, handled weird-looking critters, and used a knife with the kind of artistic swordplay seen in a Three Musketeers story. Emeril's enthusiasm was irresistible. When TVFN ran ads looking for people to show up for the taping, the children demanded to go, just as children for centuries have begged their parents to see the traveling circus when it came to town.

The set was cheaply decorated with a fishing net strung up behind a countertop, a vintage Coca-Cola machine to one side, and a few jars of hot sauce on shelves. But no one was disappointed. When Emeril charged out, the audience screamed with glee and kept applauding as he took his spot behind a cutting board.

"Wooooo!" Emeril shouted back, soaking up the excitement. He grabbed the raw chicken in front of him, stood it up on its rear, and began using its drumsticks to clap along with the crowd, nodding and beaming wide.

When Erica heard the audience's hysteria, she felt chills. "Most television executives never actually see an audience. You get the Nielsen ratings. So this roar went up from the audience, and I just thought, 'Oh, my God,'" she remembered. At Saatchi & Saatchi she had run its branded entertainment unit, a production arm that developed shows the company's advertisers would want to buy time on. Erica would sell the shows to networks with the promise of presold advertising. The unit's biggest success was *What Every Baby Knows*, starring pediatrician Berry Brazelton, who gave tips on raising infants. It ran in syndication on cable stations for years, providing advertising slots in which Procter & Gamble would tout diapers. Erica noticed that although the ratings were never sky-high, everywhere she went with Berry, his fans wanted his autograph. They wanted him to kiss their babies. They asked which pacifier he recommended. Erica realized ratings could matter less than usual if a show appealed to a focused demographic that advertisers wanted. Long be-

> "It was so over the top. People, they went crazy."
>
> —EMERIL

fore many others, Erica understood that someone could have this kind of narrow but valuable cable television fame without giant ratings.

As she stood in the *Ready . . . Set . . . Cook!* studio hearing the fans whoop with every "Bam!" Erica decided that Emeril could be the new Berry Brazelton.

Within days, Food Network's top staff met to try to turn Emeril's special into a regular series.

Befitting a program that was more like a concert than a studio show, the idea gained the name *Emeril Live*, even though it was not going to be broadcast live. Producing a cooking show with a live audience and a full backstage kitchen staff (which *Ready . . . Set . . . Cook!* did not need) in a studio outside 1177 Sixth Avenue was going to run about $50,000 a day. The baseline cost for shows shot at 1177 was $2,750 per half hour. Joe said that if they could do three hourlong episodes in each day of taping, you could figure the cost at around $9,000 per half hour. Still, that meant that 90 episodes of *Emeril Live* would cost $1.8 million, nearly a fifth of the network's $11 million programming budget for 1997.

As optimistic as she was, Erica told Joe the network would be sticking its neck out by committing that kind of budget to one show.

"We never spent a lot of money on anything except the James Beard awards," he argued. "We have to roll the dice with this. It is the best thing we've come up with, and Emeril is the most popular guy on the network. If we don't come up with something new for him, some other network will."

Emeril, delighted to work on the fly in front of an adoring audience cooking his own recipes, agreed to do three shows each taping day, and Erica, thinking of Brazelton, agreed to wager a big piece of the network on him.

Emeril Live, with a two-man band and an opening monologue, debuted on January 20, 1997, and it was a hit from the start, doubling the network's ratings in its 8 p.m. slot.

Erica's optimism returned when she gushed to *Multichannel News* in February 1997, "We've created a unique television form. It's a cross between *The Tonight Show with Jay Leno* and a cooking show."

As time wore on and the show's success grew, who exactly the "we" was who created *Emeril Live* became a matter of dispute—success, they say, has a thousand fathers and failure is an orphan. Years later, Emeril himself claimed the idea had come about in a meeting with Erica when he was complaining that he was bored of doing *Essence of Emeril* and was going to "retire" from doing cooking shows. "And then that's when I suggested to them that with my music background and loving people, being with people, that we should do a live show," he told me in a 2010 interview. "We should do a people show. And I expressed to them that you had Letterman, you had Leno, and there's nobody in the cooking world that was doing that stuff."

Among the many problems with this account is that Erica, not shy about claiming credit for successes on her watch, admits she was not at the network when the basic idea for the show was hatched. She says her contributions, not minor, were to exploit Emeril's talent as a drummer by including the band and to further brand him as a big personality by insisting on an opening monologue. Jeff Wayne credits Joe for the basic format—Emeril cooking as a sort of concert in front of a live audience—as do Susannah Eaton-Ryan and others. It is certainly possible that a similar idea was brewing in Emeril's mind because of his exuberant public appearances at the time, but no one at the network recalls hearing the thought before Joe put together the special. If, in the short time between the end of the *Real and Rustic* special and *Emeril Live*, Emeril pushed Erica for the band before it organically occurred to her, that is not how anyone chooses to remember it.

In any case, long before the bloom of success gave way to bickering over origins, an incident elsewhere blunted the initial *Emeril Live* high.

Around 6 a.m. on January 30, 1997, Susannah Eaton-Ryan, head of operations, was woken by a call from her overnight man. "You're not going to believe this, Susannah. We have a real problem."

She held the phone to her ear without lifting her head from the pillow. At CBGB, the punk club she'd managed in the 1980s, people had died of overdoses in the bathrooms. What could be so damn urgent? "Yeah. What now?"

"We showed porn on the air during *Too Hot Tamales*."

Susannah sat up. Showing explicit sex on the air was a federal offense.

It happened, the overnight operations man explained, during the airing of a taped episode of Susan and Mary Sue's show. The women had been preparing a dish that required tender slices of flank steak. "You've got to pound the meat," one of them had instructed. At that moment the tape had been sabotaged. It cut to a naked man and woman . . . pounding the meat.

The engineer had switched to the backup tape as quickly as he could. Food Network was at least professional enough at that point to have backup tapes lined up. Susannah had helped set up the system.

The backup tape had the identical scene of hard-core pornography on it. The engineer was powerless to stop it. For an entire minute—an eternity in TV time—an anatomical close-up of copulation streamed to TVs throughout the nation, Mary Sue offering an unintentional voiceover with instructions on the proper way to prepare meat the entire time, before the video returned to the regularly scheduled programming.

About an hour later, Erica called Mary Sue in Los Angeles, where it was 4 a.m. "Something inappropriate happened on your show."

Mary Sue's first thought was, Oh, my God, did I make an innocent racial slur or something? She asked Erica, "What happened?"

"I'm not going to tell you," Erica replied, hoping that if the knowledge stayed contained, the problem might go away. "But if the press calls, you need to be on red alert."

Mary Sue called Susan, panicked and rambling: "Erica called, I don't know what the hell is wrong, but something bad happened on the show, and the FCC may be involved."

That morning at the Border Grill, the business manager Andrea Uyeda came in shaken and asked Mary Sue and Susan, "Did you see the show?" She slid a tape into the video player in the office.

Mary Sue was far more familiar with preparing quesadillas than the intricacies of television production. Watching the pornographic snafu, she wondered, "Was there some cosmic wire crossing that caused us to get mixed up with the Playboy Channel?"

Meanwhile, FBI agents arrived at the network, grilling the employees who worked in the tape-editing room.

Those who were not at the office that day received personal visits from law enforcement. One staffer was swimming laps at the YMCA, came up for air at one end of the pool, and saw two pairs of black shoes standing there. "Get out of the pool," said one agent. Another young, off-duty staffer heard a knock on his door.

"Who is it?" he asked.

"Open up," a voice said, "it's the FBI."

He let in two men in suits and they handed him their gold-embossed business cards, taking seats on the lawn chairs the lowly paid young man was using for furniture.

"Why did you do it?" an agent asked.

He would never do such a thing, the staffer explained in earnest. "I went to Brown."

After ten minutes, they left. Despite the questioning of everyone at the network who had access to the broadcast tapes, the mystery of who had spliced in the porn was never solved, and no punishment was meted out against the network. Mary Sue and Susan decided the incident was actually pretty funny and ultimately a good thing. It had gotten people talking about Food Network.

6

Changing the Recipe

The longer Food Network could stay alive, the more chances it had to get lucky.

One day early in the run of *Emeril Live*, a television producer named Peter Gilbe tried to sell Joe Langhan a strange British show. *Two Fat Ladies* followed the journeys of a pair of eccentric, not-thin and not-young friends, Jennifer Paterson and Clarissa Dickson Wright, as they bounced through the English countryside on an antique motorcycle and sidecar. The ladies were in search of farm-raised foods and drafty kitchens in castles and cathedrals where they would cook their versions of traditional British fare, deploying as much lard, anchovy, and breading as possible while keeping up a bawdy patter in the Queen's English.

In one episode, Jennifer was preparing a pan for a sugar cake, and in a droll tone, instructed Clarissa on the proper application of butter to keep it from sticking. "Did you see *Last Tango in Paris*?" Jennifer asked, referring to the X-rated 1972 erotic drama starring Marlon Brando and its famous sex scene involving the lubricious qualities of butter. "Well, something like that."

Jennifer, the elder, favored shapeless monochrome dresses and wore eyeglasses so giant they enclosed her face from her forehead nearly to the tops of her lips. Clarissa, the weightier, often wore flowery print tent dresses. Jennifer smoked and drank. Clarissa, a recovering alcoholic, did not.

Erica Gruen was eager to add more personality to the network. And if she wanted unusual, *Two Fat Ladies* fit the bill. Joe had shown Erica the tape Peter had sent him, and she was definitely interested. In some ways as traditional as tea, in others as weird as Monty Python, it was shot on film, slowly and expensively. Gilbe had filmed a dozen episodes—two seasons' worth. Having already sold Food Network the rights to *Ready . . . Set. . . Cook!*, he pushed Joe for a big price for *Two Fat Ladies*. Peter wanted Food Network to buy the American broadcast rights and thereby help him afford a third season. "I can let you have this show if you'll finance thirty percent of shooting more episodes," Peter said.

"Well, what do you spend on 'em?" Joe asked.

"About a hundred and eighty thousand dollars an episode."

Joe laughed. Peter wanted $360,000 from Food Network for the twelve episodes. Joe pointed to the newly built *Emeril Live* set. "Those shows out there cost us $18,000 each. For an hour. You're asking us to spend, like, thirty thousand for a half hour. We just don't have that kind of money."

Although Peter over the next few months kept mentioning rival interest in the show from PBS, it turned out there were not a lot of American television venues vying to bid on a show about overweight English matrons prattling about and preparing breath-destroying dishes such as Onion Soup with Stilton. Eventually, Food Network bought broadcast rights to *Two Fat Ladies* for between $5,000 and $10,000 an episode.

The unusual name of the show began attracting media attention. Nearly every article about the upcoming cable season in 1997 that referred to Food Network made mention of *Two Fat Ladies*, and Clarissa and Jennifer came to New York to shoot promotional spots. Food Network rented them a vintage motorcycle and sidecar from a collector. Like the rock band Van Halen, which famously demanded green M&M's in their dressing rooms, the Fat Ladies had certain requirements: Scotch whiskey must be stocked on the set, and smoking would be allowed indoors. The producers complied. But on the shoot day, they were nervous because the motorcycle appeared rather compact and Clarissa was not. "Is she going to fit in the sidecar?" the crew whispered as the shot was set up. Happily the younger of the fat ladies slid into the sidecar as snugly as a buttered spatchcock into a baking dish.

The pair visited the daytime talk show *Live with Regis and Kathie Lee*, cooking their version of pork stroganoff for the hosts: tenderloin, butter, gin, and sour cream. During commercial breaks, they took note of how voraciously Kathie Lee Gifford gobbled down a plate of it. A few days later in an interview with the *Washington Post*, they talked about her some more. "She certainly looks undernourished. . . . We were told that she has troubles at home . . . you know . . . with her husband," Clarissa said, referring to football great Frank Gifford, who in the spring of 1997 had been recorded by the gossip newspaper *The Globe* being seduced by a former flight attendant in a hotel room. "Well, would you blame him? Nothing to get his hands on, poor man."

"I took home screeners and watched them on the VCR with my husband. I said, 'I don't know. I can barely understand these women. I don't know if this is going to go over . . . Plus the title, 'two fat ladies,' as I was told, is a bowling term in the UK for when you get double zeros, gutter balls. My husband said, 'It's hilarious. It will be fine.'"

—ERICA GRUEN

Outside Philadelphia, they stopped by the shopping channel QVC to promote the American edition of their first cookbook, *Cooking with the Two Fat Ladies*, and sold two thousand copies in ten minutes. That was nice. Less so was when Richard Simmons, the manic workout guru known for his ringlets of hair and terrifyingly silky shorts, rushed from the wings where he was waiting for his own selling segment and embraced them in front of the cameras.

In the *Post* article, Jennifer said, "I thought he was a lunatic. He's certainly unusual-looking."

Clarissa added, "Well, I was very glad I was not likely to be an attraction for him. Imagine fighting that off!"

Erica also gave a new show to Bill Boggs. Around the Food Network office, Boggs's narcissism was legend. One editor loved to tell the story of how Bill, a frequent name-dropper, came in to do a voice-over for a special and said to him, "You look just like Kevin Costner, and I know because I've met him." A young production assistant had made T-shirts emblazoned with Bill's face and wore one ironically around the office. Under the large head shot, it said simply "Bill Boggs."

But Bill's desperation to hobnob with the famous could be useful. Back when Bill had been at Channel 4 in New York, he'd interviewed Bill Cosby at one of Cosby's favorite restaurants, Ennio & Michael in Greenwich Village, for a series of segments Bill called "Corner Table." When the producers of *In Food Today* allowed him to bring these segments to Food Network, Boggs convinced Cosby to revisit the restaurant for another quick interview. Rochelle Brown, still a producer for the show, led the shoot. When it was done, she told Boggs, "You know, this could be a pilot."

More Boggs sounded like a good idea to Boggs. The only problem was that the Cosby segment was too short, only about two and a half minutes. He needed a few additional minutes to demonstrate a half-hour show. Asking Cosby to show up again to make a pilot for the lowly Food Network was out of the question. Boggs studied the tape over and over, trying to figure out a way to stretch the two and a half minutes. Finally, he saw a solution. He bought a sweater the same color as Cosby's, gave it to an African-American friend, and arranged to meet the Cosby stand-in at Ennio & Michael. He had a camera crew shoot the two of them from behind, so you could see an arm that looked like Cosby's in the shot with Boggs as he nodded and made up his end of a mock conversation with Cosby. The camera shot the dishes of food as they came out. Artful editing, lingering food shots, narration from Boggs, and a lot of splicing eventually produced enough footage to make a usable pilot of *Bill Boggs's Corner Table*.

Erica picked up Boggs's show and told the host, to his glee, he could make monthly specials. On one of the first, Boggs interviewed Matt Lauer, who had just taken over as the cohost of the *Today Show*. The two had worked together when Matt was anchoring the local news in New York and Bill was a lifestyle reporter. The interview was done at one of Matt's favorite restaurants, Blue Ribbon, in Greenwich Village. Over a lunch of oysters and salad, Matt, then forty and single, revealed that he liked nothing more than ordering the roast chicken with a glass of wine for dinner. It was another example of the new world of food the network was offering—real men don't just drink beer and eat pizza; spending a night savoring fine food and French wine was a perfectly cool choice for an urban bachelor.

It was certainly an alternative to what one of the most popular TV comedies was presenting. In the final episode of *The Drew Carey Show*'s first season, Drew and his friends invented "Buzz Beer," a coffee-enhanced beer. They marketed it with the slogan: "Stay up and get drunk all over again!"

Meanwhile, *Emeril Live* was still burning hot. That spring the network ran a promotion offering free tickets to upcoming broadcasts to anyone who called a toll-free number. Within minutes, so many calls were choking the line that the phone company had to shut down the Food Network's service temporarily.

At the network's May 1997 up-front presentation to advertisers, Erica told the Emeril story proudly. It was the first time a president could talk about the network being hot.

Erica launched what in the TV business are called "stunts" to inject excitement into the broadcast schedule. March 12, 1997, was "All Pasta Day." She also started pushing Joe to ask her thoroughbred, Emeril, to do even more for the network—more episodes of *Emeril Live*, more episodes of *Essence of Emeril*, more personal appearances, more of everything.

"Emeril is already doing more than he can," Joe protested. Having worked with Emeril and his team for years, Joe felt he had to protect the chef from the network making too many demands. Emeril was not being paid very much and his shows were valuable to the network, but Joe thought Emeril was more interested in spending time at his restaurants than in devoting more time to television and he felt that the most important consideration was not to drive Emeril away.

But Erica kept pushing Joe to push Emeril. Joe understood that things at the network needed fixing, but he believed some things did not. He stiffened and simply did not make the calls. Reese and Jeff Wayne, who were still on the Food Network board, were telling Joe that the board was not very happy with Erica. Joe, who'd seen three chiefs in two years, thought he might be able to outlast her reign and deal more easily with whoever was next in charge.

Erica was frustrated that Joe was not able to get more out of Emeril and threatened to quash the informal deal Reese had made with Shep allowing Emeril to mention his spices on the air. He could be more famous, she said, and richer. When Emeril protested that he did not want to fly around the country making more appearances to promote the network, because he wanted to spend time in his restaurants, Erica responded with the same faux pas that Reese had made early on, insulting the chef's craft and using a lowbrow name for the profession.

"What do you want to do, be a cook all your life?" Erica asked.

"Yes, I do," he said.

Soon there was only one recourse: money. "Okay, here's the concept," Erica told Susannah Eaton-Ryan, testing the idea. "If Emeril gets paid a million dollars, it doesn't matter how long his deal is, or anything about it, but he can say he's the first chef ever to get a million-dollar deal." One million bucks—however big a stretch—would do triple duty: it would placate Emeril's ego, tie him closer to the network, and demonstrate to cable operators, advertisers, and the public that the network was on a solid financial footing.

There was little dispute between the network and Emeril's business manager, Tony Cruz, over the financial terms of the new contract. In exchange for being paid triple what anyone else was getting, Emeril would appear in around ninety episodes of *Emeril Live* a year, plus a certain number of episodes of *Essence of Emeril*. Betty was a trained accountant, not a lawyer trained in negotiation. But Tony, who had dropped out of accounting school before he went to work at Emeril's New Orleans office in 1990, tried to extract the most for his boss's talents and rising fame. At one point in the negotiation, over this contract or another, Emeril's team inserted some language deep in a revision of the contract that would eventually grant Emeril the rights to all the episodes of *Emeril Live* and *Essence of Emeril*, past, present, and future. Nobody at Food Network got a deal like that. After all, the network was paying all production costs, so why should the star retain any rights?

Tony and the team knew the rights clause was a long shot, but they figured Food Network might either not notice it, or just give in. "They're happy Emeril is not pressing for even more money than they are offering," Tony thought. "Maybe they'll think, 'Hey, if he wants to keep the rights to some low-budget cooking shows that have questionable future value and will forgo some salary in exchange, it's a great deal for us.'"

However it happened, when the smoke cleared, Emeril had won the rights to own his shows. In the years to come, this would come to matter a lot.

Another of Erica's first moves was deciding not to renew Sue Huffman's contract. Although Sue was titular head of programming, Sue's main task had been to foster relationships with foodies, not to shape shows. She spent a lot of time having dinner and chumming up to chefs. She had forged important connections between the network and the food world elite, including Julia Child and Marion Cunningham, but Erica wanted to jazz the programming up, à la *Emeril Live*, and let her go.

Joe, vice president of production, liked this move at first. With Sue gone, he was clearly the senior programming executive in the hierarchy, and Erica was taking steps to free up money that promised to give him resources to bring in other deals like *Two Fat Ladies*. But he also noticed that when Erica discussed programming, she expressed disdain for the way the network had been doing things and the low production values. Joe thought she did not understand there were reasons many of the shows were cheaply made. Joe had been following Reese's commands to make as many new shows as possible, avoid repeats, and do it all under a starvation budget.

Joe stewed quietly under the criticism, knowing that if he had more money he could do more. He also knew Erica was unlikely to get much more money for programming. She found this out herself at board meetings when she asked for more resources. Reese would explode at her, "This isn't what you were hired to do!" She was going to destroy the network! And in the process, he let it be understood, ruin his chances of ever taking his profits. On this point, the other members of the board, some upset over her killing the Scandinavian deal, some weary of losses, agreed with Reese.

Erica started pressing Joe for more detailed accounting about how much was being spent on the production of each show. Joe tried to explain to her that most of the cost of producing each show was inextricably tied to the expense of keeping a full-time production studio staff at the network. The whole setup was to do nearly everything in-house, like a news operation, taping cooking shows all day and broadcasting live shows through prime time. The only cost unique to each show was the food—about $125 per half hour, not an amount it would be easy to trim.

Erica kept asking Joe for more explanation, asking how to slash each show's individual budget. Joe, frustrated, began steering conversations away from programming and toward what he thought were areas Erica might be able to do something about if she wanted to tackle the dire state of the network's finances—eighteen months behind earnings projections of the original business plan, he'd point out. For a time, Erica, whose title was CEO of the network, seemed to Joe to be properly occupied with nonprogramming matters like advertising, bringing in more cable providers, and—at least it kept her off his back—her office decoration. She was letting Joe operate as the go-to man at the top of the programming chain. But then Erica asked him and Susannah to start a search for a new VP of programming.

Joe was furious.

"We can't let her bring in someone else!" he sputtered to Susannah.

Susannah tried to reason with him: "Joe, if it's good for her, we have to do it. I'm not going to have private agendas."

Characteristically, Joe tried to manipulate the situation from behind the scenes rather than risk confrontation. He felt he was owed the programming job. At least, he wanted things to stay as they were. He had started the damn network! He had come up with *Emeril Live*! But he never actually asked for the job. Instead, with every candidate Erica sent to them, he reported back unfavorably.

Erica, flabbergasted, decided to pick a candidate on her own. She was an admirer of television executive Geraldine Laybourne, who had led the transformation of Nickelodeon into a top-rated cable network with movie, toy, and theme park spin-offs. In the 1980s, Eileen Opatut had worked under Gerry when the network brought *You Can't Do That on Television*, a Canadian sketch-comedy show with child actors, to the U.S. Whenever one of the actors on the show uttered the words "I don't know," a gush of chunky green slime would glop down onto their heads. Young viewers loved the show, especially the slime, and *You Can't Do That on Television* became a foundation for the fledgling Nickelodeon to build on.

On that show's heels, Nickelodeon's programming team developed *Double Dare*, a game show that required families to answer trivia questions and occasionally perform stunts with slime. *Double Dare* and its slick but fun-loving host, Marc Summers, became essential after-school viewing for a generation. By the late 1980s, almost every show on Nickelodeon seemed to involve dousing children in green goop. Eileen, a New Yorker with a sardonic wit who was part of the Nickelodeon programming team, came to think of her place in the cable programming industry as "a Slimer." She was now working for the BBC's North American division, helping to sell its shows to other networks.

When Erica approached her about the programming job, Eileen said she was interested in moving back to the creative side, and admitted that she found Food Network difficult to watch at times. Some of the talent was good, but most of the shows were too similar. Nearly everything was shot in the same tiny studio, "Kitchen Central." Every broadcast day looked like the next.

"The only difference is one day is pot roast, another day pasta," Eileen said. The subject of food had vast potential, she argued, especially if the network could bring in outside production companies and shoot in different locations. "The network is not expressive of all food can be for all people." Eileen liked the idea of supplanting a run of instructional in-studio cooking shows with programming that was more fun and free-ranging. Food does not get divorced, nor thrown in prison, but there had to be a way to inject more drama into it. Both Erica and Eileen agreed that Food Network should be aimed not only at those who loved to cook, but also—and more broadly—at those who liked to eat.

Not that Joe wasn't already trying in his own way to stretch the programming. On Eileen's first morning as Food Network's vice president of programming in August 1997, she walked into a conference room and was stunned to find two men and a herd of dogs. She had just met the stars of *Three Dog Bakery*, a fitting introduction to the chaotic way shows were being acquired and produced. For every *Two Fat Ladies*, there were a handful of *Three Dog Bakeries*.

Eileen, eyes wide, backed slowly out.

Joe had brought the dog show to the network. In 1989, Dan Dye and Mark Beckloff had founded a retail shop called Three Dog Bakery in Kansas City, selling all-natural dog treats. Their dogs—Gracie the Great Dane, Dottie the Dalmatian, and a black Labrador named Sarah Jean the Biscuit Queen—were the faces of the company: Sarah Jean held the enviable title of Executive VP, Tummy Rubs. After Dan and Mark appeared to promote a cookbook on *In Food Today*, Joe had asked the pair to come to his office. "I love your energy," he told them. "And I think that you guys could really do something. You are genuine, a little rough on camera, not super-polished, but that makes you interesting."

They drove from Kansas City to New York with the big dogs in a van for the taping of their show. The only suitable hotel that would give rooms to the entourage was in Fort Lee, New Jersey, across the George Washington Bridge from Manhattan. It required a harrowing daily trip through traffic for the pack to get to the studio. By the time they arrived at 1177 Sixth Avenue, their energy was flagging.

There was little rehearsal or prep time. While they were having makeup applied, Dan and Mark received instructions about the premise of each of the day's five or six shows—"Birthday cakes for dogs," "Western medicine for dogs," and the recipes: Grrrrrrranola, and German Shepherd's Pie. The set was designed to match the aesthetic of the thirty-odd Three Dog Bakeries now franchised around the country—rawhide bones for door handles and cartoonish multilayer cakes adorned with biscuits. It looked like a very cheap, beige-and-brown version of *Pee-wee's Playhouse*. For dogs.

During taping, the hosts had to remain on slobber alert, keeping rags on their belts to wipe up any trails the elderly Great Dane left behind as she poached ingredients off the counter.

After stumbling onto the cast of *Three Dog Bakery* in the conference room, Eileen called the network staff together in the studio area to introduce herself. "I have an open office," she told them. "If you have any ideas, I don't feel competitive. I'm only as good as everybody's ideas. So, please, if you've been thinking about anything and want to talk about it or you don't like something, please tell me. You can tell me now or later on your own."

The only one who spoke up was Matt Stillman, a production assistant who had started at the network a year earlier. His first job had been emptying the slop buckets from under the fake sinks, and he had since been promoted to managing the tape library for *In Food Today* and seating the audience for *Ready . . . Set . . . Cook!*

"I totally have ideas," Matt said. "I'd like to talk to you."

She looked at the twenty-four-year-old. He had black bushy hair and the kind of oil-brown Dr. Martens shoes artsy types were wearing in New York in 1997. Eileen had two toddlers at home, and Matt struck her as what they might look like grown up. She deduced from his features that he shared her Eastern European Jewish heritage, reading Matt as Yiddishkeit at first sight.

After the meeting, Eileen called Matt into her office. He told her he was taking night classes in comedic improv performance at the Upright Citizens Brigade. In college at the State University of New York at Geneseo, Matt had started a sketch comedy show called *Nocturnal Transmissions*, which had been broadcast on local cable. The show managed to be simultaneously clever and stupid, a kind of mind candy for geeks.

He told Eileen he thought the network too often treated its own viewers as stupid. Too many of the shows addressed people as if they had never cooked before. Even those that offered a peek into highbrow cuisine were presented in cheesy formats. Upright Citizens Brigade had always instructed improv actors to "play from the top of your intelligence."

Eileen was nodding. "Yes," she said. "I want to make smart television."

"I think it's better if you assume people are smart," Matt went on. "This network could be for smart people." He told her that even while he emptied slop buckets, his mind gestated ideas about offbeat, ambitious programming the network could try.

Their minds began to fuse. "Yes, that's totally what I want to do." Eileen smiled and nodded. This kid had a fresh point of view. "I need an assistant," she said.

When Eileen said that she wanted the channel, reaching seventeen million homes in 1997, to appeal to those who eat, she meant humans, not dogs. After a production run of just thirty-nine episodes, *Three Dog Bakery*, Food Network's only show focused on cooking for animals, was put to sleep.

Within her first few months, Eileen canceled many shows. She called the crew of *Dining Around*, the restaurant show starring Nina Griscom and Alan Richman, into a conference room. Eileen thought Alan a genius, but the show with its warmed-over fare and chintzy set, unbearable.

"We just want to let you know that ratings are a bit down," she told the crew. "And with that, you know, we had to look at the expenses of the show and, we've decided to, to uh, discontinue *Dining Around*."

There were gasps in the room, shock from those who had worked hard to deliver the best show they could for three years. They had developed a micro-culture replete with inside jokes about the peccadillos of the stars, a certain way of doing things, gossip, flirtations, and artistic effort expended on a starvation budget. *Zzzfffwipp!* All of it, gone. Most of the crew of *Dining Around*, *Three Dog Bakery*, and the other killed programs would find other TV gigs, other little work families, to join. Some were on staff, others freelancers who would not find their way to Food Network again. For some, those shows, small as they were, stale as the food could be, would be the most fun they'd have in their careers. Others would nearly forget they'd ever worked on them.

Under Eileen, the programming department developed a rule: every program had to show food within the first thirty seconds, grabbing the viewer by the stomach. She continued Reese's policy of forbidding credits at the end of shows, but this was less to protect moonlighting crew members than to squelch any signal to the viewer's brain that this TV meal was ending. Seamlessly, a new show would start and there again, in the first thirty seconds, would be the image of something delicious, an apple pie à la mode, a beef shoulder with sage.

If Joe did not like the idea of hiring someone to take control of programming away from him, he liked it even less when Eileen was actually there. What had been calculated avoidance and simmering frustration with the network head Erica Gruen turned into the outright silent treatment of her new hire Eileen Opatut, who was canceling shows Joe had helped create.

When Eileen would try to ask him who certain members of the staff were, how the infrastructure of the network worked, and how the production of a certain show was done, he would look past her and walk away. At staff meetings, he overtly read magazines when she spoke and refused to address her.

Since Joe was the head of production, his icy silence made Eileen's job difficult, and she was not privy to the reason for it. She knew little about his history at the network. It was frustrating, but early in her tenure, she had other problems to deal with. Behind the scenes at *Emeril Live*, a mutiny was brewing. In the rush to get the show into production in the fall of 1996, Joe quickly hired Darlene Hayes as head producer. She had worked on *Donahue*, the groundbreaking free-form talk show, and on *Montel Williams*. When Joe interviewed her, she had explained her vision for *Emeril Live*. "You need to look at it like it's a party, like Emeril is throwing a private party in his restaurant and you're invited." She wanted Emeril to wear a stylish outfit, a dark blazer and nice jeans. But Emeril always, always, always, saw himself as a chef, and he wanted to wear his chef's coat from start to finish.

"It looks much too formal when there's a band and an audience and he comes out in a chef's coat," Darlene groused. "It ruins the whole mood."

She and Joe came up with a compromise. Emeril would greet the crowd in a blazer to the side of the kitchen set, and explain what was coming up with a brief monologue. Then, as he moved toward the kitchen island, an assistant would take the blazer from him and help him slip into his chef's coat, ready for business.

Emeril accepted the compromise, but he never felt warmly toward Darlene and her showbiz approach. Nor did he like the way *Live* was being run as a food operation. Emeril ran tight ships at his restaurants. On the show, the backstage kitchen staff was constantly running out to buy ingredients at the last minute. Delays were regular. Emeril was not given advance time to hone his recipes. Bills were not being paid. At one point, Leonard "Doc" Gibbs, the percussionist in the band, called a production assistant saying he was owed money. The assistant began sending Gibbs's calls to voicemail. The messages turned increasingly angry: "This ain't how we roll in Philly!" Doc barked on one message. "I am gonna come up there and we're gonna get it on!" Emeril knew that if the show were a restaurant, this kind of carelessness would put it out of business.

It was obvious that they had to make the show work. From the first day Eileen went to see a taping, the audiences were not the moms and grandmoms she had expected. Men of all ages were in the crowd, some wearing jackets emblazoned with the New York Giants logo. When Emeril dropped garlic onto roasting meat, they whooped like they were watching a sporting event, and shouted with glee when he yelled "Bam!" and chucked more spices down. Oh, my God, Eileen thought. These guys want to cook a standing rib roast, too.

New categories for advertisers do not come around the television universe often. Emeril had opened food to an entirely new demographic, men who cared about good food.

The most obvious way to stem the production chaos was to let Darlene go, which Eileen did after the first season. She then called a television producer she had known for years, Karen Katz, the former director of original programming at Lifetime. Karen's dream was to produce quality documentaries, like the ones she had overseen at Lifetime on AIDS and child labor abuses. When Eileen explained the potential job, Karen was reticent. She had never heard of Emeril, never produced a food show, and was not particularly interested in doing so, but she agreed to a meeting.

Eileen and Emeril, with his assistant, Felicia Willett, met Karen for breakfast at the Mark Hotel, Emeril's regular Manhattan residence. Eileen and Felicia peppered Karen with questions. Emeril burrowed his face down into his chest, listened intently but made no eye contact, and didn't join the conversation. He did not even bother to recommend the thick, smoky bacon, one of the reasons he always stayed at the Mark.

While Emeril sat, silently, Felicia asked Karen, "Do you see this as a cooking show with entertainment or is it an entertainment show with cooking?"

Karen knew they had interviewed other producers. Her competitiveness kicked in. Emeril carried himself like someone important. She suddenly wanted this job. What was the right answer? Well, this guy is supposed to be some great chef. . . . "It's a cooking show with entertainment," Karen answered.

Emeril looked up. This was not the answer Darlene would have given. He finally spoke. "Do you like food?" he asked. No matter what kind of carnival the Food Network intended to build around him, making food was going to be the center of what he did. If you didn't like food, what good were you?

Karen looked directly at him. "Have you seen my hips?" she asked. Emeril smiled. She got the job as executive producer, and the team fell into place.

Karen immediately promoted Rochelle Brown, who had moved to *Emeril Live*, to producer. Her assignment was Emeril: prepping him before the show, tending to him during it, making sure he was happy. Susan Stockton ran the kitchen. Karen insisted that episode themes be scheduled far in advance to allow plenty of time for Emeril's team to plan recipes and for Susan to do the necessary shopping.

The changes increased efficiencies, but the schedule that was established to maximize Emeril's limited time in New York was brutal. They were regularly shooting three hourlong episodes a day. That's a lot of television, and things sometimes got loopy, especially with a roster of celebrity guests that seemed so random it had the air of stunt-casting: the Broadway actor Harvey Fierstein one afternoon, the morning news host Deborah Norville another. His audiences were increasingly rowdy. People showed up in T-shirts that said "BAM!" They went wild when Emeril said, "Hey, now!" One night Emeril held an arm-wrestling contest with some Giants fans in the crowd.

A steady diet of crowd adulation and espresso sometimes drove Emeril to the edge. One example came to be known as the Bologna Incident. The show started innocently enough, with a big uncut roll of bologna on the counter. But when Emeril began to work with it, he stood the pinkish roll on its end to peel the casing from the tip.

"After you pull back the skin on your bologna . . ." Emeril began, hearing the audience laughter building. He picked up the meaty cylinder and held it at waist level and looked down at a baking dish on the counter. "See, this bologna is so big, it won't even fit in this pan. What you want to do . . ." His smile grew and he glanced up at the audience. "Ladies, watch out over there," he warned. He peeled the casing off, and coated the meat with oil, using his palms, set it in the pan, and walked back toward the oven. "After you've got it rubbed up nice," he said, pulling down the door, "you put it in there. If it will fit in there." The thick, long bologna, flopping over the sides of the pan, would not fit in the oven. He tried to cram it in.

Off camera, Susan Stockton and Felicia yelled into their headsets, "Emeril, get away from the bologna. Get away from the bologna!" He could not hear them, and Karen let him run with it. Just before the commercial break, he stood in front of the oven door, which still would not close around the bologna.

"Sometimes," he said. "You just gotta say, 'Hey, don't mess with my bologna.' You know what I mean?"

Karen had learned something. Emeril had a showman's instincts. He could play with a moment, take it to the edge, but not push it over. He'd been a bad boy and gotten away with it—and the audience had stayed with him the whole way. The Bologna Incident showed her he could be trusted. Emeril learned something, too: that Karen would let him have some slack to improvise. He would not get the hook when he took chances. The two of them could relax.

> "I thought a cooking show was the kiss of death for my career."
>
> —KAREN KATZ

As far as most viewers were concerned, Emeril could do no wrong. Every time he declared, "Time to kick it up a notch!" the audience roared. Erica and Eileen began moving Emeril's show later in prime time, hoping viewers would tune in to other Food shows as they waited for *Emeril Live* to start.

As the show became more prominent, it became a target for critics who felt the original mission of Food Network was being betrayed. The assumption was that the original mission was to spread a refined gospel of fine dining. Of course, it had not been. The original mission had been to take advantage of changes in the cable television industry by finding a new idea for a network that promised to make a lot of money. When that idea had turned out to be food, the people available to be put on the air at first were generally those passionate about the subject. The original talent had an interest in spreading the news of fine cuisine—as did Emeril, in fact, with his own panache—but those who financed the network would have been just as devoted to a pet channel if that had turned out to be a winning business idea. There was no foundational principle to betray other than "Let's make money without putting porn on the air." And yet, not four years into its existence, Food stood accused of selling out.

In a July 1997 *Christian Science Monitor* article exploring the issue, a "former Food Network executive" griped that the channel "lacks food credibility." Another noted that the network's quest for ratings had made recipes incidental.

Countering these criticisms, Erica responded in the piece, "We're not trying to be the *Gourmet* magazine of the airwaves. Our shows are chock-full of recipes but reinterpreted in television terms for our audience, which is young, urban, and more interested in food as part of their lifestyle. It's up to us to be bold."

Julia Child came to Emeril's defense, emphasizing that Food Network was a for-profit business. "Unfortunately, it's entertainment programs that bring in the money," she told the reporter. *The French Chef* was not so different. "You have to make teaching an entertaining thing to watch," she said. "It has to be lively and fascinating."

Erica hired some new talent to promote the network's big story. She tapped another of Gerry Laybourne's former lieutenants, Heidi Diamond, the former head of marketing at Nickelodeon. Impeccably turned out with expensively cut blond hair and sharp Armani suits in gray, navy, and black, Heidi was known for her sharp wit and bawdy personality. She often quoted a piece of business advice she had once heard: "Whoever says 'fuck' first at a meeting controls the meeting."

She was not interested in food or cooking. When she bought a new apartment, she had the kitchen torn out to make more space for a clothing closet. Prada shoes and cashmere sweaters were more important to her than eggs. But she was a TV person; what the network was about did not matter. She had no children and had promoted Nickelodeon. She could adapt to food.

As she told *Brandweek* magazine when her hiring was announced, "I can't wait to get dunked in the sauce. What an incredible opportunity to build the brand, and have people see, smell, touch, and taste the Television Food Network, on air and off."

A pro, Heidi quickly set about building morale in the office. After a group came to visit the network from a cable provider in Pennsylvania and Heidi showed them around, they sent a thank-you gift. It was a giant bologna—yes, another one. Working late when it arrived, Heidi instructed a young staffer to take the sandwich meat to the nearest deli on Sixth Avenue and trade it for as much beer as possible. When the staffer returned, de-bolognaed and carrying armfuls of cold beer, a late-night office party ensued.

Heidi oversaw the rebranding of the network and there was serious work to be done. Aside from sprucing up the logo and tightening the name from TVFN to Food Network, almost nothing had been done to establish the brand. Interesting things were happening on-screen but they needed to be gussied up and sold to the world. By June 1997, she produced an internal document, the "Current Situation" at Food:

- Current positioning murky
- Alienating to some, as well as skewing older (both look/feel and words)
- Tons of work still to be done in honing in on a solid brand position for network

- Tons of new "stuff" to launch
- Need to begin to move audience to younger, more contemporary view of Food Network
- Resources scarce—limited funds left

What the network needed, she said, was a "Big Idea," that

- Unifies and ties all elements together
- Works on air as well as off
- Communicates a benefit to viewer/consumer
- Visually and audibly captures attention
- Is evocative . . . leaves the consumer feeling something—is fulfilling a need/want/desire

Heidi's presentation concluded with a list of words associated with "Full of Flavor" that the network's marketers and programmers should try to include in every advertisement, promotion, and show. They included *fresh, zesty, smoky, juicy, succulent, aromatic, luscious, chewy, chilly, saucy, nutty, fruity, spicy, crunchy, gooey, tart, creamy, oaky, sweet, smooth, meaty.*

The words could have been used to describe Heidi.

Like the other start-up types who thrived in the early days of Food Network, she was willing to do what it took to get the job done.

Shep had sought to tie chefs to rock musicians. Heidi wanted to go even bigger. The key at Food was to get the stars of the shows everywhere.

Without receiving or paying for permission from the National Football League, Heidi managed to attach the network and its star to the biggest pop-culture and advertising event of the year. Emeril's Bam! Bam! Tailgate Jam was a sweepstakes promoted on-air in which the grand-prize winner received a trip to the Super Bowl in San Diego complete with a pre-game tailgate party prepared by Emeril himself.

The Food Network could not actually use the words *Super Bowl.* The winner would receive "tickets to the big game." Local cable providers could attach themselves to the glory of the sweepstakes by advertising it across all their channels. On the open market, Heidi bought the tickets for the game on January 25, 1998, airplane seats, and a hotel room for the winner. The tailgate party was held in a parking lot of Qualcomm Stadium in an area not covered by NFL broadcast rights. Media circling around looking for things to cover mentioned the Food Network tailgate party in their coverage, and the party was filmed for use in later promotions. Total cost for the Super Bowl promotion: less than $30,000, including the zero dollars the network paid the NFL.

It worked out well for all involved. At the game itself, Terrell Davis of the Denver Broncos scored repeatedly, leading his team to victory. The night before the game, Emeril and fellow chef Todd English, a rising culinary star from Boston, found themselves at a restaurant in nearby La Jolla with a group that included a young marketing woman from the NFL and her friend, a technology consultant. Emeril sat next to the dirty-blond tech consultant, instructing her on the proper wine to have with each course. She had not heard of him before the evening, but the staff of the restaurant had. They paid the increasingly boisterous chef lavish attention. When he said, "Don't you think you could kick it up a notch?" with each bottle of wine he ordered, the tech consultant was horrified, thinking he was insulting the restaurant staff. She was mystified when they laughed heartily and patted him on the back.

It is good to be king. The evening continued later at a quiet bar on the top of a hotel, just the two chefs and the two young ladies.

The process of turning chefs into stars was well under way. From the music business came yet another component, putting television chefs on tour like rock stars.

Rich Gore and Joe Allegro were partners in a company that paired sponsors with rock concert promoters. They had, for example, brought stereo-maker Pioneer Electronics to Ron Delsener for a Rolling Stones tour in the 1990s. But they wanted to be more than middlemen. They could not break into the concert promoting business themselves; veterans like Bill Graham on the West Coast and John Scher and Delsener on the East had it sewn up.

Rich was channel-surfing one Saturday morning when he noticed how many cooking shows there were. People might pay to see these chefs in person, he thought. Here were stars no one was doing much with. Rich and Joe booked conference rooms at the New Brunswick, New Jersey, Hilton and hired three PBS chefs, Nick Stellino, Nathalie Dupree, and Caprial Pence, along with David Rosengarten from Food Network, to do cooking demonstrations. They found sponsors: Land O'Lakes butter, Kikkoman soy sauce, Progresso soup, Food Network, Comcast cable, and *The Home News* newspaper. The sponsors covered the cost of producing The Great Chefs of TV Festival.

It sold out—1,000 tickets at $45 each. Easy math: $45,000 profit for their first event. Shep thought the Miami Feast on the Beach was another Woodstock. Rich and Joe envisioned new events as versions of the traveling pop-music festivals of the times: Lollapalooza and Lilith Fair. After each twenty-minute demo, audience members could have books signed and take photos with chefs or mingle in an area where sponsors' products were displayed.

Erica, a former concert promoter herself, was so impressed by Jeff and Rich's enterprise that she suggested the network buy it. The deal worth more than a million dollars brought Joe and Rich aboard Food Network to head an events department. Jack Clifford, who negotiated the deal and who controlled enough seats on the board to outvote Reese, was especially enthusiastic because he planned to run chili cook-offs at some of the events.

The name was changed to *Cooking Across America*. Sissy Biggers, who had replaced Robin Young as the host of *Ready . . . Set . . . Cook!*, would preside over local versions of the competition when she was not taping the original in New York. Sissy had become a popular figure among male viewers of every stripe, from teens to more nefarious sorts. She received a lot of fan mail and read every piece. Apparently prison wardens approved of Food Network's family-friendly content and allowed inmates to watch the shows. Even on the profanity-free, sex-free network, men behind bars managed to find objects to fetishize, among them Sissy's shapely legs. She would often linger over fan mail from prisoners praising her gams.

The *Cooking Across America* chefs, who came to include Bobby Flay, Mario Batali, Emeril, Sara Moulton, and other Food Network personalities, along with popular chefs from PBS like Jacques Pépin, were paid around $2,000 each plus a free flight and a hotel room for appearing. Ticket prices were raised to as high as $120. By 1998, 75 percent of attendees were buying merchandise, including chef's jackets, cookbooks, and T-shirts.

The rising stars played the part. After a show was over, the troupe would usually head to the trendiest restaurant in town. Joe Allegro noticed that more and more "chef groupies" were tagging along. At a tour stop in Las Vegas, Sissy stripped down to her underwear and dove into a fountain at the Bellagio Hotel. Others followed her.

"We were having an Upfront party at the Roxy in New York near the Village. It was open to media, advertisers, some fans. Emeril is there, myself, Michael Lomonaco, Bobby before Bobby became Bobby. The people that liked my show just wanted to get a hug. But Emeril was a rock star. There were these three drop dead gorgeous women. One comes up and she says, 'Oh, Bam, will you sign my breasts?' Emeril looked at me and then back at her. 'If you let Curtis hold them, I'll sign them.'"

—CURTIS AIKENS

New Owners Again!?!

Even as Food Network under Erica Gruen had haphazardly found a hit in *Emeril Live* and was finally establishing such critical components as an effective marketing department, HGTV, Scripps's own lifestyle cable channel, was quietly executing the vision Ken Lowe had laid out for it from the start. Three years into its launch, it was enjoying far more financial success than the investors in TVFN were. There may have been no parties where stars stripped down to their underwear in public, but under Lowe, the Knoxville-based channel was soberly attracting advertising dollars at a record pace. Researchers reported that viewers were "addicted" to shows such as *Room by Room*, a half-hour interior makeover, and *Gardening by the Yard*, shot in a Tulsa backyard. By 1998, two years ahead of schedule, HGTV was on the verge of turning a profit.

Ken had been ahead of the media game for a long time. As a boy in rural North Carolina, he had set up a pirate radio station in his backyard. After graduating from the University of North Carolina, where he became fast friends with a future disc jockey named Rick Dees, Ken joined Scripps in 1980 as general manager of the company's radio properties. In 1988, he was promoted to VP of television programming, promotion, and marketing.

In a Scripps culture where many of the top brass were old newspapermen, Ken stood out as a media futurist. With a shock of brown hair over a heavy brow that seemed to provide cover for his narrow gray-blue eyes, Ken had a gaze so steady it bestowed an anchoring gravity. He was so good at selling his ideas that he achieved at Scripps what Tryg had not been able to do at ProJo: convince the moneymen that cable networks were potential gold mines.

Tryg had succeeded in getting ProJo to invest in two lifestyle TV ventures, Joe Langhan's food channel and a health network, but that was as far as he had gotten. And Food Network's failure to meet its earning targets had not helped his campaign.

Ken had conceived of a home and garden network after he visited a Home Depot and realized that each aisle could be its own television show, and then pitched the idea to the Scripps board around 1993. Ken had brought in two big magazine racks covered in blankets. During his presentation, he had dramatically unveiled the racks; they were full of lifestyle magazines—home design, gardening, food, family travel, and others. They were all thick with advertisements, and, unlike the categories of other successful magazines—news, sports, and music—no one had created cable channels to mine these rich veins of popular interest. He thought each lifestyle topic could be its own channel, and he believed that Scripps should have multiple lifestyle networks, a cable empire. But initially his goals were modest; he wanted the board to green-light just one channel focusing on home and garden projects. HGTV would be a good place to start, Ken told the board. Home repair and remodeling were a $106 billion business; lawn and gardening, $75 billion. A lot of that money was being spent by women. Besides Lifetime, there were no established networks aimed at women. He wasn't proposing more soap operas and tearjerker-of-the-week movies. He wanted to give women news they could use and sell advertising on the back of it.

"Look, this money is going to end up somewhere in television," he said at presentation after presentation. "And a cable network is the place." The Scripps board went for it, granting him $25 million and agreeing to upgrade a production facility Scripps had bought in Knoxville, Tennessee, to serve as HGTV headquarters.

Ken had long appreciated Food Network's focus on the advertiser-friendly female market, even if he'd disagreed with Scripps's decision to invest in it early on. He did not like the CNN-with-stoves approach. He insisted HGTV shows, including its own handful of cooking shows, be softer and more elegant. He made sure HGTV producers spent time choosing fun background music and gentle tones for voice-overs, believing these touches mattered to women.

Ken occasionally heard that Scripps-owned cable providers were not impressed with Food Network and that subscribers were complaining about it, asking for other channels to take its place. He also knew that without subscriber fees, the food channel was floundering financially.

Back in May 1996, the Scripps board took ProJo's offer to buy their small stake for roughly what they had invested, $11.4 million. But Ken, who had not been consulted on the sale, was disappointed, wishing there was a way Scripps could have taken control of it rather than backing away. He foresaw Scripps as the master of "category television," and he and Frank Gardner, Scripps's senior vice president of television, had regularly talked about adding channels. If Scripps could bring its solid middle-America sensibility to Food, they could remake it into a blockbuster, Ken thought.

Then the opportunity to snatch it fell into his hands. In February 1997, A. H. Belo Corporation, a Texas media conglomerate, bought ProJo for $1.5 billion. Belo's CEO, Robert Decherd, wanted ProJo for its broadcast stations and its still-profitable newspaper, *Providence Journal*. During the purchase negotiations, however, Tryg and the ProJo board had insisted that its 56 percent stake in Food Network be valued at a whopping $300 million. Decherd, eager to own the other assets, agreed to the valuation, over the objections of his investment bankers that Food Network was not worth nearly that much. The stake in Food Network was barely mentioned in news coverage of the sale.

After the deal closed, Decherd had sent several lieutenants to Food

Network headquarters to go over the books. Joe Langhan got the sense that the Belo people did not understand the cable business or like it much. Knowing their own staff lacked expertise, Belo hired Jack Clifford as a consultant. Always one for bold statements and full of belief in any project with which he was involved, Jack told the Belo executives at one point, "Someday, this Food Network is going to be bigger than your whole company put together."

They laughed.

Decherd's reps communicated no vision for the network's future. They left Erica in charge and told her to do what she'd been doing. The Food Network staff wondered if Belo might shut the money-losing network down. "This party might be over," Joe confided to a few staffers after the visit.

Tryg wound up with a lot of Belo stock and went to Texas to meet with Decherd. Always on message, Tryg told him that profits of the "mature" broadcast and newspaper businesses were "due to fall off a cliff" as new technologies like cable and the Internet rose. He argued that Belo ought to use Food Network and other cable ventures ProJo had been exploring to build a third leg of its company—Internet and cable. They would all profit from this approach.

But Decherd was uninterested in the business of cable networks and he expressed his resentment over what he said was ProJo's extortionate valuation of Food Network. After Tryg made a second trip to Texas, it was clear that Decherd wanted to get out of cable. Tryg thought that was a huge mistake, and since he owned a chunk of Belo stock, it could hurt him badly. He promptly sold all of his stock and told his ProJo associates to do the same.

In the summer of 1997, Belo hired investment bankers to unload their stake in Food Network. When word reached Scripps, Frank suggested to Ken that Scripps offer to trade a recently acquired San Antonio station to Belo as part of a deal for Food Network. It could be attractive to Belo because it would give them stations in major

> "Today it is bigger than their whole company put together."
>
> —JACK CLIFFORD

Texas cities and they could then spread the costs of news coverage throughout the state.

The Scripps board was thrilled with what Ken was achieving with HGTV, but they had seen the mixed bag of shows on Food Network and were skeptical that it could become profitable, despite Emeril's budding success. Belo seemed interested in making a deal, but Scripps executives remained far from sure, especially since Reese would not be bought out as part of it. His 5 percent share had always been separate from ProJo's stake; he'd kept it even after the Belo takeover. Scripps managers who had dealt with Reese in the early days were telling stories of his irascibility. Why take on a money-bleeding cable channel with the troublesome Reese attached to it when moneymaking, unhindered broadcast stations were such cash machines?

Ken confided in Frank just how frustrated he was at the internal resistance to the deal. "Oh, my God, I can't believe we got Belo convinced. Now we've got to convince our own guys? Don't they understand the opportunity here?"

The two men realized they were sticking their necks out. Food might take Ken's focus away from HGTV, and no matter how right the idea of making a play for Food Network seemed, there were serious hurdles, some swiftly jumped, some stubbornly high.

Meanwhile, Tribune, which had maintained its 30 percent stake in Food Network, had the first right to buy a majority stake if it came up for sale. Ken flew to Chicago and met with Jim Dowdle, still the Tribune CEO. His son had become an advertising salesman for Food. But since helping put the initial deal together, Tribune itself had invested few manpower resources and little attention in Food Network. As of 1997, there had been no profits.

"Jim, here's the deal," Ken said. "We need you guys to step aside, pass on your right of first refusal and let us buy the network."

"Yeah," Jim replied quickly. "You know, we wouldn't know what to do with it. You guys go ahead. We'll be good partners."

In fact, Tribune was willing to divest itself entirely, and Dowdle let it be understood that for about $50 million, Scripps could have its

30 percent stake. But Ken's bosses at Scripps nixed the idea. Why take on almost total ownership when the risk could be spread? If Food kept losing money, part of the burden would fall to Tribune's deep pockets, and if it tanked completely, the $50 million would be good money after bad. Scripps's executive team was not even squarely behind buying Belo's 56 percent stake.

Before the board was to vote on the Belo deal, William Burleigh, the CEO of Scripps, called Ken to warn him. "Hey, I just have to tell you that this is not going to go very well. I've already heard from two of the directors who are going to vote it down."

Ken wanted this deal. Building a fleet of cable networks was his mission, and he had staked a lot of his reputation on making it happen. If the Belo deal failed, he'd be in the same boat as ProJo had been, holding one network and no leverage, operating a sideshow, HGTV, alone down in Knoxville.

Burleigh, a former newspaper reporter, continued, "Look, I'm for it. You know that. But, you know, my CFO's not. Corporate development is not." The corporate development guy was the one who had bad memories of dealing with Reese from the early days.

When Ken dialed into the conference call a few minutes early, he heard some board directors engaging in typical pre-meeting chatter.

"What's this call about?" one director said.

"I think we're going to talk about the Food Network," another responded.

"Food Network?" the first director said disdainfully. "That sounds like something my wife would watch."

Ken heard the men laugh. "Ha ha ha."

When Ken's turn came to make his pitch, he seized on what he'd just heard and made it the very reason for making the deal. "The reason you guys approved HGTV," he said, "was you saw very clearly the opportunity to target women. Women are going to have more buying power. There's very few networks, hardly any in the whole cable lineup, that target women. This will complement HGTV."

George Babick *(left)*, the network's first head advertising salesman, and Reese Schonfeld, the founding president, in front of the original Television Food Network headquarters on West 33rd Street in Manhattan, 1993.
(Courtesy George Babick)

The
Food
Channel

The name and logo for
the start-up network as they appeared
in the original business plan, 1992.

A meeting between Ken Levy and Joe Langhan, shown at his desk at the first home of TVFN, created the spark that started Food Network.
(F. Heaney)

Mary Sue Milliken and Susan Feniger, Los Angeles chefs who became known on Food Network as *Too Hot Tamales*, made their first major TV appearance on Julia Child's *Cooking with Master Chefs* on PBS.
(Courtesy Mary Sue Milliken and Susan Feniger)

Cookbook author Marion Cunningham hosted an awkward but charming TVFN show that bestowed a sheen of food world credibility on the network in its early days. Shown here in her home kitchen with her calming dog, Rover, whose photo she kept on set.
(Scott Mitchell)

Debbi Fields taping a promotional segment with Steven Jon Whritner, vice-president of creative services, 1995.
(From the collection of Steven Jon Whritner)

A cake celebrating one year of survival. Notice that the TV is tuned to channel 50, where the network was still carried part time only by Time Warner Cable in Manhattan.

(© Connie Simmons 1994)

Early advertisements for the network. One touts a short-lived fitness show starring the Olympic gymnasts Nadia Comaneci and Bart Connor.

A young and game crew set out to start a new network, including Rochelle Brown (with newspaper), a producer for *Food News & Views*, and Susannah Eaton-Ryan (in newly installed control room), the director of operations.

(Top photo: F. Heaney. Bottom photo courtesy Susannah Eaton-Ryan)

Providence Journal executive Jack Clifford *(center)* leads a chili cooking contest with Jack McDavid *(left)*, Bobby Flay *(right)*, and emcee Robin Leach. On the photo banner behind them are Emeril Lagasse, Curtis Aikens, Mary Sue Milliken, Susan Feniger, and David Rosengarten.
(From the collection of Steven Jon Whritner)

Trygve Myrhen, CEO of the Providence Journal when TVFN was launched.
(Allen Salkin)

Jack McDavid and Bobby Flay during a break taping a promotional spot for *Grillin' and Chillin'*, 1996.
(From the collection of Steven Jon Whritner)

The Two Fat Ladies, Clarissa Dickson Wright *(sidecar)* and Jennifer Paterson *(saddle)*, squeeze onto a motorcycle and sidecar for a promotional shoot during a New York visit as network staffers grab a chance to be photographed with the rising stars.
(From the collection of Steven Jon Whritner)

Dan Dye *(left)* and Mark Beckloff, stars of *Three Dog Bakery*, with Sarah Jean the Biscuit Queen, Dottie, and Gracie— Executive V.P., Eating.
(Photo by Tatiana)

The on-screen name and logo changed in 1996.
(Photo by Chloé St. Etienne/ © Allen Salkin)

Erica Gruen, network president when *Emeril Live* debuted in 1997, with Emeril Lagasse at the James Beard Awards, 2009.
(Courtesy Steven Rosenbaum / @Magnify)

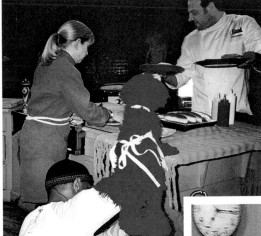

Elmo has been a frequent cooking show guest. Behind the counter with Elmo and Muppeteer Kevin Clash on Sara Moulton's *Cooking Live*.
(Courtesy Sara Moulton)

The intended perspective.
(Courtesy Sara Moulton)

Matt Stillman *(top left)*, creator of the Bill Boggs shirt, former slop bucket boy, *Iron Chef* and Alton Brown evangelist, New York, 2013. He was on his way to pitch himself as a potential producer for a start-up Web TV show.
(Allen Salkin)

Heidi Diamond *(top right)*, inventor of the term "chunks."
(Courtesy Heidi Diamond Archives)

Eric Ober *(center)* in his CBS News publicity head shot.
(Tony Esparza/ CBS News/ © 1992 CBS Worldwide, Inc. / All rights reserved)

Judy Girard *(bottom left)*
(Courtesy Judy Girard)

On the set of *La Cocina de las Estrellas* *(The Kitchen of the Stars)*, a cooking show pilot directed by Brent Keast *(left)* and improbably starring Charo, Ed McMahon, Chef Claud Beltran, and Frankie Avalon.
(Courtesy Brent Keast)

Chefs Ming Tsai and Masaharu Morimoto sing karaoke at the Harvard Club, New York, 2010.
(Allen Salkin)

Bob Tuschman, a longtime programming executive—known to viewers as a judge on *Food Network Star*—is credited with bringing Rachael Ray to the network.
(Allen Salkin)

Sandra Lee, one of the non-chefs who became network stars after 9/11, sometimes seems to have more detractors than fans, but has done notable work for hunger charities.
(Allen Salkin)

Pulling off the South Beach Wine & Food Festival requires creator Lee Schrager to do a lot of schmoozing. Here, in 2008, he explains how the day will go to Arthur Agatston, author of *The South Beach Diet*; rides a cart along the beach, checking tented venues; instructs hospitality staff at the Loews hotel to make sure Paula Deen has a smoking balcony and Alice Waters an airy rotunda room; and takes a call backstage as Rachael Ray, her husband, John Cusimano *(seated)*, and festival manager Devin Padgett await her appearance at the annual Burger Bash.

(All this page: Alex Quesada, Polaris Images)

Paula Deen and her agent, Barry Weiner, greet each other backstage in South Beach, 2012, shortly after the bad publicity she received for endorsing a diabetes drug. Sixteen months later, with her empire crumbling after even worse publicity, she severed their relationship.
(Allen Salkin)

Jamie Oliver and Alice Waters at the South Beach festival. The network and its personalities fed the wave Alice and other pioneers began.
(Allen Salkin)

Shep Gordon, inventor of chefs as rock stars, in New York City, 2012.
(Allen Salkin)

No doors! Few drawers! Fantastik? What Rachael Ray saw from behind the counter of *30 Minute Meals*.

(Allen Salkin)

Tyler Florence's fame has survived his much-criticized Applebee's endorsement deal. Here, he is greeting fans at the Culinary Institute of America at Graystone in St. Helena, California, during the Flavor! Napa Valley festival 2011.

(Allen Salkin)

The photo of Giada De Laurentiis from the February 2002 *Food & Wine* magazine that caught the eye of Bob Tuschman.
(Victoria Pearson)

During the holiday shopping season in 2010, the New York department store Barney's gave its windows over to a food TV theme, praising and lampooning the constellation of established stars. Here are Rachael Ray, Ina Garten, Paula Deen, Martha Stewart, and Sandra Lee.
(Allen Salkin)

Robert Irvine prepares for public appearances by doing push-ups to pump himself up. Yanked from appearing at the South Beach festival in 2008 following a controversy over his credentials, he was a featured attraction by 2012, bigger than ever.

(Allen Salkin)

Anthony Bourdain performing at the South Beach festival. Audience members spin the wheel and Tony delivers what it decrees, from "Dick Joke" to "What's Your Problem With . . . ?" Along with his TV shows and books, Tony, whose first show was on Food Network, has made a side career as a sort of dastardly Mark Twain, delivering pointed oratory—and Food TV criticism—onstage in a never-ending theatrical tour.

(Allen Salkin)

Gordon Elliott *(tall with gray hair, left)*, producer of *The Chew* on ABC—and onetime star of *Door Knock Dinners* on Food Network—gives instructions to one of his stars, Michael Symon, while Mario Batali awaits the start of taping. Food Network faces increasing competition from all directions: networks, YouTube channels, and cooking apps— many of them featuring stars the network helped create.
(Allen Salkin)

Brooke Johnson
(Allen Salkin)

Martha Stewart's company bought Emeril's catalog of cooking shows and lines of spices, books, and cookware in 2008 for $50 million. Here, he bends to listen to her at a 2011 event honoring him in Sagaponack, New York.
(Allen Salkin)

Trying to create new food stars for the spinoff Cooking Channel at a 2012 event, including Debi Mazar, Gabriele Corcos, Chuck Hughes, Roger Mooking, Eden Grinshpan, and Ben Sargent.
(*Allen Salkin*)

It's just business: Anthony Bourdain has written of Guy Fieri, "If I had to be him for five hours, I'd hang myself in a shower stall," but the two mug following a 2012 charity roast of Bourdain in New York—during which Guy briefly forced Tony to wear a blond spiky wig.
(*Allen Salkin*)

Susie Fogelson outside Guy Fieri's Times Square restaurant with Justin Warner, winner of season eight, *Food Network Star*.
(*Allen Salkin*)

Some directors continued to protest. This was not HGTV, which they had shaped from the start. Food Network was broken, they said. And in New York. "How are we going to fix it?" asked one director.

Frank and Ken chimed in. "That's our job. We'll take care of it, we'll fix it."

In the end the board voted unanimously in favor of buying Food Network.

After the investment bankers held negotiations in New York, Ken and his team were allowed to inspect the studios Reese had built at 1177 Sixth Avenue, and see exactly what it was they were about to buy.

Riding up the elevator to the thirty-first floor, Ken wondered about getting supplies upstairs, and asked himself who in the world would put a food network up in a high-security office building in Midtown Manhattan? When he was shown the kitchen, his nose curdled. This looked nothing like the modern new studios HGTV had in Knoxville. Here there were fruit flies, a rank smell of seafood, drying meat, stale spices, trapped smoke, all wafting through the ridiculously cramped office area. College radio stations were more professional-looking than this.

Oh, my God, he thought. What are we buying? The fact that the mayor's wife was working there only added to the swirling, illogical miasma. Ken's inner dialogue continued, even as his face betrayed nothing. You really think you can make this work? This thing is broken.

His team headed back to the offices of Scripps's investment bankers. The team—Ed Spray, the programming chief of HGTV, Mark Hale, the head of production, and Susan Packard, in charge of selling the network to cable providers—were so shell-shocked that they tried to talk Ken out of the deal, arguing that the purchase would take away their focus from HGTV. Food would be a burden to fix. "Things are going so well at HGTV, why in the world would you want to buy this broken-down network?" one of them asked.

Inwardly, he had the same argument with himself: This is a bigger bite than I thought it was gonna be, he thought. Ken did his best to fend off the doubters, not letting on about his own misgivings. It would have been difficult for him to take any other position. He was the networks guy. One was not enough. As imperfect as this was, who knew when another chance would come?

"Don't worry about what you just saw," he told them, steeling himself. "Don't think about a cable channel. Think about a brand, how many places we can get this network, how many things we can attach to it."

By the end of the conversation, nobody was thrilled about the deal, but they were swayed by Ken's conviction. He had proved naysayers wrong before, so his people would wade into this fruit-fly-infested place.

When Ken had first pitched HGTV, focus groups had come back highly negative about every aspect of it. One researcher said, "The name HGTV sucks."

Ken had thrown the research in the trash. He had heard a quote years earlier from the management guru Peter Drucker that he repeated often: "The best way to predict the future is to create it."

Back at his hotel, Ken put doubts about Food Network into the mental trash. Once he brought it into the Scripps family, a smart bunch of Midwestern and Southern folk, it would be able to flourish, he told himself. It just needed a bit of scrubbing and healthy guidance. Ken could create its future.

The deal was announced in September 1997. In exchange for KENS-TV, a broadcast TV station in San Antonio, and its companion AM radio station, Scripps received from Belo 56 percent of the Food Network and $75 million. Analysts valued the TV and radio stations at $200 million and calculated that Scripps had paid $125 million for a majority stake in a financially unstable, niche cable network. In announcing the acquisition, Scripps said it expected Food Network to turn "cash-flow positive" within three or four years, but that it expected to lose $10 million in the current year.

> "I wondered, 'How is this thing even legal? Why did the Health Department not shut it down?'"
>
> —KEN LOWE

Privately, Scripps offered to buy out

Reese for $6 million. He considered it, but one of Ken's lieutenants quietly told Reese that if he held on, profits would come soon. "Just so you know, we're going to make you very rich." Reese decided to keep his stake.

One night, Eileen called Susannah Eaton-Ryan at home. In the brief gap during which Belo let the network run itself, Eileen had reveled in the freedom of her job, and Erica had encouraged her to experiment. But now news articles about the sale were mentioning the economic sense of meshing HGTV and Food and producing shows at Scripps's 45,000-square-foot production facility. Eileen fretted. What would become of her show ideas, of her whole career?

"They bought the network," Susannah told her. "If they want to paint the walls yellow, that's their prerogative."

Ken understood that the appearance of a new boss from the provinces would spook the Food Network staff. He did not want them to bail before his team figured out what changes to make, so he gave a speech at the Sixth Avenue offices shortly after the deal closed, and assured them that nothing had been decided. "Okay, you know, here's the deal," he said. "We're buying you guys. I think we're your third or fourth parent. But welcome to this family, a sisterhood of networks. We like what you do. That's why we bought you. We want to grow this network.

"And by the way," he said, trying to defuse their anxiety with a joke, "pay no attention to that convoy of pickup trucks circling the building downstairs and the rumors that you're all moving to Knoxville next week."

Maybe they weren't all moving immediately, but Susan Stockton was asked to fly to Knoxville and check out the studios and the local food scene in anticipation of producing cooking shows in the Volunteer State. She discovered a fast-food hell. Chains and more chains, all serving food trucked in frozen by mega-suppliers from Chicago. You could buy butter and flour, but almost no fresh vegetables could be found at the markets. There was no Chinatown for interesting produce, or Little Italy for fine grades of pasta flour. Finding an apple that didn't break apart in your mouth like dry pebbles was a challenge. And fresh seafood? Fuggedaboutit.

Back in New York, she reported to Erica Gruen, "We really limit ourselves down there. We can do baking shows, but I can't get vegetables. I can't get bok choi." Plus there was no food culture, so there were few chefs around to bring in for guest stints.

It was a hard argument to dispute, and Ken saw its logic. HGTV was a Middle America channel spreading a native you-can-do-it gospel so home owners could take on building projects and urban dwellers could enjoy the fantasy of yard work. Knoxville had hardware stores and rhododendrons aplenty. High-end cooking was still an art form best practiced in the major cities on the coasts. Urbanites who could score fresh grouper and suburbanites entranced by the foodie life watched Food. Ken's colleagues at Scripps weren't food people and were not likely to comprehend why the network should stay where it was. Cincinnati was a city whose main culinary claim to fame was a local form of (admittedly delicious) chili served over spaghetti with a mound of grated cheddar cheese.

At a meeting with CEO Burleigh, Ken asked for time to let things settle before making big moves with Food Network. "Look, I know I told you initially that we'd be producing a lot of programming in Knoxville," Ken told him. "But we're gonna tear the hearts and guts out of the place in New York."

Ken was already figuring he would need to install someone more familiar with the Scripps way to transform the network. He asked Erica to stay on, perhaps for as long as a year, keeping her management team in place, while he figured out how to best digest the acquisition. Hiring someone immediately in New York made little sense if the network was going to be forced to move to Knoxville.

Erica did love the job she had held for about a year and a half, but understood how unlikely it was that she would keep it with the ownership turnover. She agreed to stay for the year, keeping the agreement private, but insisted she be paid for the entirety of her five-year contract.

Burleigh told Ken he could have a bit of time, but that the sooner things moved to Knoxville, the better. Ken continued to stall, allowing designers to draw up plans for Food Network's new kitchens and slowly migrating some of the business and technical operations to Knoxville.

Joe Langhan was listening carefully to Ken's speech to the Food Network staff. Less concerned about a geographical move, he was keen to know what personnel changes Ken might make at the top. What Joe heard disappointed him: Erica and Eileen would be staying. The buyout left Joe without his old ProJo patrons. Reese was still a part owner and on the Food Network board, but Scripps could now outvote him on anything. Jack, Jeff Wayne, and Tryg were out. With or without Eileen and Erica, Joe understood that Scripps would never promote him to a big programming job. Food Network was not going to be a seat-of-the-pants operation anymore. It was getting corporate, and Joe had no allegiances within this new corporation.

Eileen made efforts to involve Joe in what she was doing on the programming side, but his resentment at being passed over for her job had calcified. Still trying to find a role for him, she asked him one day, "Who do you want to work with?" He mumbled something and wandered off. Longtime staffers told her how creative Joe was, what good ideas he always seemed to have, but Joe treated her with seething silence.

She finally told Joe that if he didn't open up to her, his job was in danger. At network planning meetings in late 1997, Eileen was told that the network had overspent the year before and that new ownership was not yet opening the spigot, so the programming budget would be especially tight, just $10 million. Unsaid was that the overspending was at least partly Joe's fault.

He was increasingly convinced that no one wanted to hear his ideas anymore. Erica and Eileen, and now Ken, had their own ideas about how it was going to go, and it didn't matter what he thought. He would not help Eileen calculate budgets for the in-house shows, making it nearly impossible for her to figure out what she could do with the $10 million.

After months of buildup, Eileen called him into her office. "This is not working out," she said. It would be better if he resigned, she said, and a severance package could be worked out.

Waves of shock coursed through him. Joe walked out of the building without telling anyone what had happened. He phoned George Babick, who met him for lunch; two of the original hands at TVFN. Joe had started the network, the website, and *Emeril Live*. His severance was about $100,000—nine months' salary.

A few days after he left, Eileen asked Matt to call everyone on the thirty-first floor in to the conference room.

"Should I get Joe?" he asked.

"No. Don't get Joe," she said.

Eileen addressed the staff. "We're really appreciative of how much Joe has done for the network," she said. "But we're going in a new direction, and he's out, effective immediately."

There was no farewell party, no toasts to what he had accomplished. When he returned the many calls on his answering machine, the friends and colleagues who had barely been able to reach him for four years because he was working so hard were outraged at how he'd been treated. He should have been paid millions, they said. He should sue.

"That's the television business," he told those who called. Joe was like one of those Yankee tinkerers who are always working on ten different projects in their basement workshops, only rarely lifting their heads to survey the bigger picture. "Things change fast," he explained to friends. "You can be pushed out anytime."

As Erica tells it, Joe returned to the network for one more meeting with her, during which he demanded he be further compensated with an ownership stake. "The Food Network was my idea and I am owed a piece of it," Erica recalled Joe saying.

She recalled asking what he meant, and that he said Sue Huffman and George Babick had gotten pieces and he wanted his. She replied that it wasn't hers to give.

Joe disputes this recollection, saying no such meeting ever happened. In fact, Joe insists that he had an agreement entitling him to a tenth of one percent of the network, negotiated years earlier with the start-up consultant Stephen Cunningham—not long after Joe had asked Reese for a stake and been rebuffed. Joe says he was in line to collect on this stake should Reese ever sell out. It would therefore make no sense that Joe would come around the network asking Erica for what he already had.

Steve has no memory of such an agreement from the early days.

A creative and hardworking genius who could fight like hell behind the scenes for a project he believed in, Joe had certainly never been adept at championing himself. In the hours and days after he left the network, Joe was left to think about the difference between an "intrapreneur" and an "entrepreneur." An intrapreneur was someone who invented things for the company he worked for. He didn't get rich or any control over what he invented, but he got a salary for as long as the company wanted him around. An entrepreneur was like Reese, who owned what he created, or a good part of it, and could control his own time. Joe decided he would go the entrepreneur route from here on out. It was too late to get a big piece of what would probably be his greatest creation, but he tried to move on. He did ask for and receive from Reese some office space to start on a new project he had in mind related to licensing digital music.

"I started thinking, well, jeez, what am I going to do now? . . . I mean, you're upset a little bit—in a lot of ways. But then on the other hand, I was never the type, under any circumstances, just to sit around and mope about it. Even within the company, when one of the projects I was trying to develop or create didn't work, or somebody killed it or something, I didn't sit around and mope about that. I just went to the next one."

—JOE LANGHAN

About a month after the purchase, Ken flew Food Network's top managers down to the Great Smoky Mountains for a retreat with the managers of HGTV. It was not unlike sending the Little Rascals to the

Little House on the Prairie. A bus met Erica, Eileen, Susannah, Joe Allegro, Rich Gore, and Heidi Diamond at the Knoxville airport and whisked them to Blackberry Farm in Walland, Tennessee.

Ken was at the door of the Blackberry Farm lodge to greet them. He addressed the two groups, HGTV and Food Network, cheerfully. "Okay, your mom and dad just got married. And you're one family now. So you guys are going to have to get along."

Later that evening, everyone was asked to gather around a campfire and sing songs together. The New Yorkers exchanged looks. A campfire? Heidi's Prada heels were of no use here. "Let's sing 'Rocky Top Tennessee!'" one of the HGTV people suggested. Someone from the operations department at Scripps took a guitar out and played the country chestnut as his colleagues sang along.

The New Yorkers were trying not to let their eyes pop out of their skulls. "Is this what they call a hootenanny?" snickered one. Joe Allegro gamely took a turn on the guitar. He played "Piano Man" by Billy Joel.

The Scripps people exchanged their own looks. "Makin' love to his tonic and gin?"

Breakfast the next morning was country huge. The Food Network people poked at the grits. Ken suggested to Eileen that the chef at Blackberry Farms would make a good cooking show host. She found him bland. The Food folk nervously joked that the weekend was like the episode of *The Twilight Zone* in which seemingly benevolent aliens come to Earth "to serve man" and end up eating everyone. "They're going to have us for dinner," the Food people whispered, worried that the weekend was a formality and that they'd all be canned at the end of it.

Although they were not fired or filleted, the Food people left believing that Scripps did not understand them and this marriage wasn't going to work. The retreat was a disaster. Ken knew it, too. Food Network had had three owners in two years. The staff distrusted ownership. Most of them wanted to keep doing it their way. They feared losing their identity.

Ken started thinking more pointedly about who might replace Erica, someone more Rocky Top. Keeping the peace was not easy. In the weeks that followed the retreat, nearly every time Ken asked Food Network executives to consider something, he was told why it wouldn't work. A few weeks after the retreat, he got tough during a meeting back in New York.

"You know what?" he said. "You have to understand something. We bought you, okay? We now own you."

The city folk understood that straight talk. Soon, they saw that there was at least one advantage to being owned by Scripps: the company would spend money. Scripps did agree to increase the Food Network production budget between 10 and 15 percent. It wasn't a huge leap— Ken was still deciding whether he would be able to keep it in New York—but it was something, and programming executives ran with it. The network made plans to produce 1,200 episodes of original shows during 1998—none of them in Knoxville—and in the spring announced it had three new series ready to go on-air, nine in development, and new episodes of *Two Fat Ladies*.

Eileen and Erica began to focus more clearly on dividing the broadcast day between daytime and prime time, just as most networks did. Cooking shows were always considered solid daytime fare, so they had that covered. The question was what to put on in prime time. *Emeril Live* pointed the way. Other prime-time shows should be similarly fast-paced and entertainment-driven a formulation Erica described to a reporter as "TV Food Lite," which did little to mollify critics of the changes at the network.

The new focus allowed some familiar faces to flourish, Bobby Flay for one. Long after he'd finished *Grillin' and Chillin'*, the network was still showing reruns of the forty-two episodes and using him in promotional materials, but his efforts to reach out to Food Network about making another show had failed. Calmly, Bobby had been applying pressure and gathering intelligence. Every time David Rosengarten, who had two series in production, *In Food Today* and *Taste*, stopped at Mesa Grill during 1995 and 1996, Bobby peppered him with questions about what was happening, who was running things, and what sorts of series they were looking for. "I'd really like to do more on the Food Network," he confided to David.

Meanwhile, Bobby followed a second track. Through Joe Bastianich, the scion of a New York restaurant family, Bobby had become friends with a talent agent named Richie Jackson. Richie also knew Mario Batali and another young New York culinary star, Tom Colicchio, and like Shep, he had realized that, similar to the other celebrities he represented, chefs had the kind of big personalities and charisma that could lead to show business careers. They were stars. And few of them were represented by entertainment agents.

One night, Richie tried the idea on Bobby. "I would love to work with you and see what we could build."

Bobby told Richie what he had told David Rosengarten: he was looking to get back into television. He liked being on camera, and it helped his restaurant business.

Richie said if the Food Network wasn't calling back, it was time to look elsewhere. He knew people at Lifetime and, soon after that network's executives met Bobby, they signed him to make a year's worth of cooking shows called *The Main Ingredient with Bobby Flay*.

Lifetime paid for Bobby to visit Lou Ekus's TV training facility. There Lou loosened Bobby up on camera. "Let me guess," Lou said to Bobby on the first day of training. "You're looking at the camera and you're going to teach America to cook, right?"

"Yeah."

"No."

Bobby was, as always, prepared to soak up useful information. He listened.

"Here's the deal," Lou continued, sizing up what might motivate Bobby. It wasn't dogs. "Think of the girl that you never got. You have twenty-two minutes to seduce her with your food. Do it. You're talking to her, only her. Pick up the fruits and vegetables and the meats and talk about them like they're the greatest thing you've ever had in your hand. An onion? Why are you using it if it's just any onion? You have to really explain it. Words like 'great,' 'fantastic,' and 'delicious' mean nothing. Talk about it. It's a Spanish onion and it's 'picante.' Seduce her."

This Bobby could understand. Picante.

That trip and the experience of making more shows for Lifetime helped Bobby sharpen his TV skills. Having two popular restaurants kept him in the media. With their new budget and desire for big personalities, both Eileen and Heidi considered Bobby prime-time material, although Eileen did not think he had the goods to do it solo. He spoke too fast and he still seemed uneasy on-screen to her, but those deficiencies were outweighed by his compelling story as the New York boy who had become a success cooking Southwestern food, by his unflagging passion, and by his charisma. Eileen called Richie. Soon she signed Bobby for a new series, *Hot Off the Grill.*

She paired him with Jacqui Malouf, an edgy but chipper comedienne from Ontario. To differentiate it from a daytime cooking show, Eileen had *Hot Off the Grill* shot on a roomy set that featured an open living room in front of the kitchen. Cameras could pull back from the cooking area and catch an array of good-looking people arranged on couches and chairs nibbling what was coming from the kitchen. Jacqui was the cheerful host of this party, while Bobby cooked.

One of the first guests on *Hot Off the Grill* was the comedian David Brenner. As Bobby dished out salmon tartare–stuffed piquillo peppers, Brenner told a story about the time his mother cooked liver so tough his frustrated father nailed it to the sole of his shoe with a hammer. "He sat all night with the liver hanging off of his shoe," Brenner said, insisting it was a true story. "And all my mother said was, 'There are other ways of expressing your dislike for my cooking.'"

Hot Off the Grill ran at 8:30 p.m. every weeknight as a lead-in to *Emeril Live,* at 9 p.m.

Heidi brought Bobby in to make new "Full of Flavor" on-air promotions. Bobby was shot in front of a green screen and when the promos were broadcast during commercial breaks throughout the day, viewers saw Bobby pointing at a giant, brilliantly yellow lemon that exploded when he touched it and formed the word *juicy.*

You could do anything with food, Eileen thought—travel shows, comedies set in a restaurant, documentaries. Like nearly every executive who had passed through Food Network, she agreed that Mario Batali was a star. He was cooking a creatively authentic version of Italian food few people had ever seen and explaining it with the flourish of a gifted storyteller. It was smart, but for some reason, Mario was attracting plenty of press but not many viewers, far fewer than Emeril and, still, not the female demographic the advertising department was selling. The ad men continued to pressure the programming department to let Mario go.

Mario had his defenders. Joe Allegro and Rich Gore of the events department argued for him to stay. On their tour, he was a big draw, a leading star, no matter what the ratings were saying. If the network wanted to continue to make profits from their road shows, they could not lose dependable talent. Mario had his own interest in staying on TV. First, he liked showing off what he knew. Second, in 1998, he and Joe Bastianich opened an ambitious restaurant in Greenwich Village called Babbo Ristorante e Enoteca, which won three stars from *The New York Times*—certainly good publicity, but so was a cooking show on a growing network.

Eileen tried to widen Mario's appeal. She spent some of her increased programming budget sending Mario to Nice, Barcelona, and Valencia for a food travel show, *Mediterranean Mario*. She changed the set of *Molto Mario*, adding three stools to the kitchen so three guests—friends, food experts, journalists—could taste what he cooked and fire off questions for the maestro.

On one of the new *Molto* episodes, the three stools were occupied by Bill Buford, who was writing a book about his experiences working in Mario's kitchen called *Heat*; Ed Levine, a food writer; and Anthony Bourdain, the head chef at New York's Les Halles bistro and an aspiring author.

"My friends Bill, Ed, and Tony are here," said Mario at the top of the half hour. Bill and Ed managed to fire off questions amidst Mario's cascading patter of stories and instructions. Tony did not get a word in edgewise.

Even with the warmth of the new format, Mario and Erica Gruen battled when it came time to negotiate a new contract for *Molto*. Tired of answering to the network's whims, Mario wanted full creative control. Erica refused and ended production. The shows kept running on the air, but for a time he was out.

> "They were just my friends. People I could count on. People I knew would show up. They would also not vomit when they ate tripe at eight o'clock in the morning."
>
> —MARIO BATALI

The network staff remained worried about the changes Scripps might make, but tried to function normally. There had been so many ownership changes in such a short time that coping amid flux came relatively easy.

To promote the forthcoming season to advertisers and journalists, Heidi produced a sharp-looking promotional book. The cover had images of the network's universe of stars: Jennifer of *Two Fat Ladies* in a hunting cap, pointing a rifle at the viewer; David Rosengarten and Donna Hanover; Robin Leach in a tiki shirt touting *Gourmet Getaways*; Sara Moulton; Mario Batali in a pineapple-print Hawaiian shirt holding a fishing rod with a sausage and a tomato baited onto the hook; Emeril; Curtis Aikens; the Too Hot Tamales; and Sissy Biggers.

The copy began, "Feel it. Taste it. Smell it. See it . . . Anyway you sense it, Food Network is sizzling with success." There was a "lift and sniff" tab covering the image of a cup of coffee. A strip of packing bubbles was glued over the image of an ear of corn. "Press," the instructions went, "to hear the corn pop."

Food Network was the second-fastest-growing cable network, lagging behind only HGTV, the promotional book bragged. Its audience was wealthy, married, and had young children and plenty of expendable income, the sort of people one would expect to be drawn to information about fine food. Research from Nielsen and Mediamark found that, compared to other networks, Food's viewers were more likely to be part of couples with two incomes over $50,000 a year than any other network, and were far more likely to own a luxury imported car. Internet traffic was way up: 11,000 unique visitors a day in 1997 to 44,000 in 1998. Daily page views had risen from 131,000 to 422,000. Heidi dialed up her media assault. In an article in the *Los Angeles Times* in February 1998, she noted that men made up 40 percent of the audience, a surprise to some who viewed cooking as women's work. She created a clever phrase to explain it: "I think men have childhood memories of their families gathering in the kitchen, or maybe it's a nostalgic thing with their mothers preparing meals for the family. I call it the edible complex."

The article reported that Food Network was attracting "blue chip advertisers" like American Express, Toyota, and General Mills, but noted that some were asking the same questions the men of ProJo had faced when they first pitched the network to investors: Was food too narrow a subject to thrive 24/7 and would "viewers eventually . . . tire of such narrowly focused programming?"

If being criticized is a sign of respect, Food was given an Everest of respect in November 1998, a few weeks from its fifth anniversary, when Amanda Hesser, an influential dining reporter at *The New York Times*, paid a visit to *Emeril Live*. The resulting article was a butchery lesson. The reporter was passed a turkey sandwich Emeril had made for the cameras: "I took a bite," Hesser wrote. "It was a bad turkey sandwich. A very bad turkey sandwich. The bread was greasy, the turkey was dry, and the orange mystery cheese wasn't even melted."

She called Emeril "more jester than cook," "a zookeeper," and "the antithesis of the thoughtful, methodical Ms. Child." She quoted food-world luminaries, including Michael Batterberry, the founder of *Food Arts* magazine, who said: "A lot of professional foodies are a bit dismayed at the tone of the program. It really smacks a little bit of the wrestling ring or the roller derby."

Someday, such criticisms of Food Network chefs would be numbingly familiar and glance off toughened flesh, but this was a cutlass gash across the tender belly of the young network.

At a book signing in Chicago two weeks after Hesser's article, Emeril, hurt, told a *Chicago Sun-Times* reporter, "Just because I have fun don't mean I'm not serious. I take my reputation seriously. I've been working on mine for twenty-eight years." His show did have a useful message, he said. "You should have fun in the kitchen. . . . That's who I am. Most people get it, some don't."

Hesser had written that Emeril's shows were reaching up to 294,000 households a day in 1998, far more than Julia Child in her heyday. Erica was still hoping Julia could be lured to make more appearances on Food Network, and that her halo of food world credibility might keep critics like Hesser at bay. But it was Erica's decision to get rid of Sue Huffman that cost the network a few more years of Julia's semiregular presence. Shortly after Sue left, Julia's assistant sent a letter to the network canceling a Thanksgiving special she had been contemplating.

Julia remained interested in the fate of the network, however. In 1998, she wrote to Erica complaining that she couldn't see Food Network at her home in Cambridge or in Santa Barbara, California, where she had begun spending winters. The cable providers in those cities did not yet carry it.

On April 9, 1998, Erica wrote to inform her that Cox Cable was adding Food Network to the channel lineup in Santa Barbara, where Julia would be able to watch her own classic PBS shows Monday through Saturday at 6:30 p.m. and Sunday at noon.

"We'll get to Cambridge someday! The network is doing very well, though—we'll be in thirty-five million by year's end. . . ." Later that year, Erica wrote another letter, almost pleading, "Thank you for your constant support and inspiration. We'd so love to see you here again on your next New York visit."

Erica believed that she had accomplished much at Food Network, steering it toward a new era in which the entertainment value of shows was higher and the personalities of the stars memorable. She'd brought veteran talent into the executive ranks. She'd recognized the promise of

Emeril Live and helped shape it. She'd stemmed the financial losses and managed to keep things going well enough through a period of turmoil that a solid company like Scripps was willing to buy it. During her reign, the channel's distribution had grown from sixteen million homes to thirty-four million, and its prime-time ratings had tripled.

It wasn't losing Julia, by then in her mid-eighties, that cost Erica her position at the top of the network, or Reese's disdain for what he saw as her overspending ways and fumbling of valuable marketing opportunities. In Reese's 2001 book, *Me and Ted Against the World: The Unauthorized Story of the Founding of CNN*, which was largely focused on his years at CNN, he never mentioned Erica by name but referred to her as "a disastrous president," and remarked that after he left, the network lost Julia.

Even if she had somehow forbidden Amanda Hesser from ever visiting the *Emeril* set and never hired a feng shui consultant, it was very unlikely that Erica would have kept her job for long once Scripps became the majority owner. Ken needed his own person in there.

Finally, in November 1998, the time came for Ken to make the switch at the top he had planned. It had become clear that he would not be forced to move the network to Knoxville anytime soon, and he had someone in mind to take her place who appeared to be a good blend of New York and Tennessee—Eric Ober, a former CBS news executive who was commuting from New York to Knoxville four days a week to run the Scripps television production facility. Although news articles about Erica's departure in November 1998 noted that it came shortly after the Hesser piece, negotiations over Erica's severance had been going on long before that, and Eric had known for weeks beforehand that he would be entrusted to carry the network to its next stage.

> "The idea was just to settle the place down a little bit. Eric was used to dealing with chaotic newsrooms and there was a feistiness at Food. It was too intense."
>
> —KEN LOWE

"*Allez* Cuisine!"

say unto you: *Allez* cuisine!

All this buying and selling, firing and hiring, wouldn't mean much if the network couldn't put great shows into viewers' homes. But as the songwriter Leonard Cohen often says, "If I knew where the good songs come from, I'd go there more often." In late 1998, Food Network had Emeril. But after him, it had pretty much a gang of nobodies and a few half-somebodies on the air. Even as Scripps installed a new president, the business was doing only slightly better than breaking even.

The person in charge of a television network, and his or her team, approves or rejects ideas when they come knocking. Too conservative in placing bets on new shows, and it's unlikely anything original will make it through. Too chance-taking, and money will be squandered and viewer patience exhausted before the miracle of a hit arrives. Ultimately it comes down to gut instinct. Take the right chances and the kingdom of TV riches opens. Stumble and you're crocodile food in the moat. Everybody eventually stumbles.

Into this moment ambled the former slop bucket boy, Matt Stillman, who was about to reach into the mysterious realm of creativity where the hits live. For a time, when he came knocking with ideas, the people in charge were willing to listen.

Growing up, Matt played Dungeons & Dragons and his father inculcated in him a fascination with Greek, Indian, and Norse mythology. Matt also watched martial arts movies by the Shaw brothers, who combined heroic conflict with underlying romance. His upbringing, in short, was a brew of geeky obsessions.

In college, Matt found a bizarre cooking competition series from Japan called *Ryori no Tetsujin*—literally translated as *Ironmen of Cooking*—on a public access channel in upstate New York. Each episode—with English subtitles—was centered around an hourlong culinary battle between colorfully attired chef/warriors and presided over by a histrionic "Chairman" who wore a bejeweled cape and announced his presence by taking a loud, crunchy bite from a yellow bell pepper. The basic setup was enticing, but Matt went bonkers for the show's underlying mythology. The Chairman was presented as a real person who had used inherited wealth to build a kitchen stadium. His stable of "Iron Chefs"—one specializing in French cuisine, one in Italian, one in Chinese, and one in Japanese—would take on challengers and, under the pressures created by competition, invent new delicacies. At the start of each show, the four Iron Chefs would rise onto a stage on hydraulic lifts, smoke billowing, their satiny robes gleaming. The challenger, whose biography was carefully told and used as explanation for his desire to test himself in this arena, might be from a popular restaurant in Japan or from another country. He would pick one of the warriors with whom to do battle, saying, for instance, "I choose Iron Chef Japanese!" The chosen Iron Chef then stepped forward. The Chairman unveiled the day's secret ingredient, say cuttlefish, or pork belly, or apples. The timer was set: one hour to prepare a meal based on the secret ingredient.

"*Allez* cuisine!" the Chairman would shout, a declaration that the battle was joined.

Osamu Kanemitsu, an executive at Fuji Television, created *Iron Chef* around the same time Joe Langhan was concocting a food channel. Osamu's boss, Yoshiaki Yamada, had issued a seemingly simple order: "I want you to air a culinary program on Sunday nights at 10:30." In that era, Japanese television programmers generally had the same attitude as their counterparts in the U.S: cooking shows were for house-wives and there was no audience for them at times other than on week-day afternoons or weekend mornings. Osamu decided to violate two cardinal rules of traditional cooking shows: that recipes should be set in advance and the shows set in a sedate kitchen. His new show would be improvisational and held in a busy, chaotic environment. Osamu's concept, he explained in the fastidiously detailed *Iron Chef: The Official Book*, was to "create a culinary program where the menu hasn't been decided on in an atmosphere like the Harrods food emporium."

It was sort of about cooking, but it was really about the construction of a pressured situation where the only solution was creativity.

Another Fuji Television programmer, Takashi Ishihara, proposed casting for the Chairman the musical actor Takeshi Kaga (born Shigekatsu Katsuta), who had played Jean Valjean in the Japanese pro-duction of *Les Misérables*. The format evolved to include a team of scur-rying assistants for each chef, a play-by-play commentator assisted by a roving reporter, and a shifting panel of judges who offered com-ments during the cooking and at the end tasted each dish and declared a winner.

Mirroring Food Network, *Iron Chef* debuted in the fall of 1993—and faced low ratings. But with format tweaks, *Iron Chef* became popular in Japan, breaking the same ground as *Emeril Live*, showing that by inject-ing entertainment into a cooking show the audience could include men, women, and children.

A few years after its Japanese debut, *Iron Chef* first started attracting notice in the United States when it was aired with subtitles on KTSF 26, an Asian channel in the San Francisco Bay Area, and other Asian television outlets in Los Angeles, Hawaii, and parts of New York and New Jersey. Soon calls and letters poured into the San Francisco station from viewers of various ethnicities, expressing how much they loved it. It moved *Iron Chef* to an 8 p.m. slot on Saturday nights, and by 1998, the show had become a local cult phenomenon. In the bohemia of Oak-land's warehouse district, a fan staged a mock *Iron Chef* battle, attract-ing three hundred partygoers. Sake and soy sauce companies had long advertised, but soon American Airlines and computer makers bought time. An English-language fan website was launched and a drinking game developed: take a sip every time a judge says, "I think he may steam that."

Matt saw the show as a medieval martial arts series with specialized weapons: gleaming sushi knives, stone pestles, whirring quick-freeze ice cream makers. The secret ingredients—salted salmon! eggplant!—were like things decided upon by the roll of a twenty-sided die in Dungeons & Dragons. He saw each challenger chef as a knight arriving from a far-off kingdom to challenge a master warrior on his home turf, the hallowed jousting ground of Kitchen Stadium.

Unlike the show's fans anywhere else, Matt worked at a place that had the power to spread the good news of *Iron Chef*—if only he could convince management to put it on the air. When he was still a new hire making $17,000 a year, he'd shown Joe Langhan a videotape. Joe had recognized the wacky beauty of *Two Fat Ladies*, but nixed *Iron Chef*: "Too weird." Soon after Eileen took him on as her assistant, he began gushing about the show to her.

Others at the network were noticing the show independently. Erica Gruen's husband had seen it on a Japanese channel carried in Kew Gardens, Queens, where they lived. One evening, he called Erica into the living room. "Oh, my God," her husband said. "You've got to come in and see this show. It's *Ready . . . Set . . . Cook!* on speed!" Erica asked Eileen to reach out to the show's producers to see if broadcast rights were available. Eileen had seen Fuji Television reps pitching it at a national cable convention in New Orleans. She figured that if the show was running on an obscure Japanese channel in Queens, American rights couldn't be too expensive. She made inquiries.

Nevertheless, Eileen was skeptical. *Iron Chef* was a bizarre program made in a foreign language and the chefs used many ingredients Americans had never heard of. In the late 1990s, not many supermarkets carried kale, let alone sea urchin. Eileen knew that the odds of *Iron Chef* getting on the air were slim. Still, the show, as weird as it was, fit in with what she said she was trying to do, namely, expand the network from cooking to food in all its aspects. *Iron Chef* was certainly, as Heidi's slogan had it, "full of flavor."

Matt's enthusiasm for *Iron Chef* motivated her. "You have to do this," he beseeched her. "This is what you want to do." Eileen wanted Matt to feel he was important at the network. She knew Fuji had been shopping the show around, but she encouraged Matt to think it was his baby. If she let her young, curly-haired charge think the idea was his, he'd work hard on it. In the unlikely case that the show landed on the air, it could give him confidence and help his career.

"This is amazing," Eileen told him. "How did you know about this?"

He told her how he'd seen it in college and had been a believer in its potential for years.

"Okay," Eileen said, trying to be a good mentor. "I'm going to help you, but you have to help me pitch this. It's great, but it's going to be a hard sell here."

Before they could sell *Iron Chef* inside the network, they needed to find out how much it would cost. Bruce Seidel, whom Eileen had hired from Discovery Channel, had been appointed head of acquisitions and she assigned him to negotiate with Fuji. The Japanese company said the least it would take was about $25,000 an episode, a price that would include dubbing and editing to fit the ninety-minute show into an hour of American commercial television. This was far more than Food Network had ever paid for an outside production. Yet Fuji also had conditions. It wanted *Iron Chef* to be treated with respect, not as some kind of foreign freak show. Japan had long been showing dubbed versions of American imports like *Dallas*. In Japan, spending money on good dubbing was a show of respect.

As talks continued, Heidi had to make a trip to Japan on other business. She visited the Fuji offices and, following Japanese tradition, she bore gifts, ties and scarves printed with New York icons like the Twin

> "I was just so passionate about it, so into it, totally lit up by it, by doing all this cool programming stuff. It felt like this was my creative moment. I was so sure this was going to be a breakout. I knew I was responsible for making it come to pass, to be the best show it could be."
>
> —MATT STILLMAN

Towers and the Statue of Liberty. Heidi had her own ideas for how to broadcast *Iron Chef* in the United States. She was a fan of the show *Mystery Science Theater 3000*, in which a man and his robot friends were shown in silhouette at the bottom of the screen as if they were sitting in a theater watching old science fiction movies. They would heckle and snicker at the film. Stoners and college students loved the show; she thought the same audience would like *Iron Chef*. Heidi told the people at Fuji that she wanted to keep the main soundtrack in Japanese and run a humorous voice-over in English. As her words were translated, the executives' faces dropped. Her suggestion was sacrilegious to them. The show was a celebration of the artistic mind, not something to be ridiculed. The Fuji executives quietly showed Heidi the new *Iron Chef* cookbook. It was one of the most beautiful books she had ever seen. The photography was of the highest quality. The Japanese words were rendered in precise calligraphy. The layouts were as good as any the finest design firms in New York could produce. It made her understand what Matt had known from the first time he saw the show: *Iron Chef* was no joking matter to the Japanese. She bowed deeply as she left and dropped the *Mystery Science Theater 3000* idea.

Back at the network, Matt, Eileen, and Bruce were trying to keep the project alive internally in the face of skepticism from Ed Spray, the Scripps executive Ken sent to oversee Food Network. At a meeting in the fall of 1998, Ed said he could not believe anyone in their right mind would consider putting a foreign-language show on an American channel in prime time. "What do you mean, Japanese?" he asked her with scorn in his voice.

Eileen chalked his attitude up to the cultural differences between the Midwestern Scripps and the coastal Food Network. But when Ken was shown a tape, he also told Food Network programmers, "You've got to be out of your mind."

But the Scripps people did not kill the show outright. They allowed the Food Network staff to keep tinkering with it, which was a victory of sorts.

Had the new president of Food Network known how deeply Matt was tied to *Iron Chef*, he might have nixed it pronto. Before he was named president, Eric Ober had set up meetings with Eileen to suggest ideas for shows the Knoxville facility might produce. Eileen, the hootenanny at Blackberry Farms still vivid, was wary of Scripps's influence and told Matt, her assistant, to stall Eric. He was good at it. When Eric called, Matt, speaking with brusque officiousness, explained how busy Eileen was.

When Eric arrived for the meetings, Matt would tell him Eileen was unavailable.

Shortly after Eric knew he was going to replace Erica Gruen, but before anyone at Food had been told, he got off the phone after jousting with Matt, turned to a colleague, and said, "I'm gonna fire Matthew my first day. I'm just going to walk in there, stride over to Matthew, and say, 'Matthew, I don't even want to bring you to my office. I'm just firing you right here. Just for being an asshole.'"

But by the time Eric took the job, he had a slight change of heart. He knew Eileen mothered her assistant, and Eric didn't want to antagonize the head of programming off the bat.

Eric spent most of his first week as president of the network hanging around the studios watching shows being made. After decades in the news business, he believed you could really tell who was competent and who wasn't by observing the action from the control room and the studio floor.

During that week, Eileen pulled him aside. "We have a show from

> "I said, if we do the show, we need to keep the parts that are keeping the sense of this larger arc, the origins of the battle, in place. . . . Here's how it needs to be subtitled, here's how we'll edit it, here's why cutting is important, here's how we'll make a story arc still fit, as opposed to just chopping it up so we can make it a one-hour show. . . . The show was about a particular sect of Japanese food traditionalist—in all seriousness, they would challenge Morimoto and say, 'We have a serious bone to pick with you, and we're going to battle you. Your French-Asian cuisine is BS.' There were real rivalries. That's what made it compelling. . . ."
>
> **—MATT STILLMAN**

Fuji that we have to make a decision on by tomorrow because we have an option at a really good price," she said. She did not describe *Iron Chef* as Matt's baby.

Eric watched an episode in her office. It was in Japanese, without subtitles or dubbing. Eric stared at it, taking it in. He thought, This is fucking hysterical. Screaming chefs! The guy with the pepper!

"What is this?" he asked Eileen.

"It's produced in Japan. It's very popular there. We suspect that somebody like Discovery will pick it up if we don't buy it."

Eric thought the Food Network had plenty of room to experiment and even fail on air. After all, almost no one was watching, so almost no one would notice. The important thing, he thought, was just to make decisions fast and to try new things. It wasn't like launching a prime-time show on CBS where millions were at stake with every gamble. *Iron Chef* might cost a lot in Food Network terms, but Scripps had pledged to increase his budget. He had the money and, he thought, the autonomy to green-light it.

"I'm in," Eric said. "Let's just buy the show."

Eileen explained there was still the question of whether it should be subtitled as Matt wanted, and as it had been successful on public access, or dubbed as the Japanese wanted. The Scripps executives had said the only way they'd ever consider it was if it was dubbed. Eileen was not sure what to do.

"I don't want subtitles," Eric said. They were difficult to read. In 1998, almost no one had wide-screen TVs; high-definition was a thing of the future. Eric also remembered going to Godzilla movies when he was fourteen. He knew comedy was inherent in the flaws of dubbing, and he saw comedy in Kitchen Stadium. It would work.

"Dub it," he said. "I don't give a shit whether it's good dubbing or bad dubbing. Even if it ends up with a lot of lip-flap while the judge says in Japanese, 'This tastes most delicious, very piquant,' and the dubbing says just 'I like this,' I don't give a shit. It will be funny, like Godzilla movies."

The decision to dub *Iron Chef* pleased the Fuji executives, but they did not trust the Americans to do it: they might do something disrespectful. Fuji insisted on doing the dubbing themselves.

Bruce worked out the final price—around $10,000 an episode with an option to buy more at a higher price later, and the papers were signed. Eileen approached Matt with a little smile on her face. "We did it," she said. "You did it, we did it."

Matt resisted the urge to cry or jump up and down. "Yes," he said quietly.

Around the time of the *Iron Chef* purchase, network executives thought they had identified a chef who could capture the same crossover audience as Emeril and create a solid evening programming block. Chef David Ruggerio, a Brooklyn native and former boxer who'd started his food career cleaning sidewalks outside a fish restaurant in Sheepshead Bay, had blue-collar charm and a serious cooking pedigree. He was running Le Chantilly, a high-end French restaurant in Manhattan, but could also sling entertaining stories about his outrageous family, such as yarns about his grandma's gambling junkets.

> "It was not by focus group. When Eric came on, I loved his style. He said, 'Hey, there are only twenty thousand viewers watching us on any night. It's not going to be big news if we pull a show.' He said, 'Let's try it and if it doesn't work, we'll pull it.'"
>
> **—JOE ALLEGRO**

The network had developed *Ruggerio to Go*, intending it to appeal to the same Giants-jacket guys, grandmothers, and children as Emeril did. The show was shot in the same studio as *Emeril Live*, with most of the same crew, and by the time it debuted in October 1998, the network had produced dozens of episodes and spent a fortune marketing Ruggerio. But just a few weeks after the first episode ran, Ruggerio was arrested and charged with $221,000 in fraud. According to the Manhattan District Attorney's indictment, Ruggerio had been submitting charges to credit card companies far in excess of what the restaurant's customers had signed for. In one case, he added a $30,000 tip to a $1,000 dinner tab. Facing up to fifteen years in prison, Ruggerio eventually pleaded guilty and was sentenced to pay over $100,000 in restitution, spend five years on probation, and do 500 hours of community service.

The morning after Ruggerio's arrest, Eric met with Eileen, Heidi, a Scripps programming consultant named Judy Girard, and an in-house lawyer. Ken Lowe attended by conference call. Eileen and Judy argued to keep the show on the air, contending that they had spent heavily on it, only a few episodes had aired, the network was badly in need of new content, and the charges did not impugn the chef's cooking credibility. Heidi was vehemently opposed to keeping the show. No matter how famously thick the foie gras at Le Chantilly, no matter how charming his patter, Ruggerio's arrest would be awful for public relations. "He has stolen from our viewers," she argued. "Whether or not they were there. He has broken the law." Eric and Ken agreed with her, and Heidi's argument won the day. Ruggerio was out—and, with a hole in the schedule, the idea of airing a wacky show from Japan suddenly seemed less wacky.

Hit-making is not a repeatable formula. It can't be bottled; a set of people at a certain point in their lives meet in a certain place under certain circumstances. They will never meet again in this way with exactly the same powers, nor will the world again be in just the same state of receptivity. Crucially, the show, the song, the sculpture must find a way to be seen, heard, or experienced by others in its moment. As Linda McCartney once said, "You can't reheat a soufflé."

> "I am absolutely petrified by people in white coats. I don't care if it's a dentist, a doctor, or a chef. They all scare the hell out of me. I don't hang out with chefs. They frighten me."
>
> —ALTON BROWN

Matt was regularly on the phone to the American office of Fuji TV, discussing *Iron Chef* edits, and choosing which actors would dub which characters. David Rosengarten adopted him. He took Matt to Kurumazushi, where they ate hundreds of dollars of raw fish and quaffed sake, all paid for by the critic's expense account from *Gourmet* magazine. Macallan sent

David a 140-year-old bottle of Scotch to taste on *In Food Today*. After the show, he walked a glass over to Matt. "You have to try this!"

Fuji, eighty-dollar toro, and antique Scotch—Matt had made it. He just knew that he was a genius, that rare person who was ahead of the curve—even though, truthfully, he had not invented anything. He had just recognized something good, understood what was magical about it, and advocated for it with all his might. This was a talent, unquestionably, but it was not the same as the talent of actually giving birth to an idea whole as Osamu Kanemitsu had. Likewise, Matt took pride in having been a part of Upright Citizens Brigade from its early days. Some of those from his era had gone on to perform on *Saturday Night Live*. But he hadn't.

It didn't stop his ego from growing due to the feeling that he was on a winning streak—because in a way he was. His particular talent for recognizing and associating himself with brilliance came in to play again when he was sitting at his desk outside Eileen's office one day paging through a film trade magazine and saw a small mention of a pilot food television show shot on a new type of Kodak film. Matt went to the Kodak website and read a little bit more about the pilot's star, a former cinematographer named Alton Brown.

Alton's father had worked in radio in Los Angeles in the late 1960s. At one of his parents' cocktail parties, he'd met the producer Gene Roddenberry, spurring his interest in science and television. Gene was working on a new show called *Star Trek*. On a napkin, he drew for Alton, wide-eyed, a picture of the starship called *Enterprise*.

His parents moved the family back to their native Georgia when Alton was seven. Alton Brown Sr., a workaholic, became a local media mogul, buying a radio station, a newspaper, and three printing shops. His death at home at thirty-eight, when Alton was eleven, was ruled a suicide. The son retreated into science fiction television and movies. He hated high school. He viewed the teachers as regurgitation machines uninterested in inspiring students. It took him seven years to finish college, flunking science and math and changing schools twice before graduating from the University of Georgia with a degree in drama.

Along the way, he spent a summer in Italy studying bilingual drama, learning how to communicate with an audience by performing in Italian even though he didn't actually speak the language. His interests had expanded to include cooking. For dates, the awkward young man taught himself to make a meal he called "The Closer," sole au gratin Florentine, which was designed to be impressive, inexpensive, and suitable for serving as leftovers for breakfast. He found work as a cameraman. In 1987, he landed a gig as the director of photography on the video for R.E.M.'s song "The One I Love," became a cinematographer and then a director. He worked on small television commercials until he burned out, telling himself the world had enough radial tires and diapers.

At the age of thirty, he was dreaming of what he might do next. What didn't the world have enough of? Alton's mind brought together the things he loved: cooking, science fiction, and theater. He wrote on a piece of paper a rough idea for a television cooking show he'd like to star in: "Julia Child, Mr. Wizard, Monty Python."

Man, he thought, I could really make something out of that.

This is part of what makes the alchemy of a hit unrepeatable. It's easy to say, "We need more groundbreaking shows!" But go find yourself another director of an R.E.M. video who met Gene Roddenberry as a boy, studied bilingual drama, and was so lame with the ladies that he learned to cook out of desperation but ultimately found a wife who would support him.

His wife, DeAnna, was skeptical, pointing out that watching a lot of cooking shows wasn't much of a credential for being the host of one. They made a deal. Alton could apply to three culinary schools. If he got into one, they would sell their Atlanta home, and she would support him. He got into the New England Culinary Institute in Montpelier, Vermont, and attended in 1995. After graduation, he worked as a grill man at a North Carolina restaurant and wrote scripts for the show he imagined. DeAnna came up with the name *Good Eats*.

Alton had been befriended by Chris Gyoury and Sarah Burmeister, a team of television commercial producers in Georgia. Also bored of the work, they wanted to expand into something more creative and took to Alton's idea, a sort of comedy focused on the science of cooking. Not only did they finance two pilots, which together cost around $150,000, but Sarah invited Alton and DeAnna to live at her house in Roswell, Georgia, an Atlanta suburb. The pilot shows were shot on film, not video, in Burmeister's home kitchen, which had a picture window overlooking a garden. Chris removed the backs of ovens and refrigerators, allowing Alton to open a fridge door, poke his face in, and speak directly to the camera. The effect lent the show one of its distinctive looks. They completed two pilots for *Good Eats* in 1997, "This Spud's for You" and "Steak Your Claim." In the latter, Alton showed viewers, via chalk marks on a live cow, where steaks came from, instructed how to shop for them, and finally, how to best cook one (sear in cast iron, then bake).

More alchemy: have producers bored with their day jobs hire a fiendishly smart salesperson, Tara Burtchaell. A New York University graduate who worked for advertising producers in Manhattan, Tara brought the city hustle with her when she moved back to her native South. Tara was baffled by Alton and his show, but put everything she had into selling it. She created a "bible," basically a pitch book, for it, putting *Oh, No! Not Another Cooking Show!* on the cover, and a list of potential future episodes inside. She brought it to the cable TV convention in New Orleans and stopped at the Food Network booth. She was told she ought to contact Eileen Opatut and that it would help if she could add information about audience response to the pilot episodes. Tara had heard that a PBS station in Chicago was looking for new programming, and they agreed to run the *Good Eats* pilots a few times to gauge if ratings were going up or down. Meanwhile, she contacted Kodak and pitched the idea that there might be an interesting story in the fact that the producers had shot the episode with the company's film instead of videotape. The strategy came together when WTTW aired it, good ratings resulted, and the *Tribune* ran a review praising Alton and "the spiky, energetic camera work." The review by Steve Johnson concluded, "This lively, well-made and refreshingly different show deserves a place at a television table overcrowded with cookie-cutter cooking programs."

All good news, and yet when Tara prepared to reach out to Food Network, she admitted to Chris and Sarah, "I don't know if we're going to get our money out of this one." Tara knew that programming chiefs are always overwhelmed with unsolicited pitches, so she found out who Eileen's gatekeeper was and targeted him.

Either Matt called Tara or Tara called Matt. Matt says when he called, Tara said, "Wow, Food Network is calling us?" Tara says when she called, she opened with, "I know you get bombarded, but . . ."

Either way, it was oil and oil. Matt had already been reading up about Alton because of the Kodak article and told Tara he was definitely interested. She sent a tape and the updated bible with ratings information and the *Tribune* review. Watching *Good Eats*, Matt felt that same flush he'd had when he first saw *Iron Chef* in college: "This is going to be amazing." Dozens of pitch tapes were coming into Eileen's office a week, but he dashed into Eileen's office with this one. She liked it and told Matt to set up a meeting. Not a week after the tapes had been sent to Food Network, Alton walked into the little Atlanta production office and asked Tara, "Has anything happened?"

"The Food Network wants to meet with us," she said, smiling.

"Let's go!"

"We're working on getting flights booked right now."

At the network headquarters, Tara began the spiel she'd practiced.

"Eileen, I'm sure you've been charged with wrapping shows around personalities. You've got Emeril. That's one guy and he's awesome. This is a new fresh way of looking at things. We're not talking about recipes. We're not talking about restaurants. We're getting inside the food. We'll do angles from inside the refrigerator. We'll do things upside down. We'll . . ."

Eileen was sold. She asked for them to come back with a bid to produce thirteen episodes.

But would Scripps go for another weird show? *Good Eats* would cost around $35,000 a half-hour episode, even more than the rights to *Iron Chef.*

"We already have *Taste!*" someone protested at a planning meeting.

The premise of David Rosengarten's show was to look deeply at one ingredient. It was produced in-house and cost less than half of Alton's show.

"On the most superficial level, they're similar," replied Matt, who was so eager to speak at meetings that Eileen, after allowing her mentee a few minutes to make his points, often told him, "Shut up, Matt. That's enough." In this meeting, he was allowed to continue. "But they're totally different in approach. Everyone loves David and, yes, there is a similarity. But David stands in a white room and talks about the cultural significance of a recipe. His show doesn't move around. It doesn't look at science. It's not really comic."

Word came that ad sales thought *Good Eats* was too weird. Advertisers wouldn't get it. Eileen argued that *Good Eats* might be unconventional, but it fit in with *Iron Chef* in that they both treated the viewer as smart and delivered offbeat entertainment. And its high level of inside humor could give the network a certain voice of geeky intelligence.

By late 1998, Eileen and Matt won the day again. Eric said, "Why not?" and Scripps agreed to give it a shot.

Matt flew down to Atlanta to oversee production of the first shows.

> "I'm standing in the middle of a cow field with a farmer and a big chalkboard and you've got chalk all over the cow and I'm going, 'Who in the heck is going to watch this show?'"
>
> **—TARA BURTCHAELL**

As his programming budget increased to a workable but still tight $42 million, Eric, a fan of *New York* magazine's annual "Best of New York" issue, created a show called *The Best Of.* Two local news reporters, Jill Cordes and Marc Silverstein, narrated short segments on the best entrees, confections, and delicacies from around the nation. Simple, but with *The Best Of,* Food Network entered new territory, sending cameras and reporters out into the country. Eric funded another "road show" called *Door Knock Dinners,* hosted and produced by Gordon Elliott, a former Australian talk-show host. Elliott, accompanied by a different chef or food personality each episode, would knock on people's doors offering to whip up a meal for the family using whatever was in their refrigerator and pantry. Other new shows followed, including *Legendary Hangouts*, in which Ober's former CBS colleague Morley Safer would sit in a booth at an old restaurant like Chasen's in Hollywood and narrate a half hour on the joint's legendariness; *My Country, My Kitchen*, which took chefs to their native lands; *Melting Pot*, featuring food experts like Padma Lakshmi and Aarón Sánchez cooking ethnic cuisines; and *Taste Test*, a corny game show hosted by David Rosengarten.

Question: "What is the official definition of pâté?"

Answer: "There is none!"

Eric was a supporter of David's. He authorized the production of new episodes of *Taste* and brought in a new producer for *In Food Today*, Bob Tuschman, a former producer for *ABC News*. Bob's first assignment was to modernize it. Before him, *In Food Today* had the look of a news program from the early 1960s hosted by people who hadn't bought clothes since the 1980s. He brought in more light features and cooking demonstrations and ushered out breaking news.

Eric meanwhile took David to a tailor and bought him a well-fitting suit, something to frame the network workhorse as a thinking person's food maven. Eric's philosophy was that people watch people. Even in something as serious as news, people did not tune in to a particular show because of a deep affinity for CBS or NBC. They tuned in to see Dan Rather or Tom Brokaw.

Or Mario Batali. The chef had been without a show since he and Erica had fought, and now Eric told Eileen to bring him back. Mario always got good buzz and often showed up on gossip pages. He was a great self-promoter; even people who were not in the food world knew who Mario was. Batali did not win the full creative control he'd wanted, but after time away from the cameras, he concluded that he and the network were better off together than apart.

Eric's philosophy was at odds with his bosses at Scripps. The parent company was less interested in personalities, more in formats. From his first pitch for HGTV, Ken had said programming would be inspired by the aisles of a home improvement store and articles in shelter magazines. HGTV, the flagship channel, was not about celebrities and buzz; it was about sinks and rosebushes. Eric saw the logic: networks that made stars would eventually be at the mercy of those stars. A show with a winning format would survive even if you cut high-priced talent loose.

But even though he understood it—and knew that he had been brought in partly because he understood it—he did not agree with it. His experience was that TV needed stars, especially cooking shows, where one person addressed the camera directly. In New York, instead of looking only for formats that would be hits, he and Eileen looked for stars that could make something a hit. *Melting Pot*; *Ready. . . Set . . . Cook!*; *Chef du Jour*; *My Country, My Kitchen*; and *In Food Today* functioned like a minor league farm system where new faces could be tested and budding stars could gain valuable on-camera experience.

One of the first talents to emerge from the system was Ming Tsai, a young chef who paired Asian ingredients with classical French technique. Ethnically Chinese, Ming was born and raised near Dayton, Ohio. His father was an engineer and his mother ran a modest takeout Chinese restaurant where Ming worked after school. He went to Yale to study engineering, but he played a lot of squash and skied as often as he could, and he spent summers in Paris apprenticing at bakeries and restaurants.

The summer of his junior year, he took classes at Le Cordon Bleu cooking school in Paris and, after graduation, he spent two years in France working in restaurants. After earning a master's degree in hotel management from Cornell University, and cooking in San Francisco, he was hired at Santacafé, a restaurant in Santa Fe, where his "Southwest Asian Cuisine"—dishes like coriander-crusted tuna with carrot-daikon salad and chile-cilantro vinaigrette, and grilled lamb marinated in Dijon mustard, ginger, and Chinese rice wine—attracted notice from national food writers. Ming first appeared on Food Network when cameras from *Dining Around* visited the restaurant where he was executive chef. His first words on camera were, "Hi, my name is Ming Tsai. I was born Chinese. I'm still Chinese! Now today I'm going to make you grilled lamb."

The executive producer of *Dining Around*, Marilyn O'Reilly, was also overseeing *Ready . . . Set . . . Cook!* Impressed with Ming's deep voice, strong jaw, and shy smile, she asked him to come to New York to compete on the show in 1996. After taping five episodes in a day, winning two, losing two, and tying one with Susur Lee, a Hong Kong–born East-West "fusion" chef six years Ming's elder, Marilyn gave him a turn on *Chef du Jour*. The network featured few Asian chefs, and producers were weary of hearing viewer complaints about foreign-accented chefs, especially French ones. No matter how expert Eric Ripert, Jacques Pépin, or Wolfgang Puck were, people griped, "I can't understand what he's saying." Ming spoke English like the Midwesterner he was—mixed with a bit of East Coast prep, like he had just come off a tennis court.

But even with his dimpled grin and unique ethnic appeal, he fumbled on camera. Unlike *Ready . . . Set . . . Cook!*, *Chef du Jour* had no studio audience. There were four cameras and a few crew members. Ming's jokes were met with silence. He failed to move recipes forward quickly enough to finish on time and neglected to explain unusual ingredients with sufficient depth. Why are Asian peppercorns different from black peppercorns? What is ponzu?

"You're not great," Marilyn said. "But you're better than most."

"Thank you," Ming replied. "I guess."

He wanted to be as good at television as he was at everything else he put his mind to. He noticed what others who have spent time on TV usually notice, that appearing on the screen sprinkled some magic on him in other people's eyes and made them want to listen. Ming moved to the Boston area to open a restaurant, and whenever Food Network called, he went and performed without pay. David used him on a dim sum episode of *Taste*. Marilyn offered him a chance to do *Cooking Live* during Sara Moulton's annual vacation on one condition: "You've got to get media training if you're going to do this. Get the training and you'll become the network's Asian expert, and then maybe we can get you a show."

Ming made the pilgrimage to Lou Ekus, spending $3,000 for two days. He was stiff until Lou, pulling out a favorite trick, told him to seduce the camera by imagining he was speaking to someone sexy.

"I have a picture of someone I think is absolutely gorgeous," Ming said. He taped a photo of his puppy Jasmine to the camera—the same trick Marion Cunningham had used years earlier with Rover. Every time he looked at Jasmine, he'd smile and relax.

In February 1998, his restaurant Blue Ginger opened and he got strong reviews: "The first spoonful of a spring pea soup, brilliant green as grass, fragrant as the first mowing, explodes in my mouth," critic Allison Arnett wrote in *The Boston Globe*. Soon after, Eileen offered Ming his own series on the network, *East Meets West*, a straightforward cooking demonstration show. On May 15, 1999, Ming, then thirty-four, won an Emmy for *East Meets West*, beating Julia Child and Martha Stewart in the category of Service Show Host. Nine days later, a profile by freelance writer Kathryn Matthews went out over the Knight Ridder wire service, noting that Ming is "tall with broad shoulders, boyish good looks, and surefire confidence in the kitchen."

Commenters on the fan forum section of the Food Network website gushed: "Ming is a talented babe with a great personality"; "He looks hot in that one pair of shorts he wore when he went to Hawaii." And from an Asian fan: "I'm very proud of you and your heritage."

> "TV has an irrational power . . . When you're in that black box, the average public just assumes you are the authority on that subject. I'm happy to admit that I think I'm as good as two thousand other chefs in this country. But am I in the top twenty? No. Hell, no."
>
> **—MING TSAI**

In the two years since Tyler had first appeared on *In Food Today*, he had faithfully come every time the network called. But none of his on-screen work gave him what Bobby, Mario, or Emeril had—his own show. Tyler came to understand that each had a compelling and easy-to-digest personal story to tell about his relationship to food and cooking. Mario had spent time cooking in small Italian villages. Bobby was the urban dude who knew how to start a party with a grill and some peppers. Emeril was a blue-collar guy who had put in the time to learn New Orleans cooking but stayed loyal to his mom, Hilda, back in Massachusetts.

Audiences, Tyler noted, felt bound to chefs with good back stories the way sports fans root for athletes. Success on-screen is not just about cooking the lightest soufflé, doling out the cleverest shortcuts, or even being the best-looking. Lou Ekus could teach someone how to have an ease on camera, but that wasn't enough. You needed a story that touched people.

Tyler pondered his own story. Money was scarce when he grew up, and as a toddler, he was allergic to milk, chicken, and many other foods. After his grandmother died, Tyler got his hands on her box of home recipes. Tyler's mom needed help around the house, so he taught himself to cook like Grandma. He followed the interest born from that recipe box and earned a culinary degree from Johnson & Wales in North Carolina. When he was named executive chef at Cafeteria, a booming new restaurant in Manhattan's Chelsea neighborhood, he brought his grandma's recipes with him. Cafeteria had a sleek all-white design, model hostesses, a techno soundtrack—and Grandma's meat loaf on the menu.

Diligent about networking, Tyler was at a cocktail party celebrating *Food & Wine* magazine's annual "Best New Chefs" issue when he spotted Eileen Opatut and took the opportunity to chat with her. He had no "Bam," nor the unique look of Ming. But he had a box of recipes. Tyler told his story. "And those," he said, concluding his life story in food, "are the same recipes I put on the menu of Cafeteria."

Eileen's heart swelled. Even as this handsome young man with a cute smile and big brown eyes was cooking at one of the hippest restaurants in New York, he was thinking of his beloved grandma and dishing out her home-style cooking. Eileen cherished her own grandmother's recipes and it occurred to her that a lot of people probably did the same. Tyler's story conjured nostalgia for a simpler time when kindly matriarchs cooked comfort food for their extended families and everything was right with the world.

Eileen's oldest daughter was going to school with a child named Yuki

O'Brien—half Japanese, half Irish. How would Yuki connect with his heritage? Maybe, Eileen mused, Yuki's parents had a Japanese grandmother's recipe for beef soup, or an Irish grandmother's recipe for biscuits. Those old recipes were bonds to the old country, to a dimly remembered way of life that gave people identity in the present.

Here it was again: the right personality meeting the right executive who is in the right position and the right frame of mind at the right time. Eileen called Tyler at Cafeteria. "Listen, Tyler. We want to give you a twenty-thousand-dollar development deal."

Tyler was thrilled. He was being paid what nearly everyone in the restaurant business is paid: peanuts. He'd been working in restaurants since he was fifteen years old. He had had one New Year's Eve off in the last decade. He got Christmas or Thanksgiving off, but never both. This was okay money and a promise at the big time. He resigned from Cafeteria immediately.

"We've got this concept where you would travel around the country and help everyday people out with their food emergencies at home," Eileen explained at a meeting. "And it's something, you know, right now, we got a working title, it's like *Food 911*. Like, you call 911, the cops show up. You call *Food 911*, and you show up."

Food 911 was set to debut around the same time as Bobby's new road series, *FoodNation*, another effort to bring sunshine to the schedule. In anticipation of the big, dual launch, Bobby and Tyler were summoned to the Venetian Hotel in Las Vegas to help present the upcoming season to advertisers. Standing outside the hotel with Tyler, Bobby dispensed some advice. "Take a look around. 'Cause there's a couple of chefs, and I'm not gonna mention their names, they were on the network at a very early point, that weren't invited here because of their antics, their prima donna attitude. Everything had to be about them. If you notice, they're not here right now? Just notice that, all right? The network wants you to be here, then you need to be here."

Tyler nodded.

"You see all this?" Bobby continued, "you see all these limousines? You see these big parties? You see these airline tickets? You see all this stuff? Like the exposure you get? It's a gift. Don't ever blow it. Don't ever, ever, ever blow it."

Bobby had learned from the best about how to treat people when you are a famous food person. Shortly after he opened Mesa Grill, Julia Child had come to the restaurant. Before she sat down to eat, she went into the kitchen and shook everyone's hand, from the dishwasher to the chef. She exhibited grace. Bobby watched and learned.

A few years later, Bobby had dinner with Julia in New York. She ordered an upside-down martini.

"Ms. Child, what is that?" Bobby asked.

"Well, it's a lot of vermouth and a little bit of gin," she answered with a laugh.

When, after months of waiting, Food Network finally received the edited and dubbed episodes of *Iron Chef* in the spring of 1999, Eric, Eileen, Matt, and the others were beside themselves with glee at the campy results. "Oh my, the chef trained in America is adding dried mullet roe," went the dubbing of one character. "What more can you expect from a man from the land of freedom?"

Somehow the Japanese, consulting with Matt on their voice-over actor choices, had managed to imbue the dubbing with exactly what Eric had wanted, the comedically wooden quality of *Mothra*. The edits, also done with the help of copious notes from Matt, who spent weekends studying every second of every tape, maintained the logic and high drama of the original. Fuji and he had produced a sweet-bitter confection that tickled the taste buds and left a craving for more.

The combination of debuts and new seasons of *Iron Chef*, *Good Eats*, and Ming's, Tyler's, and Bobby's series were part of an official "relaunch" of the network set for June 1999. For many of those hired over the past two years—Eric, Eileen, Bruce, Bob, and Heidi among them—it felt like a launch. They had never seen Reese barking orders, or Robin

Leach stumbling onto a set drunk, or an explosion in Kitchen Central. A former stripper no longer kept the books. The first show of the relaunch was a special episode of *Emeril Live*, taped in front of a thousand people in Chicago. Despite all the changes, Emeril was still the king—and he knew it. In one 1999 broadcast, he led off the show saying, "I'm Emeril Lagasse—in case you just landed on the planet."

Reviewers had mixed reactions to the new shows. Most loved *Iron Chef*, though a reviewer for Toronto's *The Globe and Mail* found Alton Brown's *Good Eats* vapid, writing, "It's hard to believe hungry viewers can be any wiser about good eating after half an hour spent in the company of a comedian who defines steer as 'basically a bull that's been . . . well, let's say that they don't make much time with the ladies.'"

Rick Marin, a trend reporter for *The New York Times*, took a longer view—whether or not the shows were good, people were talking about them, and that was new. When he asked the Food Network spokesperson to explain how chefs had managed to rise in the pop culture pantheon, Heidi extolled the sex appeal of her male stars. She referred to them as "hunks" and then immediately coined a term for the phenomenon of chef-hunk: "Really, you could call them 'Chunks.'"

Wrote Marin, "The chef-hunk—'chunk,' if you will—is visible on almost every other page of Bobby Flay's latest cookbook, *Boy Meets Grill* . . . Recipes aren't the only things viewers request, said Heidi Diamond, senior vice president of marketing. 'Indecent proposals' are not uncommon, she said. 'They're passionate about these cute-boy chefs for a variety of reasons,' she said. 'Food is so sensual. There's something magic about these people's hands and the way that they caress a knife or handle a naked potato.'"

Next Heidi got *People* magazine to profile Ming Tsai in its "Most Sexy" issue:

It's that playful smile—in addition to his five-peppercorn grilled steak, Asian gazpacho, and Jasmine tea soufflé—that leaves fans of the Food Network's Emmy-winning *East Meets West* with Ming Tsai hungry for more . . . "I don't think of myself as a true celebrity,

like Ricky Martin or George Clooney," he says. Perhaps not. But
Tsai can do something neither of those guys can: deliver both the
sizzle and the steak.

By mid-1999 Food Network was on the air in about 40 million homes,
making it one of the rare start-up networks to find a toehold in the
national cable lineup. About 67 million homes subscribed to cable television. In the fourth quarter of 1998, the network averaged a 0.3 rating.
That meant roughly 130,000 homes, an increase of 50 percent from the
previous year, were tuned in at any given time. Advertising revenues
were up 80 percent to $36 million.

Ken and others at Scripps thought that they would be able to quickly
improve the bottom line at Food Network by using their track record
with HGTV to convince cable providers to start paying subscriber fees.
They were wrong. Cable operators who had been carrying Food were
happy to continue paying nothing until around 2003, when the original
agreements negotiated under Reese and his immediate predecessors ex-
pired. DirecTV was the first to pay a few cents a month for Food, starting in 1997, but that was only after the network kicked back $7.6 million
in "launch incentive and advertising fees" to close the satellite deal, according to filings made with the Securities and Exchange Commission.

For new providers, Ken and his deputy, Susan Packard, offered to
bundle HGTV and Food Network together for a package price. The
price wasn't much higher than it had been for HGTV alone, a few pennies at best, but at least it cemented a practice of cable providers paying something for Food. The idea was that in the future it would be
easier to ratchet fees up from two cents to five than from zero cents to
anything.

Although Tryg and others who shaped the original TVFN business
plan had hoped to find a dependable second revenue source beyond
advertising, they never had. The magazine, food brands, and Couponix
that Jack, Joe, and Tryg had imagined had not been developed. Blame a

combination of never-ending management and ownership turmoil, the exigencies of the original rush to put out a signal, an ongoing inability to step back and think strategically, and the fact that no one else was exactly stepping forward and offering to start a magazine or a brand of chocolate bars with a financially troubled brand. Bobby and Mario's restaurants were booming, Emeril's spices were selling, but the network had not figured out how to extract its cut. As a result, the Food Network gambit had become to keep the business painfully trim but ticking, trusting that it would teeter slowly into profit someday, at which time it could begin to grow more vigorously.

Food Network did survive, but the model was frustrating. For years, the network's executives had to go to its owners, whoever they happened to be at the time, begging for every significant expenditure, a few hundred thousand for *Two Fat Ladies*, a few for a new logo, a few more to try *Emeril Live*. Even if the network was marginally earning more than it spent by 1999, it had not earned back its start-up costs. On paper it was still in the red, and Reese, for one, had not started receiving dividends.

He was not happy with the new owners. First, Reese became concerned that Scripps was going to make drastic changes in the advertising department where he still had friends. Under the name of his holding company Pacesetter, he sent threatening letters to Scripps. In one, dated August 17, 1999, he announced that Pacesetter would resist the company's attempts to move the advertising traffic department from New York to Knoxville and asserted that HGTV's ad salespeople were illegally selling spots to national advertisers that were supposed to be reserved for local cable providers to sell on their own.

Ken tersely replied, ". . . we fail to see how Pacesetter can 'resist' moving the Food Network traffic function or why we need to report to you or convince you of anything related to HGTV."

After an angry meeting in early September between Reese, Ken, another Scripps executive, and Eric Ober, Reese filed for an injunction on September 24, 1999, to prevent the move of the advertising traffic department. Reese's lawyers offered as evidence the claim that Scripps had already "defrauded" the ABC television network "through a similar scheme. If Food Network's national advertisers are defrauded in this manner, the damage to the reputation, goodwill, and profitability of Food Network and its investors, including Pacesetter, will be irreparable and incalculable." The matter was settled without court action, but then through a clerical error, Reese got his hands on an internal Scripps strategy document, which said that the company intended to leave Food alone to teeter forward with little new investment until they were sure that HGTV was officially profitable.

Reese did not realize how close HGTV was to black ink. To hell with it, he thought. Who knows when that will be. He was tired of waiting for profits and decided to get whatever he could right then for his stake.

The CEO of Scripps, Bill Burleigh, a news industry veteran like Reese, met with him to discuss a buyout man to man. Basic terms were agreed to, but as negotiations were wrapping up, Eric received a call from a Scripps executive in Cincinnati. Reese had a special request he wanted included in the deal. "He wants two tickets to every *Emeril Live* taping," the executive said. "Is that okay? Can that be worked out?"

Eric laughed. *Emeril* tickets were at a premium. There was a lottery for seats. Tom Brokaw's daughter had called him personally to request tickets. But Eric understood how these things went. The ducats would allow Reese to demonstrate he still was somebody at Food Network.

"That's fine," Eric told the Scripps man. "We can always give him two tickets."

On December 16, 1999, a Scripps press release announced: "The E.W. Scripps company has increased its controlling stake in the Food Network by acquiring the 5 percent share held by Pacesetter Communications, Inc."

Scripps now owned 64 percent of the network. Terms of the sale of Reese's stake were not publicly disclosed, but it is believed the total paid to Pacesetter was between $10 and $20 million.

Eric was surprised Reese had taken so little. When he eventually found out the approximate price, Eric did the math—$10 or $20 million for 5 percent meant Reese was accepting a valuation of between $200 and $400 million for the entire network. Eric believed the network's prospects were bright and it was worth far more.

Reese got two-thirds of the price himself after paying off those he had cut in at the start. He sent George Babick around $700,000. He also sent checks to Sue Huffman, the original head of programming; Connie Simmons, Reese's executive assistant and lawyer; and Stephen Cunningham, the ProJo consultant who had brought Reese aboard. Steve got $1.5 million. As Steve remembered the transaction, it was only around this time that Joe Langhan came forward suggesting that Steve consider cutting a check to him for a small portion of the proceeds. Steve talked it over with his wife. Joe had hired Steve in the first place, and it did not seem fair that the man who had done more to start the network than anyone else should receive nothing from this sale. Steve's wife wasn't so sure at first, but told her husband that if he thought it was the right thing to do, he ought to do it. Reese did not contribute, but a check was cut to Joe for around $200,000.

New York charities did well in the deal. For years, Reese and Pat could be counted on to donate a pair of *Emeril Live* tickets to benefit auctions.

On August 10, 1999, Jennifer Patterson, the spectacled half of *Two Fat Ladies*, died of cancer. Heidi phoned Eric with the news. Food Network had made Jennifer famous in America. "We have to do something," she said.

He sent Heidi to England. "I'm dispatching you like the president dispatches the vice president," Eric said. "You're on funeral duty."

> "Turned out to be perhaps the most foolish financial move I ever made . . . If I'd hung around long enough, they would've made me very rich. As it is I did fine, but it's just a matter of impatience."
>
> **—REESE SCHONFELD**

The funeral was as bombastic as Jennifer. Her casket was preceded by pallbearers carrying her motorcycle helmet.

Back in New York, Eric met with Eileen. *Two Fat Ladies* was still one of the network's highest-rated prime-time shows. Eric wanted the show to continue, death be damned. "You know, it's like Menudo!" Eric said, referring to the popular Mexican boy band that retired members when they reached puberty and replaced them with new boys. "Why don't we find another fat lady and just make it the *Two Fat Ladies* again?"

Eileen was appalled. She had known Jennifer and Clarissa since she'd worked at the BBC. "We can't do that!" she protested.

Eric was dispassionately calculating: Hits are hard to come by. "Well, why don't you call the producers and find out?" he pushed. "Because I'm sorry she's dead, but there's no reason not to try to continue the show."

Eileen stopped protesting, but she ignored Eric's order and he did not bring it up again. With Reese on his way out of the picture, Scripps was promising to loosen the purse strings, trusting that they would be able to wrest Food from its troubled path into the sunlight of the Scripps way.

Even without new episodes of *Two Fat Ladies*, the network's cultural cachet was rising. More than one teenager in the late 1990s was indulging in the after-school habit of grabbing a bag of chips and watching Food Network after school. There they would sit, shoveling Doritos in their mouths while imagining that they were actually eating ravioli with sage, flourless chocolate cakes, and colorful fizzy cocktails. Food Network was small enough to still be cool, and you didn't have to hide it like porn.

The ongoing road show overseen by Joe Allegro and Rich Gore, rebranded as Food Network Live, was profitable and drawing crowds at its stops around the country. Tyler, Sissy, Mario, Boggs, Emeril, and Ming were all making regular appearances, each pulling in a few thousand dollars a night and selling stacks of cookbooks along the way.

Even with the debuts of *Iron Chef* and all the other new shows, the cultural cachet was only rising so far. Food was still a minor cable player at best. When Eric pulled Joe and Rich into his office and demanded to know why they were still featuring PBS stars on the road shows, Joe explained that they needed them to sell tickets. He showed Eric a marketing survey that showed only 17 percent of households had ever heard of Food Network.

The network president didn't want to hear it. "Meeting's over," he said, furious.

Eric had been doing his best to professionalize the operation. He saw the old F.O.R. hierarchy as antithetical to a serious enterprise. He had rooted out nepotism in previous jobs, and managed to force Reese's wife, Pat, out of the network, despite her contributions, by not assigning her to any new productions. A $5 million marketing campaign debuted in the late fall of 1999, timed roughly to coincide with the network's sixth anniversary. Heidi put together the media, which included "Let's Talk Turkey" ads in newspapers and bus shelters, over an image of a well-fed bird and the lines "Great legs, tender breasts. Recipes, menus, and more at foodtv.com."

Nevertheless, Eric got a rude taste of the disdain held for the network by one person in the lifestyle TV establishment during an uncomfortable meeting with Martha Stewart. The Food Network had negotiated with Martha to buy the rights to thousands of her old daytime shows, which they could strip the cooking segments from and assemble into half-hour blocks to run late at night, early on weekends, or wherever they might fit. It was a good deal for both parties. Martha and her company would make a few million dollars for old content and the Food Network would get thousands of hours of evergreen shows for a low per-hour cost.

In the final meeting at Martha's offices, the lifestyle queen let her representatives shuffle the papers around as she stood facing the opposite direction, alternately looking out a window and poking at her mobile phone. When it came time to sign, she strode to the table, signed the papers, and strode out of the room without gracing Eric or his team with a handshake or even a glance.

Eric turned to his Food Network lawyer and said, only half joking, "The only other thing I want in this agreement is I don't ever want to have to see that woman again for the life of the contract."

Like most of the others who had been at the network since before Scripps bought it, Matt had been worried about the corporate parent draining the network of pizazz. Eileen assured him it wasn't going to be so bad, and they'd proved it with *Iron Chef* and *Good Eats*. As Matt and Alton worked together to make *Good Eats* even funnier, they grew closer. They joked about both being "smart nerds" and shared recommendations about favorite books of philosophy. Matt and his mom sewed a pink and blue quilt for Alton's daughter Zooey when she was born. Alton confided in Matt that he hoped they could someday make an episode of *Good Eats* in which Alton's grandmother would show how she prepared biscuits. It would be a love letter to "MaMae," who had helped raise Alton after his father's suicide.

Matt and his brother Daniel were cast in two episodes of the second season of *Good Eats*. Matt played a scientist and Daniel a physicist. They sat on a roof with Alton talking about chicken bones.

But with Matt now appearing on camera and seeing good ratings coming in for *Iron Chef*, his baby, his sense of his own genius was starting to grow out of proportion. Eileen hadn't meant to, but, not unlike a mad scientist, by coming to depend on Matt, she had tinkered with something unstable and was in danger of creating a monster. The success went where it often goes in a brain untempered by age: straight to the ego. Matt was walking tall, sure that he knew best and that whatever he touched would turn golden.

Eric Ober was planning to address the entire staff of the Food Network at a party to celebrate the results of the relaunch. To inspire the troops, he wanted to focus on a particularly hard worker. He asked Eileen who he should shower praise on.

She asked him to give it to her project, Matt.

And so in the ballroom of a glittery Times Square hotel in front of the entire staff of the network, Eric singled out Matt, the upstart he'd once thought of as a little shit. "I just want you all to know that a lot of the success of Food right now comes from the effort and dedication of one young man, Matthew Stillman," Eric declared, raising a glass. "This is the golden boy of Food Network."

The applause rang for a long time in Matt's ears.

You Reap
What You Sow

When *Iron Chef*'s ratings doubled the network average, Ken admitted that he'd been wrong about the Japanese show and that Eric had been right to approve it. In New York he told Eileen, "Hey, that's great stuff, keep on doing your magic." But overall he was less thrilled with the pace of progress at Food. Back in Knoxville, Scripps's head of investor relations was reporting to him that big stockholders were perplexed at the direction the company was taking by pouring money into a cable network that might—might—earn profits in three or four years. When Ken would be trotted out to face the investors, they'd pepper him with questions about low subscriber fees. "What are you going to do, young man, if this doesn't work?" one asked Ken, then in his late forties.

Criticism came from all directions. He and his corporate colleague Ed Spray were still hearing from cable operators about the quality of most of the programming, and from some of the internal people at the network about the squalid state of the facilities. Ken agreed with most of it. Before Scripps bought majority ownership of Food, when Ken was on the road trying to sell HGTV to cable operators, the operators argued that they only had room for one lifestyle channel and Food Network was free. Ken's comeback about the competition and its low-budget content was, "Well, yeah, it's free, but it's not good."

Now that Food Network was a Scripps property, the corporation's head of distribution, Susan Packard, was out on the road trying to squeeze subscriber fees out of operators, promising, "We're going to fix this thing, we're going to make it a network you can be proud of."

But the network had not changed enough in the year or so Scripps had owned it, and Ken yearned to deliver results fast to quash skeptics. He started chumming with the talent, seeking to understand kitchen culture. This could be tougher work than it seemed. Drinking ouzo with Mario Batali into the wee hours yields regret upon waking. After a long night of wine and feasting at Emeril's house in New Orleans during a Super Bowl weekend, Ken woke with a pounding headache while Emeril was already out doing morning television. But Ken was learning. And plans were made for new, better spaces for the headquarters and the kitchens in New York, even if they would be temporary.

Ken's ideas for the network began to collide with Eric's. Eric had spent time prior to his Food stint working in Knoxville, but he was still far more a product of his two decades at *CBS News*, a sacrosanct division that corporate usually left alone. Scripps preferred to deal with the press carefully, routing reporters' calls through its corporate public relations department. Eric, who seemed to know every journalist in New York, answered their calls directly and gave on-the-record quotes without corporate permission.

Often when Eric did ask superiors for approval for a move he intended to make, he was not always gracious about it. In one case, Eric had an idea to buy broadcast rights for food-related movies, everything from *Eating Raoul*, a comedy about a couple trying to make money to open a restaurant by robbing and killing swingers, to *Tom Jones*, a period drama with a famously lusty feast scene. The movies would be hosted by one of Eric's favorite Food Network personalities, David Rosengarten, who would cook a meal leading into and out of commercial breaks. All together, the show would take up a three-hour programming block on Sunday nights where ratings had been languishing. When Eric presented it to Ken and Ed Spray for a final sign-off, he considered it a mere formality. He explained that with good films, they could sell the commercial time at a premium. The rights were cheap and they could air the films as many times as Food Network wanted.

Ed shook his head. "No."

Eric was flabbergasted. "Why wouldn't we do this?" he asked roughly. "We could make money. It's unique programming. What's the down-side?"

Ken signaled to Ed who said, "It's not the spirit of the Food Network to do movies," explaining that this was not the vision Scripps had for its channels.

Eric thought, "What the fuck is he saying?" and began to formulate a theory that Ed had it out for him personally. Before Scripps, Ed had worked at *CBS News* under Eric. But Eric had never promoted him to general manager of a local station, a coveted job, because Eric didn't think Ed was leadership material. Eric found it infuriating that this former underling whom he'd viewed as a wimp now had power over him. After the meeting, he asked Ken, "What really happened there?"

"Well," Ken replied. "Ed really doesn't believe in it."

Ed. What did Ed know?

The Scripps team had been pressuring Eric to get rid of those who they thought would never mesh with their corporate culture. They did not like Heidi's bawdy way of doing things—breasts and legs! Not Mid-western family-friendly! Nor, despite what they said to her face, were they enamored of Eileen Opatut, the head of programming, associating her with the wild pre-Scripps days and noting how ill at ease she'd been in Tennessee. She had not gotten into the spirit of the hootenanny. But Eric refused to let either of them go.

With HGTV edging into the black, Ken steered the company's money behind Food. In 2000, Scripps planned a 30 percent increase in spending on the network. Eric had been a great choice to mollify the troops at 1177 Avenue of the Americas—a New Yorker who understood the energy of the place and allowed the creative people to experiment. But now his occasional surliness and go-it-alone attitude was leading those around Ken to think that Eric was in danger of violating some-thing Ken shared with very few people outside Knoxville: the no-assholes rule. Ken did not want to work with people he defined as assholes—non-team players common in the media world who tried to make their marks by stepping on the backs of others in their ambitious scrambles. Ken tried not to hire them, and if one got in, he disposed of the offender quickly. Eric, who was secure with what he'd achieved in his career, was well liked by those below him, but those above him in Knoxville, while they did not think he violated the no-asshole rule, recognized that he saw himself as his own man, not a prized Scrippsian trait.

There was a potential replacement waiting in the wings. Soon after Scripps bought Food Network, and as it was preparing to launch a spin-off to HGTV, the DIY Network, Ed had suggested that Ken hire his friend Judy Girard to consult on programming across Scripps's existing and proposed cable channels. Judy had made her name as the top programming executive at Lifetime, where she was known for adept scheduling. She had helped develop the channel's flagship original movies-of-the-week, though some TV critics derided them as "women-in-peril" films: the main character was always having her baby stolen or being stalked by a deranged ex-con who had seemed so nice on their first date.

After she left Lifetime and then a telecom start-up, Judy took a break to consider her next step. She was taking a walk on the beach near her home in Los Angeles when Ken called and offered her a job working on Food's programming. Ken's pitch was that he was giving her the opportunity to be at the start of something big.

Judy had just left two high-pressure jobs and wasn't interested in eighty-hour weeks anymore. She told Ken she would maybe think about it.

"Judy, you and I both know, if you pass on this, you're never going to forgive yourself because you're too interested. Go walk on the beach tonight and let's talk tomorrow."

They both knew he'd set the hook. "I hate you," Judy said. "I want this decision behind me."

"I'm not going to let you put it behind you," Ken said.

Ken told her she could start slow. She would not have to work long hours and could stay in Los Angeles. If she liked Scripps and they liked her, there might be more opportunities. She accepted, and became Scripps's senior vice president of programming and content development in August 1998. After Judy consulted primarily on DIY for a year and got used to the culture—and did not seem to be an asshole—Ed asked her to move to New York to work full-time on Food as a programming and scheduling consultant.

Ken explained to her that Food was not Lifetime. He thought Lifetime spoke down to women by appealing to their fears. There would be no women-in-peril nonsense at Food Network. It was certainly aimed at women, but it had to appeal to them the same way HGTV did, with dignity. "This is about grabbing women's attention, and saying, 'Hey, we get you.' Okay?" Ken said. "There are certain things about Lifetime that don't appeal to women. Being told that it's a network for women doesn't appeal to women."

That said, Food was not another HGTV either. Some New York sass was okay. "I want a completely separate brand here," he instructed. "I want the graphics to look different. I want it to pop. But you're gonna have to walk a little bit of a fine line here, Judy, because this is a Midwestern company."

Eric didn't think he needed a consultant looking over his shoulder: He had Eileen and her growing programming team—Bruce Seidel, Bob Tuschman, Kathleen Finch, and others. Judy did have some ideas Eric agreed with—the Martha Stewart deal was her initiative—but she did not like David Rosengarten and didn't think he was attractive or smooth enough for TV. "Why is he on the air?" she asked Eric more than once.

"Because he's smart and he's interesting," Eric responded.

He came to view Judy as a corporate suck-up with strange habits. She chomped carrots compulsively like grizzled newspaper editors used to work cigars. She had gone to a renowned Manhattan nutritionist complaining about having a lack of energy, and the doctor prescribed raw vegetable snacks, saying they would give her pep. Every pronouncement she made seemed to be punctuated by the "crunch!" of a vegetable.

Otherwise, she had little love for food. At business lunches, she ordered a plain hamburger on a bun adorned only with ketchup.

Eric also noticed how she punctuated certain statements by turning her palms up, as if signaling that she wanted to be inclusive. Eric had hired performance coaches for on-air reporters and he detected coaching in this gesture. It was all a show, he thought.

Judy called Knoxville every single day. And in those calls, Ed would reveal to her his frustrations with Eric: He was spending money without permission, bucking personnel decisions, and yakking to the press. Eric believed too much in food news. His Food Network reminded Ed of Reese's TVFN: CNN with stoves.

Seeing the growing tension between Eric and Scripps, Heidi Diamond sensed changes on the horizon. She believed that her years of experience at cable starts-ups and her success at producing marketing miracles on almost no budget at Food entitled her to be considered for the top job at the network. Heidi found an opportunity to make her case to Ken, suggesting that if Eric left, she should be elevated.

He told her he was open to the idea, but he knew he was not going to make that move. Judy was being eased into Scripps; Heidi never had a chance.

In January 2000, Ken was named president and chief operating officer of E.W. Scripps Co., the parent in Cincinnati. In just a few years, cable television revenues had grown from nearly nothing to 18 percent of E.W. Scripps's revenues. His baby HGTV was in 61.7 million homes. Food had expanded into 47.3 million, its annual revenues were up 60 percent to $66.6 million, and it had become profitable a year earlier than Scripps had projected. Even with the success, Ken knew he would have less time for day-to-day involvement in Food Network and wanted to make sure it was in trustworthy hands. Eric had brought order to the chaos, but now it was time to install a true loyalist at the top. Ken felt that Judy understood his thinking so well she completed his sentences.

On Eric's last day, Ken asked him to come to the network-wide meeting where they would announce that Judy was being put in charge. Eric refused. He knew that people he had protected would be fired, and he didn't want to smile and pretend he liked it.

"Make up whatever bullshit you want," he told Ken, "But I don't want to be there. That would be endorsing her, and I'm not going to endorse her."

When Judy heard Eric was not coming, she went to his office and told him she was sorry about how it had all played out.

"You reap what you sow," he said.

Before he left Food Network headquarters on his last evening, Eric dropped an autographed photo of himself on each desk as if to say, "Remember me. Remember when times were good."

> "If the only way I'm going to keep a job is kissing ass, I don't want to keep the job. Life's too short. If you don't like it, fire me. But don't be unhappy because I don't call you every day with gossip."
>
> —ERIC OBER

Through the changes of the first seven years, one show had held on, the news broadcast first called *Food News and Views* and later *In Food Today*, airing in 2000 daily at 5:30 p.m. When Bob Tuschman came in as producer, he had lightened the show; policy debates on farm subsidies were out; "A Salute to American Food" was in. A chef showed Donna Hanover how to skewer a corn dog with a chopstick.

Offstage, Donna's marriage was disintegrating in very public fashion. The city's tabloid newspapers were filled with gossip suggesting that her husband, Mayor Rudy Giuliani, was having an affair with his director of communications, Cristyne Lategano. In May 1999, Lategano resigned from City Hall and later married a sportswriter. But Donna and Rudy's problems persisted. One time network staff heard Donna through the walls of a conference room screaming at Rudy on the phone. The makeup department learned to wait for the mother of two to stop crying before getting her ready for the cameras.

In the spring of 2000, the mayor was spotted at public events with a new female companion he'd met at a cigar bar, Judith Nathan. It all famously exploded on Wednesday, May 10, 2000, when Mayor Giuliani, locked in a U.S. Senate race against Hillary Clinton and having revealed days earlier that he was being treated for prostate cancer, decided to come clean. At a press conference in Bryant Park, he announced that he and his wife were splitting: "I, um, this is very, very painful. For quite some time I, it's probably been apparent that Donna and I lead, in many ways, independent and separate lives . . ."

Donna was unprepared for the announcement. When the press showed up at Food, Heidi Diamond snuck her out a side entrance. Outside Gracie Mansion, Donna gathered herself enough to tell the press, "Beginning last May, I made a major effort to bring us back together. Rudy and I reestablished some of our personal intimacy through the fall. At that point he chose another path . . ."

One day, Susannah Eaton-Ryan found her crying in a hallway. "I'm really sorry," Donna said. "I really cared about my marriage and this is very hard for me."

But Donna's public divorce did not doom the show. Rather, it was done in by Judy's dislike of it and of cohost David Rosengarten. Just before Eric Ober left Food, he had told David, "You have a Judy problem."

He also had an Eileen Opatut problem. She was doing her best to see eye-to-eye with her new boss. Eileen called David "the thespian" when she'd see him around the network—"Oh! It's the thespian!" She'd never been a fan of *Taste*. David tried a lot of wacky gimmicks, none of which were to Eileen's taste. In the final segment of a show he once did about California salads, he sat at a table eating a Cobb salad and wearing sunglasses as the production staff shook the whole set to simulate an earthquake until it came crashing down. She also thought that *In Food Today* was looking increasingly chintzy, and did not see the point of spending to improve a 5:30 p.m. show when she could invest in prime time instead.

David remained convinced that he was part of the bedrock of the channel. He decided to use his proven charms to win Judy over—food and schmooze. David managed to entice her to lunch at Estiatorio Milos, a fancy Greek place in Midtown where the Mediterranean scent of fresh crusty bread, grilled fish, and lamb usually soothed the most cantankerous soul. It didn't do much for Judy. David started talking about ideas he had for new shows.

"You know," Judy said after listening for a spell, "you seem obsessed with having a TV show."

"I'm not obsessed," David said, flummoxed. "This is what I've been doing for the last seven or eight years of my life. I just want to discuss with you the—"

Judy cut him off: "Why are you always talking about shows? You should think about something else sometime."

David stopped talking. This isn't going well, he thought.

Judy and Eileen tried to ease David into the realization that his time at Food Network was coming to an end. But he did not want to take the hints—until a meeting was scheduled for him with Judy, Eileen, and Bob Tuschman. Nervous and wanting to be prepared, he went into Bob's office the day before. "What's this meeting about tomorrow?" David asked.

"Oh, I don't know. I think they just want to talk about the future of the show." Bob may not have agreed with Judy that David could not work on television, but he did agree that the era of high-falutin' food talk aimed at a narrow audience was coming to a close. He and other newer executives at Food Network were extolling "accessible" programming like *Iron Chef* and *Emeril Live*, hits that worked the trick of making food shows palatable to a broad audience who might never make their own chocolate mousse.

David well knew that Emeril was king, and he had been warned by Eric and all but told by Judy that his days were numbered, but his ego was impregnable. *Taste* was not in a cycle of production at the time, but David had been the dependable in-house go-to man for everything since the moment the network flickered to life on November 23, 1993.

Seven years of good luck and high status in the food world he loved had followed.

"Uh-huh," David replied, "you sure that I'm not walking into a mugging here?"

"No! No, no! It's not a mugging," Bob assured him.

David didn't entirely trust him and figured he would adapt, simply finding an idea for an "accessible" show—perhaps a spin on *Taste* as he'd done a few years earlier with *Taste of the Orient*.

The next day at the meeting, Judy got to the point. "We're going to cancel *In Food Today*."

David pivoted. "Okay! Well, that's fine, because I've got a couple of other shows that I'm really eager to work on and talk over—" Eileen broke in. "No, no, no. I don't think you understand. We're actually not going to work with you anymore."

David looked at Bob, who was staring at a corner of the room. Judy was the boss, and he and Eileen both wanted to survive in the new regime. They had been around the TV business long enough to know that cancellations are always hard to break to the talent, but every show ends. There was nothing anyone could have said to make things any easier for David. Better to look away as the killing cut was made.

Donna, however, understood more about the business, and had sensed for months that the show might be on the way out. In the midst of dealing with her dying marriage, she had been pursuing other options, doing guest stints as a morning host on local channel 5's *Good Day New York* and talking with production companies. Eventually, she landed a gig hosting an A&E design show, *House Beautiful*.

David did not land another show. He met with Erica Gruen, who sympathized with how unfair it was. "What a crazy thing in the TV business," she said, "to build somebody up for seven years and then just cancel the franchise."

As Judy prepared to make other drastic and difficult changes, a gift arrived. One day in late 1999, before Judy took over, Eileen Opatut called Bobby Flay with some news.

"I got this phone call," she said. "I wasn't even going to tell you about it, but I feel like I have to. Fuji Television called because they were look-ing for you, and they thought they could find you here. They want to come to the United States, and they want to challenge an American chef, and Tim Zagat [copublisher of the Zagat restaurant rating guides] told them that you are the quintessential American chef. I'm sure you don't want to do this."

Bobby had been a fan of *Iron Chef* even before it debuted on Food Network. In the mid-1990s, he'd watched it in Japanese at 3 a.m after he got home from Mesa Grill. He loved competing in any game he had a chance of winning and he understood the mythic quality of the show. He would be defending his home territory, New York. This was epic.

"Give me the number," he said.

He called Fuji. They explained that they were bringing the whole circus to New York for a special battle. Four Iron Chefs would be in attendance, and, if he accepted the challenge, he would be cooking against Iron Chef Japanese, Masaharu Morimoto, who happened to be living in New York at the time. Did Bobby want in?

He was way in. "Tell me what you need from me."

Weeks before the scheduled battle, a crew of around fifty began ar-riving from Japan. They stayed at the Kitano Hotel on Park Avenue, and dozens of them showed up at Mesa Grill every night, tasting the food and asking Bobby what ingredients he used and where to buy them. Fuji had rented out the downtown nightclub Webster Hall to stage the battle. Soon the Chairman and the four Iron Chefs joined the entourage in New York.

The coming together of the Iron Chefs at the Kitano in the spring of 2000 was not unlike the gathering of little people at the Culver Hotel in Hollywood in the fall of 1938 for the filming of the Munchkin scenes in *The Wizard of Oz*. According to legend, dozens of the cast members drank heavily, swung from chandeliers, and engaged in bacchanalia. In an infamous TV interview years later, Judy Garland professed that one of the diminutive actors asked her on a date.

Kaga stayed in character as the Chairman at all times, on camera and off. From the moment he emerged from his hotel room, he was in his shining bejeweled cape and his hair was pomaded into the Dracula-on-steroids pompadour he wore on the show. When he spoke, even if it was to ask for someone to pass the soy sauce for his breakfast bento box, he did so in the same booming voice he used for the character.

Heidi saw a big promotional opportunity in the *Iron Chef* cast and lined up a full schedule of media interviews and photo shoots. She also dispatched a young Food Network public relations assistant, Amy Voll, to mind the visitors.

The very first morning, Amy called Heidi from the chefs' hotel suite and stammered, "They're all drunk! They're smashed. They're beyond, they're just totally drunk!" At breakfast, the Iron Chefs had quaffed sake and devoured bento boxes of sushi, yakitori, and sashimi. They were speaking Japanese, so Amy did not understand what they were saying, but sensed from their throaty laughter that they were telling dirty stories. They occasionally cast a long glance her way.

Amy typically wore formfitting jeans and a tight T-shirt to work. On the second morning at breakfast, Amy found herself standing not far from Honorary Iron Chef Japanese Michiba, the eldest of the Iron Chefs. Michiba was known for cooking with a strongly flavored stock of dried skipjack tuna and kelp, called in Japanese *Inochi no Dashi*, and, in English, Broth of Vigor. Apparently, his famous broth was keeping him in working order. Amy heard the sixty-nine-year-old say something in Japanese which sounded like "humm, huuuuuh, hoooo," and then he lunged at her, grabbing her rear end. Amy, horrified, stepped back. Michiba attacked from the front and grabbed at her breasts. It looked to her as if he intended to twist them like old radio dials.

Amy swatted his hands away and fled from the room, shocked and upset. She was a professional and understood how much had been invested in the Iron Chefs' visit. She was trying to mind these esteemed visitors and now one of them had molested her. Amy phoned Heidi again. "Oh, my God, I can't believe this just happened!" she sobbed. "What am I going to do?"

Heidi told her to get out of there. Back at the office, Amy met with Ken, who was in New York for the Iron Chef visit. He told her he would order the entire shoot and publicity campaign shut down if that was what she wanted. He put no pressure on her to continue with her work.

"No," Amy said. "Anytime you halt production, it costs money." She told Ken the show must go on. Although she went back to minding the chefs, including Michiba, from then on she was never alone with them. Another assistant was assigned to stick by her side and step in if any of the chefs tried to demonstrate their vigor again.

The night came for the big battle. Gordon Elliott was the master of ceremonies. Judges included Tim Zagat and Donna Hanover. Bobby's adrenaline was pumping and his mother and girlfriend were in the audience (he and Robin "Kate" Connelly had split).

At the top of the show, the Iron Chefs who were not competing, including Michiba, hit their marks and stood regally as smoke machines set a dramatic billowy background. The Chairman bit a pepper and the secret ingredient descended from the ceiling of the dance club in a disco ball. Before it was low enough to see, Bobby smelled shellfish, recognized it as lobster or crab (it was rock crab), and started thinking about how to prepare it. He quickly formulated his menu. Four dishes: crab and scallops in cilantro sauce; crab and avocado salad in a coconut shell; spicy saffron soup; and a potato and crab cake. About five minutes into the battle, Bobby was so hyped, he stuck his hand into a food processor. It was not running, but he cut his thumb badly.

I don't fucking believe this, he thought. He wrapped his hand in a towel and continued to cook as best he could with one hand.

Twenty minutes later, Bobby felt water at his ankles. The sinks were leaking. He saw the wires to the ovens running through the water. When he put his hands on a stainless steel table, an electric current shot through him and vibrated hard in his cut thumb, throwing him back. At first, he did not realize what had happened, and thought the shock was a sign that he'd severed a nerve.

When his assistant chefs discovered that electricity was running through the kitchen station, they wanted to walk off the set.

Bobby, red hair standing on end, thumb throbbing, commanded,

"We're not fucking going anywhere. This is it. We have forty minutes to finish these dishes, let's go!"

On the other side, Morimoto and his two assistants were busily constructing five dishes: crab brain dip; rock crabs grilled in seaweed; crab rice in sour soup; a double hors d'oeuvre of claw meat in bean paste along with crab and asparagus with mint; and Japanese crab salad.

The crowd was chanting. Those from outside New York yelling, "Mo-ri-mo-to!" those from the city, "Here we go, Bob-by, here we go!" With just seconds to spare, Bobby and his team finished.

"It's the Comeback Kid!" Tim Zagat cried, the pride of a New Yorker in his bellow. As the clock reached zero, Bobby's sous chefs lifted him up and he stood on a cutting board. Bobby could barely breathe. His mother was crying. His thumb felt like it was hanging by a thread, and his body was reeling from the shock. The judging was still to come, but he lifted his arms up in joy. "Raise the roof, yo!" he yelled. "Raise the roof!"

A reporter walked over to Morimoto and asked, "How did you do?"

"I did my best."

"And, what about your competitor?"

"He's no chef."

"What?" she asked, as if mishearing.

"He's no chef."

"Why?"

"He stood on the cutting board. In Japan the cutting board is sacred to us."

Bobby lost in a unanimous vote, and the cutting board incident sparked an international scandal because Japan's national pride had been offended. The media loved it. Within days of the show's airing in June, CNN, *Newsweek*, *The New York Times*, and the *New York Post* ran stories casting Bobby as the bad guy for breaching international cutting board etiquette—something that before that moment no one knew existed. *Time* magazine called Bobby "a big whiner."

As far as Judy was concerned, six months into her tenure, Bobby, in one stroke, had drawn more attention to the network than all the other celebrity chefs, even Emeril, had in years of trying. In 1999, about 84,000 households tuned in to Food at any given hour; a year later 1.5 million viewers watched the Flay-Morimoto battle. By that October, the network was available in 52 million homes and was projecting annual advertising revenue to reach a record $91 million.

"You took it on the chin for us," she told Bobby. "I will never forget this. You have changed the Food Network."

That fall, Bobby was in his office at Mesa Grill and heard his assistant, Stephanie, take a call.

She stuck her head in Bobby's office. "You're not gonna believe this."

"What?"

"It's Fuji Television. They want a rematch. In Tokyo. We're not going."

Yes, they were, Bobby said. Another chance at supremacy.

"Tell them we want six first-class round-trip tickets and we'll be there."

Fuji brought Americans from a military base to cheer for Bobby at Kitchen Stadium, Japan. This time he won.

> "Of course, I had no idea my action would become such a big deal later on. It was my natural reaction to what Bobby did. To me, a cutting board is a place where you prepare food for customers. So stepping on it with shoes is just something I would never do."
>
> —MASAHARU MORIMOTO

Iron Chef exemplified the move away from traditional cooking shows and sober formats. Amidst the flush of success, Judy was following Ken's mandate to make the network more fun and less focused on education. "The more that we can convince people that we're not a cooking channel, the better," Judy told a trade magazine. She also had her favorites and, as David had been, her not-favorites. Sara Moulton—Saint Sara the educator—of *Cooking Live*, Sissy Biggers of *Ready . . . Set . . . Cook!*, Bill Boggs of *Corner Table*, and others knew they were vulnerable.

One of her first decisions was to move *Emeril Live* to 8 p.m. every weeknight, where the most popular show on the network could build an audience that might carry through prime time. Heidi launched a pub-licity campaign: "Emeril at A-T-E."

In order to do this, Bobby's show *Hot Off the Grill*, which aired five nights a week, would have to be moved. Judy, expressing her newfound confidence in Bobby and aware that *Iron Chef* had put Food Network on the cultural map, and made Bobby a star, went to Mesa Grill for lunch to explain what she planned.

"Look," Judy said, "I just want to let you know something. I'm taking your cooking shows out of prime time. I'm putting you in daytime."

"What?" Bobby said. He had fought his way back onto the network. He liked things how they were.

"We're going to do the cooking shows in daytime. I'm going to put more entertainment-driven shows in prime time."

"You're out of your fucking mind. This is the Food Network. People want to see cooking."

"Well, that's what I'm doing," Judy said.

She told him that shows with more entertainment like Alton's *Good Eats* and *Iron Chef* were the type of thing that would be on in prime time from then on.

Bobby liked Alton's show. When Judy first showed him a tape of *Good Eats*, he'd told her, "This is a talented guy. We don't have anybody like this on the network. He's on his own planet." But now she insisted that "dump and stir" cooking shows—the kind that Dione Lucas, Julia Child, the Frugal Gourmet, and others had delivered for nearly half a century on television—would no longer be in prime time.

It meant a lot to Bobby that Judy was taking the time to explain the direction of the network, even though he was losing his evening spot. After all, she wasn't canceling his show. After *Iron Chef*, there was no question that Bobby could be fun or that he'd be a good soldier. He would survive.

Others would not. David's and Donna's heads were already in the bag. Next Judy came for Sissy Biggers, the host of *Ready . . . Set . . . Cook!* Sissy liked her role as a game show host. She liked being on Food

Network Live tours. She liked making appearances on other network morning shows where she was billed as "Food Network's Sissy Biggers."

Then she received a phone call from her agent. "I just got a call from Judy Girard's office. She said there's no reason to come in for a meeting." Judy had assumed Sissy would know what it meant.

"What does that mean?" Sissy asked. She knew, but needed to hear it.

"Judy's taking you off the show."

"Babette," Sissy said, her tone sharpening, "I'm having that meeting. If she wants to take me off the show, she has to do it in person, because I want to see what it's like to be fired twice by the same person, and she'll probably never get to do that again in her career, so why should we deprive ourselves of this opportunity?"

On the train into Manhattan from her home in Connecticut, Sissy thought back a half decade to her time as cohost of a cheerful morning talk show on Lifetime with Marc Summers (the former host of *Double Dare* on Nickelodeon) when Judy was in programming at the network. One day, immediately after a live broadcast of *Biggers and Summers*, Judy called her into a meeting.

Sissy, ebullient from the day's show, walked into Judy's office and complimented her. "I love that suit!"

"You just did your last show."

"Forget what I said about the suit," Sissy responded, keeping her wits despite her disappointment.

Now Sissy steeled herself for another visit to Judy's office by wearing her best outfit, a dark navy skirt-suit that showed her famous legs. When she was shown in, Judy said, "Sissy, I don't think you work on television."

Sissy tried to stay calm. "Judy, you're certainly entitled to your opinion." She told the network chief that *Today* had booked her for a number of upcoming food segments and that she was an integral part of the Food Network's traveling road show. It was the best Sissy had.

It wasn't enough; Judy said she was not going to change her mind.

Sissy was out, but the network still thought there might be an appetite for a food competition show that was more straightforward than

Iron Chef. And the premise of *Ready . . . Set . . . Cook!* was tidy: two chefs with two audience members as assistants, a bag of groceries, and eighteen minutes to make the best meal they could.

Sissy had feared for weeks that she'd be replaced by someone younger and prettier. When Bobby called to tell her he'd heard that her replacement was the host of *Ready . . . Steady . . . Cook!* in the UK, Ainsley Harriott, who was four months older than Sissy, she breathed a sigh of relief.

Judy was more gentle with Curtis Aikens. He had been earning around $200,000 a year for the programs he was still making for the network, including cohosting *Calling All Cooks*, a showcase of recipes from home cooks. When his contract expired, Judy offered him a third of what he'd been getting. Predictably, he said, "No hard feelings," and informed the network he'd be moving on.

Judy flew out to Los Angeles to tell Mary Sue Milliken and Susan Feniger they were finished, too. The name of their show had been changed to *Tamales World Tour*, but to Judy, it was still an instructional show. All together, they'd made four hundred episodes, more than enough to use as reruns if the need arose.

Susan was bummed out, but her girlfriend, Liz Lachman, had always told her, "You just need to do the show and know that at any point it could end. These things come and go."

The day Bill Boggs was told he was out, he left Food Network and walked over to the 21 Club and ordered his favorite: a cheeseburger with grilled onions and a glass of wine. As he sipped his drink in the late afternoon, he stared at the empty booth where a couple of years earlier he had interviewed Deborah Norville for *Corner Table*. He raised his glass and toasted the air.

As the cancellations mounted, so did complaints. What was left of the network's old guard told Judy that something essential was being lost—the world of fine food that Alan Richman and Nina Griscom had presented, the intricacies of French wines David Rosengarten knew so much about. The grousing droned on, but had no effect on Judy.

The cultural change at the network was underscored when it moved

> "I'm a television person, not a food person. So my job was to take it to the next level in building it as a television network. The food thing was secondary to that, it really was. The other point of view is from the foodie point of view of what the network did and didn't do, its effect on food culture, blah blah blah blah blah blah blah."
>
> —JUDY GIRARD

out of 1177 Sixth Avenue to more spacious and modern offices across the avenue at 1180, which had desks for the advertising sales and marketing departments that had previously been relegated off-site. It was more professionally decorated. In-house production and the kitchen moved to professional studios at Fifty-seventh Street and Tenth Avenue, a twenty-five-minute walk away, meaning there were fewer fruit flies, and the executive suites no longer smelled like whatever was being cooked in the central kitchen. *Emeril Live* was shot on the ground floor at the studios, and Sara Moulton, whom Judy found appealing for her simplicity and for the economy of her show, finally got her own permanent *Cooking Live* set that was scaled to her height so she could cook safely. The professional ovens had doors that did not shatter, and more space to cook. The quality of the recipes and the appearance of the finished dishes improved dramatically.

By the spring of 2000, Judy's new programming schedule began taking hold. The programming day was now segregated into three clear parts: straight cooking shows, cooking shows with strong personalities, and cooking as entertainment.

Emeril Live ran at 8 p.m. every weeknight, followed at 9 p.m. by a variety of shows, including *Door Knock Dinners* on Mondays, *Good Eats* on Wednesdays, and *Food 911* on Thursdays. They would in turn be followed by *The Best Of, FoodNation*—the road show following Bobby Flay around the country—and *It's a Surprise!*, in which Marc Summers, Sissy's old partner, would travel around the country helping regular people throw surprise parties.

She put *Hot Off the Grill*, Ming Tsai's *East Meets West*, and *Molto Mario* in late-afternoon/early-evening slots known as "Early Fringe," with *From Martha's Kitchen*—cooking segments strung together from the purchased Martha Stewart shows. She populated the morning with straightforward cooking shows that cost the network almost nothing: Julia Child, *The Galloping Gourmet*, and archived episodes of Sara's *Cooking Live* and Curtis's *Pick of the Day*. Overnight hours generally featured long infomercials that allowed advertising salesmen to collect the kind of commissions that create loyalty and the network to extract revenue from thinly watched periods.

Since Eric Ober's departure, Matt had grown increasingly uneasy with the direction of the network. Eileen, his ally and protector, was trying to align herself with Judy's vision, but he had a harder time.

He was astonished at the bland ideas he was seeing. Whenever he was in a meeting where Judy was discussing potential new series, he had a hard time holding his tongue. "Does this really look like a good thing to you?" Matt would ask. He came to meetings armed with his usual quiver of unusual ideas, but not one hit the mark. He pitched a strange Japanese animated cooking show called *Mister Ajikko*.

No go, he was told.

After MTV did a "Wanna Be a VJ" contest, Matt wrote a production budget and a pitch for a show in which people who dreamed of hosting their own cooking shows could compete for a chance to do one on Food Network.

It was a nonstarter.

Judy knew that Matt had done a lot for the network. If she could bring his talents into line, tame him just enough, he could remain useful. She told Matt that he had a good nose for new shows and was gifted at honing ideas. She met with him one-on-one and told him, "We appreciate how much you've done for this network, but you have to understand that the network is headed on a slightly different tack. You need to get on board with the direction this network's programming is going in."

Matt told her he understood. He would try to mutter less at meetings and not criticize other people's ideas so much.

Judy summed up her message in terms she thought Matt would understand: "You need to be less creative."

One day in the new main conference room, Judy showed Matt and Eileen a tape that had come to her attention of a woman who was appearing on segments of local news in Albany, New York. The woman, a cheerful native of upstate New York named Rachael Ray, was demonstrating how home cooks could make quick meals for their families.

"Do you like her?" Judy asked.

Matt did not think Rachael was terrible, but she was not groundbreaking television like *Iron Chef* or Alton Brown. She was pleasant. There are so many good people we should put on before we put on Rachael Ray! he thought.

"See if you can find a place for her," Judy said.

Heidi had been making plans to leave since Eric had left, and she finally did in May 2000. Her farewell e-mail to her comrades praised the network and concluded, with sass, "Can't help but leave with a few 'Heidi-isms.' These thoughts have guided me throughout my endeavors, and perhaps they'll guide/inspire you, too . . ." Characteristically, these included:

Wear black to the office. Wear leather to big meetings. Don't answer to "honey." Always accept cashmere. Use perfume as a weapon.

They make an interesting contrast with the "core values" of the cable division of Scripps: "Diversity, clarity in communication, integrity, compassion/support, shared responsibility, work/life balance, openness, and humor."

Judy's management style may have lacked ideal measures of Scrippsian compassion and humor, but she certainly was clear and open about what she wanted: broader appeal. As the old shows and established personalities were ushered out, Judy began reshaping the network. In Heidi's place, Judy hired Adam Rockmore, a marketing expert who had been working for the chocolate giant Godiva. Adam gravitated to a show the network had begun developing for Marc Summers to host called *Unwrapped*, in which the ever-chipper host traveled the country explaining the origins of popular food products. Eileen had been pushing hard to do more productions outside the studios, and the increased programming budgets were allowing it. A show already being shot on the road was *Food Finds*, focusing on obscure delicacies.

"I want to get behind *Unwrapped*," Adam told Judy soon after he arrived.

"Why?" she asked. "*Food Finds* is similar. Why wouldn't we just continue to invest in that show, versus a new show?"

"*Food Finds*," he replied, "is pretzels from Amish country." If you asked consumers which show they'd want, the answer would be clear. "You can learn about Twinkies and about Junior Mints, or you can learn about pretzels from Amish country?" Judy loved the logic. *Unwrapped* wasn't about food. It was about nostalgia and pop culture, and Marc, fondly remembered for *Double Dare*, was a perfect pop nostalgia fit for it.

Eileen delivered a British show called *The Naked Chef*, starring a young chef named Jamie Oliver. He had come to fame when he happened to be working the risotto station at the trendy River Café restaurant in London the day a TV crew came to make a documentary about the Christmas season. In his early twenties, Jamie was funny and had the kind of blond tousled hair and cheerful, rumpled features that gave him the general air of being comfortably in his pajamas no matter what he was actually wearing. To complete the picture of a carefree hipster chef, a category that had rarely if ever been presented before in the mainstream media, Jamie played the drums in a band called Scarlet Division.

After the documentary, Jamie received calls from a number of production companies interested in developing a food show with him. At first, he thought his friends were playing a joke, and cursed out one caller. He decided to go with Optomen, the company that had produced *Two Fat Ladies*.

Patricia Llewellyn, the producer who had given *Two Fat Ladies* its name, suggested to Jamie that he call his show *The Naked Chef*. It would grab attention and convey the basic message of the show: don't get too fancy, use good basic ingredients and don't muss them up with sauces and difficult preparations.

First broadcast in April 1999 on BBC2, *The Naked Chef* introduced a heartthrob young chef with a working-class accent tooling around town on a scooter, charming his hot girlfriend with a chocolate tart, whipping up Thai Green Curry Chicken for his band, and baking focaccia with rosemary and garlic for his sister's "hen night." The same year *Naked Chef* debuted in England, hearts were aflutter over the star of another new show, *Nigella Bites*, on BBC 4. The daughter of a prominent politician, Nigella Lawson was a voluptuous beauty with thick brunette hair, massive brown eyes, and a seductive way of saying *butter*, *sauté*, and *luscious*. An American journalist wrote that Nigella cooked dinner like it was "a prelude to an orgy."

When Nigella's British production company shopped American rights, Food did not bid. Tempted though Judy was, her willingness to dollop British talent into the schedule only went so far. *Nigella Bites* was snapped up by the Style Network in the States.

In the meantime, Food set about making the most of Jamie, and Adam hired an outside advertising agency, G Whiz. The first thing everyone asked when they heard the name of the show was, "Is he really naked?" so the ad men decided to work with that misconception. A nationwide advertising campaign that was unfurled in the fall of 2000 played with the idea that something naked was coming to Food Network. Bus shelters and billboards, some in Times Square, 240 in Los Angeles alone, showed posters of fruit and proclaimed, "Naked Chef Coming to Food Network." One displayed two cantaloupes that looked like breasts. The second showed a peach, photographed in soft-focus so it looked not unlike a naked derriere, delicate fuzz on pinkish lobes. The third showed a rigid half-peeled banana.

Incensed residents of a Philadelphia suburb considered the suggestive cantaloupes, bananas, and peaches too risqué for children, and called their cable company, demanding that they take down the fruit ads.

Word of the uproar reached the chairman of the Scripps board, who called Ken. He remembered, "The chairman of our company saw it before I did. So I got a phone call. He was not pleased." When Ken saw the ads for the first time, he thought they were *not* Scripps material. What were those insane people in New York doing?

He called Judy and cautioned her, "You can go right to the edge, but don't go over the edge. This is a Midwestern, family-controlled company."

"Okay," she apologized, "so I went over the edge on this one." She pulled a full-page ad that had been set to run in *USA Today*.

Ken mollified the Scripps board. "You have to understand," he told them. "Food is always going to have a better sense of humor than our other networks. If you attach a personality to HGTV and a personality to Food, Food's the one you're always going to invite. And here's the reason. Remodeling, building, this is serious stuff, okay? You screw up a bathroom remodel? It's thirty grand. You mess up an omelette? I'll make it again. So this will be a little edgy. This will be more fun. We'll try different things with this."

As much as dedicated viewers bemoaned the loss of food experts like David, there was something exciting about the new versions of a food-centric life Jamie and others were presenting. Jamie with his curries was not the food world equivalent of Bob Dylan in his brilliance, but both performers opened up what a star could be in their respective fields. Dylan self-consciously (and with the help of a manager) created the poet rock star. Jamie, partly by chance, partly by natural temperament, partly thanks to Patricia Llewellyn, was the prototype hipster-chef. Of course, there had been earlier models—Chef Marco Pierre White, for instance—but none so famous. Jamie opened up the field to new for-mulations of what a chef might be, and, more broadly, what a foodie's lifestyle could entail. The fruit campaign, despite the protest, worked. *People* magazine named Jamie one of the sexiest men alive and photo-graphed him in a bathtub deep in bubbles, surrounded by grapes. The article reported that he had actually cooked once wearing nothing but an apron. "Not a good idea," Jamie was quoted as saying. "The steam from the convection oven got through and burnt me old fella." At a Food Network party to welcome him to New York, Jamie, clad in a blue corduroy suit, joked about his inability to keep his mouth shut and laughed about the time he was being interviewed and confessed to once eating "codfish semen."

The network was stretching the definition of food programming, but only to a point. There were aspects of the chef's life Food was not showing: the occasional bacchanalia, the long, hot-tempered hours in the kitchen, and the burnout. Ken had said Food was always going to be edgier than HGTV. He had seen for himself through ouzo goggles that the chef's life was not only about properly seared steak. The people drawn to the restaurant life are often more adventurous and passionate than your typical air-conditioner installer. It attracts adrenaline junkies.

This image of the life was rising in pop culture. In 2000, *Kitchen Confidential: Adventures in the Culinary Underbelly*, a tell-all book about the sex, drugs, and seamy side of the business, became a best seller. It cast the life of a line cook in an appealingly gritty light and made a bad-boy star of the author, Anthony Bourdain. Meanwhile, Richard Gere handsomely played a chef in the movie *Autumn in New York*, and even a commercial for Viagra starred a knowingly smiling restaurateur cooking with fire while his wife extolled his virtues.

Tyler Florence was one of those starting to live the more devilish life available to a chef freed from the kitchen. One incident demonstrated that his own appetites were leading him to ignore some of the advice Bobby had given him in Las Vegas—to remain humble and contained when it came to his dealings with the Food Network. In December 2000, the network sent a hired car to pick Tyler up at his one-bedroom apartment on Chrystie Street. He was due at a studio for a publicity photo shoot.

Susie Fogelson was assigned to oversee the photo shoot with Tyler. She was a brand-new public relations department staffer with auburn curls and a trim figure, who had just been persuaded to leave Nickelodeon, where she'd promoted *SpongeBob SquarePants*, by the promise of working with flesh-and-blood TV stars at a network that was still young and rough enough to offer the promise of quick advancement. The network needed shots of Tyler to use for advertisements and other marketing. It was simple, but the only substantial shoot Susie had seen before was for *Rugrats*, a show about the adventures of rambunctious toddlers. Chefs are more mischievous. Tyler was drinking wine, and his teeth were stained red, but instead of telling him about it so he could drink water or brush his teeth, Susie just dreamily stared at him.

Oh, we can fix it in Photoshop, she thought, looking at his brown eyes.

When the shoot was done, Tyler, picking up on her attraction, gave Susie a kiss on the lips that was slightly too long for an appropriate work kiss, and asked if she wanted to come out that night with him and some friends.

Serious about her work, Susie declined.

"Oh, well, is it okay if I keep the car for a while?"

"Um, okay," the starstruck new hire answered. She wanted to give him what he wanted where possible. But the car had been intended only to pick Tyler up for the shoot and take him right home, a few hours max, a total cost of $150 or $200.

Tyler kept the car and driver all night. The tab came in near $1,200.

Susie quietly submitted the expense and vowed to be more careful around chefs in the future.

As the status of chefs rose, eager producers rushed into the food TV business with every kind of show idea. Matt was still working as Eileen's assistant, screening pilot tapes. One day a tape came in embossed with a fancy label—*Suzanne DeLaurentiis Productions*. She was pitching a food show called *La Cocina de las Estrellas* (*The Kitchen of the Stars*) featuring Charo and Ed McMahon. Charo was the bubbly Spanish performer known for giggling "cuchi-cuchi!" during guest stints on the 1970s show *The Love Boat*. Ed McMahon was Johnny Carson's straightman sidekick on *The Tonight Show* with a well-known affection for alcohol. *The Kitchen of the Stars* had been shot in a few hours at a small studio in an industrial stretch of North Hollywood. When McMahon showed up for the 8 a.m. call, he told the director, a hastily hired television arts teacher at Pasadena City College named Brent Keast, "I have a golf date. You have to finish this thing by eleven."

Matt was impressed by the label. De Laurentiis is a famous name in the movie business: Dino De Laurentiis was a legendary movie producer, though Suzanne was, at best, a distant relation (his granddaughter Giada, three years away from being a cooking star herself, was working as a caterer in Hollywood at the time).

Matt slipped the tape into a video player. On-screen, Chef Claud Beltran, a Los Angeles caterer, prepared spicy dishes. Next to him, Charo and McMahon hammed it up in the blindingly bright kitchen, sticking spoons in dishes and trying to be funny. For some reason, Frankie Avalon, the singer and actor known for his early 1960s beach movies, came on the set, too. Chef Beltran attempted to explain everything he did in English and Spanish. Ed said little more than "Oh," "Yes," and "Looks good," and held up a copy of his recently published autobiography, *For Laughing Out Loud: My Life and Good Times*.

Charo shimmied. "Oh!"

The Kitchen of the Stars was execrable.

Matt took the tape to Eileen. "You have to see this," he said. They laughed hysterically at the show and agreed that it may have been the worst pilot they had ever seen.

Ken had instructed Judy to think of Food Network not only as a cable channel, but as a brand. The founders of the network had seen the possibilities, but no one had chased them as hard as Ken now wanted to. Think Food Network–branded utensils, he told Judy, selling shows internationally, cookbooks, and more. Judy was not an expert at this kind of brand extending, but she understood Ken wanted shows elemental enough to cross borders and talent that could be trusted in front of advertisers.

Eileen was trying to fall into line with the new leadership, but Matt's tastes had not changed. He continued to suggest the kind of unusual ideas he always had. He wrote a pitch for a series on molecular gastronomy and presented it at a programming meeting. He argued that a science-focused cooking program on what was happening at a molecular level would be cool.

"Interesting," one executive said. "Are people really interested in science when they are here for food?"

"Well, they like it on *Good Eats*," Matt parried.

"That has Alton."

He wanted the network to do documentaries on food and social issues. He pitched an idea similar to *Behind the Music* called *The 100 People Who Changed the Way the World Eats*. It would feature a countdown where historians would discuss everyone from Christopher Columbus to Count Rumford, the pioneer of the temperature-control stove. Matt did financial projections for a book and a DVD box set.

He suggested a show similar to Dave Attell's *Insomniac*, in which a comedian would tour late-night drinking and eating haunts.

"Not our demographic, Matt," Eileen said.

Back when Eric had called him "the golden boy of Food Network," the network president also told him that if he played his cards right, he might one day run the network. Now, making $67,000 a year, Matt was not interested in playing things right. Under Judy, it wasn't working.

Matt began using a company credit card to pay for lunches and dinners with oddball production companies. He thought they would lead him to his next killer idea, the one that would bring him back to the center of the network's creative attention. Not authorized to incur expenses by meeting with representatives of companies Eileen had not approved in advance, he hid his tracks and did not document these meetings in proper expense reports.

He believed he was defending the soul of the network against the dark forces arrayed around him, and he saw that soul as more than just a connection to food. In his experience the network was a place for experimenting and scoring big with avant-garde forms of television. One day in October 2000, Kathleen Finch, a programming executive, asked him to come to a meeting. He walked into a room, and Eileen, along with the head of human resources, confronted him about the expenses. They had tracked his e-mails and his unauthorized expense reports. The expenditures were not allowed, they said. He had broken company policy.

Matt tried to defend himself by arguing that he was meeting with people the network ought to know. But Eileen had had enough. His ideas and enthusiasm had made her look good and inspired her, but things had changed at the network. In the Scripps culture, Matt was making her look bad.

They told him they were firing him.

"Is there anything I can do to make it up, to keep my job?" he said through his tears.

"No," they told him.

Matt had made the mistake of thinking the network had a fixed identity and tying himself to his idea of it. Facing reality burned.

With all the changes and the new conservatism, Food Network was delivering food knowledge to more people than ever. In 2000, foodtv .com soared past a million visitors a month. Mario was still cooking, as were Bobby and Emeril, all award-winning chefs. Jamie was making the profession hipper than ever. Marc Summers was showing the fun side of food. Cat Cora, Padma Lakshmi, and chefs like Michelle Bernstein, Ceci Carmichael, and Aarón Sánchez were showing its diversity on other shows throughout the schedule.

Judy had some successes in her first year, but Eric Ober's "let's give it a shot" attitude was what had allowed for the bold experimentation that led to *Iron Chef* and *Good Eats*. Bobby's Webster Hall battle against Morimoto had been set in motion before Judy's reign. The most significant thing she had done so far was to clear the decks, making space for something new.

Comfort Food

As Food Network approached its eighth birthday, it had fewer swashbucklers on staff to yank it in unexpected directions, but Scripps was investing in it, and *Iron Chef* was attracting heat. Chefs were sexy, and entertainment industry players were picking up the scent. One of them was Barry Weiner, who had started his career at the William Morris Agency in the late 1970s. After eight years there, he'd grown disillusioned. Convinced that his colleagues were more interested in flipping quick deals to earn commissions than in patiently nurturing their clients' careers—an approach he believed would pay off bigger in the end—he set out on his own. Rather than competing in the fields that William Morris and other established agencies dominated, like news, prime-time television, and movies, he sought his own niche. The rise of gossip TV shows in the 1980s such as *A Current Affair, Hard Copy*, and *Inside Edition* offered a new form of lowbrow television that repelled some agents, but Barry swooped in. He began representing and socializing with a New York–based cabal of hard-drinking reporters and on-screen personalities made up of the Australians and Brits who worked for Rupert Murdoch's newspaper and television empire: Steve Dunleavy, Neal Travis, Charlie Lachman, and Peter Brennan among them.

Barry and his business partner Jonathan Russo represented Robin Leach, and when Robin received his seven-figure payout at TVFN, they took their 10 percent cut. His next Food Network client was Gordon Elliott, who had his own afternoon talk show on CBS and had gained fame in New York City with his outrageous "Door Knock" features on the local Fox channel's morning show. Gordon once brought more than a hundred members of the New York Choral Society to Bill Cosby's apartment to function as a live alarm clock and wake the comedian. After *The Gordon Elliott Show* was canceled, Barry suggested they take the "Door Knock" concept to Food, and *Door Knock Dinners* was born. When Tyler Florence, who had appeared on *Door Knock Dinners*, was offered the $20,000 development deal from Food Network that led to *Food 911*, Gordon sent him to Barry: "He's the greediest man in the business."

Paula Deen, a Georgia restauranteur, had done a turn on *Door Knock Dinners* as well. For it, she, Gordon, and the TV crew had talked their way into a young housewife's kitchen in Las Vegas, found chicken, ground beef, and tomato sauce, and Paula had turned it into a spaghetti casserole. Apple pie filling and canned refrigerator biscuits became fried apple pies.

After the shoot, Gordon and Paula had stayed up until 5 a.m. playing casino craps. When Gordon took her and her sons Bobby, twenty-nine, and Jamie, thirty-two, to the Las Vegas outpost of the renowned New York restaurant Le Cirque, the maître d' had ordered them into jackets and ties and sent the boys to a wardrobe room. Gordon was charmed by her energy and wit. He wrangled Paula a turn as a competitor on *Ready . . . Set . . Cook!* and aimed to pitch Paula as the host of a cooking show on Food Network.

"Paula, you need representation," Gordon said, not long after meeting her.

"Gordon, I wouldn't know who in the world to call," she replied in her Southern drawl—WHO in the whir-urrrld to caw-awl—"I don't know anything about that stuff."

In 1999, Gordon arranged for her and Barry to meet. Barry had a

Jewish name and a hard-consonanted Bronx-Jewish accent, but he was of Chinese heritage and had been adopted by Jewish parents. When Paula met him, she exclaimed, "You don't look like Barry Weiner!"

A decade earlier, Paula Deen, fifty-two, had rebuilt her life. After her father had died at forty following heart surgery and her mother at forty-four from cancer, she'd been beset by panic attacks. For years she had barely left her house. It was only in 1989, after she divorced her alcoholic husband, that Paula had found the strength to start a catering business (on $200 in savings) and eventually break her phobia. The business was called The Bag Lady. She would wake at 5 a.m. and make 250 meals in her kitchen—ham salad sandwiches, banana pudding, fruit salad—and her then-teenaged sons would deliver them to local businesses at lunchtime. That led her to open a restaurant in Savannah, Georgia, called The Lady & Sons, which became a huge success. In 1997, she had self-published a cookbook featuring the not-entirely-wholesome recipes she served at The Lady & Sons, like fried chicken battered with egg and self-rising flour, and butter cakes made with Duncan Hines yellow cake mix, butter, cream cheese, and a box of powdered sugar. One day, Pamela Cannon, an editor at Random House who was visiting Savannah, ducked into Paula's restaurant to escape a thunderstorm and noticed the cookbook. Random House paid Paula a $7,500 advance to publish a polished version of it and added a foreword from Savannah writer John Berendt, author of *Midnight in the Garden of Good and Evil*: "Ms. Deen is an irresistible example of that extraordinary phenomenon of Southern womanhood, the steel magnolia," Berendt wrote. "She is always appealing and gracious but possessed of an unfailing survival instinct—a necessary trait for a Southern cook to make it."

A vivacious, heavy-set former model with bouffant white hair and blue eyes, Paula had an inner will and energy most people don't have at twenty-two. She could get people talking about anything one-on-one, and also could make an entire room laugh. Her family and friends had always said she was like Oprah Winfrey, but Paula had read Martha

Stewart's decorating and cookbooks in the late 1980s and was impressed at how seamlessly Martha's business flowed from her life, how she'd turned her lifestyle into a business.

"I want to become the Martha Stewart of the South," Paula Deen told Barry when they first met. "And I'll work as hard as I need to to make that happen." Paula was promoting her cookbook on QVC, and the two were having lunch at the Sheraton Great Valley Hotel in the suburbs outside Philadelphia, near the channel's studios. Paula did not have a big team. Jamie and Bobby helped run the restaurant. Her public relations strategy consisted of walking the floor of the dining room every day speaking to customers.

> "My parents died very young. My daddy was forty and my mother was forty-four. And there was nothing I could do for my parents. Nothing I could do for 'em. But the only thing that I could do, and this sounds crazy, but the only thing I could do was say they produced a winner. They did not produce a dud."
>
> —PAULA DEEN

Barry saw a sizzle in those steel-blue eyes and was charmed. He also was frustrated with his client Bob Vila, the home renovation star, who, Barry felt, was balking at cashing in big on his fame. In Paula, he saw a person with ideas like his own. He told himself there was something magical and magnetic about her, something alive at her core. Barry could work with this.

"You know what," he said. "You're going to be bigger than Martha Stewart. Why don't we do it?"

"Wonderful," Paula replied.

One young and ambitious talent agent had started circling the network even before Judy Girard took over. When Ming Tsai was offered *East Meets West* in 1998, his literary agent at William Morris, Michael Carlisle, referred him to a young agent in the television division, Jon Rosen. At the time, the movie and TV divisions focused on servicing big stars like Clint Eastwood and paid no heed to people in the food television business. No senior agent was likely to take on a first-time host on a small cable channel. But a junior agent might, especially since Ming had an offer on the table waiting to be negotiated.

But, like Paula, Jon was stoked with an inner hunger. Growing up in working-class Leonia, New Jersey, Jon saw his father and stepfather work their way into the upper middle class only to be beaten down by bad luck and changing circumstances. Jon kept a photo on his desk of his father in his twenties, face unlined, dreams in front of him. Jon had decided early that he was going to dig in and get back what his parents lost. Like thousands of yearning guys from New Jersey and elsewhere, he identified with the characters in Bruce Springsteen's songs who are fueled by a sense that something's gone wrong and a seething desire to make it right. Jon especially loved a less-well-known Springsteen song called "The Promise," which included this line:

"Inside I felt like I was carrying the broken spirits of all the other ones who lost."

Jon had been a striker on the soccer team at Boston University, but not good enough to turn pro, so he'd decided to become a sports agent. Out of college, a family connection helped him land an internship at the Fifi Oscard talent agency, then an aunt helped Jon land a job in the William Morris mailroom, where would-be agents at the company traditionally started. The salary was not enough to support him, because he was sending money home to support his mother and sister, so he took a second job working nights and weekends as a stock boy at a Macy's in New Jersey.

Upon his promotion out of the mailroom, Jon became an assistant to Jim Griffin, who represented Regis Philbin and Geraldo Rivera, among others. Jon was promoted to a full agent at William Morris in 1997, and when Carlisle walked Ming into his office on West Fifty-fifth Street, he was eager to listen.

Jon was still a striker; he strutted around the office as only a muscle-bound five-foot-eight-and-a-half-inch man can. "This guy's a go-getter, a hustler," Ming thought. "He's a bulldog."

Jon thought big quick. This wouldn't only be about the contract with Food Network, Jon told Ming. Jim had taught him about licensing riches. Food celebrities could fit into certain marketing opportunities better than actors could. Bill Cosby could do pudding commercials because he was funny and famous. But it wasn't like Cosby was known as a culinary expert or had invented his own pudding flavors. Ming was not as famous, but he was known for a specific style of cooking and his expertise was clear and sellable: Ming was Asian fusion.

Within a few months, Jon had swung his first endorsement deal for his new client. A potato chip company was coming out with an Asian flavor and marketing it as gourmet. They wanted a quote on how the chip paired with wine, for their bags and press materials. Ming was on a ski vacation in Utah when Jon reached him with the news. The company would pay Ming around $2,000 for the quote. While riding a chairlift, Ming texted something along the lines of, "I love this chip. It goes great with Bordeaux." After he hit Send, Ming sat in the chair watching pine trees and white snow pass under his skis, occupying his mind with pleasant calculations about his hourly rate. Sending the text had taken two minutes. A thousand dollars a minute equals $60,000 an hour. Nice.

Once William Morris had one happy client in-house, it started attracting more, some to mutual profit, others to mixed results. In 1999, Emeril's three-year deal for roughly a million dollars was coming to an end. Emeril was opening his fifth and sixth restaurants that year, one in Orlando and one in Las Vegas. He had cookbooks and spices, and cookware companies were clamoring to make deals. It was time to go pro. Shep still collected profits on Emeril's spices, but was focused again on his music industry clients. "We really need some support," Tony Cruz said. "I'd like to bring in somebody who has expertise in the entertainment business."

They scheduled an appointment with the television division at William Morris. In the sixteenth-floor conference room, a group of agents gathered to discuss with Tony and Emeril what they might do for the undisputed heavyweight champion of Food Network. Emeril was interviewing the agents, but the agents were also interviewing him. Jon already knew that if he could get Ming potato chip deals, he could bring Emeril the entire state of Idaho, served three ways. Unfortunately for Jon, Jim Griffin had done a bit of research into the food field, and quickly recognized in Emeril a star with big pop culture appeal who would fit in with his high-profile clients. Jim began to charm Emeril by telling his best stories. After the Jets won the Super Bowl in 1969, he'd represented "Broadway Joe" Namath.

The young agents had all heard the story before of how Joe Namath had come to don panty hose and show his legs for a television commercial. "One day I get approached by this agency called Long Haymes Carr, in Winston-Salem, North Carolina," Jim began. The agency had sent Jim the storyboards for a commercial they wanted Joe to do. They'd been sitting on his desk for weeks when photographer Harry Benson stopped by his office and saw them on the desk.

"Harry asked me, 'What's this?'

"I said, 'It's just they want Joe to do this commercial. I don't know about it.'

"He said, 'Well, it's got a homosexual overtone. A man and panty hose?'

"I said, 'Well, maybe that's it. Maybe that's what's been troubling me about it.'

"He said, 'Well, it's real simple. Just have two pretty girls come on in the last frame and kiss him on the cheek. Takes away the whole thing.'"

Griffin made the deal.

"On the way to the shoot, I said, 'Okay, Joe. Here's the copy. And there are people from the agency that are going to be there. And then they're going to take you into makeup and they'll shave your legs—'

"And he said, 'What?'

"I said, 'Yeah, well, you know, panty—'

"He said, 'Pull the fucking car over.' Thirty-ninth and Park, I swear to God. And I had to talk my way into it at that point, 'cause I hadn't told—it was not unusual for him to get his legs shaved during the football season because of all the tape. The problem was this was summer and nobody had told him. So finally I talked him into it, and we went down and did it, and it was a very famous television commercial."

Namath, Griffin confided, had been paid $75,000 for the ad, a huge payday at the time. Jim suggested that Emeril could likewise change what chefs were worth.

"Most of my clients are one-name celebrities: Regis, Geraldo," he boasted. "They don't need to have anybody say their last name 'cause everybody knows who you're talking about. Emeril has that." He said he could work a big deal with the Food Network contract and bring in new merchandise—"but," he added, tailoring his message for his audience, "it's important for Emeril to only be involved in something that he actually would use."

Jon saw Emeril and Tony nodding across the conference room table. Jon respected Jim, but he considered himself the in-house food celebrity expert. He'd identified this new breed of star as his ticket, the way he would escape the fate of his father and stepfather. He might lose Emeril to Jim, but he was going to stay in this field and work it hard, and when the next Emeril walked in, he'd get him.

Tony and Emeril left William Morris impressed and went to dinner at Sant Ambroeus, near the Mark Hotel. They talked it over, but it was clear that Jim could do for them what they could not do for themselves. The next day, Tony told Jim that they wanted to take the next step as long as he agreed to one stipulation: they would only deal with Jim, no one else there. "I do not want all of a sudden to have a bunch of agents running out trying to sell Emeril, and trying to get Emeril into different businesses. We want to work with one person and be strategic on what we do."

Within months, Tony was meeting with executives from B&G, a specialty foods maker that wanted to buy Emeril's spice business. Shep had arranged for Emeril's spices to be sold via an 800 number flashed at the end of Emeril's Food Network shows and through small distributors. B&G had a national sales force and massive distribution deals with supermarkets. "You guys have a nice little small, niche business," a B&G executive said.

Jim helped work out an arrangement in which both Emeril and Shep continued to be 50/50 partners collecting licensing profits from the spices, and B&G took over the job of running the business. The spice deal stipulated that if the product hit certain sales targets within five years, B&G would have the right to automatically renew. They hit the five-year sales targets within a year and have renewed ever since.

These endorsement deals for Emeril, and in smaller ways for other network stars like Ming, were an unmistakable marker of the rising status of chefs in pop culture, particularly chefs who carried the imprimatur of the Food Network. Success as a host could spark success on the commercial side, which created more media exposure, and more potential eyeballs for the network and the host, all of it a positive fame cycle. Shep, seeing that Emeril and other chefs were indeed becoming the popular artists he had worked to make them, stepped further away from the business.

Not every agent after him possessed his uncanny instincts. It is easy for a celebrity to say he or she will only endorse products that fit his or her image. It is another thing to turn down money when it is offered. Woody Allen once pitched Smirnoff vodka, and Groucho Marx sold Frosted Flakes. Jim brought Emeril to Elmo for the straight-to-video feature *Elmo's Magic Cookbook*.

A far riskier decision proved disastrous. In the fall of 2000, in Los Angeles, Linda Bloodworth-Thomason, a television producer whose credits with her business partner and husband, Harry Thomason, included the CBS hits *Designing Women* and *Evening Shade*, found herself watching *Emeril Live* on Food Network. Since the late 1980s and early 1990s hits, she and Harry had stumbled with unmemorable shows such as *Women of the House* and *Hearts Afire*. With the loss of their development deal at CBS, Linda knew A-list stars would be resistant to working with her. But an unorthodox talent like a chef might be more open. Linda was impressed by the chef's charisma, and, with her showbiz radar, she saw Emeril as a blustery Jackie Gleason type—beefy but vulnerable. Watching Emeril clown during his cooking show, she wondered, Can he do comedy?

She and Harry reached out to Jim and Emeril about the possibility of a sitcom—a half-hour comedy in which Emeril would play a chef named Emeril who had a television cooking show. The star didn't say no, although it seemed strange to Emeril, who still saw himself as more chef than entertainer. Linda wrote a few lines of sample dialogue, and Harry asked Emeril if he would mind reading for the part.

Harry came to New York to hear Emeril read. Back in L.A., he told Linda, "Honey, I think he can do this."

Emeril had taken over Julia Child's role at *Good Morning America* as a food correspondent, so Bloodworth and Thomason tried pitching the show to ABC. The network passed. In December, the executive producer of the *Today Show*, Jeff Zucker, was named president of NBC Entertainment. Zucker had long been an Emeril fan and had unsuccessfully tried to lure him to *Today*. Before he moved to California to take up his new post, Jim pitched the sitcom to him and closed the deal.

Overcoming Emeril's doubts, the producers assured him he did not need the acting chops of Robert De Niro for the show to work. Around the William Morris offices, Jim bragged to Jon and anyone else within earshot, "You can have all the other food stars. I have Emeril, the biggest of them all."

Within a few months, it was clear that Jim had led Emeril into troubled waters. Linda and Harry quickly created a pilot that network executives and a few critics saw in the spring. TV critics were savage. One called it "a train wreck." Others noted Emeril's obvious lack of acting experience and declared the scenes with his "wife" and "young children" at home screamingly dull.

Production on the series proceeded anyway, but in the lead-up to the debut, scheduled for fall 2001, Zucker spoke to the press and offered faint praise: "It's not embarrassing. It may not be everyone's cup of tea. But we're betting that it's going to appeal to a lot of people."

Producers tweaked the show so that most of the action happened on the set of the cooking show. Two characters were added, a food stylist and Emeril's talent agent, played by the veteran actor Robert Urich. In one of the advance ads for the September 25 debut, Urich was shown sitting around with too much makeup on his face. When Emeril approaches, Urich explains, "It's just a little bronzer."

"You look like a penny," Emeril replies, emphasizing the punch line with a stiff forward roll of his shoulders.

Barry may have believed that Paula Deen was a great candidate to host a cooking show, but no one at Food Network or any other place seemed to agree. At meeting after meeting throughout 2000 and 2001, he heard excuses like, "She speaks Southern," "Gray hair," and "She's not really a size two now, is she, Barry?" In other words: She sounds like a hick, she's old, and she's fat.

Barry had dealt with rejection plenty of times before. His client Peter Brennan had created *Judge Judy*, featuring a former family court judge from Brooklyn who tartly dispensed justice and life lessons in a mock small claims court. When they were shopping the pilot, naysayers dropped uncouth dismissals—from the broad "Are you out of your mind?" to the bigoted "Who's going to watch a show starring a loud-mouth Jew from Brooklyn?"

Doggedly, Barry had insisted, "You know most of the things that really worked well on TV were things that people never anticipated." By 2000, *Judge Judy*, picked up in 1996, was profitably on the air nationwide in first-run syndication, breaking ratings records and earning Emmy nominations. The star, Judith Sheindlin, would build a fortune estimated at more than $100 million.

When Barry pitched Paula at Food Network, Eileen Opatut told him, "You just don't get our business anymore." Times had changed, she said. The network was trying to get smarter, not dumber.

The programming department was not in the mood for fried chicken. But with the network's talent ranks thinned by Judy, something new certainly was needed. As hard as talent agents like Jon and Barry were working, there were still precious few of them in the food

TV field pitching clients. Most of the latter came to the attention of the network through their own hard work and determination. Luck helped, too. And, doubtless, fate.

After Judy had seen Rachael Ray's first pitch tape and recommended it to Eileen and Matt, the cook and her tape had vanished into the cracks of the network. It had been a hell of a journey for her to get to the point where she was even noticed by Food Network's president.

Rachael was a petite, stocky young woman with thick brown hair, a quick smile, and a naturally hoarse voice, the aftereffect of a child-hood battle with croup. Her family was in the restaurant business, and growing up, she'd washed dishes in the summer and worked the waffle iron. Her parents had divorced when she was thirteen, and her mother, Elsa, moved Rachael and her siblings to Lake George, New York, where Elsa helped manage a chain of Howard Johnsons. Rather than hire a babysitter, she often took Rachael and her older sister and younger brother to work with her. Rachael helped out in the restaurant. She donned an unbreathable polyester uniform that got so hot in the sum-mer, it was like wearing ten layers of garbage bags, except uglier—the uniform was burnt orange with a button-on plaid apron. At five foot three, she had to leap into the ice cream chest to reach the tubs and scoop out cones. Balancing on the edge of the freezer, where a trail of ice water and melted ice cream collected, would leave her with a malty-colored stripe across her chest.

Every Christmas, she visited New York City with her family. They took her to the toy store FAO Schwarz, where there were five floors of dolls, musical instruments, and puzzles to play with and a hair salon. Paradise. She began to form fantasies about moving to the city when she grew up, and decided that something magical would happen to her there.

At twenty-three, she made the move and got an apartment in Queens. A guard dog named Lisa lived chained outside the front wall of her apartment building and Rachael befriended her. She felt sorry for the dog and would bring her food, wash her face, and sit and pet her.

She found a job running a candy counter in the gourmet-foods Cellar at Macy's. When store managers tried to transfer her away from the food department, she left and found a job at a gourmet market opening uptown, Agata & Valentina. A fiercely hard worker who could fix a meat slicer and unstick a balky cash register, she'd be at the store receiving deliveries at 4:45 a.m., which meant waking up at 3 a.m. in Queens, and would stay past midnight. One night after her boss dropped her off at home, Rachael was mugged. Two young men had been hanging out in her building's vestibule out of sight of the dog, and as her boss drove off and she fumbled for her keys, one pulled a gun and demanded her money.

She screamed, "Please don't kill me!" as she pulled out a tiny canister of pepper spray her father had given her and aimed it at his face. He screamed, covered his face, and ran. The police drove Rachael around for hours looking for him, to no avail. She slept an hour and a half and went back to work.

A few days later at work, she was sitting cross-legged when the wall phone rang. Her foot had fallen asleep and when she got up, she stepped down wrong and snapped her ankle. Her difficulties deepened from there.

Ten days later, the attacker was back, waiting for her outside her building. It wasn't clear what he wanted this time except to hurt her. He dragged Rachael off her crutches into a dark spot and began beating her with the gun.

This time she yelled, "Lisa! Lisa!"

The dog came charging up the alley on her long chain. The mugger ran off. Rachael, hobbling on her broken foot, fell hard on the ground.

Rachael called her mother every day, and that night she made the call from a hospital.

"I think I have to go home," Rachael, beaten and bruised, confessed. Elsa agreed. New York had not been magical.

Friends helped her load up her possessions, and Rachael, twenty-seven, moved in with her mother, two hundred miles from the city. She found work at Cowan & Lobel, a gourmet market in Albany. Driving to work one morning, Rachael swerved and flipped her truck. Soaked in gasoline, she climbed out and called her mother, who drove her to work. She was in charge of receiving perishable goods at the market and was afraid that if she did not show up to log the deliveries properly, the cheese order might get messed up.

Her relentless "I'll handle it" work ethic led Rachael to take on yet more responsibility at Cowan & Lobel. Her mother sometimes suggested that she work a little less and take some time for herself. But Rachael considered herself a pale comparison to her mother, who had worked hundred-hour weeks throughout her childhood. At the store, she noticed that some ingredients were not selling and suggested to Donna Carnevale, a member of the family who owned the shop, that they promote a twist on Domino's Pizza's promise to deliver a pie in thirty minutes or less by hiring chefs to teach classes on how to use the store's products to cook a meal at home in thirty minutes or less. The store started selling gift certificates to the classes, but couldn't turn a profit because of the cost of hiring chefs. Rachael was already in charge of making their ready-to-eat takeout meals—lasagnas, chicken dishes, and the like. She seemed to know what she was doing. "Why don't you teach the class?" Donna asked.

"No, people are going to want the whole chef experience," Rachael protested.

"They are eating your food already," Donna replied, winning the point.

The classes were popular. Dan DiNicola, a reporter for the CBS-affiliated TV station WRGB, took one, and was so charmed that he offered Rachael a weekly three-minute cooking segment on the local news. Over time, the segments were filmed at viewers' houses. Rachael drove her pots, pans, and ingredients around in her car and cooked dinners in their kitchens. She loved the work, but she was paid around $50 a segment, far less than each cost her to make.

At dinner with the WRGB news director Joe Coscia, she bemoaned the situation: "Joe, I don't have enough money to pay my rent."

He helped her produce some local travel advice segments, getting her on the air more and creating content he thought they might be able to sell to other stations in the area. They also made a pilot of a cooking show, shot at the cabin in Lake Luzerne that Rachael shared with her mother. On a wall was a painting of her late grandfather, an Italian immigrant and a stonecutter who babysat her as a little girl. It was a homespun little show, showing food and family and a smiling young woman working to make everyone happy. This was the pilot that had not impressed Matt Stillman and Eileen. But local viewers regularly asked her if she had a cookbook. Rachael cold-called Hiroko Kiiffner, a one-woman publishing house. Hiroko was skeptical—she'd heard fifteen-minute meals and twenty-minute meals and half-hour meal concepts before—but eventually was willing to take a shot. The book, *Rachael Ray's 30 Minute Meals*, published in 1999, sold ten thousand copies in two weeks at Albany-area supermarkets, a wild success. Hiroko put the book into a second printing after only three months.

Luck favors the extremely well prepared and talented. Early in the spring of 2000, Lou Ekus, the cooking show coach who had trained Ming, Bobby, and Sara, was driving to the Culinary Institute of America in Hyde Park. He was listening to a local radio station and a woman he had never heard of was being interviewed about her cookbook. He was so transfixed by how natural she was on the air that after he pulled into the parking lot at CIA, he sat in the car to listen to her. She did everything he would have coached someone to do—be charming, reveal personal details, be concise, and be clear. Lou did what he had never done before—he picked up the phone and called Bob Tuschman at Food Network to recommend someone.

"I don't know who this woman is," he told Bob. "I have no idea what she looks like, but here's a name you need to look into—Rachael Ray. Her shtick is thirty-minute meals. I just heard her do a perfect interview on a local news station in Albany about her cookbook. She was so much fun and so energetic, you should check her out."

Bob had not heard of her either, but he went to the network's cookbook library. A copy of Rachael's book was on the shelf. Her photo was on the cover. She looked fresh and happy. The recipes appealed to him. Bob never had time to cook complicated meals at home during the week and he thought the thirty-minute concept was good, as was her promise that she only used ingredients people could buy at a regular supermarket.

He called Hiroko and asked about meeting Rachael.

"That's so funny," she said. "I've got a call from Al Roker also. And he's going to put her on the *Today Show*. She's going to be in New York in a week."

Roker, who had a country house in upstate New York, had seen Rachael on local TV. "There's this really cute girl on Albany television," he told a *Today* producer. "I think she might be kind of fun to be on our show." It took Rachael and her mother nine hours to drive down to the NBC studios in a blizzard for her appearance on March 6, 2001.

From her first pop on national television, Rachael was gold—so obviously appealing that you can sense what Lou had heard on the radio simply by reading the transcript from her appearance on *Today*.

AL ROKER: This morning on *Today's Kitchen*, comfort foods of the century. With the kids home from school and a winter that just won't go away, neither will my friends, there's nothing better than cuddling up in your flannels with some hot and tasty comfort food. Rachael Ray, author of *Comfort Foods: Rachael Ray's 30 Minute Meals*, is here—you got very excited when I said that.

RACHAEL RAY: Yeah, it's cool. Al's saying my name. Groovy.

ROKER: She's here to show us how to make one-pot dishes.

RAY: Yeah.

ROKER: So, now what's the deal? Why are we so excited about comfort foods these days, Rach?

RAY: Well, because they bring everybody back to their beginnings, you know. Comfort foods are as different as wherever you grew up, you know.

ROKER: Right.

RAY: My grandfather is from Sicily, so for my mom, a big pot of escarole and beans is comfort food. My dad's from down South, so for him, jambalaya is comfort food. Me, I've always lived in the Northeast, so what we're going to make right now is comfort food for me.

ROKER: Chicken and dumplings.

RAY: Chicken and dumplings soup.

ROKER: All right. How do we get started?

RAY: Okay. Well, I know you know how to cook, but can you just pretend you don't for a minute, okay?

ROKER: Okay. I have no idea.

RAY: Quick—quick chopping lesson.

ROKER: Uh-huh.

RAY: If you're not comfortable in the kitchen, first thing to do, get a firm grip about whatever you're chopping, curl your fingers under so they don't call you lefty.

ROKER: Okay.

RAY: Okay? Get a nice sharp knife. . . .

That, my friends, is how it's done. Within two minutes, you've learned about where she comes from, what she's going to make, and why she's going to make it. In the process, she has captivated her interviewer, told a joke, and taught a lesson. It's not as easy as she made it look, but after a childhood in restaurants and years of work, it was easy for her.

The day after her *Today* appearance, Rachael met Bob, Eileen, and Kathleen Finch in a Food Network conference room.

She had them charmed immediately, especially when she tried to talk them out of hiring her. She had been watching Food Network. She knew the big stars were respected chefs like Mario, Bobby, and Emeril.

"Listen," Rachael said. "You're champagne, I'm beer out of the bottle. I clearly don't belong here, I'm not a chef. You've been duped."

She got out of her chair, sincerely prepared to leave.

"No, no, no, stop," Bob said, laughing. "That's what we like. We don't want you to be a chef." Nigella Lawson wasn't a chef, and she was a star. The network was prepared to expand the roster a bit in its instructional programming. A cookbook writer like Nigella or Rachael could work.

Bob was sold. She had enthusiasm, charisma, and a down-to-earth quality. She may not have been exactly what Eileen was looking for, but Eileen did not find her nearly as objectionable as she had Paula. The busy New Yorkers she knew certainly could use tips on how to cook meals quickly. Although Eileen had recently signed one of the founding fathers of celebrity chefdom, Wolfgang Puck, for a cooking show, she understood that Judy was willing to serve both champagne and beer as long as they both had fizz.

Rachael was asked to make a pilot. They paired her with a producer, Mark Dissin. Dissin—most everyone at the network called him by his last name—was a former sports documentary maker who had inherited the role that once belonged to Reese's wife, Pat O'Gorman, the go-to in-house producer. Having worked with the revered Olympics storyteller Bud Greenspan, Dissin understood how to trim a production down to elements that would capture and hold a viewer, even a cooking show.

He and Rachael disagreed on the format of her show. She wanted to demonstrate three recipes for every featured ingredient, an approach with roots in both her demos at Cowan & Lobel, whose original intent had been to move a certain product, and her three-minute news spots.

He insisted that a show called *30 Minute Meals* should present one meal cooked in thirty minutes without the shortcuts that would be required if three thirty-minute options were presented. He won.

Before shooting the pilot, Dissin gave Rachael one instruction: "Do not stop tape under any circumstance, period. It's not your job. You keep going, no matter what."

In the hallway before taping began, Rachael met Sara Moulton, who added another bit of advice: "Smile all the time for no apparent reason."

Rachael's nerves were not helped when she saw where they were taping her pilot: Emeril's set. His name was projected onto the floor and it spun and stopped, spun and stopped: Emeril . . . Emeril . . . Emeril . . . Everything looked enormous to her. A radio bud was placed in her ear. Voices were speaking in it. They told her that they would instruct her when to look to camera one, two, three, four, or five, and when to wrap up for a commercial break.

She did not know which camera was which. "Can you call the camera people names instead of numbers? I'm confused. I don't know what all the numbers are. I mean, I know that's Jay." She pointed to one of the cameramen. She'd met them all earlier. "Can we just call Jay, Jay? When you want me to look at Jay, just say, Jay!"

"Okay, you can call them by their names," a voice said into her earpiece.

The kitchen staff had been prepping what they could for her, but there was not much they could do. Rachael had to pull all of the ingredients out of the on-set refrigerator, chop, measure, cook, and plate everything in thirty minutes. Someone in the backstage kitchen would be cooking along with her in case she burned or spilled something, but it was not like a traditional cooking show where, through "the magic of television," the host would slide a chicken raw into the top of the oven and slide a duplicate out, fully roasted. Instead of trussing birds, prechopping onions, and measuring tablespoons of salt into little glass bowls, the only thing the kitchen staff did was preheat Rachael's skillet. The light on the camera in front of her went on.

"Hey, everybody, I'm Rachael Ray and I make thirty-minute meals. Now that means in the time it takes you to watch this program, I will have made a delicious and healthy meal from start to finish." That was the extent of the script that had been written for her. She had to ad-lib the rest of the banter.

During the discussion about what to call the cameras and through her introduction, a flame had been burning under her skillet.

"Now," Rachael said, grabbing a bottle, "just gonna put a little bit of olive oil in the pan. Like one turn of the pan. About a tablespoon."

She tilted the bottle. The instant the olive oil touched the skillet, which was now preheated to the point of combustion, FOOOOOM! A jet of flame shot four feet into the air.

WHOOOOSH!

Rachael jerked her head out of the way in time to avoid burning her eyebrows off.

She thought, I just set Emeril's set on fire, and remembered Dissin telling her, "Don't stop under any circumstance. We will tell you when to stop."

Rachael smiled just like Sara had told her to, and threw salt on the burning oil, extinguishing the flame, and pushed the skillet off to the side. She grabbed another pan, a cold one, poured in a tablespoon of oil, and kept going.

Despite the conflagration, Rachael had been unfailingly chipper on camera. The network green-lit her show, ordering twenty-five episodes. As she shot her first season, Bobby, having grown into the role of shrewd big brother among the ever-shifting Food Network family, was asked to go watch her and offer whatever advice he could. He stood in the wings for twenty minutes. Her own set was a mélange of oranges, saturated teals, and canary yellows. The toaster was bulbous like a child's toy. Even the microwave oven with a little circular window managed to be cute. It was all irrepressibly bright and bouncy.

Bobby did what Bobby does: made a snap judgment that turned out to be right. He focused on the star. She just gets it, he thought. She's just who she is. She doesn't make any false moves. You can tell she's going to be good.

Between episodes, he introduced himself. Rachael was still overwhelmed by her success—from local news to Food Network in a matter of months. "Bobby Flay is coming to see me?" she said to him as he approached her.

"You're not trying to be anybody else," he praised her. "People will relate to you immediately."

As she continued shooting episodes in the summer of 2001, Rachael developed a tension-loosening ritual called Dollar Fridays. Everyone on the crew—twenty or thirty people at that point, including camerapeople, culinary producers, back kitchen staff, the director, the set dresser, hair, and makeup—would write his or her name on a dollar bill and put it in a bin. Before the lunch break, Rachael would pull out one bill and read the winning name. The winner had $20 or $30 to buy a nice lunch.

Despite her efforts to spread charm, not everyone at the network was a fan. Many of the kitchen staff were miffed that someone with less expertise than they had was giving cooking advice in front of the camera. If Bobby was the brother figure in the Food Network family, Emeril was still the patriarch, the Godfather. Judy regularly asked his opinion about new talent. "She doesn't know anything about food," Emeril griped. "I would not put her on. She dilutes what Food Network is all about."

But to Judy, Food Network was about good television, not evangelical proselytizing about the wonders of food culture and how to avoid lumps in your béchamel. Her approach would soon bear fruit, but not in a way she or anyone else would have wanted. Nevertheless, it must be said, as dreadful as it sounds: From a profit perspective, the best thing to ever happen to Food Network was September 11, 2001.

The national catastrophe created opportunities for men like Barry and Jon, and vindicated Judy's approach, opening space for a wide range of TV-friendly talent, some with only filament-thin tethers to the world of fine food. But the client who had brought Jon Rosen and William Morris into the network would not benefit.

Ming Tsai's latest show, *Ming's Quest*, took him on the road internationally, cooking in exotic locations. After a long day of shooting that Tuesday, he and his crew were unwinding at the bar of the Four Seasons hotel in Bali. It was just after 9 p.m., twelve hours ahead of

New York. The general manager of the hotel came up to the group and announced, "There's been a horrible accident. A plane hit World Trade Center One."

There was no more information. A member of Ming's crew was a little freaked out because his sister lived close to the tower. But what could they do? They were on the other side of the earth. It sounded like a terrible accident. They kept drinking.

Twenty-two minutes later, the GM came over again. "You need to get to a TV. A second building was hit." The crew walked to the hotel's TV room. Two Americans were crying. The news showed a tower collapsing and a massive cloud of dust.

"What movie is this?" Ming asked.

They caught the first flight to Taiwan, where they began a long wait for a flight home.

Within forty minutes of the second plane hitting, Ken Lowe, Ed Spray, the president of Scripps's cable television division, and Frank Gardner, the board chairman, held a conference call with Judy and the presidents of Scripps's two other networks, HGTV and DIY, to talk over what the networks should do. Should they continue with their scheduled programming? Wouldn't any commercial seem grotesque in the horror of the attack—even an ad for a laundry detergent's power to remove stains would seem inappropriate. What sort of stains? Bloodstains? Should they break in and make public service announcements? What other options were there?

Every non-news station faced similar choices. ESPN switched to a feed from *ABC News*. MTV carried *CBS News*. The Home Shopping Network showed Canadian network news, and TLC picked up the BBC World Service. The History Channel, Comedy Central, Travel, SciFi, E!, and Lifetime stuck with regular programming even if some resorted to reruns.

At Scripps, Gardner, who had worked in television news, said, "We have to do something drastic. Let's just go to a slide with music."

For twenty-four hours, Food pulled everything. Over gentle music, a single slide was shown with a purple lily and the text "Due to the nature of today's tragic events, the Food Network is suspending programming."

The studio had been preparing for a three-week shoot of *Emeril Live* when all production was canceled. The Food Network kitchen staff cooked all the food they had stocked for the shoot and donated it to St. Luke's Hospital.

Early viewer reaction was positive. Judging by e-mails and calls, viewers felt it was appropriate to pull the programming. Who could stomach anything except news during those first few hours? But within twelve hours, after nothing else had blown up, people's brains were beaten senseless from watching loops of the planes, the towers' collapse, terrified workers running for their lives through ash clouds in downtown Manhattan, the smoldering Pentagon, and aircraft wreckage in rural Pennsylvania. By the first night, a trickle of viewers was asking to see people cooking on television. Devoted fans wanted to retreat to the hearth, even if the hearth was a television showing a hearth.

After one day of darkness, Scripps decided that its programming, safe and nonviolent, generally focused on home and family, would offer a needed distraction. In the days that followed, news stories reported that couples who had broken up before the trauma of 9/11 had decided to get married. Soup kitchens saw an influx of volunteers. There was talk everywhere of "cocooning" with one's family. It was clear to Judy and her team what they had to do. TV audiences wanted TV that nurtures. Food Network could become an oasis; the network would air as much television comfort food as possible.

Ming, marooned in Taiwan for four days, caught a flight to Toronto, and hired a car to drive him thirteen hours home to Boston. A new season of *East Meets West* was scheduled to begin shooting the next week in New York. His wife told him he wasn't going—the towers were still smoldering.

The pause in production gave the network time to reconsider. It had many seasons of *East Meets West* in the can. Now that they were no longer putting straight instructional cooking on in prime time, Eileen figured they could rerun what episodes they had more frequently in daytime, especially since the Asian ingredients Ming was using were still esoteric to most viewers. As Eileen saw it, most people who owned woks had been given them as wedding gifts, stored them in a closet for a few years, and then tried to off-load them at yard sales. If Ming had convinced viewers to oil them up even once, that would have been a lot. A little *East Meets West* went a long way. Meanwhile, *Ming's Quest*, part of the effort to try talent outside the studio, had been getting middling ratings in prime time, nowhere near those of *Good Eats*.

Ming had worked hard to get on the network and spent thousands of dollars of his own money for media training. But it had served him. His restaurant in Wellesley was a success and he would soon land a deal to make a show called *Simply Ming* on public television. Food Network had helped turn him into a star, Jon had helped monetize it, and Ming had no intention of relinquishing the status.

Barry Weiner saw 9/11 not as a problem for Paula, but as an opportunity.

His office was near the Carnegie Deli, the landmark Theater District restaurant famous for its gigantic sandwiches: piles of pastrami and corned beef so rich they threatened to send most diners into a food coma. Many a tourist has been forced to cancel afternoon plans in favor of a nap after a battle with a Carnegie Deli sandwich. In the weeks after the tragedy, Barry noticed two things around Midtown. First, there seemed to be a funeral every two hours at St. Patrick's Cathedral. Second, there was a constant line of 150 people waiting to get into the Carnegie Deli. The city's fine-dining establishments were suffering, as were many other businesses in the city, but not the Carnegie.

He made an appointment to see Judy. She had grown weary of him pitching Paula, but she respected Barry's TV acumen.

"Judy," he said. "Do me a favor. Walk home from work." She and Barry happened to live in the same apartment building on West Fifty-seventh street. "I want you to walk along Seventh Avenue. And when you walk along Seventh Avenue, take a look at the Carnegie Deli. The only thing that might be a little unhealthier than fried chicken is corned beef and pastrami. I am willing to bet you that there will be at least ten times as many people outside waiting in line at the Carnegie Deli as there are in any of those so-called fancy restaurants that you believe your audience wants."

Judy laughed at him.

He called her the next day. "Well?"

She had seen the line.

"You know something," Barry said, pressing his case, "one thing that we've all learned because of 9/11 is we're all going to die. We know that. Whether we eat corned beef, or we don't eat corned beef, or whether we eat fried chicken, or we don't eat fried chicken, or whether we eat macaroni and cheese or we don't, it's not going to make a difference. But the fact is, you want to know something? We're in a world right now where you see a funeral every three hours, you want to feel good. They're not locals outside the Carnegie. Those are tourists from the Midwest. All of those people who you believe aren't going to want these sorts of things are standing outside because they want to eat a three-pound corned beef sandwich, and they're also going to watch Paula Deen on your network."

Judy sighed. "Okay, come and talk to me."

She relented enough to approve paying for two pilots for Paula, closely overseen by network staff.

Eric Ober, the deposed network president, watched the Emeril sitcom when it debuted on September 25. He cringed. One crucial mistake was obvious immediately: Emeril had been cast with taller performers. On his cooking shows, Emeril prowled his kitchen station with commanding intensity. On NBC, dwarfed by Urich, he looked dumpy and out of it. Emeril's awful in this format, Eric thought, and it's not going to work. He believed that Jim, in the quest to earn his commission on a fat network TV contract, had put his client into a position he should not have been in.

Critics brought out their knives again. Neil Genzlinger in *The New York Times* called the show "a hacking, sputtering mess."

Viewers agreed. Ratings declined nearly every week.

Zucker invited Emeril to his office. "It's nothing wrong with the show, nothing wrong with the cast," he told the chef. "We've got some really great people. But I can't do another season of it. The numbers are not there, and I've got to answer to the board."

Emeril the sitcom was off the air before November.

Emeril did not like to see any venture bearing his name fail, but he still had *Emeril Live, Essence of Emeril*, restaurants, new cookbooks on the horizon, and a growing line of pots and pans called Emerilware.

Emeril's ultimate judgment about the sitcom was the same as his appraisal of other important business endeavors in his life: It was about the relationships. Everyone had tried their hardest. To his mind, no one had betrayed him. Even when he agreed to try a cockamamie show like *How to Boil Water*, he had met people he liked, put his trust in them, and found things to enjoy about the experience. One had led to great things, the other had not.

"It was awesome," he remembered of the sitcom cast and producers, "having a relationship with Robert Urich, Sherri Shepherd, Lisa Ann Walter, Jeff Zucker, Harry and Linda." Emeril did not blame Jim. He chalked the failure up to debuting so soon after 9/11. "Not a good day for comedy," he said.

Jim also interpreted the quick cancellation not as a verdict on Emeril as a star, but as a result of the changing appetite of viewers after 9/11. To this day, he does not allow that it might have been partially his fault for allowing his client to get involved with it in the first place.

While Judy had denigrated the concept of the network as a cooking school, she understood that there was still a place for instruction, as long as it wasn't in prime time and the hosts were telegenic. She and

Eileen created a programming block for Saturday mornings that the network advertised as "Cooking School." The eight half-hour shows started being rolled out around the network's eighth anniversary in November 2001. In its first iteration, the block included mostly existing shows, but it also had three new titles. In order, the schedule was: *Molto Mario*; *Cooking Thin* (a new show starring Kathleen Daelemans); *Sara's Secrets*, a recorded show Sara Moulton was making in place of *Cooking Live*; *30 Minute Meals with Rachael Ray*; *From Martha's Kitchen*; *Sweet Dreams*, a dessert cooking show starring Chicago pastry chef Gale Gand; Wolfgang Puck; and *Melting Pot*.

Rachael's show was quickly a standout. She was delivering a message for people who were disconnected from their kitchens, and in the wake of 9/11 yearned to find a way back. She told them it was not so difficult to cook—if she could, they could. In thirty minutes, anyone, even a working mom, even someone who didn't know an amuse-bouche from an amusement park, could pull off a little miracle that would allow her to spend "quality time" with people she cared about.

At the time of Rachael's debut, the network was expanding its reach dramatically. Between August and November 2001, it added four million new subscribers, and two million more came in the first four months of 2002, bringing the network into seventy-two million homes. Food Network programs had a better chance than ever of reaching enough eyeballs to make a significant cultural dent. Prime-time ratings increased 25 percent in 2001 over 2000.

More attention was heaped on Rachael when her domestic travel and dining show, *$40 a Day*, debuted in April 2002. "Bubbly," the *Los Angeles Times* reviewer called her. "The host seems to be having the time of her life as she tours points of interest, learns the history of the various dining spots and then invades the kitchen for recipes. Along the way, she . . . thanks a man for taking a photo for her with a hearty, 'Yeah! You rock!' and high-fives a chef while shouting, 'Right on!' . . . Watching Ray at work within the *$40 a Day* system is a real treat."

Jon Rosen was watching. He'd never met Rachael, but his assistant tracked her down on vacation in France.

"Your personality translates directly across the screen and makes me feel like I'm in the room with you," he said when he reached her by phone.

As soon as she was back in the States, she came in to William Morris and signed. Before Jon could start bringing deals to her, Rachael, characteristically, figured out a way to bring in her own. Soon after the debut of *30 Minute Meals*, a friend invited her to a birthday party. Everyone there seemed to be a model or an actor, the kind of Manhattan fashion party where everyone was gorgeous and a foot taller than Rachael. Across the room, through a sea of shoulders and scarves, she spied another vertically challenged head. It belonged to John Cusimano, a distributor of independent films. They got to talking. She said she was the host of a show on the Food Network. He'd never seen her show, but he told her he loved food.

"Oh, yeah?" Rachael asked. "What was the last meal you cooked?"

He knew she assumed he would say something like chicken parmesan or chili.

"Last night I went to the fish market," John said. "I got a piece of tilapia and I sautéed some tomatillos with some jalapeños and cilantro and deglazed the pan with a Negro Modelo. I served some mâche on the side."

"Wow!" Rachael replied. "I have a great guy for you, 'cause you must be gay if you're cooking so great."

"No," John said, sensing his opening. "Actually, I am not."

Hours into the nonstop, easy-flowing conversation, the host of the party came up to them and said, "Dummies! This is the person I was trying to introduce each of you to for a year!"

They were rarely apart after that. But to be rarely apart from Rachael meant participating in her career. *30 Minute Meals* was just starting, and Rosen had not developed any product endorsements for her yet, but after a few months, Rachael told John that her fans were writing to the Food Network and telling her at book signings that they wanted to know where they could buy Rachael Ray products. On her show, she always mentioned how useful it was to have a "garbage bowl." Instead of taking the time to dump every carrot shaving and orange peel into a trash bin across the room, Rachael kept a bowl on the counter to fill up with discards while she cooked quickly. She also used a Santuko-shaped knife that was unusual for trained TV chefs. It was a Japanese-style blade that had a scalloped face and a long, flat bottom edge, making slicing easier for amateurs. She also used what she called a "moppine," an all-in-one oven mitt and kitchen towel. They were all helpful time-savers she used at home. And none of them was available branded with her name.

One night after shooting at the Food Network, she and John sat at a hotel bar having a vodka, club soda, and lime, and on a cocktail napkin, she sketched an idea for a cooking pot she'd like to own. It was oval and just longer than a piece of dry spaghetti. "You're a lawyer," she told him. "Can you figure out a way that we can sell my products?"

John had marketed small films like *My Life's in Turnaround* and *Conspiracy of Silence* and worked out licensing agreements. He did some research and found out that the Cannes Film Festival of kitchen products was the Chicago International Home and Housewares Show. He put together fifty homemade press kits containing articles about Rachael and the Food Network. Rachael had torn out an article about Anolon pots. She liked the weight and the look of them. She asked him to find the Anolon booth at the show and find out if they'd be interested in making an oval spaghetti pot. Her little drawing of it was in the press kit, too. Although they were not married yet, Rachael felt comfortable entrusting John. They had been together nearly every free moment since they'd met. And their relationship would help their marketing efforts. People will be interested in the fact that we're together, she thought. It has sort of a mom-and-pop feel to it.

In Chicago, John found the Anolon booth and met the vice president of product development, Suzanne Murphy. He showed her the pasta pot drawing. "As an added bonus," he said, "if you have a small, narrow stove, like you do in an apartment, and Rachael does at her cabin upstate, you can fit two of them easily next to each other and still have just as much cooking space."

Susanne had heard of Rachael and liked the pot idea. They agreed to speak about it further.

John hung up his film hat. This was easier than flogging little movies.

Soon, John and Rachael, with Jon Rosen's help, launched a series of new products: garbage bowls with Meyer, spaghetti pots with Anolon, and knives with Furi.

The success made Jon Rosen bolder. In regular brainstorming meetings at William Morris, he told anyone who would listen, "I want to go after Bobby Flay." Outside of Emeril, Bobby was the biggest fish at Food Network. Jon knew Bobby was with Richie Jackson, but Richie was a boutique agency. Jon could do stuff for Bobby that a small company never would. How could Jon get into a room with him?

Jennifer Rudolph Walsh in the literary department told Jon that a girlfriend of hers had worked for Bobby. "I can get to him," she said.

Bobby agreed to a meeting. He walked into the same conference room Emeril had walked into years earlier, except this time, Jon was ready. He had assembled a group of people he felt were loyal to him, people from the books division, the speakers division, commercials, scripted television. He'd seen what Rachael and John Cusimano had done, and it had expanded his vision even further.

Thanks to his assistant's research, Jon knew that Bobby had played basketball growing up, that he had developed a taste for the world of fashion, that he liked to travel, that he had a daughter from his second marriage, and that he was interested in horse racing. Jon had this all written out on a notepad in front of him. "You're a star," Jon said. "You're phenomenal. And I want to bring you in."

He told Bobby he could be a massive brand, that all of his interests could be leveraged into endorsements and businesses. "All you're really doing right now is television. How about a turkey endorsement deal? Maybe a board game deal? Big-money corporate speaking engagements? I know I can call up about you," Jon said, "and say, 'Guys, here's why you should do this endorsement deal with Bobby. Did you know that he is a father, and did you know that Thanksgiving is the biggest day of the year for him, and he has forty of his family and friends over and there's a Trivial Pursuit match?'"

Bobby left and talked it over with his girlfriend, actress Stephanie March, who was then costarring on *Law & Order: Special Victims Unit.*

"I think I'm gonna make this move," Bobby told her. "Nothing against Richie, I just think that this machine is bigger. You know they have Emeril, they have Rachael, but I don't mind being third in this deal."

She agreed. She'd been around Hollywood long enough to know that a powerful agency can open doors.

When he broke the news to Richie, who had recently negotiated his new three-year deal with Food Network for around $800,000, his long-time agent told him, "I feel like we've done a good job for you."

"You have," Bobby said. "There are limits to a boutique firm like this. You know, just where all the media's going now, and endorsements and books and everything else, I just need to be in a more encompassing place."

That was that.

Soon Jon made a deal for Bobby to endorse Butterball turkeys. A luxury car company called William Morris: they wanted to hire a celebrity chef to cook a special lunch for the wives of its top salesmen. Was Emeril available? No, but Bobby was.

He didn't mind playing second fiddle to the king. Especially when the car company was willing to pay $30,000 for an afternoon's work.

Paula Deen shot the two pilots in Savannah, but the producers assigned to the show brought the network's prejudices with them. They dressed her in cashmere and pearls. They tried to make her look like a refined Southern lady and coached her relentlessly. One pilot was called "Afternoon Tea."

When Barry saw the tapes, he was appalled. This wasn't the gutsy woman with an inner magic. This woman was cowed and bland.

Before Judy had a chance to see them herself, Barry went to her office. "Do me a favor," he said. "You can't watch the pilot."

"You're out of your fucking mind," Judy said. "Why shouldn't I?"

"I'm telling you," he said, "it's the worst thing you've ever seen. So you don't have to watch it just so you can tell me it's the worst thing you've ever seen. I'm already telling you it's really that bad, but it's because you fucked it up. You sent all your people down there, and they didn't allow her to be who she was! They tried to turn her into your version of what she should be in Savannah, Georgia. But that's not it! Let her be who she is! Don't gentrify her—and don't bother looking at the show."

If there was a lifetime achievement award for chutzpah, Barry Weiner deserved one. "We'll do a show for you at cost," he pressed. "Give me any time period, I don't care where it is. You have nothing to lose! You have time periods on your network right now when nobody is watching. So you might as well let somebody not watch one of my shows instead of yours."

After two hours, he wore Judy down. "Just get the fuck out of here," she laughed. "You got thirteen."

Months before the first of thirteen episodes of *Paula's Home Cooking* aired, Paula fussed over TV critics at a promotional lunch in Los Angeles. She served them creamed corn and fried chicken and peered over their shoulders "to make sure you're cleanin' your plates." The show's debut in November 2002 was part of the still-chugging "Cooking School" block on Saturdays. Critics raved, notably those outside New York. "Her show is like watching your favorite aunt whip up a yummy banana split cake or lemon chess pie while you sip coffee at the kitchen table," wrote Reagan Walker in the Atlanta *Journal-Constitution*.

Judy called Barry to thank him. The network's programming had been too focused on the taste of the coasts, she said. It was like the famous *New Yorker* cover by Saul Steinberg where the city is the center of the Earth and everyplace else on the planet is a tiny sliver.

"You proved something to me," she said. "You proved that we have an audience beyond the Hudson River. Thank you."

Soon, endorsement offers for Paula were coming in, small things, regional brands. Barry told her to say no for now.

"But they're offering cash money!" she said more than once.

"We're not doing it," he said.

"What do you mean, we're not doing it?" she asked, incredulous.

"You said you wanted to be Martha Stewart," he said. "We're going to be bigger than Martha Stewart. If we take every offer now, all that'll happen is it's like you're becoming a whore." He told her to wait until the endorsement offers were for millions of dollars, not a few thousand.

"I hope you know what you're doing," she said. But she agreed to keep doing it his way.

Players like Barry, Jon, and others, who had found their ways to the launching pad, were poised to propel the network and its stars into a celebrity stratosphere that few besides Shep had envisioned. But first, they needed more talent that was capable of making the journey.

Noodle Roni with Blue Eyes: A New Kind of Star

When Food Network executives traveled the country conducting audience research at the turn of the millennium, they asked a cross-section of Americans: What do you cook? How does food play a role in your life? Who cooks in your household? How often do you cook? How much prepared food do you buy? Do you cook "family recipes"?

It turned out that a lot of people thought making a box of Noodle Roni was cooking. Many did not know what a scallion was. The definition of a "family meal" had different meanings. It could refer to a takeout rotisserie chicken brought home and served by a single dad to his three kids around a table at 6:30 p.m. or a dish of "grandma's lasagna" cooked from scratch by a mother and left on a counter for busy family members to eat as they arrived home. No matter what the family looked like or how far-flung, separated, or busy, food could be its glue.

A man in St. Louis talked about how he had prepared a book of family recipes, which he planned to hand off to his daughters when they got married. A bus driver in Philadelphia said that his kids were getting older, he was about to retire, and the best gift that he could give them was the feeling that they could still come together as a family around food. He loved to cook, and it was a household pillar that gave everyone security.

These stories, not unlike the one Tyler had told her, reminded Eileen Opatut of being taken to the Lower East Side as a little girl to watch shows at the last surviving Yiddish theaters. Afterward, she and her parents would walk down Orchard Street and go to kosher restaurants like Ratner's. The food—soft onion rolls, cheese blintzes—meant love and comfort to her and connected her to what her mother made at home—Mrs. Opatut boasted that she could make potatoes twenty-eight ways.

Not everyone was telling warm stories. In the focus groups, many people revealed that the traditional connections conjured by food had been unintentionally broken. Family members had moved away from one another, and no one knew what had become of Grandma's old recipe box. Anyway, who had time to make their own piecrusts, grate their own potatoes for latkes, or roll sheets of pasta? Cooking for most of the busy, younger generation was something only for people who bought high-end magazines like *Gourmet* and *Food & Wine*. In those glossy pages were photos of whole fish served seaside on white platters, and chilled bottles of white wine beading on beautiful tables lit by candles in hurricane lanterns and set with vases of bellflowers. It was elitist.

Food Network's viewers were reporting that all the cooking they were seeing kindled a desire to reclaim a connection to something they had lost, a time when meals were the center of the family—even if it was not a time they had ever personally experienced. For younger people, whose parents had fed them from boxes and takeout containers, cooking was almost an act of rebellion.

This sociological data might seem self-evident in retrospect, but it was not obvious at Food Network, even in 2001. Eileen interpreted the focus groups' responses to mean that many Americans craved a simple way back to the kitchen—or, at least the feeling of being back in the kitchen. Sure, Food Network could lay down the bread crumbs for people to follow from their televisions to their cutting boards, but the business of food TV was not to get people to cook—it was to get people to watch more food TV. Rachael, the smooth storyteller, was doing something intimate, with none of Emeril's yelling or the callers who peppered Sara Moulton—just calm, comforting small talk as a hot dinner came together on a set that looked more like a real kitchen. How could that warmth be stoked? What more could Food Network put on the air that would strike those crucial inner chords?

Rachael and Paula came across as members of a viewer's family. Rachael looked the part of a neighbor or a young mom. Paula played the indulgent grandma. She signed off shows with the catchphrase, "With love and best dishes from my kitchen to yours." No cashier at McDonald's, no newscaster on CNN or star of *Friends* ever looked into the camera through the steam of a hot apple pie and sent love to customers or viewers so directly. And as the years unfolded, these kitchen scenes were beamed into America's homes on larger and larger high-definition televisions, reinforcing the illusion that viewers were somehow looking through a window into their own kitchens, except the ones on TV were homier—their own might have discarded takeout containers from Boston Market. For the purpose of conjuring warmth, it was becoming clear that it was better if the on-screen cook was more a seasoned amateur than a smooth pro, someone who was like a friend or family member whispering tips and sharing her own secret recipes, binding viewers to her like the man in St. Louis was trying to do with his daughters.

High-end cooking demonstration shows were still on the network. Eileen had brought in Jacques Torres, the dessert chef from Manhattan's Le Cirque, for *Chocolate with Jacques Torres*. Michael Chiarello, a Napa Valley stalwart, was developing a show called *Easy Entertaining*. Wolfgang Puck was part of the "Cooking School" block on Saturday mornings. But complaints about Puck's dense Austrian accent and Torres's French pronunciations would eventually come in. Viewers could not connect with the foreigners.

Fittingly, amidst the changing focus, Julia Child made her last appearance on Food Network on the episode of *Wolfgang Puck's Cooking Class* that aired Friday, November 30, 2001. It was the same month that Rachael's *30 Minute Meals* debuted. The world had been created and paradise lost since the elemental black-and-white days of *The French Chef*. Julia was now a visitor in a strange land where cooking was less important than the cook. She had appeared on an episode of *Emeril Live* earlier that year, helping Emeril prepare a roasted chicken—"That's pretty scrawny," Julia remarked about Emeril's bird. "Well, we have no budget this week," the chef laughed.

Julia and Wolfgang prepared a guinea fowl and white asparagus gratin. As the Austrian-born chef explained the recipe, he paused and said, "I can't believe I'm telling Julia Child how to cook. That's like telling God how to create the world."

Viewers, whether they knew it or not, were connecting with a number of stars who had grown up in difficult family situations, with bad divorces, alcoholism, or worse. This was true of Rachael, Paula, and Alton. It was as if their own deprivations created a desperation to bond through the comfort of food, one so strong it could reach through the television screen and grab hold of whoever was watching.

Sandra Lee, known as Sandy to colleagues and friends, was looking for her own way up and out. She was also ferociously driven.

Working on one of her first cookbooks, she asked her recipe writer, Denise Vivaldo, about Nigella Lawson. Sandy was interested in understanding how the sultry Englishwoman had managed to transform herself from a journalist into a television star. It was well known that Nigella had perfected her cooking skills while taking care of her husband who was losing a battle with throat cancer. "She has that great backstory—husband died of cancer," Sandy said. "How do you beat that?"

Sandy had her own backstory. According to her memoir, *Made From Scratch*, her mother was a prescription-drug addict who once beat her so badly her body was covered in welts; her stepfather was inappropriately sexual with her; and her father, with whom she moved in at sixteen, was arrested for raping his twenty-five-year-old girlfriend. The one pleasant period of Sandy's childhood was between the ages of two and six, when she and her sister lived with a doting grandmother in Southern California, who kept a clean house and baked for them. She and her grandmother watched *The Lawrence Welk Show* together. Little Sandy liked how the band's outfits, often powder-blue suits with ruffled shirts, matched the pastel stage sets. When she and her sister went back to live with their addict mother, Sandy, the eldest, spent her preteen years taking care of her sister and three half siblings.

"Many times in life I have looked up at the sky," she wrote in her memoir, "and said aloud, 'Why do I have to go through this?'"

Sandy left college in the middle of her junior year. Tall and blond with high cheekbones and icy blue eyes, she first found work at a clothing store, then sold security systems and 90,000-volt stun guns at home and garden trade shows. Living in an apartment in Malibu, she improvised ruffled curtains out of coat hangers and fabric, and with her trade-show experience, managed to turn her homemade curtain system into a business called Kurtain Kraft. Selling at county fairs, she scrounged together the money to hire Florence Henderson to sell the product on infomercials and, as the business grew, she took on the role of pitch-woman herself on QVC. She was hit with patent infringement lawsuits, and diversified the brand into gardening, scrapbooking, and crafts.

In the late 1990s, Sandy met television host Dick Clark through a talent agent. Impressed by her looks and her poise, Dick's production company signed her to create a "How-To" lifestyle television show and suggested food should be a focus of it. Sandy enrolled in a two-week course at Le Cordon Bleu, a cooking school in Ottawa, Canada. She learned cumbersome techniques such as how to scrape tendons from a veal chop. When it took her an hour to do four, she decided that this was too time-consuming for many women. Back in L.A., she decided to write a cookbook based on the idea that using some commercially pre-pared products would give busy women an easier way to cook that would yield gourmet results fast. At a supermarket in 1998, she found herself standing in front of bags of Nestlé's semisweet chocolate chips. She had a brand name for her approach: "Semi-Homemade."

Romantically involved with a rich Los Angeles businessman, Bruce Karatz, Sandy hired a series of food experts to work on the book, eventually turning to Denise, a well-known Los Angeles area recipe writer who had helped a number of celebrities write cookbooks, among them the ThighMaster queen, Suzanne Somers, and the Fat Ladies' nemesis, Richard Simmons.

She self-published *Semi-Homemade Cooking* in 2001. Her concept was that the recipes would include 70 percent store-bought packaged foods and 30 percent homemade ingredients. The book told people how to make Meaty Microwave Lasagna with a packet of French's spaghetti sauce mix and Beer Margaritas with Corona, tequila, and Minute Maid limeade. Sandy was featured on the cover, smiling angelically in a cloud-white sweater and a blond bob. "Nothing is made from scratch" the cover copy proclaimed. Dick Clark gave a blurb: "Sandra Lee showed me an amazing new way to cook that everyone can enjoy . . . delicious and quick!"

She followed it up with a new edition of the book in 2002 with a glowing introduction by Wolfgang Puck. Kathleen Finch, of Food Network's programming department, who had created *Unwrapped*, saw a magazine article about Sandy the same week she made a promotional appearance on a Halloween edition of *Today*. Dressed up as Sandra Dee, Sandra Lee was so moved by the sight of Matt Lauer's bare pectoralis majors in his Siegfried & Roy costume that she placed her hand flat on his chest and exclaimed, "Oh, my God!" as he turned beet red. At one of the Food Network programming department's regular meetings to kick around new ideas and potential talent, Kathleen pitched Sandy hard. "She's the answer to working mothers' prayers," she said.

The network didn't want a duplicate of Rachael. They wanted to complement her, to build a stable of approachable new kitchen talent. If the trail back to the kitchen had to be made of Noodle Roni, so be it. The audience research had shown that was enough.

"This seventy-thirty concept is so smart," Kathleen continued. "And I'd love to make a television series with her."

Eileen, Kathleen's boss, agreed. She liked the concept and Sandy's previous TV experience with Kurtain Kraft.

Although she had been preparing for a breakthrough for years, Sandy was surprised by the call from Food Network. She was calling herself a "lifestylist," something broader, she thought, than a food expert, and she wanted the show to include more decorating tips. There was some dispute over the format, but in the end every episode of *Semi-Homemade Cooking* featured a "tablescape," a fussy-as-Lawrence-Welk decorating scheme for the dining room table—themed napkin rings, color-coordinated tablecloths, printed name cards—to match the food she'd just semi-made. In the first episode, Sandy demonstrated how to wrap a marshmallow with fondant.

Sandy was Noodle Roni with blue eyes, on-camera charm, and a fierce will to create a beautiful dinner table that looked as complicated as something from *Gourmet* but promised to be easier than a trip to Kmart. It didn't matter if it was that easy or not. It was a fantasy for those career women who yearned to fulfill some 1950s version of being the perfect housewife, even if, exhausted, they never budged from bed while watching it on weekend mornings.

The name of the Saturday-morning cavalcade of cooking shows was changed to reflect the pedigrees of the new hosts who had not gone to cooking school: In the Kitchen.

In the same vein, another cookbook author came to Eileen's attention: Ina Garten, the former owner of a gourmet shop on the East End of Long Island, had published *The Barefoot Contessa Cookbook* in 1999. Eileen spent time in the summer in East Hampton near the shop of the same name, and was a big fan of the ease, class, and repeatable success of recipes like Perfect Roast Chicken and Pasta, Pesto, and Peas.

And yet, Eileen and Judy had resisted when Eve Krzyzanowski, Martha Stewart Living Omnimedia's head of television, had first pitched Ina as a potential cooking show host prior to 9/11. Just as they had argued against Paula at the time, Ina was neither young nor model-slender.

Ina, fifty-one years old when her book was published, had never envisioned herself on television, but she had been a high achiever her entire life. Before she'd opened the food shop, she had been an analyst in the White House Office of Management and Budget during the Carter administration. Her husband, Jeffrey Garten, whom she'd met when she was fifteen and visiting her brother at Dartmouth, had worked in Henry Kissinger's office. In D.C., she'd hosted Saturday brunches, practicing a cooking hobby stoked by her interest in *Mastering the Art of French Cooking*. Then, sitting at her desk in the spring of 1978, she'd seen a tiny ad in *The New York Times* for a specialty-foods shop that was for sale in Westhampton, New York.

Now that's something I'd like to do, she thought. She was burned out by Washington and, like a lot of urbanites, dreamed of a more grounded life in the country.

She and Jeffrey drove out to Long Island that weekend. The place was a small shop called The Barefoot Contessa, named after a 1954 movie starring Ava Gardner. It was a tiny operation: one person tended the front of the store, one worked in the kitchen baking bread, slicing salmon, and preparing soups.

She bought the shop with money she'd made buying, fixing up, and flipping two row houses in D.C. The East End of Long Island was idyllic. Its famous beaches and proximity to New York attracted the wealthy during the summer months, and its rich farmland and a long tradition of fishing meant access to amazing gourmet spoils: oysters, fresh corn, tomatoes, and striped bass.

Over the next two decades, Ina moved the store twice to bigger spaces, settling it in East Hampton, a more established year-round community where she and Jeffrey bought a home. By the mid-1990s, with around a hundred employees, she was struck with a feeling similar to the one she'd had in D.C.: I can't do this one more minute, she thought. I need to do something else.

A friend had told her, "Type-A people think that they can figure out what to do next while they're doing something, and they can't." So she sold the store to two employees, keeping ownership of the building, and made herself an office upstairs. Ina was flummoxed when she faced an empty schedule. She had gone from being responsible for a thousand baguettes at three o'clock in the morning to idling. One Monday morning, when Jeffrey was leaving for work, she said, "I have nothing to do this week."

"Nothing?" he asked.

"Well, I have a manicure on Wednesday, but that's it." From the office, she ordered magazine subscriptions and made lunch dates. One day, Jeffrey suggested she write a cookbook, something many customers had asked her to do over the years.

Well, I'll just start the process, she thought. It was something to do.

She wrote a proposal and sent it to Roy Finamore, an editor at Clarkson Potter. He had edited cookbooks for Martha Stewart, who had a house in the Hamptons and frequented the shop. Roy bought it. The recipes were based on the ingredients Ina found around her: Corn Cheddar Chowder, Lobster Pot Pie. Martha wrote the book's foreword.

Ina's cookbook presented food that looked and tasted great, but was easy to make. In *The New York Times*, Florence Fabricant wrote, "This is an excellent starter cookbook to set the novice on the path to successful dinners and parties. . . . Bright photographs, by Melanie Acevedo, show exactly how most of the food should look, and illustrations show the differences between mincing, dicing, julienne, and chiffonade."

The book quickly sold out its first printing of 15,000 copies, eventually selling 100,000 in its first year. Stewart, whose company had gone public in 1997, was trying to get into the business of producing television shows other than her own. Seeing Ina's sales figures, the Stewart people gave her a column in Martha's magazine. Eve and Martha also pushed her to try a cooking show. Ina was reluctant, worried about whether she'd be able to cook on camera, but was finally persuaded.

Eve and Ina decided that the most authentic way to present the recipes was to show Ina making them in her East Hampton home. It would give her the air of being a nice home cook, a friendly neighbor who might ring the doorbell and present you with an apple tart.

Ina did not fully realize what shooting at home would mean. A production team showed up at her house in East Hampton in early 2000. A prep kitchen was set up in her yard under a tent. She thought she could protect her rugs and floors from the muddy comings and goings of the crew by putting out a bin of socks and insisting everyone wear a pair when they were inside. But there were more than a dozen people in the crew, and they found it too cumbersome to keep taking off and putting on their shoes every time they ran into the house. The carpets started to fill with dirt, and the lawn under the tent was damaged from all the traffic. Worse, most houses in East Hampton had their own septic systems, and few were suited for heavy use. Within a few days, Ina's system backed up and the toilets gurgled with brown water. The would-be star of *In the Kitchen with Ina* was frantically unhappy, and it showed in her performance. She had been given little training—no trip to Lou Ekus. What is the hardest thing for most first-time cooking show hosts to do? Cook and talk at the same time. Ina couldn't do it. She mumbled and cut her finger badly the first day while slicing vegetables on a mandoline. For some people, the pleasure of cooking is the meditative quality of quietly peeling, slicing, and straining. They don't have to talk. That was being taken away from Ina. At least one producer got the impression that the real problem was that Ina's food stylist had done most of the cooking for the book and Ina lacked the kitchen chops to produce camera-ready food, no matter how much time the production crew had given her.

Even if it wasn't true, the mood was sour. Ina sobbed between takes, upset that she'd agreed to do this, frustrated at her performance, and in pain from the cut. She did not want to be on television anymore and felt that she'd been badgered into it. She was curt with the production staff, who were themselves disgruntled at her inability to stick to the tight shooting schedule, originally aimed at completing two half-hour shows in a day, a tight pace even for a seasoned pro, an impossible pace for someone who needed to stop talking and watch herself chop if she was to avoid cutting herself again.

At the end of the shoot, someone brought in champagne. There was a toast. Ina gave the producers signed copies of *The Barefoot Contessa Cookbook*. Then she raised her glass and, not joking, said, "Now get out of my house."

Back in New York, the production team edited together a few weak half-hour episodes. They bought her new carpets. Ina sent the production company a bill for the signed cookbooks. Then Martha saw the tapes. She did not like that Ina was using Fiestaware plates, which looked similar to the dinnerware used on Martha's show. She did not like Ina's performance. Martha also seemed unhappy that another woman was going to be the star of a show produced by her company.

"I don't want to be representing Ina," Martha declared to her staff at her television studio in Westport, Connecticut. She issued an order. "I don't want this shown. I want the tapes of this whole series destroyed."

Eileen had been invited out to watch the taping of the pilot. She saw all the problems, but came away with the impression that there was a way to do something with Ina that would work. The Martha production was awful, but after 9/11, as Rachael Ray's show became popular, Eileen grew sure that Ina was the kind of cookbook star she wanted to add to the Saturday block, someone who, handled right, could come across as classy and competent. Eileen spent more than a year trying to convince her to try again. But Ina didn't want to have her carpets ruined again, or spend weeks away from home taping in a studio.

Then Eileen found what she thought was a potential solution. Rachel Purnell produced Nigella Lawson's cooking show in England, and shot the episodes at Nigella's home. It showed Nigella's life, the smart friends she had over to dinner, and her late-night fridge raids. Viewers aspired to live that lush cosmopolitan life.

Nigella Bites looked great because it was not made like a traditional cooking show with four cameras positioned in front of a kitchen counter and taped as the host cooked, shot in real time, and divided into four segments separated by commercials. Rachel Purnell's company, Pacific, shot the episodes somewhat like a movie. There were only two cameras, and they taped three takes of every move the host made. If Nigella sliced an onion, the cameras might take a long shot. Then she'd do it again and a camera would follow her hands. The third take might be a medium shot, during which she would speak to the camera about what she was doing. The script was more thoroughly written out, requiring less extemporaneous speaking from the host. Because there were multiple cuts and the shape of the episode was determined when it was edited together, many takes were done without any talking. Voice-overs were used. It took two to three days to create twenty-two minutes of television, not including postproduction editing and fine-tuning. The visual result, with its lush cinematic quality and an appealing narrative, showed the care that had gone into its production.

Most important from Ina's perspective, Purnell's method required a smaller crew. There were two cameras, one piece of lighting equipment. Six or seven people could make the whole show. Eileen was able to convince Purnell to come to New York for a meeting with Ina. The cookbook author was still very wary of trying TV again, but after seeing how elegant Nigella's show was, she was willing to listen. Purnell told her that the slow process would bestow a richness on the show that would be more representative of her food and lifestyle. It would have the quality that Ina demanded of the photos in her books.

"Please," Eileen said again and again. "It will be better this time. I promise."

Ina relented. Purnell and her crew went to Long Island to produce the show, now called *Barefoot Contessa*. The Pacific crew, as promised, did not destroy the house. The storyline, similar to that of Nigella's shows, showed Ina living her life, being a hostess in a country setting that seemed like a dream come true for a lot of people.

> "I never watch my own shows. Never. I have no idea how it comes together. From day one, I always had enormous confidence that they knew what they were doing. They're extraordinary. But no, I can't. If I ever watched a show, I think I'd probably never do it again."
>
> —INA GARTEN TO INTERVIEWER MAILE CARPENTER

At a luncheon to unveil Food Network's forthcoming season, Eileen introduced Ina and told the assembled TV critics that her show "speaks to people who want to entertain with simplicity." Her appeal was deeper than Eileen anticipated. Rachael Ray, with her blue-collar upstate roots, showed hardworking moms how to make miracles with supermarket ingredients. Paula delivered comfort from the South. Ina let viewers into a relaxed, refined life of fresh ingredients and airy spaces. It was the best kind of fantasy and it was real for Ina and Jeffrey. Although he was now a dean at Yale, spending weeknights during the school year in Southport, Connecticut, where he ate at Chinese restaurants and small diners, he came home to East Hampton on the weekends. He often appeared at the end of the show as part of "the beauty shot," sometimes along with Ina's friends, happily digging in to what she'd just made in the kitchen for viewers.

It was such a compelling vision that some fans began parking near Ina's house or even poking through her hedgerow, aching for a peek into Ina and Jeffrey's happy life. Some knocked on her door. It came to be a nuisance. But she became a fixture of the In the Kitchen—ITK—block, and the network agreed to her requests to do as little media as possible. Rachael, Paula, and Sandy were already on their way to becoming national brands, but Ina continued writing her own cookbooks and living the life in East Hampton that viewers saw on the show. She hardly remained an unknown. She continued publishing cookbooks and even starting making some endorsement deals, but she refused to join the celebrity chef festival circuit and, for the most part, sidestepped the fame machine the others were eager to step aboard. Of course, she and Jeffrey had not come from the same humble circumstances as most of the others.

The new hosts were helping the network break into new television territory. When Comcast added Food Network to the lineup for 70,000 subscribers in the South Bend, Indiana, area in November 2003, a year after Ina's show debuted, a reporter at the *South Bend Tribune* wrote a primer "to help you figure out the tempting but unfamiliar at this 24-hour, all-you-can-watch buffet." By the network's tenth anniversary,

South Bend's cable population was part of around seventy-nine million national subscribers.

Meanwhile, the success of the easy meals–easy comfort hosts was beginning to provoke a backlash on chefs like Mario Batali who were still emphasizing more sophisticated cuisine. Batali had been sent to Italy to film a new show, *Mario Eats Italy*, in which he'd visit off-the-track villages and trattorias, the sort of places where he had learned how to cook the Italian food he brought to Babbo and *Molto Mario*.

> "And they didn't want me to do rabbit, they wanted me to do chicken breast."
>
> —MARIO BATALI

Shortly before the crew was about to film Mario demonstrating how to make tripe stew—the cow's stomach is a staple of Roman cuisine—the producer Sarah Burmeister received a call from Jeanne Shanahan, an executive in the programming department. "Don't do a tripe stew," Jeanne told her. "It's disgusting."

Sarah was taken aback. To her, chefs of Mario's accomplishments were artists who used a plate instead of a canvas. They needed to be treated with sensitivity. "That's one of the lead dishes at Babbo," Sarah said. "You're basically telling him his food is no good."

The tripe survived, but the programming department began thinking about finding someone else to explain to the public how to cook Italian food. Perhaps an orange-clog-wearing, erudite storyteller who made pastas from chestnut flour was not the man to kindle a newfound appreciation for Italian cooking in states where you could still find only one kind of mushroom in the supermarkets.

Despite the programming department's second thoughts, Mario was a pop-culture phenomenon. In Bill Buford's 2002 *New Yorker* profile of Mario, later expanded into the book *Heat: An Amateur's Adventures as Kitchen Slave, Line Cook, Pasta-Maker, and Apprentice to a Dante-Quoting Butcher in Tuscany*, he observed Mario walking the sidelines before a New York Giants game as a guest of the commissioner. Football fans in the stands recognized him.

"Hey, Molto!'" one of them shouted. "'What's cooking, Mario?'" "'Mario, make me a pasta!'"

Soon the football crowd had started chanting, "Molto! Molto! Molto!"
Mario had leveraged this mainstream fame into a series of successful
new restaurants in New York with his business partner, Joe Bastianich,
and others. Those places, Osteria Lupa Romana, Esca, and Otto Enoteca Pizzeria, received strong reviews, but the power of Mario's celebrity helped draw all sorts of customers, not just well-heeled New Yorkers
who always flocked to the hot new restaurants. If you were coming into
the city from Pine Brook, New Jersey, or Hewlett, Long Island, you
would be likely to swap your Giants—or Jets—gear for a blazer and
consider trying one of Mario's places.

It was good restaurant business, but for its In the Kitchen block, the
network was not looking to appeal to Giants fans in the way *Emeril Live*
had done. Ina, Sandra Lee, and Rachael were aimed primarily at women
who dreamed of getting food on the table fast, not an audience who
wanted to learn about which dried and salted parts of the pig Italian
shepherds carried with them for snacking. If a few men wanted to pause
on the channel to bask in the intense gleam of Sandra Lee's smile or to
fantasize about having a mother who was as good a cook as Ina, well,
that was fine, too.

Bob Tuschman found an alternative to Mario in the February 2002
issue of *Food & Wine* magazine. An article entitled "Let's Do Lunch"
featured Giada De Laurentiis, who appeared ready for her close-up.

(That issue of *Food & Wine* also contained a feature on Maria Guarnaschelli, a renowned cookbook editor, and her daughter, Alex, a rising
New York chef. Bob was not moved to call the less ethereal Alex, and it
would be a few years before she found herself a network fixture.)

The article of interest explained that Giada, inspired by her grandfather Dino's love for the Neapolitan food of his youth—he had lost a
fortune opening upscale Italian markets and restaurants called DDL
Foodshow—had enrolled in Le Cordon Bleu cooking school in Paris.
She had done stints at a hotel restaurant in Marina del Rey and at Wolfgang Puck's Spago in Beverly Hills before tiring of long restaurant
hours. Her catering company, GDL Foods, was known not just for Italian food but also for California comfort staples like turkey meat loaf

and chicken pot pie, made for clients like the actor and director Ron Howard. For the photo shoot at a lunch in honor of Dino, Giada, thirty-two, was photographed with a sweater over her narrow shoulders, smiling wide and holding a little furry white dog on her lap. She had made baked rigatoni, pork loin with spinach and ham, and a ricotta tart.

Bob could not phone the gorgeous, petite, honey-haired caterer fast enough to discuss a cooking show. She was open to it, even if it had not been her intention to be in show business.

Bob talked it over with Eileen. Her concern was that despite Giada's Italian food heritage, she had been trained in a different tradition at Le Cordon Bleu and then had cooked generic fare for her catering clients. How exactly could they present her? She wasn't the expert that Mario or any number of Italian chefs were. Ina, Rachael, and Sandra Lee had cookbooks. Giada didn't. From their conversations came the idea that Giada could be the personality who represented "everyday Italian" cooking. She would make dishes regular people could make, not just admire as part of the sport of "armchair cooking." This would allow the network to carry two Italian experts—Mario, the professor, and Giada, the home ec teacher.

Bob asked Giada to make a test video. A friend in TV production filmed her making a baked rigatoni, but she did not look very comfortable on camera. Eileen asked Bobby Flay to take a look at the test. "What do you think of this girl?" Eileen asked him.

"She's really pretty," Bobby said. "She seems like she's good."

"I think I'm going to give her a chance," Eileen said.

It made sense to him. Giada seemed to know something about food. She came from Hollywood royalty and probably had an intuitive understanding of show business. Bobby understood better than most of the old guard chefs that show business was what the Food Network was in now.

Eileen had a solution to Giada's on-camera stiffness: Nigella again. But cheaper. She asked a young Food Network staff producer, Irene Wong, to study the *Barefoot Contessa* tapes. They could borrow some of the production technique and do a lower-budget version with Giada for a show they decided to call *Everyday Italian*. Irene did not consider what she was doing as stealing the Nigella formula. Yes, there were multiple takes from different angles of each cooking move, and there were close-ups of Giada explaining to the camera what the actions were, so the talking could overdub the action. But an important difference was that Irene was shooting with just a single camera, giving the director even closer control over every shot, and they rented a neutral location instead of shooting in Giada's home, so there was less narrative backstory required.

Giada's famous grandfather, Dino, had always questioned whether his five-foot-two granddaughter could stand up to the rigors of the kitchen—how could she even lift the heavy pots?—and the harshness of a twelve-hour shoot day could be even more brutal. Irene, accustomed to training new talent on *Melting Pot*, instructed Giada to smile whenever she spoke on camera, no matter what was happening around her— the same advice Sara Moulton had given Rachael. However, the space was strange to Giada, as were the borrowed cooking utensils, the water pressure, and the stoves. Trying to remember what she was supposed to say and keeping a cheerful expression on her face while occasionally burning things was a challenge. Smiling widely throughout a twelve-hour day under lights made her cheek muscles ripple with pain. But like any other new workout, her system adapted to it, and soon Giada could smile effortlessly, no matter what the circumstances.

Once her show aired, viewers asked their own questions. Some wrote to the network criticizing it for hiring a pretty young actress to host a cooking show rather than someone who knew something about cooking. Even those who liked her show began asking how she could cook so much pasta and stir in so much panna and yet stay so thin. Was she spitting out food when the camera stopped?

Giada always told people that the secret to her slender figure was that she ate small portions throughout the day rather than big heavy meals, and that she hit the gym regularly. Those who worked with her on the set knew that that was basically true—salads for lunch and only small tastes of finished dishes. But Irene and the production crew did have a secret weapon: they kept a stash of bittersweet chocolate in the freezers for Giada. When they needed to pep her up for a segment, they'd feed her a fortifying nibble of chocolate. On some twelve-hour shoot days, the little bits of chocolate seemed to be the only food she took in.

This was talent an agent could do something with. Jon Rosen, who by now had gained a reputation for making money for his Food Network clients, received a call from a lawyer in Los Angeles. "Would you be interested in Giada De Laurentiis?"

She was represented by International Creative Management, but was considering making a move. The lawyer arranged a video conference, and during the meeting, Giada told Jon she was satisfied with her book agent at ICM, but she complained of her TV agent. "I asked what he thought of my show, and he hadn't even watched it."

Jon told her she did not need to be treated that way. He gave her a version of the pitch he had made to Bobby: she had enormous potential, she could be a brand, there was a lot to do, and he would do it with her.

Giada signed with Jon.

The In the Kitchen block running on Saturday and Sunday mornings was solidifying, but prime time was not as set. New research from focus groups was confirming Judy Girard's instinct that after 7 p.m., viewers wanted more entertainment. *Emeril Live* filled an hour every night and was solid. *Cooking Live* had filled up a lot of time, and Judy found Sara's pluck appealing, but the instructional show ended in 2002, when *Sara's Secrets*, an ITK show, began taping. *Unwrapped*, *Good Eats*, and *Iron Chef* were slotted on various nights. But there were still hours in the schedule filled with one road show or another—*$40 a Day*, *Food-Nation*, *Food Finds*, *The Best Of*—but begging for programs that could make more of a cultural and ratings mark.

Ready . . . Set . . . Cook! was gone, but Eileen believed there was still potential life in food competition and game shows. She gave the green light to *Date Plate*. The premise was that two young bachelors would watch a clip in which a young woman described herself, and each would then prepare a dish she would like so much she'd go on a date with the guy who made it. Each competitor was paired with a professional chef and given $50 for ingredients. On the premiere episode, an opera lover named Joshua, twenty-seven, competed against a bartender-actor-weightlifter John, twenty-two, for the affections of Hallie Sherard, twenty-five, a TV producer whose hobby was said to be sculpting rear ends out of wood.

Joshua and Cat Cora made Crazy Water Fish Stew. John, with Daisuke Utagawa, cooked Elvis-Inspired Lamb Chop. Hallie chose Joshua's stew. The reality of the show was less than real. The men were cast from modeling and talent agencies. On their off-camera date, Josh took Hallie to a ceremony with a friend of his father's who was a shaman. A ritual was performed with burning sage. Josh told her he was very interested in theater. She drove her own car home. The show lasted twenty-six episodes—thirteen fewer than *Three Dog Bakery*.

Eileen also tried *Food Fight*, which pitted two teams of amateur cooks against each other in themed episodes. In one, Jill Kelley and her twin sister, Natalie Khawam, battled a pair of brothers to see who could make the best dish using alligator meat. The show was canceled and forgotten until 2012, when Jill's complaints to the FBI about receiving threatening anonymous e-mails ultimately led to the revelation of General David Petraeus's affair with his biographer, Paula Broadwell, and his resignation as CIA director. Suddenly the media was begging Food Network for archived copies of *Food Fight*.

Eileen also tried something Matt Stillman might have liked. *Dweezil and Lisa* was a reality show starring Dweezil Zappa, the son of the musician Frank Zappa, and his girlfriend, pop singer Lisa Loeb. Eileen hoped *Dweezil and Lisa* would appeal to hip young urbanites. The pair traveled around the country, sampling food and wine, cooking, and playing music. Eileen was correct that hipsters were becoming more interested in food, but this was not the show to capture that demographic. Reviews were mixed, and after ten low-rated episodes, the show was not renewed; the bickering couple broke up shortly after taping it.

These awkward, low-budget shows looked increasingly dated by 2004, when broadcast networks were showing more outlandish and sophisticated reality competition shows like *The Bachelor* and *Joe Millionaire*.

Even as her programming department was delivering these duds along with Giada, Rachael, and Ina, Eileen was making her most ambitious post-Matt attempt to shake up expectations about Food Network.

In Anthony Bourdain's 2001 best seller, *Kitchen Confidential*, he ridiculed Food Network, mocked Bobby, and compared Emeril to an Ewok—one of the glassy-eyed band of alien teddy bears in *Return of the Jedi*. Tony quickly inked a follow-up deal for a book called *A Cook's Tour*, for which he intended to travel to far-off lands, eat interesting foods, and write about it.

One day, two TV producers, Dan Cohen and a colleague, came to Brasserie Les Halles, where Tony was still working as a chef. They looked dodgy to him, but he sat down. They said they were fans of *Kitchen Confidential* and were interested in working with him, but he told them he'd already sold the film and TV rights to New Line.

Tony, tall, lean, and disturbingly still at times, like a blank-faced poker player giving nothing away, could come across as simultaneously shy and intimidating, as if wheels were grinding underneath the surface calm. He concluded that the producers were the types who talked big and delivered little. He gave it to them straight. "I can't give you *Kitchen Confidential*," he said, "but I just sold a book idea for a cook's tour." He explained the concept and said he was about to leave, making him unavailable.

He grew colder when they suggested that if they developed a show idea together, they might all pitch it to Food Network.

They haven't been reading my book too closely, Tony thought. Food

Network? I've been going around making fun of Emeril, for chrissake. These guys are full of shit. They don't even know me. He glowered at them and they went away.

He was shocked when they called back a week later and said a meeting had been set up at Food Network to discuss the idea of doing *A Cook's Tour* as a TV show.

Tony had appeared as a guest on *Molto Mario* and as a chef demonstrating a salmon recipe on one of the early newsy shows. He had been as appalled as Ken Lowe had been at the filthy kitchens, the tiny sets, the electric stoves, and the production values that were no better than porn. He had to wash his own pan.

But at this meeting, the situation seemed to have changed. Judy and Eileen seemed to be professional, smart, and, most surprising of all, genuinely interested in him and the kind of show he might like to do. He was impressed, but he tested them. "I make fun of Emeril. Why do you want to talk to me?"

They told him they were eager to hear new ideas.

He rattled off some of the countries he intended to go to as part of *A Cook's Tour*: Cambodia, Vietnam, Russia, places he could not imagine the network of Rachael Ray being interested in.

"That's fantastic," Eileen said. "Do the show!"

> "I got the impression, I'm sure a highly subjective one, that they were really sick of their own programming. And they were looking for something a little subversive."
>
> —ANTHONY BOURDAIN

Something was going on that did not make sense. Why would these two very smart, successful women want to risk their reputations on him? But if they really were as willing as they said they were, to send cameras on his tour and allow him to do it his way, then okay. Why not?

Eileen was genuinely entertained and interested in Tony. He fit her urban sensibility. Of all the shows she developed, she really wanted this one to work. Judy was willing to take a few chances. The network was on firmer ground, and she was starting to grow a bit restless, despite the raw fennel she munched to maintain mental clarity during the day.

Tony certainly seemed a more likely TV star to her than Rosengarten had.

With the network's money behind him, Tony set off on the first stop
on his television journey with a husband-and-wife production and camera team of Chris Collins and Lydia Tenaglia. In that first season, he
ate cobra heart in Ho Chi Minh City, iguana tamales in Mexico, and
drank a lot of vodka in St. Petersburg. "Look at that; it's sex, man," he
said, peering at slices of fresh tuna in Tokyo. He drank, smoked, and
even cursed on camera. The curses were bleeped out, but Tony received
none of the negative feedback from the network that he'd anticipated.
He never called the network and appreciated that they never called him.

Ratings weren't spectacular—*Good Eats* and *Emeril Live* were beating
A Cook's Tour in prime time, as was Marc Summer's lower-budget evergreen, *Unwrapped*—but reviews were strong, and the network sprang for
a second season, shot in 2003. Tony went to Brazil, where he sampled
seafood stew and many caipirinhas, and to Kansas City, Houston, and
North Carolina for a show on barbecue.

Eileen wanted the network to be smart and risky and was emotionally invested in the show, but during the second season she started hearing from Scripps that a cigarette-puffing, vodka-swilling Lou Reed of
the planet's fire pits and stillhouses might not be the right direction for
Food Network. Nevertheless, she believed in the show and spent personal capital arguing for it as a counterbalance to the light and wimmy
ITK fare.

Perhaps she should have saved up some of that capital.

In early 2004, Ed Spray, who oversaw the company's cable channels,
offered a consulting job to Brooke Johnson, a veteran in the business
who'd been program director at WABC in New York, where she had
launched the show that became *Live with Regis and Kathie Lee*. Most
recently she had been the head of A&E, until she was pushed out in
2000. Brooke was widely credited with helping A&E grow from a fringe
cable channel that ran British coproductions in the late 1980s into a
major player that reached seventy-six million homes. Although her departure was called a resignation so she could spend time with her

teenage children, she had been shoved aside in a complicated corporate power play. When her three years of severance ended, she called friends in the TV industry about a new job.

Ironically, Brooke had discussed taking the top job at Food nearly a decade earlier. She knew Reese Schonfeld, and when he was starting CNN in the early 1980s he had tried to bring her to Atlanta, but Brooke had declined. When he was leaving as head of Food Network in 1995 and Brooke was rising at A&E, he'd floated the idea of her taking his place.

"I'm in a position to influence the board, and if you were interested, I could probably make that happen," Reese had told her.

Like most people in those days, Brooke thought that a 24-hour network devoted to food was a nutty idea. It was doomed to failure. Known to deliver her unvarnished thoughts in a straight monotone, she told him plainly, "I am not interested."

But when Ed offered her the job of being a general consultant across all the Scripps networks, she'd been out of work for three years and it sounded like an ideal way to reenter the business and survey the cable landscape.

One day she received a call from Judy, whom she'd known over the years. "You're a consultant to us, right?" Judy asked. "Well, let's have lunch. I have a problem."

The problem was Eileen. The head of programming griped about the lack of funding to try more experimental pilots, even though her overall budget had increased dramatically—58 percent in 2003 alone, with twelve new series and sixty specials. There were solid TV veterans on the programming team now: Bob Tuschman, Kathleen Finch, Bruce Seidel, Alison Page, and others. It wasn't just about following hunches anymore. It was about managing a team. Judy liked Eileen personally, but she didn't think she could run a department the size of Food's. She thought Eileen had made a mess of some presentations to the Scripps board. Budgets and show ideas were not being teed up clearly enough to receive easy approval and, while she did have many successes, *Barefoot Contessa* among them, many of Eileen's hunches weren't working out.

At lunch, Judy told Brooke she was thinking about restructuring the department, wanting to somehow keep Eileen but ease her out of responsibility.

One of the reports Brooke had written as a consultant noted that Food Network was doing nothing to capitalize on the growing success of its stars. By January 2004, Food Network was reaching eighty million households. Its website had four million regular users who were accessing a recipe library that had reached 25,000 entries. The site had a store selling Emerilware pots and pans, Bobby Flay pear margarita mix, recipe cards from Ina, and roasting pans from Jamie Oliver—none of them official Food Network products, but a testament to the growing power of the brand. Was Food Network the pivotal factor in American culture's increasing fascination with all things food-related or did it happen to come along when that interest was increasing for other reasons? From the perspective of the people inside the network, it was not their job to tease out how many tablespoons of the new gourmet-obsessed nation were added by Food Network and how many by other societal factors. They just kept putting out shows that they hoped the culture would eat up. They used focus groups to help them understand the new order so they could cater to it, but full comprehension of the phenomenon was a complex exercise best left to university Food Studies departments (New York University had started one in 1996). TV people were too busy trying to turn a profit.

Brooke was appalled that such profit opportunities were being left to the talent and their proliferating agents to figure out haphazardly. Ed agreed with Brooke, and before her lunch with Judy had suggested she head up a department of ancillary business. Even though the creation of such a role was her idea, Brooke admitted to herself, Man, I'm so bad at this kind of stuff. At the same time, she had received an offer from Laureen Ong, the president of the National Geographic Channel, to become her head of programming. Brooke was tempted to jump ship, but the NatGeo job would require a weekly commute to Washington, D.C., and Scripps had been so generous, hiring her as a consultant.

All of these pressures erupted at lunch with Judy when Brooke spontaneously said, "I have the solution to your problem, Judy. You don't need to restructure, you should hire me. Hire me as head of programming."

By then, Brooke had come to admire the kind of foresight that Ken had and that she did not, seeing the potential in Food Network in the mid-1990s. Judy said she'd think about a programming role for Brooke, but Ed nixed it, insisting it was ancillary business or nothing. Brooke was close to jumping to NatGeo, but after sleeping on it one night, decided to stick with Scripps. A week later, Judy, having talked it over with Ed, offered Brooke the top programming job, installing her above Eileen and giving her the title of general manager in charge of programming and creative services. Judy hoped that Brooke could organize the department and make strong presentations to the Scripps board, leaving Eileen to continue developing show ideas with her team.

At A&E, Brooke had invested in a few major shows rather than a lot of minor ones, as Food was doing. Her first ratings breakthrough was with a series called *Biography*, documentaries about historical figures and big celebrities like F. Scott Fitzgerald, Bob Hope, and Calvin Klein—and eventually nearly everyone you could imagine. Running every single night at one point, it made A&E a prime-time force on cable.

Now she wondered, why not place a big bet by investing in one of the most successful shows on Food?

She asked Eileen, "Why don't we do *Iron Chef* in English?"

"Because it would cost so much money!" Eileen replied.

In 2001, Food Network had turned down the chance to buy the American rights to an English-language version of the show they'd made famous. The struggling broadcast network UPN bought them instead and produced a version called *Iron Chef USA*. It starred William Shatner as the Chairman, who managed, in a glittering purple coat and frilly vest, to channel Takeshi Kaga's histrionic original in a uniquely Shatnerian way: "Totally rad!" the former Captain Kirk and T. J. Hooker exclaimed at one point.

Iron Chef USA tipped too far into camp. Instead of carefully follow-ing the evolution of each dish, the show searched for one-liners. The through-line of watching the competitors' creations evolve—crucial to the mythology of the show as a pressure cooker that would drive chefs to new heights of creativity—was lost in the noise.

Sissy Biggers found work on the show—she and two others were out-fitted in gold blazers and cast as roving reporters and commentators. An exchange about sea urchin roe was typical:

"What? It's the sperm? We eat that?"

"Yes, it's like the love juices of the sea urchin."

Bruce Seidel, the programming executive at Food Network in charge of *Iron Chef*, attended the taping of the UPN version. "We should have bought this," he said to a colleague. "We could do better."

After two low-rated episodes, UPN surrendered.

As head of programming, Brooke knew that she had a short honey-moon period with Judy and the executives at Scripps in which they would allow her to take a few chances. It might require building an expensive new Kitchen Stadium set in New York, wrangling live audi-ences, developing a big cast, and asking the network kitchens to source obscure ingredients, but she was confident it would all be worth it for a big hit.

Bruce put it together, producing the pilots in Los Angeles. He cast the American Chairman, and since Food Network was still running the Japanese version, he saw it as an opportunity to link the two shows, and sought an ethnically Asian actor as the nephew of the original Chair-man. Many actors answered the casting call in Los Angeles, but when Mark Dacascos walked in and started speaking, Bruce turned to a col-league and said, "We've found our Chairman."

Mark's father and stepmother were both kung fu champions and teachers. He was raised in Germany and spent long hours training in martial arts and attending tournaments. As a boy, he'd seen a kung fu movie in which powerful fighting monks defended a small village, and he developed a fantasy that he could become a warrior monk who would be a gardener and teach philosophy and history to children. Before Bruce cast him, Mark had found work in a few martial arts movies but little else.

Brooke asked Bobby Flay to help create the match-ups; he chose Mario Batali and Wolfgang Puck. Bobby was matched against one of the original Japanese Iron Chefs, Hiroyuki Sakai. Wolfgang beat Masaharu Morimoto. Michiba, he of the grabby hands and the "broth of vigor," did not attend. For his two sous chefs, Mario had chosen Anne Burrell, who was the chef at Italian Wine Merchants, and Mark Ladner, the chef at Casa Mono in Manhattan. Both had serious technical skills, and Mario enjoyed hanging around with them. Anne screamed so loud with joy when Mario told her she was in that people nearby thought she was hurt.

When Mario was pronounced the winner of his battle with Morimoto, he turned to Anne and Mark and said, "That's it. You're on my *Iron Chef* team forever!"

"The judges of the original Iron Chefs were all Japanese, so they understood what I cook, or do in terms of technique. That doesn't mean they are better, but at least they know what I am doing, which is in a way satisfying for me, even if they vote for my opponent. Also, I feel more comfortable explaining my dishes in Japanese to them, which is far better than explaining my concepts and dishes in my broken English. I always feel terribly frustrated when I cannot convey my thoughts to American judges."

—MASAHARU MORIMOTO

The conflict between Eileen's gut and Brooke's more clinical thinking came into play as the network negotiated with Tony about a potential third season of *A Cook's Tour*. Eileen continued to believe that his voice was good for the network's identity and well worth keeping, even if the ratings were not at *Unwrapped*'s level.

Judy, eager for Brooke to shoulder some of the decision-making load, had taken a step back. Never a food person, she was starting to dream of resuming the long beach walks Ken had interrupted when he hired her. Brooke wasn't totally opposed to *A Cook's Tour*, but she had already decided that it needed to change if it was to survive. In his book *Medium Raw: A Bloody Valentine to the World of Food and the People Who Cook*, Tony described the jolting moment when he met Brooke, when the good feelings of working with Judy and Eileen were replaced by a new mood: "There was a limp handshake as cabin pressure changed, a black hole of fun—all light, all possibility of joy was sucked into the vortex of this hunched and scowling apparition."

While visiting Spain on a book tour, Tony was invited to the workshop of the groundbreaking chef Ferran Adrià. The Spaniard had heard that Tony called him "bogus" in *Kitchen Confidential* and wanted to set the author straight. Over glasses of cava and slices of ham in Barcelona, Ferran invited Tony to film the creative process in which Ferran developed new dishes for his restaurant El Bulli. It was a once-in-a-lifetime invitation. No one had ever filmed Adrià at work, and Tony wanted to do it for season three of *A Cook's Tour*.

Ferran was a genius who had pioneered what some called "molecular gastronomy"; Ferran preferred to call it "techno-emotional cuisine." He could turn vegetables into foams, solids into liquid suspensions, piña coladas into cotton candy. Eileen wanted to give him the go-ahead, but she was getting pressure from the network. Tony's barbecue episode of *A Cook's Tour* had outrated his international shows. Texas ribs were better for the bottom line than cobra hearts, and the network wanted him to do more shows in America.

Tony warned her, "If I don't get my way, if I don't get to do the things I want to do, I'm not going to do it."

Eileen said she understood and she fought for him. But the network wanted less foreign content, fewer foreign accents. She lost the battle. Wolfgang Puck had already been canceled. An episode of *My Country, My Kitchen* that featured French-born chef Eric Ripert visiting Andorra was used as an example of what they didn't want, because they thought Ripert's accent was too thick to be understood.

Tony, Chris, and Lydia decided to make the Ferran episode anyway. They self-financed it for $35,000, which led to the founding of Chris and Lydia's company Zero Point Zero Productions. They sold *Decoding*

Ferran Adrià, an ode to the Spaniard's artistry, to various television outlets around the world, and it became the pilot for the series Tony and Zero Point Zero made for the Travel channel, *No Reservations*—a bold and literate series that helped define the channel, though it was not fundamentally different from *A Cook's Tour*.

It soon became apparent that with Brooke on board, there was no room for Eileen. As Brooke was given more responsibility, Judy thought Eileen knew her days were numbered. She didn't imagine that Eileen would be surprised by what was coming when she asked her to lunch.

But she was. Judy wanted to get it over with, and as soon as they sat down, she asked, "How much money will it take for you to leave?"

Eileen was speechless. She loved this job more than any she'd ever had. Judy repeated, "How much will it take? Come back and tell me."

"I've learned that you're not the channel. And even if you started or built it or changed it, you don't own it, and it's not your child. And so anybody who's in that kind of position is just sitting in a chair. So it shouldn't surprise me. You can go through every other network alive, and there are a lot of changes. So it shouldn't surprise me, but it just was a surprise."

—EILEEN OPATUT

After contentious negotiations between the network and Jim Griffin, Emeril was signed to a new long-term deal for *Emeril Live* and *Essence of Emeril*. Judy had wanted to nix *Essence* because it was a pure cooking show without much Bam! and was not getting strong ratings, but Emeril, always a chef before he was an entertainer, enjoyed the low-key production of *Essence*. Jim threatened to walk if *Essence* was canceled. The network backed down, but they were not enamored of Jim and his tough tactics.

Deeply invested, the network continued to wring everything it could from the king. They shot specials in Hawaii. They did an episode in front of ten thousand people in Chicago. They went to Orlando and

Las Vegas. A Halloween special was shot at the Eastern State Peniten-
tiary in Pennsylvania. There were plans to send Emeril's food up in the
space shuttle so the astronauts could cook along with him.

Compared to the newer hosts, Emeril, with his serious cooking pedigree, was seeming, as Bourdain remembered, "like Escoffier." The network was finding success by following its Noodle Roni strategy, casting
TV-friendly hosts, but there was a price to be paid. Even before the
first episode of *Semi-Homemade Cooking with Sandra Lee* aired, the food
elite took aim. A writer for *Gourmet* magazine noted the inclusion of
Cheez Whiz in a tortellini recipe and dared to make it herself: "It takes
two days of soaking to remove the rubbery film the substance leaves on
my saucepan, so I can only imagine what it's doing to my insides."

As the network's profile rose, a counter-industry of Food Network
critics was developing. Generally, the narrative was that there had been
a golden age of foodiness, when David Rosengarten roamed the halls
in an apron, Alan Richman ruminated on runny cheeses, and Marion
Cunningham was always roasting a chicken. Sometime around the millennium, it had all been betrayed by the vixens of Velveeta, Sandra Lee,
and her evil ilk.

There was some truth to this argument. The pre-Scripps network
had relied more squarely on chefs and deeply knowledgeable food folk—
who had been watched by audiences about a fifth the size of what the
network was reaching by 2003. But you could still learn a hell of a lot
about cooking and the wide world of food by watching the Food Network at the dawn of its modern era. How Junior Mints are made is an
interesting process, as is how the chef at Lemaire restaurant in Rich-
mond, Virginia, keeps the skin on his Chesapeake Bay Rockfish crisp,
shown on an episode of *FoodNation*. The network's various road shows
were putting the evolution of American cuisine on display. In the mid-
2000s, *Road Tasted* featured shrimp and crawfish "turducken" in Louisiana, and a Danish kringle in Wisconsin.

Tony, freed from the constraints of working at the network, became
its most entertaining critic, launching a side career harpooning its stars

at every book signing and food festival he attended. In December 2004, on tour in Toronto to promote *Anthony Bourdain's Les Halles Cookbook*, he was asked by a newspaper reporter, "What's the most offensive TV cooking show?"

"There's one in the U.S. by Sandra Lee," Tony said. "She seems to suggest that you can make good food easily, in minutes, using Cheez Whiz and chopped-up Pringles and packaged chili mix."

Sandy was particularly ripe for attack. Even Sandy admitted that she had made some mistakes when she first started in the food business, especially her infamous Kwanzaa cake, which Tony called "a war crime on television."

The cake was hardly on a par with waterboarding, but it demonstrated that hosting a cooking show requires more from the talent than good teeth and an iron will. Sandy told Denise Vivaldo that she wanted to add easy-to-make cakes for every holiday, including Chanukah and Kwanzaa, in her second book, *Semi-Homemade Desserts*.

Denise wondered what she could possibly use for a Kwanzaa cake. Sandy had specified that all the cakes be store-bought angel food. The holiday was supposed to have a connection with the harvest. What semi-homemade ingredients seemed autumnal and harvest-like? She found cans of apple pie filling and a bag of corn nuts, a jar of Orville Redenbacher popcorn, and pumpkin seeds—what was more late season than all that? To hold it all together, Denise grabbed a can of Betty Crocker Rich and Creamy vanilla frosting.

When she looked at the corn nuts and pumpkin seeds sprinkled on the icing of the Kwanzaa cake, Denise thought, Those might be too hard for people's teeth. Someone will break a crown. But at that point, she'd written out the recipe and was worn out from Sandy's badgering 7 a.m. phone calls.

Most authors wanted to taste the recipes before they put them into cookbooks or at least offer suggestions. But that wasn't the case here. Denise and her assistant tossed the first Kwanzaa cake into a dumpster. A recipe tester sold the second one at a school bake sale—the first Semi-

Homemade Kwanzaa cake ever offered to the public is believed to have been sold to an anonymous buyer for less than $10.

Years later, after the video of Sandy making the cake on her show had gone viral, she admitted that she had learned from it "how in control of every single element of your show you need to be. The first couple of seasons I was not."

> "I feel bad as a professional cook that I was involved in that abortion."
>
> —DENISE VIVALDO

Denise had learned, too. It was her last project for Sandy.

As nasty as the criticism of Sandy and other stars got, Tony and other attackers were in many ways doing them a favor by keeping their names in the media. Every time he came up with a brilliant new insult—"frightening hell spawn of Kathie Lee and Betty Crocker"—it would be picked up and reposted, or dozens of commenters would share their own bile about the stars they hated so much they couldn't take their eyes off them, helping cement them as household names while stirring their fans to rise to the defense of the kitchen personalities they loved. Whether the talent was pushing pecan pie, Chicken Short-cut-a-tore, or a visit to the Butterfinger factory, fans were mad for them.

Indeed, one bad cake could not spoil the party. For those who had survived the putsches of the previous years, it was *laissez le bon temps roulez*. In November 2004, the organizers of The Great Big Food Show in Cleveland sprang for a large complement of Food Network stars to appear at the International Exposition Center. Mario, Rachael, Alton, Marc Summers, and local celebrity chef Michael Symon led cooking demonstrations, trivia contests, tastings, and book signings. More than forty thousand people attended.

Symon, who had made guest appearances on a number of Food Network shows, owned the most food-forward restaurant in Cleveland, Lola Bistro. After the second day at the expo center, the Food Network crew headed to Lola for a late Saturday-night "family" meal.

As the food arrived, Mario decreed, "Take away all the utensils! Utensils are not allowed!"

Marc picked up his steak with his hands and bit into it. Beef juice shot onto Mario's shirt.

"What the . . !" Mario yelled.

"You're the one who wanted to do this!" Marc yelled back. The meal stretched on. Eating and drinking. Eating and drinking. Laughing. And drinking.

Around 2 a.m., a few participants started muttering that maybe it was time to head back to their hotel. After all, some of them had to be onstage at 9 a.m. that morning.

"We're going to a strip club!" Mario declared.

The group poured into cars. When they arrived at a strip club under a bridge in a seedy part of town around 3 a.m., the manager warned them that it was closing in fifteen minutes. Mario ordered twenty-five shots and sent over lap dances to Marc and Rachael.

"No, no, please!" Marc and Rachael protested as the strippers sank down onto their laps and began gyrating.

"We gotta get out of here!" Rachael shouted.

Rachael and Mario said they were headed back to Lola. Marc fell into a car with people he didn't know. Back at the hotel, and nearly blind drunk, he phoned Rachael and Mario to make sure they'd be fit for the show in a few hours. No answer. He passed out.

The next morning onstage, Mario was there, hitting his mark, although his voice was unusually deep and gravelly. Alton, game and on point, made beef jerky with a room fan, three furnace filters, and a bungee cord. But Rachael, whose schedule over the three days included eight half-hour cooking demos and eight book signings, complained repeatedly from the stage about her hangover and forgot to explain many details of her recipes.

Fans waited afterward to give Rachael supportive hugs, as they would to someone they loved and forgave.

Marc asked his audience, "How many people watch us and say, 'I can do that. I want my own show'?" He told them the network was working on a new reality show that might make their dreams come true and encouraged them to send in audition tapes.

Fans adored the illusion that almost anyone might be able to leap over the bar and become a star on the network. It wasn't true, of course. But the job description had changed. Good looks, performance chops, and fierce ambition now counted for more than a degree from Johnson & Wales.

Days later, during the week of the network's eleventh anniversary, its stars gathered in New York for a live Thanksgiving special. The premise was that they were all cooking turkey and fixings together. Programming executives wanted to deepen the feeling among viewers that these stars were members of their fami-

> "I would get phone calls in NYC at 11 p.m. saying, 'Hey, Summers, what are you doing?' 'Nothing.' 'Come to the Spotted Pig.' . . . I love Mario to death, but man, I couldn't hang with him. That guy was going to kill me. I realized it after a few outings with him. He gets away with murder, but I couldn't do it."
>
> —MARC SUMMERS

lies, and that it was one big happy group. Cooking in the network kitchen were Giada, Paula, Tyler, Alton, Rachael, Emeril, and Sara Moulton. Sara had been appearing live on the network in prime time for years, and this was the most artificial show she'd ever done.

She eyeballed her colleagues and thought how strange it was that they were all pretending to be so chummy. Sara had never even seen Giada or Paula in the flesh. One taped her show in Los Angeles, the other in a New York suburb.

"I've never met either one of them before," she thought. "And yet here we are, all cooking a family meal."

Competitors Sharpen Their Knives

The Food Network's internal slogan might have been Every New President Makes Changes. Each one came to the job with a central idea about what he or she wanted to accomplish. Reese envisioned CNN with stoves. Jeff Wayne worked to rationalize the operation, Erica Gruen brought in more on-air personalities, Eric Ober boldly expanded the programming, and Judy Girard sought to broaden the network's appeal to a less food-centric audience.

By the time it entered its second decade, Food had figured out some of what worked well throughout its programming day and how to market it. It had also seeded a sprouting world of production talent and potential new stars. The foodie culture's roots in Berkeley, downtown New York, and elsewhere had now spread throughout the country, fed at least partly by the network and certainly feeding talent and ideas back into it. Whoever was in charge could reap what the network had sown and deliver its stars to a hungry audience.

But as always, getting it exactly right was impossible. The network was making some of the people happy some of the time. The task of the ever-changing enterprise was to make as many people happy as it could. The pursuit of this goal would create riches and fame, as well as failures and heartbreak. And opportunities would be missed.

Before she went to work for Scripps, Brooke Johnson, the head of programming, had rarely watched Food Network and the only network personality she had heard of was Emeril Lagasse. But she soon realized Rachael was the real rising star, a once-in-a-decade talent. She was attracting younger viewers than Emeril, and many of them had never watched a cooking show before. When Brooke extended the hours of the In the Kitchen block, ratings improved. In 2003, she invited Rachael to meet for a drink. At the Bryant Park Grill, Rachael ordered a vodka and downed it like it was cold water on a hot summer afternoon.

Hard liquor was not Brooke's thing, but she calculated, I better have what she's having.

Because Brooke had never spent much time with food folk, she had feared she would have nothing in common with Rachael, who had not gone to culinary school, but had worked in restaurants her whole life. But then the two began talking about the television business and the art of crafting a show. "It's all about telling a story, grabbing them quick, and not letting go," Rachael said.

This was Brooke's language. Her dad had produced the classic television series *Truth or Consequences*. He'd died when she was only twenty-six, but she remembered one of his oft-repeated lessons about television: "The bit has to be complete." She understood the advice to mean that stories needed a beginning, a middle, and an end, and that all three parts had to be good.

They ordered a second round of drinks, and then another. Rachael talked with feeling about her life, discussing how hard her mother still worked and how the only foods she used on her show were ingredients that anyone could buy at their local supermarket. Her focus on what you could and could not buy at the Price Chopper supermarket in Albany connected her to America's home cooks outside the urban foodie zones.

After their fourth vodka and soda, Brooke slurred, "I have to go home now." The two shared a taxi, and during the ride, Brooke kept thinking, I'm shit-faced. Don't throw up on her. Don't throw up. Don't throw up. . . .

She made it out of the cab without vomiting and concluded that the two lessons of the evening were that Rachael understood TV and that it was a bad idea to try to keep pace with her drinking.

Both were true, but Brooke missed a crucial aspect of Rachael—the same one Ken Lowe had missed in his ouzo session with Mario and his indulgent meals with Emeril, and that other programming executives apparently missed despite their expense-account nights at New York's finest restaurants. Some of the stars of food television straddle two worlds, the hard-living behind-the-scenes life of a restaurant worker and the people-pleasing world of the performer. Like great actors, the line blurs between the performance and the personal. Chefs present tripe not to be outrageous, but to reveal how humans can make something beautiful out of anything. And the great ones put a piece of themselves on every plate.

A year after Brooke's night with Rachael, Judy saw that the network was on a solid path, and concluded that her job was done. "I'm bored," she told Ken Lowe and Ed Spray. "Put Brooke in charge."

For herself, Judy figured she was about a year or two from permanently starting the "second half" of her life, when she would give up her television career and live somewhere quieter, resuming her beach walks. She and Ken agreed she would take on one more assignment, trying to turn around a troubled Scripps property, the ShopAtHome Network, a rival to QVC. There, she might be able to find profits by selling merchandise associated with the stars Food Network had helped make.

In April 2004, Brooke was appointed president of the Food Network—the first peaceful transition in the network's history.

Iron Chef America: A Battle of the Masters debuted during Brooke's first month as president and attracted spectacularly high ratings, more than a million viewers for the finale on April 25. It scored a 1.4 prime-time rating, tying the channel's highest ever, set by the original Webster Hall Iron Chef battle between Bobby and Morimoto in June 2000. It helped Food Network score an average 0.7 Nielsen household rating, a 17 percent improvement over the previous year. In an earnings conference call, Joe NeCastro, the chief financial officer of E.W. Scripps, bragged to a Morgan Stanley analyst, "We certainly did get the bang for our buck out of *Iron Chef.*"

> "Brooke is a very direct, straight-ahead person. Judy is a little bit softer around the edges. So there were a few feathers ruffled early on because Judy had her favorites and Brooke was the new sheriff in town."
>
> **—KEN LOWE**

The success of the pilots for *Iron Chef America* gave Brooke the momentum to make more changes in prime time. Less gut, more spreadsheet than Judy, she was an even bigger believer in audience studies than any of her predecessors had been.

> "Even your current fans need to be reeducated that you're not just 'how-to.'"
>
> **—INTERNAL FOOD NETWORK STUDY, 2004**

In November 2004, the results came in on one study she commissioned, "Getting Closer to the Truth: Exploring the Viewer/Network Connection." The country was hungry for the network's programming, but many potential viewers still did not know the Food Network had a range of shows, that there was more than just cooking instruction.

"Food Network is suffering from a perception problem, not programming weakness," the study reported. Even regular viewers reported wanting shows about grilling, desserts, travel, "how stuff we eat every day is made," and other areas the network already did cover but these viewers didn't seem to know about.

It also found that on the most basic level, viewers were not physically hungry late in the evening. By 9 p.m., they wanted something more entertaining than someone cooking. "It's everything I like about food without having to cook," said a noncook in the study, praising the existing lineup. "It's dinner and a story . . . the stories away from the stove."

The study included a graphic that placed viewers' perceptions of nine channels on a continuum. The History Channel had emotional appeal, but seemed a bit like "school." Food Network, perceived as something that could change someone's life, had strong emotional value, but it was considered even more educational and less stimulating. Travel and TLC were more stimulating, but less emotionally appealing. If the Food Network was to continue to grow, it would need to keep its emotional appeal but increase its quotient of "stimulating."

There were strengths. Both cooks and noncooks alike were drawn in, finding warmth. One viewer reported, "It's my living, breathing food friend. It's inspiring, comforting, and my partner in kitchen crime . . . and it lets me take the credit." Another said, "Maybe someday I'll surprise myself and turn on my stove. I don't cook, but it's fun to watch."

But others were wandering away. Cooking shows starting to appear on other networks were threatening to steal their viewers. A graphic entitled "Nibbled to Death" showed the Food Network logo as a pie. Travel Channel, with *No Reservations* in production, had bitten out a little portion. PBS had done the same. TLC and the broadcast networks were making inroads. Armed with information, Brooke and her team began to take action. By 2005, they unveiled a new slogan: "Food Network, Every Night, It's Way More Than Cooking." It was announced in ads starring Alton Brown that featured passing banners: "Discoveries. . . . Competition. . . . Style."

> "They wanted me to do Iron Chefs all the time, and stuff like that. I said, You know what, I have nothing to gain from that. If I lose against somebody, they're gonna laugh at me. And if I win, everybody would say, 'Well, we expect you to win. What do you mean you're not always gonna win?' So I think it doesn't make sense. I did one . . . And I won. So I said, That's enough. I am the only one who is undefeated."
>
> —WOLFGANG PUCK

For years, *Emeril Live* had gobbled a huge slice of the programming budget. And as of 2004, the show was still airing every weeknight, but

Iron Chef America and other shows were taking resources from it. Programming executives were no longer encouraging the producer, Karen Katz, to take Emeril on the road. Yearly specials were no longer on the docket. Karen was hearing exhortations to bring younger guests to attract younger viewers.

Emeril himself was changing. Now forty-six and happily remarried, he was confused by the change at the top of the network. He'd originally been told Brooke was being brought in over Eileen Opatut to give more attention to *Emeril Live*. But now Judy was gone and Brooke was overseeing everything? He and Karen sensed that the show was being taken for granted and agreed it could use fresh thinking. Was someone still going to be tasked with helping *Live*?

But the network's new female stars were attracting the kind of heat the men had had back when Heidi Diamond pitched the "chunks"—chef-hunks—to the media, and a breathless female reporter for the *Philadelphia Daily News* had called Emeril "cute as a butter bean." Rachael did a pictorial spread in the men's magazine *FHM* in which she was shown leaning over a stove in a short skirt and bra, and in 2006, *Esquire* called Giada De Laurentiis one of the "Fifty Reasons It's Good to be an American Man." She and Sandra Lee were following the sexy-chef trail blazed by Nigella Lawson.

A story appeared in the New Jersey paper *The Record* in the summer of 2004, headlined "TV Kitchens Turn Up the Heat; 'Food Babes' Have Taken Over." "It's clear," the reporter Charles Passy wrote, "we've come a long way from the days of a bumbling Julia Child preparing coq au vin for a coterie of public-television viewers." In a sign that the cavalcade of food babes was having a serious effect, he noted that women made up 35 percent of the student population at the Culinary Institute of America in Hyde Park, New York, up from around 20 percent of the student body in the 1990s. The article, a rewrite of a similar piece Passy had done for the *Palm Beach Post*, allowed a nod to Food Network stalwart Sara Moulton. She also had some appeal to men, he wrote, due to her "maternal comfort factor."

Sara, who had been reliably delivering cooking advice on Food Network for nearly a decade, had certainly noticed the big young person-alities and felt her own middle-of-the-roadness. But she had hoped the network would always have a place for a respected cooking instructor like her. The first day she saw Rachael make that pilot of *30 Minute Meals*, Sara recognized how young and fresh, friendly and smooth Ra-chael was. It got uncomfortable when Rachael, with Jon Rosen's help, signed a $6 million cookbook deal in the summer of 2004 with Clark-son Potter. Sara was also a Rosen client, but she was just not as market-able as Rachael.

Brooke saw it all with icy precision. The ratings for *Sara's Secrets* were only so-so. If the network decided it did want to run her shows at some point, it had more than 1,500 of them in the archive.

She broke the news to Sara over lunch soon after she became presi-dent. "We're putting the show on hiatus."

Sara's stomach sank. The *H* word. She'd been around TV long enough to know the *H* word almost always meant the *T* word: termination.

Jon, despite his negotiating clout, could do nothing to save Sara. She served out her contract, hiding the news as best she could and depend-ably producing episodes through the spring of 2005. She knew the show's producer, Georgia Downard, was also aware that the end was nigh, but Sara wanted the bad news to stay under the radar. She did not want to lower her value at *Gourmet* magazine. She had grown used to being treated like an important person there and throughout the food world because she was on television.

When they were getting around to shooting the final *Sara's Secrets*, in the spring of 2005, Sara said to Georgia, "So we're going to have a wrap party, right?"

"I don't know if they have the budget for it," Georgia replied.

Some of the cameramen had been with Sara from the beginning. After 1,200 episodes of *Cooking Live*, and 300 of *Secrets*, Sara thought they all deserved more, especially if this was supposed to be a "family," and she let Georgia know it: "Are you fucking kidding me? I've worked here for nine years and we're not going to have a proper wrap party?

They can't pony up for a wrap party? Go back and tell them we're having a wrap party."

The network finally agreed to pay the $1,500 tab at a little Italian restaurant near the studio. But on the last day of taping, a member of Sara's team kept running to Bob's office saying, "You've got to come down and say something. You've got to come say good-bye."

He sent champagne, but stayed away. Brooke did not come to the studio, either.

For nine years, she had done everything they'd asked of her. She'd been there, 7 to 8 p.m. every weeknight, and she had meant something to her audience. There had been a few profane callers on *Cooking Live*, but far more of them were like the viewer who'd called and said, "I just lost my daughter to cancer and you remind me of her." Another told her, "My mother has Alzheimer's, but she loves your show." Yes, she had benefited handsomely, but she had worked hard. Recently she had been keeping a mental file of slights. She believed she had invented the term "garbage bowl" on her show and that Emily Rieger, a culinary producer who'd first worked for Sara, had stolen the term and handed it to Rachael. She saw Rachael give viewers a tip on how to tell if oil was hot enough for frying by dipping a wooden spoon handle in it. "That's my tip!" Sara seethed. And Tyler! He was like a fame-sniffing puppy, always sucking up to everyone in power and constantly volunteering to come on anyone's show. But now the perceived bad treatment all came together and burned. It was a strange sort of family, but she realized she loved being in it. These people were still part of the network family, and she was not.

> "I knew it was going to be over sooner or later. But I have to tell you when it was over, I was devastated. I was completely devastated. It took me several years to get over it. Because I'd lost my identity."
>
> —SARA MOUL

Tyler may have come across as desperate to Sara, but his strategy was paying off. He was having a ball. By the time Sara left the network, *Tyler's Ultimate*, a travel and cooking show that brought him to Italy,

Ireland, and the South of France, was running. He was cohost of a new version of *How to Boil Water*, and his second cookbook, *Eat This Book: Cooking with Global Fresh Flavors*, had come out. When he wasn't taping for Food Network, he was traveling the country cooking at the Sundance film festival, giving holiday tips on the *Today Show*, and talking about plans to open a restaurant in New York City. He was now represented by Jason Hodes, a protégé of Jon Rosen. One day in 2006, the phone rang with a tempting but complicated offer.

It was from Applebee's, the national restaurant chain. The company wanted to improve the image of its food, and the thirty-four-year-old Food Network personality seemed the ideal pitchman. Tyler's roots in South Carolina communicated an easygoing, Middle American charm that could fit in with the company's target customers.

Applebee's proposed that Tyler come up with gourmet dishes to add to the menu and do television commercials touting the quality of its food. They were offering a lot of money, but Jason told them it wasn't enough.

The deal was not what agents call "a smash and grab," where a talent shows up at a corporate event, shakes some hands, says nice things about a product, and then flies out of town, with almost no one remembering it except the talent and his pleased accountant. What Applebee's was proposing was like Rick Bayless's endorsement of a line of chicken sandwiches for Burger King in 2003. Rick was the host of a PBS cooking show, and despite his intention to bring the best cuisine he could to the fast-food chain, he'd been savaged by the food media and fellow chefs. It was the sort of endorsement that people remembered.

Tyler and his girlfriend, Tolan, were in Tyler's home office on a conference call with Jason and Jon Rosen. An Applebee's deal might not represent who Tyler thought himself to be, a chef who wanted to encourage people to cook good simple food for themselves like the kind on his grandmother's recipe cards. But the amount the chain was offering was the kind of money that could really change his life. Then Jon and Jason told him Applebee's had gone to $3 million.

"Really?" he said. "Wow."

He talked it over with Tolan. You could do a lot of things with $3 million. "Okay," he said to Jason and Jon. "Let's do it."

The day of Tyler's first on-air appearance on Food Network, he knew the right thing for him to do with his life was to get back on that channel as much as possible. It wasn't about money.

When he said yes to Applebee's, a chill ran through him. He did not know exactly what it would bring, but he knew what the feeling meant. Okay, he admitted to himself, this officially kind of feels like selling out.

After the ads went up in the fall of 2006, Applebee's executives happily reported on a quarterly conference call with reporters that dinner sales were up and they were seeing former customers start to return to the restaurants, curious about the menu additions.

Anonymous critics from the *Philadelphia Daily News* who called themselves The Chain Gang reviewed some of the main offerings. Tyler's Herb-Crusted Chicken, topped with Italian seasonings and buried under arugula, grape tomatoes, mozzarella cheese, and a Parmesan dressing was, "not too good for you. But good." A side salad of greens, chopped hard-boiled eggs, caramelized onions, shaved Parmesan, and warm bacon dressing served with Tyler's Crispy Brick Chicken "was terrific, the best thing one Gangster had ever eaten at Applebee's."

Tyler's interaction with Applebee's culinary team and its mass-market food suppliers taught him a lot about streamlining a menu and the challenges of bringing good food to places far from fresh ingredients. And the $20 million TV ad campaign brought him fame in a way even Food Network had not, making him more in demand at food festivals and other events.

Or was it infamous? It took sixteen months for the worst to hit. At a satirical food world awards show in Miami, Tony Bourdain and author Michael Ruhlman hosted what they called The Golden Clog Awards. Ina Garten won "The Alton," for "being on the Food Network and yet, somehow, managing to not suck." But they awarded Tyler the "Rocco Award" for worst career move. It was named after Rocco DiSpirito, a New York chef who many thought had squandered his talent in the

2003 NBC reality series *The Restaurant*. Rocco, a good sport, was on hand for the presentation, but Tyler was not.

"You can get really fucked up at Applebee's for cheap," Tony vamped. "You can't do that shit at Dunkin' Donuts!"

It didn't take long for both Food Network fans and haters to take aim at Tyler in online forums.

"What a joke!" one wrote. "Talk about a sell-out. I used to think this guy was alright and passionate about food."

The network had been talking with Tyler about doing a straight cooking show, something that could fill a slot during the day. Originally it was to be called *Ty Food*. But with the blowback over Applebee's, Tyler suggested avoiding the risk and staying with the name that had proved successful, *Tyler's Ultimate*. Instead of having him travel, discovering something about food and then using it to cook a recipe at home, as he had done on twenty-six episodes over two years, he would stay in one place and cook—in 106 more episodes over six years.

> "Yeah it hurt. Of course it hurt. . . . If you take a look at Anthony Bourdain, have you ever seen that guy put anything on a plate? . . . What gives him the right to say anything about anybody? I'm just trying to feed my family, you know? And it was a really good opportunity, it was a really good business position for us."
>
> —TYLER FLORENCE

By 2007, with money in his pocket, he gave up plans to open a restaurant in New York and he and his new wife moved to Northern California, where he began to quietly plot how to remake his image into someone more down-to-earth than the grinning dude in the Applebee's ad.

When *Iron Chef America* debuted as a regular series in the spring of 2005, it cut through the stale confines of the network's kitchen sets like a jug of tart lemonade. The doings at the new Kitchen Stadium aired on Sunday nights at 9 p.m. and then reran at 11 p.m. on Wednesdays, a time slot suited to college-age viewers who'd watched the original Japanese version on other nights.

Print and bus shelter ads showed American fans who had shaved the images of Iron Chefs into their scalps and others who face-painted themselves. The new Iron Chefs were rebranded as gutsy combatants in a world of whiz-bang artistry, and if the show lacked the mythic weight of the Japanese original, it gained in vibrancy. The *Iron Chef America* producers would reveal to all the competitors three possibilities for the secret ingredient twenty-four hours before contests were shot. This was deceptive. Viewers were not told about it. The show made it seem as if the secret ingredient really was a secret until the Chairman unveiled it on set. But the deception did give the inventiveness of the chefs time to bloom. In Mario's case, he would meet with Anne and Mark and devise menu variations based on the ingredients and practice making them together. They practiced every single time Mario was on *Iron Chef America*, and their record showed it: nineteen wins against just five losses.

> "Today's food personalities are as comfortable on the red carpet as they are in the kitchen. On TV, in restaurants, on supermarket shelves . . . their phrases have become part of the American idiom."
>
> **—STERLING GROUP 2004 STUDY**

Competition was performing magic in prime time. Soon after Judy left, the network moved to a new home. As CEO of E.W. Scripps, Ken Lowe no longer had to fight anyone above him to keep Food in New York. The network signed a multiyear lease at the massive Chelsea Market building on Eleventh Avenue and West Fifteenth Street in Manhattan's burgeoning Meatpacking District, near the Hudson River.

Some of the advertising sales people remained in Midtown, but the marketing side, the studios, and the kitchens were reunited for the first time since the network moved out of the space Pat O'Gorman had found.

The proximity made one reality show idea that had been kicking around the network inevitable. *American Idol* was thriving on Fox. *Project Runway* was drawing unprecedented numbers to Bravo. Brooke and the programming department wondered why you couldn't do an *American Idol* of the Food Network.

There was opposition. One executive protested that there was not enough potential material to do a whole season. "Will it really work? Will it really be interesting?" Prime-time shows needed a focal point, a trusted Food Network personality or an up-and-comer, to be worth the expense. A standard instructional cooking show only cost a few thousand dollars an episode. A full reality show with moving cameras, shifting sets and a large cast, mostly of nobodies, could cost five times more.

But new faces were the point. Fox was offering *American Idol* winners a record deal. *Project Runway* winners got a cash prize, enough to start a clothing line. And what would Food offer? "Let's not make it a clichéd thing," Brooke insisted in planning meetings. "Let's make it real. Let's have the prize be an actual show on Food Network."

Brooke wanted ten episodes, maybe thirteen. The debate settled on six. She pushed on. "And let's make it even more real. Let's have the judges be Food Network people."

> "It's like getting the role in your high school play. It was like, 'Yay!'"
>
> —BOB TUSCHMAN

Tryouts were held. Bob, Susie, Alison Page, Michael Smith, and other executives were given screen tests by CBS Eye Productions to avoid conflicts of interest. Bob, one of the more knowledgeable food people at the network, was chosen as a judge. Gordon Elliott, the effusive Australian of the now-defunct *Door Knock Dinners*, was added to the panel. They needed a female, and Susie was telegenic. Marc Summers, ever adaptable, hosted.

For the first season of *The Next Food Network Star*, nine finalists, including a two-man team of caterers from Chicago, were chosen from an avalanche of audition tapes that poured in, some of them thanks to Marc's onstage appeals at food festivals. The show was shot as cheaply as possible the first year, most of it done in February 2005, in the smallest of the network's studio spaces, Studio B. Occasionally, the competitors and trailing cameras would venture into the office and kitchen spaces at Chelsea Market.

When it aired on Sunday nights at 9 p.m. in the summer of 2005, sliding into the *Iron Chef America* slot when that show's first season ended, ratings were excellent. The team, Dan Smith and Steve McDonagh, won (and their show, *Party Line with the Hearty Boys*, debuted in the fall of 2005, shortly before taping began for season two of *Star*).

Posters promoting the eight episodes of the second season in the spring of 2006 promised "Emotions Simmering Nightly" and pictured the new competitors. In the center was a fellow with spiky bleach-blond hair and a goatee, wearing some kind of bowling shirt. Who did this guy think he was?

When Guy Ferry (as he was known then) was sixteen, he found himself lying on a bed in a third-floor room of a cold boardinghouse in Chantilly, France, staring at a two locked wardrobes and feeling unwelcome.

> "He certainly looked very different from anybody, the nice, clean, scrubbed, people that we had before. That was a concern for me."
>
> **—BOB TUSCHMAN**

Before leaving his small hometown of Ferndale in Northern California for a study year abroad, Guy thought he was going to be living with a lively French family. But it turned out that the parents of this real family were elderly. There was a daughter at home, but she was not Guy's age, and a son who attended military school.

Guy had been in France only a few days and was coming to grips with his situation. He was a paying tenant in the house, relegated to living in what was basically a storage room. He had a desk, an armoire, a sink, and a single bed. The bathroom was two floors down. He couldn't even use the phone without permission, because Madame kept it locked. The house was near a famous racetrack, but it was empty most of the year. Guy was miserable and thought about phoning his parents, but he did not want to seem ungrateful. And the truth was that even if he had reached them, he would not have asked to go home.

Guy had been entrepreneurial and unusually adventurous since he was a child. As a fifth grader, he had talked himself into a job selling balloons at the Humboldt County Fair. It took him six years to earn the money for this trip, running a pretzel cart—that he'd built with his father—on Ferndale's main street. France was an adventure and he was going to see what there was here, no matter how mean the Madame was.

Soon, he found a pleasure that helped take his mind off the cold accommodations: school lunches. They seemed strange at first: chicken feet soup, pâté, escargots, and other inexpensive French country staples. He had never heard of this stuff, but it was delicious—mind-blowing in fact. No one ate like this at the cafeteria in Ferndale. A hippie type, his mother made his lunches on homemade bread with grains so whole the vegetarian sandwiches fell apart as he lifted them to his mouth. Instead of saying to a French girl, "Where have you been all my life?" he ate a midday meal of sheep's tongue and couscous with gusto, and thought, "Where has this been all my life? These school lunches are the bomb!"

Eventually, things got better. He met a Norwegian family with three sons and, hearing of his troubles, they took him in. His food pleasures expanded.

Before school, he went down to the local bakery to fetch bread. He was to wait in line and buy five baguettes. He bought six and ate one on the way home.

Julia Child had her fateful *sole meunière* experience in northern France. Guy had his biggest French food moment in the south. He was driving through villages with the Norwegians, and they stopped at a house for dinner. It looked like someone's home, but it doubled as the town restaurant. Soon, he was served steak frites, the beef so rich and flavorful he could think nothing other than Oh, my God! He knew meat well. The first meal he'd ever cooked for his parents was a steak when he was ten. In sixth grade, he'd worked at the Ferndale meat market. But the simplicity here, the quality of the ingredients, the setting—this was something else.

> "The vinaigrette, the mustard, the bread, the cheese—oh, God! At the end of the day, eating cheese was so overwhelming."
>
> —GUY FIERI

Instead of phoning his parents with his troubles, he wrote them with his wonder: "You guys have got to come try this food! It's out of bounds!"

In another letter home, quoted in his book *Guy Fieri Food*, he said, "I really think I know what I want to do. I want to be a chef and own restaurants."

After college, Guy moved to Los Angeles and found work at Louise's Trattoria, a string of Italian family restaurants across Southern California. He quickly became the best-known employee. At company retreats in the mountains around Big Bear, he organized all-night volleyball games in the snow, fueled by Jack Daniel's, lit by the fog lights of his jacked-up Chevy Silverado and presided over by his Dobermans, Rocky and Sierra. He was a natural-born character.

Soon he was bristling at having to take orders. Guy got into a conflict with an executive at the Louise's chain, Robert Kissinger. As the sophistication of diners in California deepened through the mid-1990s, the chain had spent heavily to improve the authenticity of its Italian menu. But Guy, who was overseeing a few locations, had other ideas about what would make regular customers happy. His food tastes had become less inspired by his French experiences than by some of the places he'd been since. He had attended a hotel management program at UNLV in the late 1980s, when Vegas was in the midst of big changes as dreamers like hotelier Steve Wynn were remaking the landscape, demolishing old hotels and building shimmering palaces in the desert. The spicier foods he was exposed to there and throughout Southern California influenced his palate and his willingness to take chances. For a cooking competition in one UNLV class, he invented a winning dish, Cajun Chicken Alfredo.

When he added tortilla soup to the lunch menu at the Louise's locations he was managing, Kissinger phoned him, furious. "What the hell are you doing? This is an Italian restaurant chain!"

Guy was unintimidated. "Listen, I got a lot of businesspeople that come in here every day and want soup and salad for lunch. And I can't feed 'em pasta fagiole and Italian wedding soup every day. I've got to branch out, man! I don't want to lose my lunch business. You know, I've got to do it."

By the age of twenty-six, he had grown weary of banging up against the wishes of the people above him. He and a friend, Steve Gruber, had been quietly plotting their departure from the company, drawing up plans for a restaurant they wanted to open together. Guy's wife, Lori, had always wanted to own a horse, and Steve had young children. Santa Rosa, forty miles north of San Francisco on the edge of wine country, not far from Ferndale, was big enough to support restaurants, but remote enough still to have acreage a young family could afford.

Guy, who'd changed his last name back to his great-grandfather's, Fieri, when he married Lori in 1995, moved to Santa Rosa in 1996. No local bank was willing to loan them restaurant start-up money. So Guy's parents, two years away from retirement, mortgaged their home and loaned him the money to open Johnny Garlic's. Guy took the menu way beyond tortilla soup. Johnny Garlic's featured the Jackass Roll, a sushi-style maki with pulled pork and green chili, and a recipe he'd been saving, Cajun Chicken Alfredo.

Thanks to good local publicity and the outrageously named menu items, the restaurant was wildly successful as soon as it opened. Early one morning in 1996 or 1997, Guy was, uncharacteristically, watching television before work. Normally, he was out the door by 8 a.m., barely pausing between waking, showering, and leaving. But Lori was watching *Good Morning America*, and as he got dressed, the *GMA* host announced, "Chef Emeril Lagasse" and mentioned that the chef had a show on the Food Network. Guy had heard of Food Network from a teenager who lived on his block, but he'd never watched it.

Unusual name, Guy thought. Then he saw a showman who stopped him cold. Emeril strutted out on *Good Morning America* to a gush of loud blues music, with a towel draped over his shoulder. The whole scene seemed to light up as he threw garlic into pans. "Oh, baby, yeah!" Emeril praised his suddenly sizzling array of pots.

Wow-ow-ow! Guy thought. That's awesome! Look at this dude! This dude can walk the talk. He's jamming! This guy must own the Food Network!

In Emeril, Guy recognized the showmanship of his childhood heroes, Evel Knievel, the stunt rider who'd jumped the Snake River Canyon when Guy was a boy, and Elvis Presley. The New Orleans chef used a sauté pan to do what Evel did with a motorcycle: reveal its inherent power.

This guy has got this down! Guy thought.

Later that week, Guy asked his teenage neighbor about Emeril. He wanted to see if the chef was having the effect on young people that Evel had had on him.

"Aw, yeah, man!" the kid replied. "Emeril Lagasse!"

The appeal for three-minute audition videos for *The Next Food Network Star* had reached a friend of Guy's, who suggested he send in a tape. He had auditioned to be on a pilot for a barbecue show in 2004 that went nowhere, so it took some coaxing to get him to try again. He used his own nickname, Guido, and demonstrated how to make a sushi roll.

> "To me, food is a party. Food is energy. Food is love. Food is excitement. Food is—I mean, I get excited about making a sandwich, you know. 'What are we gonna make happen today! Pepperoncini juice mixed with some cream cheese and some fresh cracked pepper, all right!' You know, that's where the jive starts coming down. I looked at Emeril and just said, 'Oh, there's Elvis. There's a guy that's owning this.'"
>
> **—GUY FIERI**

The *Star* producers were amazed at how calm and real Guy seemed. He was playful and humorous, talking to viewers like they were sitting having a beer with him. He didn't look like any other cooking show host, with his bleached hair and tattoos. But a couple minutes in, he seemed so likable and quick-witted that they almost forgot his weird appearance. He grabbed attention and kept it, which is what TV stars need to do.

When the network called Guy with the good news that he'd been cast, he thought it was a prank. As he left for New York in November

2005, his father told him, "Hey, the number one thing is to stay true to yourself."

Season two was really no contest. Guy bathed everyone in charisma. He had enough food knowledge to make himself a viable cooking show host; compared to Sandra Lee, Guy was Jacques Pépin.

Emeril had a bad cold, but came out to declare Guy the winner on April 23, 2006. The prize was the right to host a cooking show for six episodes, which became *Guy's Big Bite*. The day of his victory, Marc Summers, the host of *Star*'s second season, pulled Guy aside and cautioned him, "Okay, you have no idea what's about to hit you in the face. If you need some help, if you have questions, you give me a call." When Guy did, Marc told him there might eventually be some great money coming his way for doing easy things like showing up at supermarket openings and shaking hands at corporate events. "First of all," Marc said, "open a bank account that funnels nothing but personal appearance money into it. At some point, this will go away and you can have your fuck-you money, and you don't need to worry."

Guy thought he could manage his own affairs. He co-owned a number of restaurants at this point. Okay, Marc's advice that he hire a good lawyer, he understood. But he didn't need a big-city agent.

"Listen!" Marc, a showbiz survivor of more than two decades, insisted over Guy's protests. "You get yourself an agent."

This was the game now. Food Network had created contracts for its *Star* contestants that tied them closely to the network. The early business model had been to pay the hosts as little as possible and allow them to leverage their TV fame however they chose. Emeril made good money from his TV contract, but he cashed in on the spices he touted on the air, his books, and his restaurants. Low talent fees kept programming costs in line with advertising revenues and whatever subscriber fees the owners could collect. Under Scripps, the network finally started shaking off Reese's original business plan, which gave away the station for free, but it was taking years to ratchet fees up to the levels comparable networks were getting. In 2006, Food was collecting an average of 6 cents a subscriber per month. TLC got about 16 cents and Bravo 15 cents. The website was attracting 7 million unique visitors a month, advertising revenues were rising, and total viewership was up 12 percent in the second quarter of 2006 compared to a year earlier, including a 20 percent ratings rise for the In the Kitchen block on weekends. Prime time lagged with just a 5 percent improvement, despite the ratings success of the new competition shows. With that growth, the talent saw their earnings spike. Jon Rosen, Jim Griffin, Shep Gordon, and other agents had shown there were massive profits to be made on the side by food show hosts. Barry Weiner had finally declared open season for Paula Deen endorsements, allowing her to sign to produce a line of products, starting with the Paula Deen Egg & Muffin Toaster in 2006. *Judge Judy* was a great show, but she'd never created a line of iced teas. As Shep was fond of saying, you don't get rich going to work, you get rich going to your mailbox.

When she'd been a consultant, Brooke had written the memo pushing Food Network to get in on the paydays. This seemed especially obvious when the network was creating stars out of nobodies. Now the contracts the contestants on *The Next Food Network Star* signed were more restrictive, giving the network approval over future books, TV, and endorsements, and a share of revenues for all contestants. Even established talent like Bobby faced pressure from the network over royalties when their contracts came up for renewal. In the old days, the network's softhearted bookkeeper negotiated contracts with cooking show hosts. But with millions at stake, and the network reaching nearly universal distribution, around ninety million homes, a tough business affairs lawyer named Pat Guy fought hard for the network's interests. When Emeril signed his latest contract in 2003, the network extracted the video-on-demand and home-video rights to his series, gaining back a little bit of what it had unwittingly let go years earlier.

Before Guy taped his first season of *Guy's Big Bite*, he received a call from Jason Hodes. They met at the Maritime Hotel and walked over to Soho House, a private club nearby. It was a warm spring Saturday and they sat on the roof, next to the pool. Jason told Guy that he and his colleagues at William Morris thought Guy had "that one-in-a-billion spark." But there were challenges to making him as big as he deserved, Jason explained, the Food Network contract being the first problem. "It's incredibly cumbersome," Hodes said. "There isn't a lot that you're going to be allowed to do. But I have good relationships over there. And, I can be very aggressive when it comes to the representation of my clients, and I'm not afraid to push back."

If, just if, *Guy's Big Bite* was successful, they would gain leverage that could force Food to renegotiate. Selling the Jon Rosen line, Jason offered the potential for merchandise, endorsements, more television shows, and book deals.

Guy signed.

> "I know that people sometimes think that I just go like, 'Ah, yeah it's one, I think I'm gonna get up and have a mochaccino, then I'll maybe shoot an hour of *Guy's Big Bite*, and then probably just go fly my helicopter over to Cuba.' It's nothing like that, ladies and gentlemen. If you're going to be great at something, you've got to work really hard."
>
> —GUY FIERI

After the first season of *The Next Food Network Star*, Bravo announced its own food competition series. Its first major, defining hit—Bravo's *Emeril Live*—had been *Queer Eye for the Straight Guy*, and network executives including Andy Cohen, the senior vice president of original programming and development, concluded that the framework for their programming would be the categories that each of the five "Queer" characters represented: Clothing, home decoration, grooming, lifestyle/dating, and food. Bravo would focus on reality shows, and every show would be about either fashion, design, beauty, pop culture, or food.

In one of its first forays in this direction, Bravo's in-house production group developed a competition reality show around food. They soon announced a new show called *Top Chef* in which the winner would earn a whopping $100,000 prize.

A debate broke out at Food Network: Should they offer a big cash prize on *The Next Food Network Star* to match the $100,000? Should they create a rival show?

Other networks joined the food competition game. PBS created one called *Cooking Under Fire* starring Ming Tsai and Todd English, one of the Iron Chefs from the ill-fated UPN gambit. The winner would earn the comparatively meager prize of a job in one of Todd's restaurant's kitchens. Fox had debuted *Hell's Kitchen* in which British chef Gordon Ramsay berated would-be employees who were competing for the prize of working in executive positions for top-of-the-line restaurants, sometimes his own.

Top Chef worried Brooke the most, because it was from a cable channel more directly in competition with Food for viewers. To outwit Bravo, she proposed to her programming executives that they put *Star* on hiatus for a year, "then we'll do a *Top Chef*–like show to try to blunt whatever impact they're going to have." *Star* was working, so she did not want to drastically change it to make it like *Top Chef*, but producing two reality shows with full casts would be very expensive. In the end, they stuck with *Star*, because it was working. She did not suggest doing both—keeping *Star* on and asking Scripps for the budget to create a big-money rival to match what Bravo was doing.

When *Top Chef* turned out to be a hit, she scolded herself for not being more audacious. "I regard that as the single largest mistake I've made since I've been here," she admitted later. "I allowed them to develop this franchise."

But as much as Brooke rued the rise of *Top Chef*, it was not a show Food Network could have made. Putting aside that the production values were much higher than anything Food was doing, *Top Chef* showed chefs in all their gory glory. There were tattoos, real anger, and sadness. Upon its debut, a reviewer from the *Tampa Tribune* called it "a scabrous culinary contest." Such a show would never have made it through Scripps's starched culture. Bravo, in contrast, had long shown a tolerance for everything—and would continue to stretch boundaries. Nothing like *Real Housewives* has ever appeared on a Scripps channel. For all of the great shows on Food Network, has there ever been anything "scabrous"?

What *Top Chef* captured with its "quickfires," backstage jealousies, sniping, and brutal judgments, were the pressure and passion of the restaurant life, the factors that Brooke and Ken had missed when they spent time with the food people in their employ. It was there in Bourdain's book, too, and in his intense expression as he sat across from Ferran Adrià and tasted his art, but Food Network had tried to rein him in.

Doubtless, that passion was on display in Bobby's performance at Webster Hall in the Japanese Iron Chef battle, and it was captured a bit on *Iron Chef America*. But it was also hidden behind the entertaining artifice of the American creation, in the steam and the backflips, and in the encyclopedic chatter of narrator Alton Brown. Stripped of the histrionics, *Top Chef* showed something real, including the demanding critiques of the perfectionist head judge—and the show's executive producer, Tom Colicchio—who had proudly refused to go on Food Network in its messy early days. He was not a cartoon.

Once something is a hit, it's easy to imagine that you could have thought of it first. *Top Chef* would likely never have been possible if Food Network had not been on cable for thirteen years educating viewers. But Food never had the internal culture willing to put something as raw and real as *Top Chef* on the air. Bravo did.

The challenges that were flying in from many directions were flattering, since imitations signified success, but also troubling: What if a challenger figured out a better food TV formula? Worse from Food Network's perspective than *Top Chef* was Gusto, a cable channel idea that was cooked up as a partnership between the media giants Viacom and Comcast.

Starting in 2005, John Sykes, the president of network development for the MTV Networks division of Viacom, was exploring four or five possible new digital cable channels with Comcast. The idea behind Gusto was to recapture the more food-centric crowd that Food Network seemed to have abandoned as it chased a broader audience. Marketing materials explained the comparison Gusto was trying to draw: Food Network was Walmart. Gusto was Whole Foods.

Instead of Sandra Lee, Paula Deen, and competition shows, Gusto promised urbane programs hosted by personalities like prize-winning food critic Jeffrey Steingarten and wine expert Josh Wesson (one of the stars of David Rosengarten and Tony Hendra's long-ago PBS pilot *Three Men in a Kitchen*). A teaser reel created to explain Gusto inside Viacom and Comcast included a dinner party scene. Around a table imbibing leggy wines and dark meats were the kind of stars the network would tap: Gabrielle Hamilton, owner of the pioneering East Village "nose-to-tail" restaurant Prune; Pete Wells, a food writer at *Details* magazine who would soon move to *The New York Times*; Drew Nieporent, an erudite New York restaurateur; and, of all people, Susie Essman, a comedienne known for her recurring role as a profane, but clever, wife on the HBO series *Curb Your Enthusiasm*. Gusto eventually died when Comcast decided it did not want to move ahead with a Viacom partnership. But the threat of it, or of another network, like Discovery, launching a rival food channel, increased the pressure on Food Network executives to deliver what the viewer research studies had concluded was needed—shows that were less Walmart, more stimulating.

Bob Tuschman was made head of programming when Kathleen Finch became head of DIY Network. Whether it was nerves over the newfound responsibility or a bad bug going around, Bob spent some of his first days at home sick. While he recuperated, he popped pilots that Kathleen had been considering into his video player. One was called "Fuck You, Let's Bake." It was based on a stage show performed by Duff

Goldman, the irreverent owner of a Baltimore bakery, involving a sexy assistant, a punk rock guitarist, and stunts in which Duff would make soufflés while fighting ninjas. Bob didn't like the name—if Scripps had a problem with the fuzz of a peach in a bus shelter ad, no variant of *F.U. Let's Bake* would fly—and he thought the content a bit too rough for Food, but he liked Duff's youthful 'tude. The pilot evolved into *Ace of Cakes*, a show focused on Duff's workplace, Charm City Cakes, chronicling his team of wisecracking artists as they created ornately decorated cakes.

An unscripted show with so many characters was far more expensive to produce than a typical half hour, about $160,000 an episode, but the network went for it. It helped that Duff was being championed by a recent hire in the programming department, Charles Nordlander. Brought in to develop new concepts, Charles had come from A&E, which had been moving away from the biography-bound network Brooke had overseen into one more reliant on buzzy docuseries like *Dog the Bounty Hunter*, *Growing Up Gotti*, and a confection Charles had created called *Flip This House*.

Also in Bob's video player was a tape Charles and Kathleen had been developing that would become a series in which Paula Deen's adult sons, Bobby and Jamie, traveled around the country meeting homespun food purveyors.

Another, from Bobby Flay, called *Throwdown*, had been created when Brooke told him she was not interested in seeing him on another show like *FoodNation*. It might be okay for the Deen boys, but she needed something new and more complex in prime time. "Bobby," she'd said. "I'm not looking for a 'let's travel around the country learning interesting things about food.' We have a lot of those shows. We need to come up with some new concepts, be a little more compelling, a little more competitive, something that would be stickier, keep people watching longer, that would have a beginning, middle, and end."

That was the advice her father had given her. The bit has to be complete.

She gave the same speech to the other on-air talent, but unlike most of them, Bobby listened and said little.

Over the next few weeks, he thought it over. What existing show on television held the viewer's interest? What could he use as a model?

It came to him: *Punk'd*.

In MTV's hidden-camera hit originally hosted by Ashton Kutcher, celebrities were the objects of practical jokes. On one episode, Beyoncé Knowles visited a group of children for Christmas. When she attempted to put a star on the top of the tree and it fell over, ruining the presents, she was convinced she'd caused tears and mayhem. On another, Bow Wow was accused of losing jewelry he was given for a photo shoot and had to pay for it. At the end of each segment, the exasperated victim was told, "You just got punk'd!"

At the most elemental level, what Bobby liked about the show was the surprise and the ending. If only he could translate it into the food world. Okay. He broke *Punk'd* into parts. First, there was a smart host who could roll with what was happening and improvise easily under pressure. Okay, check, Bobby could do that. So what other elements are there? Ashton had celebrities. So I'll take Emeril, Mario, I'm going to take all the stars of the Food Network, and I'm going to punk them. . . . But it's limited, he thought. Why don't I go after the sort of celebrities of each community in the food world? In their own communities, they're gigantic.

Instead of a random practical joke each time and hidden cameras, which would have been a real pain to set up, the target chefs would be convinced they were going to be featured on television for cooking their specialty. This would explain the cameras. There would be a beat in each episode showing Bobby preparing for each contest beforehand at the Food Network kitchens. Then, as the target chef was setting up to cook his or her special dish on location, Bobby would walk in and challenge them to a cooking contest in front of the chef's colleagues and friends. Bobby's original title was *Cook'd*.

The ending of *Punk'd* was always the reveal that a joke had been played. In this case, the reveal to the target chef would happen halfway through when Bobby showed up. For *Cook'd*, Bobby thought the ending would be interviewing spectators at the contest as they tasted the results. Like a good movie, the show would fade to black, leaving viewers to decide who had made the better version.

He and Jon Rosen asked Food Network for funds to make the pilot. If the network didn't want to pay for it, Bobby would pay for it himself, and shop the pilot on the open market.

The programming department wasn't unwilling to pay, but they asked for changes. They did not like the name and they wanted a winner. Keep everything else, but bring in a judge or judges. It was better television.

Bobby didn't think so. "It makes you think," he argued with one of Bob's lieutenants, Kim Williamson. "*Punk'd*, what's the result? It's a laugh."

The debate lasted about a month, but Bobby finally acquiesced. During a meeting with his production partner, Kim Martin, they came up with a new title, *Throwdown*, to intensify the idea of the contest. "It sounded like a fight, or a match," Bobby explained.

Five months later, Bobby delivered a pilot in which he challenged a New Jersey barbecue champion, Butch Lupinetti. The chance to cook against a famous TV chef like Bobby clearly delighted the man. An impartial judge gave the victory to Butch. Beating Bobby gave Butch joy and eternal bragging rights. His way of life was being celebrated, and Bobby was a gracious loser, unsparing in his compliments for Butch's smoky chicken, ribs, and hog.

Throwdown included the element of competition but made it friendly. Plus, it recast Bobby as a champion of the people,

> "Let's put it this way. We gave everybody who we challenged every possibility to beat me. Didn't happen all the time. Me going around the country beating everybody is not a good thing for anybody. . . . Some other chefs say to me, how do you go around losing? How can you do that? And I'm like, Who cares? . . . It's not about winning or losing. It's about the people."
>
> —BOBBY FLAY

making him an even more appealing personality for the network to promote.

Tuschman was unstinting in his praise. "That's really a total testament to Bobby. To his ability to change, and be a partner with the network and feel like, 'If I want to stay in this network, I'm going to be a part of my evolution here. I'm not going to wait for them to come to me with an idea and feel bad if they don't have an idea for me. I'm going to create my own success. I'm going to create my own format. I'm going to create what I want to be on the network.'"

In April 2006, the network revealed a new slogan for the evening hours: "Food Network Nighttime: Way More Than Cooking." *Throwdown* and the other shows were unveiled, among them the new *Nigella Feasts*. They were finally bringing Nigella Lawson, who had inspired so many copycats, into the fold.

Personalities mattered more than ever, but those who were less motivated than Bobby to adapt lost their place. About a year after *Iron Chef America* debuted as a regular series, Bob Tuschman went to see Mario at his pizza spot on lower Fifth Avenue, Otto Enoteca Pizzeria. Although *Molto Mario* was still airing in reruns, he had not produced a new episode since around 2005. Mario thought Bob was there to offer him a new series.

"You know, I think we're done," Bob said. "I think we've run our course."

"All right, Bob," Mario said, accepting the new reality. He did not do like Bobby and invent a series to save himself. He thought the network was aiming more for college kids and tailgaters and believed his audience craved something more literate. He had already made a deal for a PBS series in which he would drive around Spain with Gwyneth Paltrow, Spanish actress Claudia Bassols, and food writer Mark Bittman, exploring the historical and artistic roots of the cuisine.

Food Network had helped him get where he was, and he liked where he was. The network called back soon after and asked if Mario would continue to appear on *Iron Chef America*. This was a place his strong personality and fame still worked on the network, and he enjoyed the competition. He, Ladner, and Anne won a lot more than they lost. If he could have fun appealing to college kids, then okay. He said he would.

Ever hungry for more studies that could help her hone the programming and marketing, Brooke authorized two more in 2007. The first, a "Food Media Platform Study," concluded that for most viewers, as long as they felt stimulated by the ideas shown during cooking shows, they were satisfied with turning to the Internet for the actual recipe details about how to reproduce what they saw.

"This integration enhances the experience and benefits of each," the study noted.

More than a thousand people who reported being interested in food were asked: "Which of these are reasons why you like to watch the Food Network?" The answers showed that some people still wanted to learn, and about the same number just wanted to be entertained.

- 64% I get inspired, ideas, new things to try.
- 56% I learn a lot from their shows.
- 54% It's just simple entertainment for me.
- 47% I find it relaxing.
- 45% It gets me excited about cooking.
- 44% I have particular chefs that I like.

For the second, a "Brand Lens Study," a group of devoted Food Network viewers were asked not to watch Food Network or use its website for two weeks. The addicts had a hard time.

"The first couple of days," said one viewer, "I kept thinking, 'Oh, this will get better.' . . . As the first week ended, my husband was ready to hand me the remote to turn on Food Network. . . . I have never seen myself walking around in circles like that!"

Another: "To not have [the Food Network] on wasn't normal. . . . I was just like, 'Oh, God!' So I wound up even switching the TV totally off, trying not to watch cooking stuff."

The visual equivalent of methadone didn't work for another either: "To fill in the time, I did get back and see some of my old series, programs that I used to watch like *ER* and a few others. But it was just . . . I knew that they were just filling in. It was this whole mental thing. It was terrible. I didn't realize it was so bad."

But foodies who felt abandoned by Food Network's "Walmart" appeal—viewers who might have tuned in to Gusto's programs, and those who were watching *Top Chef*—had some suggestions for improvement.

- "Put real people on the air that people can relate to."
- "Bring more diversity in both personalities and menus."
- "Always try and be on the cutting edge of what's going on in the food world."

The report acknowledged that the safety and comfort viewers liked about Food Network were exactly the qualities that had created opportunities for other networks. A chart showed that Food Network's programming was higher on the "family-friendly and accessible" side of the comfort continuum, while *Top Chef*, *Hell's Kitchen*, and *No Reservations* were "exciting and edgy." What's more, a significant slice of regular Food Network viewers admitted they love those edgier shows. Forty-four percent reported that they "truly enjoy" watching *Top Chef*.

> "Food is sexy and dangerous and should be reflected as such. If I wanted safe I'd watch PBS."
>
> —A SURVEY PARTICIPANT IN "BRAND LENS SURVEY," 2007

_____

Top Chef's success and the threat of a Gusto-like rival increased Brooke's resolve to do more with her network's prime-time hours. She had _Unwrapped_, _Throwdown_, the still strong _Good Eats_, the American and the Japanese versions of _Iron Chef_, and _The Next Food Network Star_, but she was hamstrung if one hour every night was taken up with the expensive production of _Emeril Live_, whose audience was getting older and whose star had an agent who kept pushing for more money.

It wasn't as if the network hadn't tried. In the last year, Emeril had been encouraged to do more away from the studio, even as the network invested in a new set. Ken considered himself a friend of Emeril, but he asked Brooke if the show needed to end. As much as Scripps had increased the programming budget over the years, it did not spend heavily on production. If Food wanted to do anything new or improve the lighting and look of its existing shows to match the sleekness of _Top Chef_, keeping _Emeril Live_ was going to be very difficult. Brooke had already tried to explain some of this to Emeril, but, unlike Bobby, he didn't want to hear that it was time to find a new act. Research confirmed that even those viewers who still wanted cooking shows wanted them in the daytime, not in prime time. _Emeril Live_ was basically a cooking show. No matter how much Jim argued that _Emeril Live_ should be considered as inviolable as _The Tonight Show_, the network was looking at the fact that _Unwrapped_, _Good Eats_, _Iron Chef America_, and _Throwdown_ were what younger audiences wanted in prime time, shows with food elements and cooking, but with interesting formats that felt more contemporary. They got higher ratings and generally cost less.

With all the evidence against keeping _Emeril Live_, the network's agonizing over canceling it showed just how strong a connection it still felt to the star and his show. No one was unaware that for years Food had been the Emeril network, and many had a hard time accepting it no longer was, especially Emeril. If he had invented a new show for himself, almost a new persona, there might have been a way to keep him center stage. But Emeril didn't. Maybe he couldn't.

Despite all the nonchefs who had flooded into the ranks of network hosts, Emeril still looked at the name *Food Network* and saw the word *Cooking* in it. He was a chef. He was the chef.

During the final season, Brooke tried to soften him for the end. "This will probably be the last run of it," she told him.

"You're full of it," he'd replied.

Emeril thought Susie's suggestion that he make an occasional appearance on *Iron Chef* was like his asking a chef at one of his restaurants to accept a demotion to dishwasher. It just wasn't done. You find a bigger role for a great employee if change is necessary, not a lesser one. Loyalty mattered.

Susie was being loyal in her own way, but Emeril didn't see it. To her, *Iron Chef* could perform the magic Emeril needed, recasting him as gritty, newly energetic and inventive, as it had done for others. From there, who knows what new ideas might present themselves for him?

Even though Emeril had been aboard from the first days of the network, he made the mistake that many others with less experience had made, believing that the soul of the place was like the soul of a restaurant—when it is really ticking it is more than a business, it is something beautiful and family-like, where the most important person (besides the customer) is the skilled chef, who delivers the culmination of everyone's efforts on the plate.

How could he have misunderstood his employer so completely? Because he had spent a decade at the center of the network, surrounded by applause, assistants doing his bidding, Super Bowl tickets, backslapping, women fawning and baring their breasts, his agent assuring he's going to work it out. It was not the network's job to teach or to have a conscience or a memory or to always put something beautiful on the plate. The network's prime directive was to sell as many Ginsu knives, boxes of detergent, Corollas, and breath mints as it could for paying advertisers. Ken Levy, the Johnson & Wales administrator who planted the seed of an idea in Joe Langhan's mind that became TVFN, had backed his school out of the deal in the early days because he recognized that it was not going to fulfill his institution's core mission: to educate.

Shortly into the run of *The Next Food Network Star*, David Rosengarten, who had been publishing a widely circulated and much-loved newsletter about the culinary scene called *The Rosengarten Report*, received a call from one of the show's producers.

"Hello, David, my name is Amy with the Food Network. We do a show called *The Next Food Network Star*, and your name has been suggested as a possible candidate."

"Really? You want me to go on a show to see if I'm going to be the next Food Network star?" He had been off the network, what, five years, and already forgotten?

"Yes! We'd like to schedule an audition."

"Amy, um, I'm not sure you're aware of this, but I have some history being on the Food Network, and you might want to just look into this before we go ahead and schedule an audition."

Two hours later Amy called back to apologize.

The fact that Emeril had retained most of the rights to his shows through every contract negotiation over the years allowed him to have a last laugh of the multimillion-dollar sort when he sold his library of shows and the rights to all of his products, basically his entire brand with the exception of his restaurants, to Martha Stewart Omnimedia for $50 million. (Yes, Shep kept his 50 percent of the spice profits.)

> "Emeril was one of the first people I met on my first day of work. He handed me a pumpkin filled with pumpkin-and-foie-gras soup. It was delicious."
>
> **—BROOKE JOHNSON**

"As soon as the deal closes, we will add EBITA to Martha's company," Emeril told a reporter soon after the cancellation in a 2008 interview outside his Miami restaurant, using a corporate term for earnings before interest, taxes, and amortization with a deftness he'd once saved for filleting haddock.

He tried to present himself as all business, but he was hurting and stayed that way for a very long time. Asked four years later why he thought the show had been canceled, he said, "I still don't know why." He still believed the network had gone nuts at some point, that when Judy Girard, Eric Ober, and Erica Gruen were presidents, the place made sense, and it no longer did. He would publicly praise Brooke, but to old colleagues like Marc Summers, he confided, "You're one of the only sane people still there."

And despite all the audience research studies and budget reasons and changing demographics, who is to say that maybe he was not right? Why couldn't the network have tweaked the show a bit, streamlined it, moved it to 11 p.m. every night, and put him up against Jon Stewart and Chelsea Handler, whose unlikely cable show debuted the same year Emeril's bowed out? The Food Network has certainly not been right about everything it's done. By 2007, they were well profitable. Why not risk a little house money in a food-mad world and try *Emeril at Eleven*?

But by the end, nobody made a strong case for keeping it, damn the cost and the risk. The network had been inexorably moving toward the decision for so long that it only heard an echo chamber of consensus inside Chelsea Market and in Knoxville that it was time for the show to go.

Not long after *Emeril Live* was canceled, William Morris merged with the Endeavor Talent Agency and Jim Griffin was let go. He went to work for a smaller agency, where he hung a photo of Joe Namath on the wall of his new office. Emeril stayed with him for a few years, but eventually returned to William Morris Endeavor.

Jon Rosen would often tell the story of how Jim used to brag that he had Emeril, the biggest food star, and he didn't care how many of the lesser lights the other agents signed. Since then, Jon had been made a member of the ruling board of the agency and represented some of the biggest earners at the New York branch of WME—Giada, Bobby, and Rachael. Agents in the Branded Lifestyle Group he oversaw had Guy, Alton, and many more.

Emeril was crushed, but for better or worse, the network was freed, lightened. With the show that had taken up an hour of prime time every night now gone, Brooke's team had a lot of work ahead of it to find something that could propel Food, and those others like Jon whose careers were aligned with the network's fate, to the new heights they dreamed of.

Channeling the
Soul of a Chef

As much as *Emeril Live* and *Iron Chef* had drawn viewers and given the channel a pop-culture identity, the research showed that Food was still saddled with the original problem of food TV—a hell of a lot of people still thought food shows were for lazy weekend mornings and housewives in the afternoons. Brooke was hell-bent to change that. By canceling Emeril, she had done for prime-time programming what Judy had done for daytime when she axed nearly the entire fleet of original network talent, from Curtis Aikens to David Rosengarten. Judy's deck-clearing had created the space for a transformative wave of In the Kitchen talent like Ina, Giada, Paula, and Rachael.

Brooke had already made major progress with *Iron Chef America, The Next Food Network Star*, and *Throwdown*, all of which were bringing in good ratings, especially on Sunday nights. But with the every-weeknight warhorse gone, she needed more category-killing content on the air as quickly as possible, especially with Bravo brewing *Top Chef* spin-offs.

Additional pressure on the network to improve upon its success came from Scripps, which was preparing to spin off its cable and interactive media holdings into a separate company, Scripps Networks Interactive. When the separation was finalized in July 2008, SNI's two most valuable assets were HGTV, with $550 million in revenue in 2007, and Food

Network with $436 million. Ken Lowe was made chief executive of
SNI, and to continue his winning record, he would need those numbers
to keep improving.

And yet as dizzying as Food's profits were becoming, the business of
television was always unpredictable, uncomfortably reliant on the miracles of creativity and chance, and on the egos of those who traffic in
them.

The good news for Brooke was that she had tools at her disposal that
no other president had enjoyed: increased budgets, nearly universal
cable and satellite carriage, and an important new arena for marketing
talent, thanks to an extremely ambitious Floridian named Lee Schrager.

One of Lee's first jobs after he graduated from the Culinary Institute
of America in the late 1970s had been in the coat-check room at the
Four Seasons restaurant in Manhattan. One night, Diana Ross came in
wearing a floor-length fur coat. After she went up to the dining room,
Lee donned the diva's fur and began vamping around the white marble
entrance area.

Diana had forgotten something. When she went down to retrieve it
and saw the young man prancing in the fur, she said, "That better not
be my coat."

Lee was fired that night, but he recovered. In the '80s, Lee, a squat,
barrel-chested man who favored open-collar dress shirts and resembled
the actor Paul Sorvino, opened a gay bar called Torpedo in the South
Beach section of Miami. Among the performers he brought in was Little Edie Beale, the eccentric star of the cult classic documentary *Grey
Gardens*. At Torpedo, she played the piano and sang "My Heart Belongs
to Daddy." Torpedo also featured the Del Rubio Triplets, who billed
themselves as "three girls, three guitars, one tube of lipstick."

After the city razed the building for a parking lot, Lee spent years as
director of catering services at InterContinental Hotels, building relationships with top chefs around the world. In 2000, the Miami-based
liquor distributor Southern Wine & Spirits hired him as director of

special events. He was assigned the task of improving the company's annual wine tasting, the Florida Extravaganza, which benefited Florida International University's Chaplin School of Hospitality & Tourism Management in Miami. In 1999, the extravaganza's first year, it had attracted six hundred people and raised about $30,000.

As a birthday gift in 2000, a friend took him to the Food & Wine Classic in Aspen. Held every June since 1982 and sponsored by *Food & Wine* magazine, it presents rarefied wine tastings and cooking demonstrations by the world's great chefs—Julia Child had been a regular, as were Jacques Pépin and San Francisco restaurateur Jeremiah Tower. In the high-altitude meadows was a privileged world of cuisine, restaurant industry gossip, and talk of *terroir*.

On the plane ride home, Lee thought, I could do that better. It was inconvenient and expensive for most people to travel to Aspen. A pass to "the Classic" cost over $1,000. He started imagining a high-season festival on the sands of South Beach where everybody could come, people who cared as much about having fun as about food education. He moved the Florida Extravaganza to South Beach and convinced his friend Jeffrey Chodorow to cajole the decorated French chef Alain Ducasse to appear. Lee was then able to leverage Alain's commitment to lure two hot Bay Area chefs, Gary Danko and Cindy Pawlcyn. His timing coincided perfectly with the rising popularity of Food Network. In the following years, Lee attracted the network's stars, seducing them with flights to sunny Miami in February, hotel rooms with fresh flowers, and promises to promote whatever book or charity project they wanted. Chefs were not paid to appear, because all the profit went to charity.

Bobby began hosting an invite-only private lunch every year at Joe's Stone Crab during the festival. Within a few years, tens of thousands of Food Network fans were buying $100-plus tickets to the raucous events Lee created—the Bubble Q, where celebrity chefs doled out heaping plates of barbecue and cocktail waitresses poured champagne; and the Burger Bash, a beer-boosted competition presided over by Rachael Ray, where dozens of chefs competed for the honor of having their hamburger judged the best in the country. Bobby would hand out his burgers at one end of the tent, Michael Symon at another, and some guys from a joint up in Boston in the middle, with the food media blogging the results of the competition. It was not Aspen, where corporate sponsors and VIPS were invited up the mountain by gondola for the annual Publishers' Party. Lee's festival was a populist good time, and offered fans of the Food Network a chance to meet the stars they had come to feel were members of their own families. There was loud live music, the bikinis of South Beach, and dozens of cooking demonstrations under vast tents on the beach all day long—along with arrests for public intoxication. By 2004, the festival was raising $600,000 annually. Giant pennants bearing the faces of TV chefs flapped from stanchions throughout South Beach. That year, a local columnist gushed, "Having the opportunity to watch my television idols perform live is the equivalent of MIT students seeing Albert Einstein solve a math problem."

It was the culmination of what Shep had started with his Miami fest in 1994 and what the Food Network Live events under Allegro and Gore had been moving toward.

Food & Wine magazine recognized that the South Beach festival could be a nice adjunct to Aspen on the annual calendar and came in as a sponsor in 2002. But Lee wanted direct access to the marketing might of Food Network. When Brooke took the helm, Lee struck, just as Shep had lassoed Reese as a sponsor for The Big Feast on the Beach a decade earlier.

"Why should I sponsor the festival?" Brooke protested when Lee called her in 2004. "All my people are there. It looks like the Food Network festival already, and I'm getting it for free."

Lee explained that the network could use the event to entertain potential advertisers and clients. "We will give you receptions. You can introduce new talent. We'll take them even though they're not well known enough," he said.

She caved in time for the 2007 festival, and Lee delivered the Food Network to its fans with even more force. He bestowed naming rights to four sponsors, and renamed the four days in February "The Food Network South Beach Wine & Food Festival presented by *Food & Wine* magazine and hosted by Southern Wine & Spirits and Florida International University." The event—referred to simply as SOBE—became the food world equivalent to the Sundance Film Festival, attracting more than 50,000 free-spending foodies annually, motivating the *Today Show* to broadcast live from the beach with a flurry of chef segments, and becoming a place for new talent to be showcased and numerous deals sealed between producers, agents, stars, and the network.

So, with the decks cleared and the launching pad set, who would be wheeled in for liftoff? A number of projects had been in development and were ready to be tried in prime time just as *Emeril Live* bowed out.

One had come from David Page, a former investigative news producer for ABC and NBC, who had moved into producing food programming in 2003, when he worked with Al Roker on Food Network specials such as "Diner Destinations." Based in Minnesota, Page had been on the phone pitching show ideas to a Food Network programming executive named Christianna Reinhardt for months. Finally, in mid-2006, she asked, "Don't you have anything on diners?"

David did not have any show ideas about diners, but he knew never to say no while pitching a television executive. "Sure," he extemporized, dreaming up a name on the spot. "I have *Diners, Drive-ins and Dives.*"

Christianna liked the sound of that. It was a Thursday afternoon. She asked if David could send over a one-page explanation of the show by Monday.

David called Richard J. S. Gutman, the author of *American Diner Then & Now*, a landmark history of the species. Richard gave David the names of a half dozen colorful diners with notable dishes that might make good profiles for television. In David's one-page summary, he suggested that they visit one each week.

Food Network agreed to finance a pilot and told David that the star would be the winner of the second season of *The Next Food Network*

Star—Guy Fieri. As his prize he had won the right to star in a six-episode season of *Guy's Big Bite*, set in what looked like a bachelor pad with a big TV and car memorabilia. Network executives loved him in it, and had concluded, like many others who saw him, that Guy had a magnetic personality. Now Bob Tuschman and Alison Page wanted to find a prime-time vehicle for him. Christianna had overseen the Al Roker show and was working on *Unwrapped*. She believed in the audience appeal of the soft road-trip format—"what's happening in your neck of the woods kind of stuff," she recalled. Out of discussions between the three programmers came the idea to try Guy in something like that.

David had not watched *Big Bite*, so he pulled up a photo of Guy on the Web and was surprised to see the spiky peroxide blond hair and multihued goatee. Guy didn't look like any creature the producer had seen on TV before. This show is doomed, David thought. But he needed the work. At the least, he'd collect some paychecks for a few weeks while they made the pilot.

When David finally met his star on the first day of production at a New Jersey diner near an oil refinery, he was impressed by Guy's energy. But it was quickly apparent that Guy knew little about the history of diners, which had a longer tradition on the East Coast than the West. Guy kept referring to diners as restaurants that specialize in hamburgers and criticized those that had very long menus, saying they couldn't be good at any one thing if the menu was so big.

In fact, many old diners have long menus because, like Alice's Restaurant in the famous song, that was their main selling point: you can get anything you want.

Green though Guy was, he was a fast learner. The pilot, which took twenty-one days to film, aired in November 2006 and was popular enough that the network agreed to finance a ten-episode season. Guy's education continued. When a chef at a deli repeated the old line that chicken soup was "Jewish penicillin," Guy mistakenly thought the chef had invented the joke. Nevertheless, zooming up to uncelebrated blue-collar eateries in a 1967 Camaro convertible, Guy seemed to bring a party with him, just as he had on those nights in Big Bear with the crew from Louise's Trattoria. As *Diners, Drive-ins and Dives* went into weekly rotation on Monday nights in April 2007, it did for Guy what *Throwdown* had done for Bobby. Guy shone a flattering light on the hard work of low-paid cooks. The people he visited were presented as artists who managed to bring passion into their special cheese steaks, seafood chowders, and meatball parms. Guy would bite into the delicacy in question and, generous with his praise, developed a lexicon of Guy-speak to bring the good times home: "That's the corner of delicious and juicy right in the middle of flavortown!" "It's not a party without Havarti!" "Pork-tastic!" "Holy crustification!"

In 2008, Lee, fulfilling his promise to the network to elevate its new stars at the festival along with the established ones, gave Guy a two-hour slot cooking for children and their parents at Kellogg's Kidz Kitchen, a $35 event at a park on Ocean Drive. Thestreet.com published an interview with the new star in which Guy, now apparently an expert, named some of his favorite dives and instructed that such places were about "a love affair with food."

Everything was so in-synch, it was easy to think a food-star-minting machine might keep rolling forever if you just added the right amounts of breadcrumbs, bacon grease, and sunshine.

Another prospect had ambushed Marc Summers one day in 2005 in his accountant's office. When Marc walked in, a hulking figure said, "Hi."

"Who are you?"

"Robert Irvine. I've been trying to attack you from three different angles." He spoke with intensity, emphasizing every word in a rounded accent particular to Southwest England. Robert, forty, had tried to reach Marc, then the host of *The Next Food Network Star*, through a mutual business associate in Philadelphia, through calls to Marc's office, and now through his accountant. The accountant had buckled under the force of Robert's personality and agreed to arrange the meeting.

Marc, fifty-four, had been in the TV business for three decades, and was so often pitched ideas for new series that he had formed his own small production company in Philadelphia. "What do you want?" he asked Robert.

"I want to be on Food Network."

"You and a million other people. What do you do?"

Robert said he'd cooked for British royalty and dignitaries in the military and elsewhere, and had an idea for a show in which he would cook the dishes he made for them.

He was freakishly fit, with the triangular frame of a bodybuilder and a crew cut. Marc decided that he appreciated Robert's persistence. It was kind of how Marc himself operated, sometimes phoning casting directors so often they would give him work just to stop the calls.

Marc went to see Robert do a cooking demonstration at a food show in New Jersey that weekend. With his muscle-head short hair, big ears, and overbite, he looked like Popeye's foil, Bluto, but he told story after story about the fabulous things he'd done. The audience was rapt.

This doesn't make sense, Marc thought. He had been at other demos where chefs offered careful technical instruction and the crowd shifted in their seats and some left. During Robert's demo, the cooking tips were squeezed in between mentions of the royal yacht. No one stirred. "What the hell do you want to do?" Marc asked again after the demo.

"I want to do a show called *Fit for a King*. I want to make food I made for people in England."

"Let me tell you, if we sign up today to do something, it's going to be two years before anything happens, if it does. Are you willing to put in two years?"

"Yes."

Marc, Robert, and Robert's writing partner Brian O'Reilly met with Charles Nordlander at Food Network, but Charles did not like the sizzle reel they produced for *Fit for a King*. Too focused on pleasing rich people, not enough mass appeal. To Charles's eye, Robert looked like a superhero. He did not look like anyone Food Network had on the air, but that did not mean it wouldn't work. What, Charles thought, could they do with a superhero chef? The four men batted it around, and out came a concept based on the old TV show *Mission: Impossible*. Why not try Robert as a kind of secret agent of food, showing up where he was needed to tackle a task he always chose to accept. The challenge, Nordlander insisted, needed to involve a time element, a deadline Robert would have to meet.

The producers arranged for Robert to go up to a training facility where the New York Knicks and the Rangers worked out. They produced a seven-minute sizzle reel showing him meeting with the teams' nutritionist and preparing meals tailored to the players' dietary requirements.

When Charles showed the sizzle reel at a programming department meeting, there was some hesitation about how viewers would feel about a British accent, but the network agreed to finance a full pilot episode for what was now called *Dinner: Impossible*. ShootersTV, the Philadelphia-based production company that Marc, Brian, and Robert were working with, was given a budget of less than $200,000 to do the hour. Shooters was so desperate to be in business with Food Network that it spent around $450,000 on a pilot in which Robert cooked for a 200-person wedding at a mansion, given only eight hours and an inexperienced staff. At one point in the pilot, Chef Irvine offered his perspective on leadership: "The chef's jacket is like a coat of arms; it makes you who you are. It turns me into this very prim and proper English guy who has no nonsense." Robert had been raised in Salisbury in southwest England, a two-hour train ride from London. His father, a former professional soccer player from Belfast, worked as a painter, and his mother, Patricia, toiled in a wallpaper shop.

The investment in the pilot worked. The network ordered a season, twelve additional episodes, although the budget was still so tight, it would take Shooters years to break even. Just as Marc had predicted, it was to be two years between the meeting in the accountant's office to the debut of *Dinner: Impossible*.

And yet something had been niggling in the back of Marc's mind: all these claims Robert had been making about cooking meals for the royal family. Marc had not exactly seen Robert chatting on his cell phone with Prince Charles. He only knew for sure that Robert had cooked for a few years at casinos in Atlantic City. It was a long way from Caesars to Buckingham Palace. But Marc dismissed the doubts, deciding, what the hell did he care if someone was fudging the truth to get on TV? Marc himself had changed his last name from Berkowitz to Summers after the Son of Sam serial killer, David Berkowitz, had made it a bad name to have.

But now, the night before *Dinner: Impossible* was to go on the air, he pulled up Robert's website and took a close look at his bio. The site said he was "chef at the Inaugural Dinner for President George W. Bush," and had done the same for George H. W. Bush. It noted that he had a B.S. degree in food and nutrition from Leeds University and had served aboard the Royal Yacht *Britannia*, "preparing outstanding cuisine for royalty, presidents, and high-ranking dignitaries."

Robert was not officially Marc's employee and Marc had not done his own investigation into the claims. If anything, Food Network, which would own the rights to the show, should have looked into his biography. Still, a pang of worry shot through Marc's mind. He and everyone else had put a lot of time and money into this show. Sitting at a breakfast bar in his production office in Philadelphia, he started thinking that if—IF—some of the biography was embellished, it went beyond the old showbiz white lies of changing your name or trimming a few years off your age. Claiming to have cooked for presidents would be considered a big lie, something that if exposed could cost you your career. It reminded Marc of an exposed truth that had nearly cost him his own show business life.

Ever since he was a boy, Marc had been obsessively neat. As an adult, he'd developed strange superstitions and rituals, such as a belief that if he booked a flight and did not read the back of a cereal box over and over again, the flight would crash. For years, he did not know he was suffering from a disease, but when he'd been the cohost of the morning show *Biggers and Summers* on Lifetime, he'd read a description of obsessive-compulsive disorder in preparation for a guest interview and recognized himself. On the show the next morning, he spontaneously revealed to the psychiatrist that he struggled with OCD. Marc described how he hung his clothes exactly a quarter of an inch apart, believing that if he didn't terrible things would happen, and confessed that he had yelled at his wife on their wedding day for being fifteen minutes late. He had been signed to host a new version of *Hollywood Squares*, but after *People* magazine wrote an article about him and Oprah interviewed him, and word started spreading in Hollywood that he was a nut job, the deal fell through. He began doing speaking engagements about his disease and wrote a book, *Everything in Its Place: My Trials and Triumphs with Obsessive Compulsive Disorder*. It was only after his old Lifetime boss, Judy Girard, went to the Food Network that he started the second phase of his career on *Unwrapped*. Marc had not deliberately lied and he didn't think Robert suffered from some moral failing if he had embellished his résumé. Marc knew simply that you had to be careful about your reputation if you wanted to survive in showbiz. Perhaps Marc should have raised his concerns earlier than the night before the show was to debut, but there was still time to change some copy on the website if necessary. He urged Robert to think through what might be coming if he was hiding something.

"You have no idea," he warned him. "I came out and started talking about OCD, the shit that started to come down."

"It's all good," Robert assured him. He was so close to the dream he'd been working toward for years.

> "I think it is worth mentioning that, as an Executive Chef, I have been in charge of kitchens in the Navy, on cruise ships and in hotels and casinos and have hired and fired hundreds of chefs and I didn't hire a single one of them based on what I might have read on their resume. I listened to personal recommendations about them from other chefs and then I found out for myself if they could cook. If they could cook and were willing to work hard, they got the job, case closed."
>
> **—ROBERT IRVINE, BLOG ENTRY**

Brooke stayed focused on shaping the network into the moneymaking force she believed it ought to be. In March 2007, the network hired

Sergei Kuharsky, a former Disney executive, as general manager for new business, finally filling the job Brooke had nearly created for herself as head of "ancillary business." Sergei had worked for Disney in the late 1990s where he helped develop the "get it before it goes back in the vault" strategy, in which DVDs of classic animated movies were sold for a limited time at premium prices. It unlocked vast millions in profits from dormant content such as *Bambi* and *Pinocchio*.

A magazine was Sergei's first priority. The network owned a treasure trove of recipes and its stars were generating new ones every day. The same year *Gourmet* magazine folded, *Food Network Magazine* was launched in partnership with Hearst. The first issue, with Bobby and Ina on the cover, featured recipes for hamburgers. Print magazines were supposedly a dying breed, but *Food Network Magazine*, leveraging its star power, was a stunning success, with a circulation of 1.25 million in its second year.

Sergei pushed for "permission research" in which the network asked its fans what sort of products they could see the Food Network brand associated with. A common answer was "a restaurant." Food Network installed a food kiosk in the new Yankee Stadium in 2008 that offered exotic dishes like a Chinese noodle bowl and jicama fries—one baseball fan asked what "Jamaica" fries were. The network kept things simpler when it opened a stand at the new football stadium at the Meadowlands in New Jersey. It served fancy hot dogs. They partnered with the national restaurant group Delaware North to sell brisket sandwiches at a stadium in Texas, and a Food Network eatery at a small airport in Florida offered turkey pinwheels with hummus. They partnered with Wente Vineyards and introduced their own wine label, Entwine, available in red and white. As he'd done with Disney movies, Sergei was making a lot of money out of little additional investment.

On February 17, a week before the SOBE festival in 2008, an article appeared in the *St. Petersburg Times*: "TV Chef Spiced Up His Past

Exploits." By then, *Dinner: Impossible* had become a successful Wednesday night staple in prime time in its third season and Robert was involved in a deal to open two restaurants in the St. Petersburg area. The paper's investigative reporter Ben Montgomery had looked into biographical claims, some on the website Marc had perused, some in Robert's cookbook, *Mission: Cook! My Life, My Recipes, and Making the Impossible Easy*, and some he had been heard mentioning around town. No matter what Irvine had been claiming, he was not a Knight Commander of the Royal Victorian Order, a spokesman from Buckingham Palace confirmed. Walter Scheib, the White House executive chef from 1994 to 2005, cast doubt on Robert's claim that he had cooked for the George W. Bush Inauguration, telling the paper that during that period Robert had had nothing to do with food preparation for the part of the White House where presidents live. A spokeswoman at the University of Leeds told the paper that the school could find no record of him. And as to his claim that at a royal school of cookery he had "aided in the construction of the cake for the royal wedding of Charles, Prince of Wales, and Lady Diana Spencer" and "participated in the design and execution of the beautifully crafted side panels," the real baker of the cake e-mailed the paper two days after the article: "He most certainly was not involved with me in making or baking the cake."

The original article noted, "Irvine's relationships have soured like month-old milk. His website consultant claims he owes her thousands. His restaurant designer has backed out. His interior decorator is suing him."

Dinner: Impossible was shooting in Puerto Rico the morning the article appeared and Robert told the early arrivals that it meant nothing.

But at 7 a.m. someone from the crew called Marc in Philadelphia. "Have you seen the article about Robert?"

After reading it, he called the star.

"What the hell is going on?"

"It'll blow over," Robert insisted.

"Robert, this is not blowing over, trust me."

Network executives quietly told Lee that Robert was not coming to the festival and to cancel his cooking demonstration. The pennants showing his face continued to flap above the "tasting village" tents along the beach as the network staff debated what to do about him. Would *Dinner: Impossible* stay on the air? Two weeks after the festival, Carrie Welch, the head of public relations, called Marc and asked him directly, "How come you didn't vet him?"

The previous June, Carrie had had to deal with allegations that a competitor on *The Next Food Network Star*, Josh "Jag" Garcia, had been inaccurate in presenting information about his background, including his military service, claiming he had deployed to Afghanistan though records were not clear that he had. He'd withdrawn from the competition. Carrie was particularly upset that in the wake of that mess, Marc had not vetted Robert more thoroughly.

"He wasn't mine to vet," Marc protested. "I would have, if I was going to sign him, but you guys took him over, so your attorney should have done it, not me."

"What did you know and when did you know it?" Brooke asked Marc in a phone call soon after.

"Brooke, I swear to God," Marc said. "I don't know shit."

"What's fake and real on DI?" Brooke pushed. She was worried the problems reached beyond the résumé and into the core of the show. What if they had to yank it from the network entirely? "Here's how I run my show," Marc said. "He has no freaking idea what the challenge is until he walks in, end of statement. Everybody knows in the office, if anybody tells Robert what's going to happen they're fired. Brooke, I swear, it's all for real. We're not giving him anything."

Frustrated, Marc reminded the chef that he had sworn to God that everything on his résumé was true. Why had Robert risked the whole enterprise on it?

"Don't you remember when we were having our private discussions?" Marc asked.

Robert replied, "I know, I know, I know."

Finally, there was a meeting at the Food Network's business offices among Carrie, Bob Tuschman, and Pat Guy, the head of legal affairs, and Robert and his business manager, Randall Williams.

Fighting for his television life, Robert brought in stacks of files and award plaques, and he and Randall pushed folders forward of British Navy papers and testimonials. But the network would lose credibility if it allowed him to stay after what he'd done.

"I'm sorry," Carrie said. "It's not going to work out." She was a little scared. Robert's muscles were bulging and the look in his eyes was alternately pleading and murderous.

Bob told him, "I'm sorry, but there's no way that we can keep you on the network with this happening."

As much as Brooke was focused on prime time, the network still filled many hours of its schedule with old-fashioned cooking shows. By this point in its history, the art of producing them had been honed nearly to perfection. Gone were the days when producers like Pat O'Gorman enforced silly rules like "no food with faces," and gone was Reese's "no stopping" dictate. The network had enough money to afford editors now—and if you wanted to use raw eggs in your mousse, go for it!

> "At the end, we hugged! I mean, isn't that ridiculous? We were like, 'Oh, good luck.' We went back to Pat's office afterwards, and we all just stared at each other for a while. I had never done that to anyone before."
>
> **—CARRIE WELCH**

There was only one problem, one wild card that prevented the production of a cooking show to reach perfection, and that was human beings, especially human beings who came from the tumultuous world of restaurants.

A visit to the set of *Secrets of a Restaurant Chef* revealed just how challenging it could be to channel a professional chef into the expensive constraints of a modern half-hour cooking show. It starred Anne Burrell, one of Mario Batali's sous chef from *Iron Chef America*, a talented and respected veteran of professional kitchens. Anne grew up in occasionally unpleasant circumstances in a small upstate New York town. In her childhood home, she would never know when her father was drunk based on his outward appearance, but then she'd realize she had no idea what he was talking about.

As a little girl, she began telling herself that she was going to be famous when she grew up. She believed that she was special, that she had a "sparkly factor." She also found succor on TV. When she was three, she told her mother she had a new friend named Julie.

"Julie who?" Anne's mother asked.

"Julie Child," Anne said. The big woman on the television who was cooking beautiful-looking food. She felt like a friend to little Anne.

The enemy of the sparkly person, Anne figured, was the mediocre person, and she knew she wasn't that. She started working in restaurants at nineteen because she wanted to buy a car, but was quickly pulled into the life. The restaurant people would go out late after work every night and get wasted, talk about all kinds of interesting things, then sleep late and do the whole thing again the next day.

A few years later, Anne found herself trying to hold down a more "responsible" job as a headhunter for doctors in a dreary office in Buffalo, New York. After work one unusually warm evening, while walking her dog, she had an epiphany: "I am twenty-three years old and I am too young to be this miserable. I will go to the Culinary Institute of America, and I will have a restaurant in Manhattan."

Thanks to her appearances on *Iron Chef America*, with her commanding personality and restaurant experience—and spiky peroxide hairdo—in 2008 the network gave her her own show, *Secrets of a Restaurant Chef*, where she would teach home cooks useful professional techniques. Programmers recognized that something about her seemed true to the frenetic energy of a restaurant kitchen, and she added something different to the ITK lineup. But she was not a smooth television presence like Rachael Ray, Giada De Laurentiis or, once she got the hang of it, Ina Garten. Anne was a handful.

When the network started in 1993, it cost about $2,000 to make a thirty-minute cooking show, including roughly $300 paid to the talent. *Secrets of a Restaurant Chef* employed a fleet of professionals and cost around $50,000 an episode. At 10:30 a.m., cameras rolled on the first of four segments for the half-hour show. When it aired, the first segment would take about seven minutes. Minus commercials, twenty-two minutes of television needed to be made. If all went according to the schedule, shooting for all four segments of episode #LR0612 would be completed in three and a half hours. The crew would lunch from two to three and begin taping another episode ("The Secret to Garlic Chicken Casserole") at 3:15 p.m.

First call in the main studio at the Food Network was 8 a.m. Anne arrived at 8:30. An hour and a half of primping later, she was due on the set, where she spent half an hour with the director and producers rehearsing.

The script for this episode called for the preparation of spinach and ricotta gnocchi with quick tomato sauce and apricot nectarine shortcake with vanilla whipped cream.

On the set, between takes, Anne needled her assistant, Young Sun, who was arranging ricotta gnocchi on a sheet pan.

"How is your boyfriend Dr. Weiner?" asked Anne. Her spiky blond hair gleamed like steel quills in the stage lights. "Paging Dr. Weiner. Paging Dr. Oscar Meyer Weeeeener."

A cameraman chimed in: "I used to go to college with a girl named Mai [pronounced "my"]. Her parents named her that. Her last name was Johnson. Mai Johnson. She's married now, so she's not Johnson anymore."

Young walked off the set toward the prep kitchen in the rear of the studio.

Upstairs in the control room, the producer and director ignored the banter and watched a replay of the segment Anne had just shot in which she made the batch of gnocchi. Was it as perfect as possible or did it need to be redone? Did the star use all the proper ingredients in the proper order? Did she stumble on any words? Did the cameras catch the dusting of the sheet pans and the squeezing dry of the spinach?

Anne called out for her hairdresser, Alberto Machuca. He ran up behind the cameras, spray can in one hand, plastic pick in the other.

"Alberto. Is there a hole right there?" Anne pointed to a spot at the back right of her head.

A "hole" meant a gap in the symmetrical pattern of spikes in Anne's mane—as if her head were a medieval mace. Alberto sprayed and teased a spike back into place.

Behind the set was a small prep kitchen where a sous chef cooked along with Anne, in case something burned and needed to be swapped out.

Beyond that sat Rani Cheema, a graphic designer whose job was to make new labels for commercial products Anne used on camera. She was a one-woman branding company. You don't want the chef to use Green Giant if Birds Eye was buying thirty-second ad spots. So every bottle of hot sauce, vinegar, wine, every can of tomatoes, corn, or artichoke hearts had its label removed and Rani made a new label with a fake brand name. When Sunny Anderson needed a hot sauce, Rani came up with the name *Nuke It* with a little mushroom cloud image on the label. Now Rani was working on a label for the white wine Anne would need in an upcoming episode. She named it Fabella, fashioning a golden yellow and black label.

Wendy Waxman, the set designer, was one of the few survivors from the network's earliest days, having worked with Joe Langhan, Reese— all of them. She had created the perfect Anne Burrell kitchen, giving the viewer a range of hints about the chef's personality, a temperamental chef-artist who surrounded herself with a mélange of the funky, the modern, and the nostalgic—vases in muted tones, a copper-colored bowl, and stacks of colorful tiles. Behind Anne's kitchen set, a wide door led to another room. The cameras occasionally captured a glimpse of a 1950s modern wooden dining room table like the one Anne might have had as a child in upstate New York. Her home had not been so sedately appointed, but it was pretty to think so.

Word came from the control room into the earpieces of the floor producers: "Moving on!" The producer, Shelley Hoffmann, a prótegé of Mark Dissin, and the director, Mike Schear, were satisfied that the segment was perfect enough.

Forty feet from the fake upstate kitchen was a cornucopia of junk food. Anne grabbed three Crème de Pirouline sticks (rolled crispy wafers filled with waxy hazelnut cream) and fed them into her mouth all at once as she padded back to the set in pastel rainbow flip-flops.

After the clacker struck and started rolling, Young quietly sat down at a production desk with two raw steaks on a white platter. They were for the show shooting the next day, but something about them didn't look right. Was tomorrow's show supposed to be about cooking T-bones or porterhouses? she asked Sarah Paulsen, the culinary producer, who checked the script for the next day's show. It called for porterhouse. But these were T-bones.

Sarah pulled up the Wikipedia entry for T-Bone steak. A porterhouse has more tenderloin, but both have a big T-bone. Young trimmed two little bits of fat from the steaks.

Up in the control room, Shelley, Mike, and a crew of eight people tethered to headsets scrutinized Anne's performance. Shelley, tall and thin in skin-tight jeans, a tailored blue blazer, and black high heels, was concerned about the shortcake-making in segment 2.

"Mike, I think she's off today in general," she said to the director. "She keeps calling it shortbread again and again. It's not shortbread. It's shortcake."

The two of them discussed whether they would have to reshoot the segment. They tried to find a spot where they could splice in a fix, but decided there was no good spot and that they would have to take it from the top.

The crew had been putting out new ingredients for segment 3, while maintaining basic visual continuity with the end of segment 2. A freeze-frame shot of the set as it was at the start of segment 2 was put up on one monitor in the control room, and Mike and Shelley compared the freeze frame to the live shot and gave instructions to the floor crew about where to place the baking powder, the butter . . . "Put the cream to the left of the Cuisinart. No, closer to the sink," Mike said. Five hours later, when Shelley was moments away from calling the work day done, Anne realized that she had forgotten the anchovies in the Caesar salad dressing. This required another major set reset. "We're going to do a fridge walk to get the anchovies," Shelley declared. "They can't just suddenly appear on the counter."

This business of the gathering of the ingredients is a serious business in the construction of a modern cooking show. It takes time to walk to the fridge. In the six to nine minutes of actual showtime between commercials, an extra trip to the fridge to fetch a forgotten ingredient can cost thirty seconds, ticks of the clock that are better spent instructing viewers how to cook. Everyone already knows how to walk to the fridge.

But it would look weird if anchovies that were not there at the start of the making of the dressing were suddenly there. So the fridge walk was the only choice.

Sink trips to wash hands are another big issue. Salmonella-mad viewers want to see those hands washed after a chef handles a chicken, but those trips are noncooking time and are carefully plotted so they don't ruin the action.

Down on the set, Anne said: "We can do a Caesar salad without Parmesan, but we can't do it without anchovies."

Sarah, in a response only the control room could hear, said, "Oh, the irony of that statement."

A few weeks later in the same studio with many of the same floor crew—sound guys and the food stylist, Santos Loo—Rachael Ray was cooking chicken breasts wrapped in prosciutto and rosemary with a side dish of cold pasta with tomatoes for an episode of *30 Minute Meals*.

The place seemed almost asleep. The whole episode took about forty minutes to shoot, flawless, Rachael keeping the banter smooth and easy as she placed sprigs of fresh rosemary between the chicken and the ham and cooked them on a stovetop griddle.

"You don't have to serve pasta hot. Room temperature is nice sometimes and you don't have to worry about everything being served hot at the perfect time." She could do three shows in a day, easy. She was Babe Ruth, a natural.

—————

On Anne's set, the question was whether any of the crew would get home in time to see any of their family members still awake.

As the gnocchi Anne had assembled in the first segment were bobbing to the surface of the simmering water, she quickly fished them out with a mesh spoon, her restaurant instincts taking over and depriving the cameras of a chance to capture a shot of the pasta floating and ready. Before anyone could react, Anne dropped the gnocchi onto a plate with tomato sauce, grated a chunk of Parmesan over it and delivered her final line: "Gnocchi Dokey!" as she stood smiling in front of her steaming pasta.

But the cameras needed that shot of the floaters. To add to the problem, Anne had come in thirty seconds under time.

As they explained all this to Anne through her earpiece, the control room team could see a close-up of her on the monitor, rivulets of sweat moistening the furrows of rage above her eyebrows.

Young brought out a pot of clean boiling water and a tray of perfect rows of uncooked gnocchi from the shadow kitchen behind the set. The star remained motionless, temples pulsing, staring down at a blank spot on the floor.

With Anne's anger and frustration apparent to everyone, Leigh Rivers, whose job it was to type text into her teleprompter, said to the control room at large, "What would JCC do?"

That morning, Juan-Carlos Cruz, a former star of *Calorie Commando*—"Keep the taste while you trim your waist!"—which had had a thirty-nine-episode run before it was canceled in 2006, had been charged with hiring homeless men in Los Angeles to kill his wife. JCC had reportedly given two homeless men the halves of ten $100 bills and told them he'd give them the other halves if they slashed his wife's throat with box cutters. The homeless men told the police, and Cruz was arrested at a dog park in Los Angeles. He eventually pleaded no contest to a charge of soliciting murder and was sentenced to nine years in prison.

Anne could not hear the comment. When the retake of segment 4 finally rolled, she was ready. She let the cameras catch the floating gnocchi as she scooped them out of the water and plated them with a ladle of tomato sauce. She cut one with a spoon and quickly tasted it, a steaming, thick ball of pasta just out of the boiling water.

"Hot, hot," Mike warned Anne in her earpiece.

Anne's taste buds were apparently made of asbestos. "Creamy, delicious," she said after swallowing quickly. "The cheese and the tomato go together so well."

"Are we still in Happytown?" Shelley asked Anne into her earpiece at 1:48 p.m.

"I live in Happytown, USA," Anne replied.

At 1:49, "Moving on" was called out, and "Lunch!"

While the grunt production work continued apace up on six, down on the third floor, programming executives were still trying to find fresh ideas for prime time as the network struggled to harness the wild energy and the soul of the chefs rather than try to force them into pre-measured formats.

As problematic as food people could be, they were often, like Anne, great characters. Mining that, *Top Chef* continued to draw huge audiences to Bravo, but Food had yet to find an answer.

That changed because of an unlikely pitch from City Lights productions. The New York–based company had conceived of a high-concept show, which took the idea of the mysterious silhouetted banker character on the game show *Deal or No Deal* and transposed him to a cooking competition. The idea was that in each episode, the banker—they did not own the rights to the character, so referred to him as a tycoon—would be planning to throw a dinner party at his castle. His butler, a snooty John Cleese type, would find four sous chefs who would compete in the castle kitchen for the privilege of cooking the dinner. The competition covered three rounds: an appetizer, a main course, and a dessert. After each round, one chef would be eliminated by a panel of judges. The food of each eliminated chef would be scraped into a dog bowl and fed, on camera, to the butler's ravenous Chihuahua.

The network was cool to the idea until Linda Lea, who had worked on *Queer Eye for the Straight Guy*, which had put Bravo on the map and inspired the creation of *Top Chef*, was attached as a producer.

When City Lights first offered Linda a producer role in 2007, she had feared for her professional reputation, asking a girlfriend, "How can I produce a show where food is being scraped into a dog food bowl?"

The network agreed to finance a pilot. On the set, Linda and the crew found themselves amazed at the passion of the chefs to win the competition, silly as it might have seemed. At the start of each round, the chefs raced across the kitchen to the pantry and seemed to forget about the cameras and all the distractions. As they furiously cooked, the cameramen and the rest of the crew placed bets on who would be eliminated.

The Chihuahua, Pico, was a problem. Pico was friendly and had a professional trainer. But it dawned on the producers that if they kept feeding the little fellow food all day long, he would get sick and not eat on cue. There was no dog double. After each round, Rocco DiSpirito, back for another try at TV, this time as a judge, was assigned to grab the rejected dish, scrape it into Pico's bowl, and place it on a cutting board under the dog's nose. They started allowing the Chihuahua only one hungry gobble for the camera before snatching the bowl away.

Soon after the pilot was done, Bob Tuschman called Linda and broke the bad news. "All that stuff, we just didn't respond to it. It's too wacky. We're sorry."

"No, no," she fought back. There were elements of this show worth saving, she just knew it. "I will be in your office Monday and we'll talk about it."

The next week, Linda explained to him and Alison Page that something magical had happened on the set. The competing chefs had yearned to show what they were made of. When the clock had started for each course, they had forgotten the loony setup and that the camera was rolling. The dog and the butler could go, but the rest had serious potential. "Let's get rid of all that nonsense and concentrate on what is working," she said. "And that's these chefs dying to play this game and compete and prove they made the right choices in their lives.

"I can do another pilot for ninety thousand dollars. Let me try."

Bob had always liked the title of the show: *Chopped*. "All right," he said. "Go do it your way."

Linda brought in Ted Allen to host it. Despite Ted's having been on *Queer Eye*, one of the most successful shows on cable, Food Network executives were concerned because he had not hosted a show solo before. But they relented, and when they saw the results, they ordered a thirteen-episode season to start. Poor Rocco, however, did not make the cut, nor did Pico.

The show was a streamlined version of the original. They kept the drama of the run to the pantry and added a mystery basket of ingredients for each round—kind of like the bag of groceries from *Ready . . . Set . . . Cook!*, but instead of being easy foods to cook at home, these typically included at least one obscure item, like Pop Rocks or durian. Three courses were each timed and judged. Ted announced that the loser's dish had been "chopped," and the loser took a walk of shame off the set, explained his or her heartbreak to the camera, and then the next round began, the whole drama moving forward relentlessly. Viewers found it addictive.

A rotating roster of judges comprised the panel, all of them prominent New York–area chefs, some who had appeared frequently on Food Network over the years: Marc Murphy, Alex Guarnaschelli, Scott Conant, Marcus Samuelsson, Amanda Freitag, Geoffrey Zakarian, Chris Santos, and Aarón Sánchez. During the long taping days, a comradeship developed between them. Aarón's flatulence, sometimes aimed directly at the stern Alex, became a running joke on the set.

After a chef was eliminated, he would stay around until a winner was named. Then each was interviewed on camera and asked to relive what he'd done and felt at each moment. For their sixteen-hour day, the losers received nothing. The winners received $10,000.

Even the losers benefited, though. Soon *Chopped* became a popular

staple of prime time. The network reran episodes frequently and ordered more. Corporate event planners offered cooking gigs to chefs
who had appeared, glad to add a Food Network touch to their dinners,
and competitors found that fans recognized them on the street.

Eventually even critics who hated the network's general move away
from foodie content into "escapist" fare were raving. "*Chopped* manages
to be absolutely riveting television that educates, informs, and thrills
at the same time . . ." Jace Lacob wrote in *The Daily Beast*. "Egos flare,
tempers simmer over, and occasionally true culinary genius and inge-
nuity is glimpsed."

It appeared that the network had finally learned the lesson it could
have learned before *Top Chef* gained its foothold: there was gold in the
fiery cave of the professional kitchen.

Difficult people often make good TV. *Dinner: Impossible* had been a
promising show and Robert, the superhero, a promising star. In his
place, Food put Michael Symon, an endlessly likable chef personality
with a quick smile and good cheer. He was fine, but DI was designed
around a demanding, relentless drill sergeant—Robert. Viewers' e-mails
asking for Robert's return poured into the network offices. Charles
Nordlander had left, frustrated over the network's refusal to pay him a
salary competitive with other cable channels, but Brian Lando, a rising
young executive in the programming department, agitated to bring
Robert back. Still, whenever the idea came up, Lando and Carrie would
engage in a conference-room war.

"We can *not* do this!" she insisted. He had swindled the network's
viewers. It was bad PR.

But Brian's argument that the show was a hit with Robert and not
one without him was in the end impossible to shout down. Plus Brian
had clout, because he was overseeing *Chopped* and other shows that were
doing well. In the fall of 2008, Marc received a call from Brian: "Are
you ready to go back to work?"

Brooke called Robert, who was still in some shock, having gone from being the star of a successful show to sitting at home watching someone else host it for ten episodes. Now he was being allowed back. He thanked Brooke profusely. The network went over every line of his biography with him, carefully checking its veracity. A few news items appeared noting the about-face and rehashing the fiasco, but there was no storm of viewer outrage over his return. His exile had lasted about eight months.

After Robert made about twenty-five more episodes, Brooke told Marc that the network was interested in seeing what Robert could do with a restaurant makeover concept. Marc's company shot a pilot of *Restaurant: Impossible* at a struggling diner in Providence. Robert's no-nonsense attitude in getting the place torn apart and remade in two days, along with his skill at psychoanalyzing the owners and trying to set them on the path to prosperity turned out to be weirdly heart-warming. And the good he was doing on the show helped rehabilitate his image.

During the SOBE festival in 2009, Carrie and Robert sat down to talk. "I would never want to do that again," she said. "I was so mad at you, and I wanted you gone. But I would never want to do that to some-body ever again."

Robert said he forgave her.

It appeared the network and its stars could get away with nearly any-thing (short of putting out a contract on a spouse) as long as the hit shows kept coming.

A Ten-Billion-Dollar Prize

I n mid-2000, Scripps had announced a new cable channel called Fine Living Network. Susan Packard, president of Scripps's New Ventures division told the A.P. that it would focus on luxury programming. If Fine Living were a magazine, it would be like *The Robb Report* and *Town & Country*, not *Good Housekeeping*. "Never has there been a moment in history," Susan explained, "where we have seen so much disposable income and yet so little disposable time."

Scripps had agreements from Time Warner, DirecTV, and a national co-op of small cable providers to put the new channel into around twenty million homes, but the timing could hardly have been worse. Yet neither the stock market plunge in the fall of 2000 nor the horror of 9/11 were enough to derail Fine Living's debut in 2002. Where Food Network had profited from the cocooning instinct triggered by 9/11, Fine Living's prospects plummeted. Shows like *Collector Car Auction* and *Bulging Brides* (a weight-loss challenge) did not win an audience. By the recession of 2009, Fine Living was the only Scripps Network Interactive channel showing a loss, with revenue falling 6.7 percent in the first quarter and *twenty-three* percent in the second, when its revenue was a paltry $11 million.

SNI executives remained bullish on Food, whose prime-time audience had jumped 15 percent in the last quarter of 2008 compared to the previous year and gotten younger. The median age of viewers fell from forty-seven years old to forty-four—good news for advertisers. SNI tried to buy out Tribune's stake, an effort that was stymied when Tribune entered court-supervised bankruptcy.

In June 2009, Ken Lowe and his team at SNI started to work out a deal to buy Travel Channel, hoping to add it to their food and shelter lifestyle channels. But they were simultaneously trying to figure how to bail on Fine Living. It was in fifty-five million homes in 2009 and Scripps did not want to give up the distribution deals with cable and satellite providers they had fought to win. Better to switch the channel's identity and keep the slot on the cable dial.

What identity? With the Travel Channel deal pending, that subject was not an option. Nor was another shopping channel. The company had lost millions on ShopAtHome and closed it in 2006, leading Judy Girard to try running one more network, HGTV, before she finally retired from television. HGTV itself already had a home-improvement spin-off in DIY, so home improvement was not an option to replace Fine Living. Dating back to Ken's original plan, SNI was in the business of lifestyle networks. It wasn't going to start the Scripps News Channel. Meanwhile, Gusto had been abandoned, but rumors were rampant that Fox and Discovery were eyeing the rising Food Network profits and plotting rival food channels.

Everything pointed to doing more with food, the proven winner. Ken, John Lansing (SNI's vice president), Brooke, and others at Food Network began discussing what kind of channel they could spin off that would not simply mimic the existing one. Where was the space to do something else?

The answer, they felt, was in the cooking shows Food had moved away from. The executives had heard the complaints about its abandonment of foodie culture and of instructional series in prime time. A channel based on them might not attract Food's high ratings, but its initial goal simply would be to improve upon the measly Fine Living. They went through a few possible names—Foodie, Dish, Eats, and Spice—before settling on the more generic Cooking Channel. In

October 2009, Scripps announced that Fine Living would become Cooking Channel the next year.

When Food was founded in 1993, the first president's wife said it was one of the worst ideas she'd ever heard. Now it was serious business, the center of a corporate machine, beloved, sometimes reviled—always cared about—by millions of people. But it had never been here before, heading toward its seventeenth birthday and about to reproduce.

It was one thing to make the broad-stroke decision to launch a cooking channel that was different from Food Network, but it was another to drill down to exactly what ought to be on that channel. In May 2010, Food Network was a top-ten cable network averaging 707,000 viewers throughout the day and 1.13 million in prime time, but it had taken four years to come up with its first defining breakthrough, *Emeril Live*.

In some ways it was far easier for Scripps to start a new food channel in 2010 than it had been for ProJo in 1993. No one needed to prove that there could be a viable 24-hour-a-day network devoted to food programming. Plus, distribution was a less desperate affair this time, simply a matter of convincing affiliates not to do anything for the time being and to give the spin-off a chance. The name would change from Fine Living to Cooking Channel one night at midnight; if ratings improved without cannibalizing ratings from Food, it would bring in more advertising dollars to cable providers and give subscribers a new channel they liked. Win-win . . . well, almost. Scripps did end up spending about $40 million in "launch incentives" to cajole carriers to make the switch. This was a drag on Cooking Channel's bottom line, as was, from Scripps's perspective, the fact that under its agreements with Tribune, Cooking had to become part of the Food Network partnership. This meant the Chicago company received roughly 30 percent of Cooking, too. Overall, though, these were still small hurdles compared to what TVFN had to overcome at its launch.

And yet, in other ways, Cooking Channel had challenges similar to those TVFN had faced in 1993. New programming was needed, fast. The channel had originally been planned to start in the fall of 2010, but it had become apparent that the launch would go better if it fit with the annual schedule of advertising sales in the spring. More important, Scripps executives wanted to make sure they scooped Discovery or Fox. As Reese had done in 1993, Scripps wanted to scare everyone else away. The start date for Cooking Channel was moved up three months, to the end of May.

It was also a challenge to Food Network itself. Part of the reason to start the new channel was to protect Food from a rival start-up, but even under a Scripps banner, this would be Food's first 24-hour competition. Would the spin-off harm its big brother by sapping resources, or show it up by being more in tune with foodie culture?

One way to ensure that the older brother stayed in charge was to keep the sibling close. Ken Lowe and John Lansing had floated the idea of creating the infrastructure of a completely separate network. What better way to assure that the new network had a separate voice from Food than to give it a separate staff? Perhaps it should be headquartered in Knoxville—the city had better food available than when Susan Stockton had scouted it more than a decade earlier. Or maybe Brooklyn?

Brooke Johnson resisted. She did not want to create a rival within Scripps that would potentially compete with her network for show ideas, talent, and budget, and she argued that it would be better to leverage the executive, marketing, and production talent in the 100,000 square feet of Chelsea Market occupied by Food. This is what they'd done at A&E when they launched History within the womb of the mother ship. It would certainly be cheaper to run the new network out of Food's Manhattan headquarters.

She got what she wanted, but the victory led to another question: whether Food Network, having evolved to deliver an ever more commercially successful product for a broad market, could now simultaneously produce an edgier product for a narrower audience. Would there be any courage to stick with riskier programming if it did not produce spectacular results from the outset, especially since everyone in the building knew what would likely work to build ratings fast—more Giada, more Paula, more Rachael?

Michael Smith, appointed from within the executive ranks of Food Network to become general manager of the Cooking Channel, said the right things in an interview for *The New York Times* before the network debut. It might provide space for riskier fare than Food Network, he said; for example, critical documentaries like *Food, Inc.* and *Super Size Me*, and shows about authentic ethnic restaurants where viewers could be shown live chickens killed before cooking.

But revealing his more conservative instincts as a Berkeley MBA, Michael also suggested that Cooking Channel would be smart to mirror some of Food's offerings. If Food Network had had a sister channel a few years earlier, when *Cake Boss* was being pitched, the fact that Food already had *Ace of Cakes* would not have militated against a second cake show. *Cake Boss* could have gone to Cooking Channel, establishing its bug-eyed star Buddy Valastro and his bickering but loving family as Scripps property, thereby keeping TLC from grabbing a thick wedge of the food television pie.

Bruce Seidel was appointed head of programming for Cooking, but he reported to Bob Tuschman, head of programming at Food, and still was expected to continue to come up with ideas there. It was an unclear role, reflecting Food's trepidation about letting Cooking Channel find its own voice.

Indeed, some of the hours of programming were filled from Food Network's archive. Like Food, Cooking Channel would start with a daily helping of Julia Child and *Galloping Gourmet* "classics." Fine Living was already running episodes of the original Japanese *Iron Chef* to fill out its nightly schedule and *Two Fat Ladies* was wheeled out for Cooking Channel's prime time as well.

This choice of shows, drawn from Food Network's less orthodox programming developed in the days of Joe Langhan and Matt Stillman, showed that Cooking Channel promised to be a departure from the middle-of-the-road programming Food Network had come to rely on as it chased—and caught—an ever-wider audience. Cooking Channel also acquired the U.S. broadcast rights to foreign series such as *Food Jammers*, a Canadian show about three artsy young men who invented outlandish kitchen gadgets, and *Chinese Food Made Easy*, a five-year-old import from Great Britain's UKTV Food starring Ching-He Huang.

"Stay Hungry" was the new network's slogan. But hungry for what exactly?

From the outset, Brooke, wanting Cooking Channel to be a quick success and prove the wisdom of her approach, could not help but tap some of Food's tried-and-true talent. For instance, Bobby had been pitching a brunch cooking show for five years. "I'm probably one of the only professional chefs who likes to cook brunch and takes it very seriously," he argued. "I do it in my restaurants very seriously, and on Saturday and Sunday mornings, when you're watching cooking shows, that's what you should be eating. Not roasted chicken."

But in meeting after meeting, he'd been told, "Brunch is too narrow." The rejection annoyed him. The programming department's protests sounded ridiculous. How many times had he proven himself? But Bobby, the old playground point guard, might be the least neurotic person who ever lived. He had literally become a professional gambler, investing in race horses (mostly fillies); eventually he would be elected a Breeders Cup trustee and write commentary for *Thoroughbred Daily News*. When Brooke asked, "Can you do us a favor, and do a show on the Cooking Channel?" he was ready. Always on point, never shaken, justice would be his.

"Sure," Bobby said, "but it's got to be brunch."

Brunch at Bobby's featured the star in a rented house in the Hamptons preparing waffles and the like. Bobby and his third wife, actress Stephanie March, were having their own country house built on the East End of Long Island the summer the show was first shot in 2010. *Brunch* would be ready for Cooking Channel's first fall. "Casual Bobby at home," Kim Williamson of the programming department explained at a planning meeting. "Rumpled T-shirt, the whole nine."

Two other now-totemic Food Network stars were cast in new productions for Cooking Channel. Rachael Ray made *Week in a Day*, a show shot on the *30 Minute Meals* set in which she would cook many meals in one go; and, back after three years away, Emeril Lagasse appeared in a small-budget six-episode run of *Fresh Food Fast* that did not exactly stretch the iconic chef—in one episode he made Kicked-up Tuna Melts (anchovy paste and Brie took it up a notch)—but it did show that the network continued to think of Emeril as a lucky charm, and that many people there missed having him around.

Despite the cold business calculus that led to the use of these proven stars, Bruce and others on the creative side also had an appetite to produce edgier programming. Developing new series to communicate that edgier voice, however, was a messy job with some strange pitches.

Shortly before the launch day for Cooking Channel, Mark Dacascos came to Food headquarters to pitch an idea called *Feasts of Fury*. With him was Ross LaManna, who had cowritten the scripts for Jackie Chan's Rush Hour films. In *Fury*, Mark, better known as the Chairman from *Iron Chef America*, would travel the world explaining how historical forces, wars especially, had shaped national cuisines.

"For example," he explained to Bruce, "if we did something in Kazakhstan, right? That's the home of Genghis Khan. You show me in their garb galloping through the plains, but later on you find out that when the horse was old, you ate it, so you ate your transportation."

"Uggggh," Bruce said. "I worry about conflict. It's such a negative word."

"We want to tweak it so it doesn't come off as battle hour," Ross offered. "We want it to always be uplifting."

"War is a bit disquieting, eh?" Bruce said, clicking his pen.

Ross kept peddling, trying to focus on the fun elements. "Every week you see a limo pull up and this incredibly good-looking woman comes out from that country and she invites him as a cultural liaison—'Come to my country.'"

The tour, Mark said, would include "fighting, eating, cooking."

Bruce asked how all the martial arts in *Feasts of Fury* would possibly appeal to women. The audience for Cooking Channel was projected to be 60 to 65 percent female, same as Food Network.

Ross parried with a joke about how the fight sequences created a context for Mark to take off his shirt and show his muscular body.

"We're a family network," Bruce cautioned.

Ross wheeled. "It's martial arts for those who want to see it as a dance expression. We could talk about the Battle of Agincourt, what Henry V's English troops ate versus the food of the French army."

Bruce had heard enough. He said he'd like to work with Mark on a new show, but with more food, less fighting.

As work continued on Cooking Channel, in January 2011 the *New York Post* reported that Food's ratings for the fourth quarter of 2010 were down 10.3 percent among viewers 25 to 54, the key demographic for advertisers. Prime-time ratings among women had also slipped badly.

An industry expert opined that in an increasingly competitive TV landscape for food programming, appetites might be changing, and Food Network might not be keeping up. "We know edgier cooking shows such as *Kitchen Nightmares* are doing well," Gary Lico, president of research group CableU, told the *Post*, referring to the Fox broadcast show with Gordon Ramsay.

A Food spokesperson argued that the network's ratings increases in 2009 had been nearly impossible to sustain. In 2009, the network had seen a 19 percent gain, led by whopping improvements in prime time. *Chopped* had been up 74 percent over 2008 and the reality series *The Next Iron Chef* attracted a total of 29 million viewers in its second season, a 60 percent ratings bump. The argument was borne out by the numbers in 2011, when the network stanched the erosion of prime-time ratings. That March was the network's highest-rated March ever, a 20 percent increase over the previous year, thanks primarily to the success of a short special series, *Chopped All-Stars*, which made Food Network the number 7–ranked ad-supported cable network in prime time. That summer, *The Next Food Network Star* on Sunday nights pulled in even stronger ratings. Brooke had overseen the development of a strategy to make Sunday nights the network's "tent pole," under which everything else could flourish. An episode of *Star* in June 2011 garnered 2.3 million viewers, and the finale on August 14 brought in 4.227 million viewers, making Food the number one network on cable that night among adults 25 to 54.

Likewise, pairing Rachael Ray and Guy on a competition show as mentors to B- and C-list celebrities learning to cook—*Rachael vs. Guy*—worked as a tent pole in January and February of 2012.

Besides promoting and expanding the tent-pole shows, another way ratings were goosed was a new trick of the cable trade, "stripping:" running back-to-back episodes from the same successful series and pushing every lagging show out of the lineup. A marathon of *Diners, Drive-ins and Dives* on Fridays was a way to feast on a hit.

But this came at the cost of the seed corn. Food was too big now to devote a half hour a day of "fringe" prime time to a cheaply produced live-to-tape proving ground like *Chef Du Jour*, where chefs used to get five full episodes to try out on the tube. Early-evening reruns of *Everyday Italian* were a better bet to sell advertising, contribute to the bottom line, and prime the pump for the sales of Food Network merchandise at Kohl's. But what was being lost was a chance to discover new, bankable stars. The network, by chucking contestants nightly on its roster of prime time competition shows, *Worst Cooks in America, Star, Next Iron Chef, Chopped, Cupcake Wars,* and *Sweet Genius,* had become expert at quickly labeling potential new talent as "losers" before giving most of them a chance to find their television voices.

No new breakout stars had been created since Guy Fieri won *The Next Food Network Star* in 2006, and Robert Irvine, who debuted in 2007. Where would the next Bobbies, Rachaels, and Paulas come from? Perhaps nepotism was an answer. Bobby's daughter, Sophie, was only thirteen when she made a poised appearance on one of his shows. After the Deen boys made the travel series *Road Tasted* together, they branched off solo. In *Not My Mama's Meals,* Bobby Deen took recipes like his mother's Deep-Fried Macaroni and Cheese and remade them in lower-calorie versions. Mama appeared remotely from Georgia and gave her honest opinion on his efforts—not always favorably! "I'll stick with mine," she said of his Guiltless Cheesy Mac, that included chopped cauliflower and reduced-fat sour cream.

Meanwhile, the weekend mornings that used to be the sweet spot for In the Kitchen were eroding. In 2008, Pat and Gina Neely's *Down Home with the Neelys* was the highest-rated debut in the block since 2003. But a few years later their show was out of production and showing only in reruns. Likewise, Anne's *Secrets of a Restaurant Chef* was kaput after 119 episodes.

The network had decided Anne was too important in prime time to be tied to a cooking show that they could easily rerun. Her sometimes tart pronouncements and unpredictability made her an ideal character for reality shows, and she started appearing more frequently on them: as a competitor on *Next Iron Chef* and *Chopped*, a mentor on *Worst Cooks in America*, and the ultimate judge on *Chef for Hire*, where the winner received a kitchen job.

In fact, Food Network had begun distancing itself from the business of producing its own television shows. At the end of December 2011, many of its production staff were let go, and over the next year, nearly all of the remaining house productions were farmed out to other companies. The network's own studio spaces, once a core part of its identity, were for hire.

A few new programs doing passably well during the In the Kitchen block were hosted by people who were celebrities already. One starred the country music star Trisha Yearwood. Another, *Pioneer Woman*, starred Ree Drummond, who had gained a huge online following on her own with a blog chronicling her back-to-basics move to an Oklahoma ranch. Maybe this was the new paradigm: the world of food no longer needed or wanted the network to make new stars or spread the basic gospel. In a country now familiar with arugula, Food Network's job was to harvest what had sprouted and display it in as fun and entertaining a way as possible.

In the fall of 2011, *The Chew* debuted on ABC. A combination talk and cooking show, it drew solid ratings out of the box, roughly equaling *Days of Our Lives*, the soap opera it had replaced. Food had not had its original talk and informal demo show, *In Food Today*, since Donna Hanover and David Rosengarten were let go in 2000 and had not ventured into anything approaching the format of *The Chew*.

Two of the show's four stars—Mario Batali, who had stopped appearing on *Iron Chef America*, and Michael Symon, a new Iron Chef, who continued to appear on Food Network—had been built by Food Network. The producer of *The Chew* was Gordon Elliott, late of *Door Knock Dinners*. Some at the network thought Food was being treated as a minor-league outfit, where fledgling cooking personalities and producers could sharpen their skills before being tapped to join the major-league broadcasters.

In December 2010, Denise Vivaldo, the recipe writer who had created the Kwanzaa cake for Sandra Lee's cookbook, wrote a column for *The Huffington Post* attacking her:

"I can honestly say Ms. Lee had nothing against African-Americans or Jews. She just has incredibly bad food taste."

Sandy's lawyer, Dennis H. Tracey, wrote to Denise accusing her of violating a nondisclosure agreement and of spreading false and defamatory statements in the column.

The Huffington Post pulled the column, but Denise never issued "a formal retraction and written apology to Lee . . ." as Tracey demanded. Eight months later, a video surfaced on YouTube and then on the food blogs *Grub Street* and *Eater* showing a series of outtakes from a commercial shoot in which Sandy appeared to be starring in an advertisement for tequila. In it, Sandy stumbled over her opening line: "Hello, I'm Semi-Homemade." She rolled her eyes and, in a tight Santa-red sweater, joked "All of me," grabbing her breasts, bobbing them up and down, and swiveling her hips. With every subsequent flub, there was a profanity, one "fuck me," one "shit," and then a request to the crew: "All these outtakes—I want them. Here's her real personality. Just splice together the curse words."

The video became an Internet sensation and seemed to confirm what many of Sandy's detractors thought—that her supersweet persona was fake. The video was pulled from YouTube "due to a copyright claim by Diageo North America," but it continued to live on eater.com.

Somehow, neither Sandra's nor any other star's personal controversy seemed to detract from their popularity with Food Network audiences. Do you cast out a member of the family because they've had a few struggles? No. You hold them tighter. Viewers' reaction to Robert Irvine's troubles was equally benign. He flourished on *Restaurant: Impossible*. His audiences grew with each new season so that by 2012, regular episodes were pulling in 1.6 million viewers. That fall, the network plastered subway tunnels and bus shelters with posters of Robert swinging a sledgehammer through restaurant walls, grinning and flexing his biceps. He was literally and figuratively huge.

Sandy won a Daytime Emmy award in 2012 as Outstanding Lifestyle/Culinary Host, an award Martha Stewart had regularly taken home. At the same ceremony, Bobby and his production company Rock Shrimp won the Outstanding Culinary Program Emmy for the latest incarnation in his cavalcade of outdoor cooking series, *Bobby Flay's Barbecue Addiction*. Sandy was rewarded with two new series, *Sandra's Restaurant Remakes* on Food Network and *Sandra Lee's Taverns, Lounges & Clubs* on Cooking Channel, a variation on *Diners, Drive-ins and Dives*, featuring Sandy traveling around to imbibe cocktails instead of cheese fries.

Still, Teflon does wear out. A never-ending series of publicity crises continued to rain on Food's existing stars, emboldening critics and potentially threatening the value of the network brands.

Ina Garten had taken a bad publicity hit in the spring of 2011, when it was reported that she had twice refused a request from a six-year-old cancer patient via the Make-A-Wish Foundation to cook with her. In 2010, she had claimed to be busy due to a book tour. The next year, after she turned down the second request outright, the boy's mother wrote about the experience on her blog. *ABC News* was among many outlets that picked up the story, and a fan website, foodnetworkhumor .com (motto: "Cook with Them. Laugh with Us") listed "Top Ten Reasons Ina Garten Rejected the 'Make-A-Wish' Foundation Boy," such as:

> 6. "Sorry, I'm too busy writing my new book, *Chicken Soup for the Nervous Laugher's Soul.*"
>
> 5. "I can't! I'm stuck in Meineke all day getting the oil changed on our fleet of BMWs."

After the bad press, Ina invited the boy to a taping of her show, but, twice rejected, he chose to swim with dolphins instead. When I requested an interview for this book a few months later, Ina's publicist agreed, then called back to ask if I intended to ask anything about the Make-A-Wish matter. I said that since I intended to ask about her whole career, it might come up. "That's old news," she told me. The interview was canceled.

When Ina's next cookbook, *Barefoot Contessa Foolproof: Recipes You Can Trust*, came out in 2012, she handpicked her interviewers. She appeared at the Food Network New York City Wine & Food Festival in front of an adoring crowd of five hundred fans. Maile Carpenter, the editor of *Food Network Magazine*, tiptoed around the issue and asked her, "I'm interested in why you've decided to sort of keep things reined in. And also I would love to hear what you haven't done."

"Oh, there are so many things I haven't done," Ina answered. "I'm very satisfied when something's done really well. And I feel like I need to have my hands in it. My book publisher will tell you, there isn't a font or a color or a recipe or an ingredient that I haven't been involved in in the books. I don't have a lot of people around me doing things. I do them all myself. So, that limits what I can do. . . . I was asked to do something with the UN. I'm like, the UN? Like, solve the problem in Syria?" She laughed. "I'll make everyone chicken pot pie and they'll be happy."

The audience of Ina lovers loved it, laughing along with her. As with

Sandy, bad publicity did not dim her. Ask random Food Network fans who their favorite star is and the most common answer will be "Ina." They recognize her authenticity. Perhaps because she says no to so much in a world that now asks much of celebrity chefs, she is able to keep living the life that her fans aspire to, roasting chickens for her husband and keeping muddy footprints off her carpets.

Some Food Network stars provided irresistible fodder. Guy Fieri imitators were cropping up. One was even interviewed by an unwitting reporter who thought he had the real Guy on live TV during a Kansas City Royals baseball game. Among Guy's growing legion of passionate fans was the Connecticut-based hedge fund titan Steve Cohen, who would become embroiled in federal investigations of his funds. The 38th-richest American on the Forbes list in 2012, worth $8.8 billion, Cohen was a fan of "Triple D" and asked Guy's business associates how much it would cost to hang out with him, driving around and visiting diners. Cohen paid Guy $100,000 to be his friend for a day. The two became close, and Guy even asked Diners' producers to feature Cohen's favorite hot dog spot in Fairfield, Connecticut, Super Duper Weenie.

After a few seasons, the relationship between Guy and the show's creator, David Page, began to sour. Guy regularly traveled with a posse of friends and hefty bodyguard types he'd known for years. During one *Diners* shoot, producers received a call from a hotel after one of Guy's entourage had gotten drunk and jumped up and down in the elevator until it broke, trapping him between floors. When the hotel staff finally freed him, he began yelling at them. It took a lot of talking before the producers convinced the hotel not to evict the whole team.

The pressures were not easy for Guy to deal with, either. A few days before the South Beach Wine & Food Festival in 2010, Guy's sister Morgan died after a long battle with cancer. Guy's Rock and Roll Beach Barbecue was scheduled along with a cooking demonstration, but Marc Summers and other friends had told him he did not need to appear at the festival that year. They counseled him to cancel; Lee would understand.

Guy vowed to make the trip despite his despair—"I made a promise." He and his business manager and entourage, which now included Steve Hutchinson, an All-Pro lineman with the Minnesota Vikings football team, arrived in time for Rachael's Burger Bash, held under a massive white tent on the beach.

Standing at the back entrance to the tent, Guy was still in mourning. "If my sister knew that I didn't come and do an event, that I didn't give back to the fans and the people that supported my career—my sister knew how I got here. She was on that road with me. Don't get me wrong, I'm . . .

"It's really a balance about, how do you focus and see and believe and, but I'm really contained, really controlled with what I'm here for— my mom, my dad, and my sister and my nephew, and my kids, my wife, and—I'm not necessarily in the same zone I'm always at when I come to South Beach.

"This is the hardest time of my life," Guy said, starting to choke up. "Oh, this is, there's nothing been like this in my life."

He excused himself wordlessly. He walked to a very dark area behind the tent near a chain-link fence and, standing with his back to the crowd, lifted his free hand to his forehead, and began to shake.

After more than a hundred episodes in which Guy visited nearly four hundred diners, drive-ins, and dives, Food Network told David Page he was off the show he had created. In May 2011, he sued the network for breach of contract. They countersued, arguing that they owned the rights to "Triple D" and the contract allowed them to replace producers. In court papers, Food Network alleged that it was David who had rendered the shoots "intolerable" because he mistreated staff and others working on the series. The network included snippets of e-mails it said David had sent to staff: "You are one fucked up dumbass loser," and "Lets assume im a genius from now on" [sic].

The lawsuit was settled confidentially out of court, and a new producer was found. But the conflicts were not so quietly settled in the media. David wrote to a Guy Fieri fan website:

Perhaps as Guy matures in his career he will come to realize that even Hemingway had an editor. And that actually listening to notes is something that can make a big difference in one's longevity. Along the way he may also learn it isn't good to get a reputation for plundering a production company's budget or for wanting to be surrounded only by sycophants, and he might even adopt more tolerant social views regarding minorities.

Next, a Minneapolis *City Pages* article included Page's claim that Guy had complained to him about being introduced to two gay men running a restaurant being profiled on the show, saying, "You can't send me to talk to gay people without warning!" and "Those people weird me out!" and "You know, it's true: Jews are cheap."

Guy's public relations team pointed out that all the claims came from a disgruntled producer. But with Guy's agent's encouragement, a crisis communications consultant with Sunshine Sachs & Associates, Jesse Derris, was hired to protect the star's image. Among Derris's past clients was John Thain, the former head of Merrill Lynch who had spent $1.22 million of shareholder money redecorating his office, including buying a $35,000 antique commode. Derris and his team explained to Guy's camp that all it would take would be a statement against Guy from Abe Foxman, the director of the Anti-Defamation League, and a gay rights leader, and Jews and gays would call Food Network, demanding that ads be pulled and calling for a boycott of Guy's shows. The damage could be permanent.

The crisis management team called reporters and pointed out weaknesses in the story. Food media blogs quoted a "source with knowledge of the situation" who noted that the *City Pages* article was riddled with "omissions," "basic errors," and "complete fabrications. As to the homophobe allegations," the source said, "Guy's own sister, who recently passed away, was gay."

Within a week, the stories died down. No boycotts or protests materialized.

But a year later, the services of Sunshine Sachs & Associates were needed again. Guy had signed a partnership with a New York restaurant company to open a Times Square restaurant, Guy's American Kitchen and Bar, that would be festooned with his image and serve Guy's signature dishes. The critics were eager to review the place and not of a mind to like it.

Emeril, who understood that exacting New York critics might savage a TV star who opened a restaurant but was not on the premises as the executive chef, had never opened a New York restaurant. Emeril knew that he did not have a trusted team in the city—the only thing that could protect the restaurant's quality and his reputation. Both Bobby and Mario had earned reputations as serious New York restaurateurs before they got on TV and had top-notch restaurant teams who helped oversee their local empires. Bobby's right-hand man is Laurence Kretchmer, the lanky son of the original Mesa Grill investor. Mario has Joe Bastianich, an author and food TV personality in his own right. Generally, Bobby's and Mario's restaurants have gotten excellent reviews year in and year out. Outside New York City, Bobby's more informal restaurants, his Burger Palaces, had been opened mostly in East Coast shopping malls and casinos, out of the range of New York critics—but still within range of his management team.

Guy should have known what was coming, but, often surrounded by people who told him what he wanted to hear, he did not. Early reviews were savage: "Of course, the Guy-Talian nachos are cold," Gael Greene, the former *New York* magazine critic, wrote in her blog just a few days after it opened. Steve Cuozzo of the *New York Post* wrote of his struggle "to extract edible elements from heaps of sugar and sludge masquerading as normal food."

When an angry Guy came to New York for the annual food festival in October 2012, he took what revenge he could, insisting that the festival's public relations director keep him away from reporters. But Guy hadn't heard the worst of it. On November 13, *New York Times* critic Pete Wells wrote what some have called the worst restaurant review in the paper's history. The entire review was a series of scathing questions to Guy, among them: "Were you struck by how very far from awesome the Awesome Pretzel Chicken Tenders are?" and "Any idea why [that blue drink] tastes like some combination of radiator fluid and formaldehyde?"

Sunshine Sachs considered suggesting to Guy that he apologize for the quality of the food and vow to shut down the restaurant until he got it right. But the decision was made to blame the messenger while simultaneously asking for more time. Flying in from California on the redeye, Guy appeared on *Today* and told the show's cohost, Savannah Guthrie, that Pete Wells wanted to make a name for himself by going "after a chef that's not a New Yorker." Then after admitting that some of the criticisms might have been accurate, Guy said the restaurant was a new concept and it was unfair to review it so soon. "Let's see where we are in six months," Guy said.

His fans crowded Guy's American Kitchen and Bar through the holiday season despite the kerfuffle, maybe even wanting to defend their man of the people against the elite critics because of it.

In the meantime, Sunshine Sachs had another Food star to rescue—or, rather, to rescue the network from. In May 2011, *National Enquirer* reported that Paula Deen, famous for using unholy amounts of butter and sugar in her recipes, had been suffering from diabetes for years. The mainstream media did not pick up the story, but Novo Nordisk, the maker of a diabetes drug, reached out to Barry Weiner. Would Paula be interested in endorsing a diabetes treatment?

He was not sure the Novo deal was a good idea, but told Paula that the company was making a good case for itself. Novo pointed out that when Magic Johnson had announced that he had AIDS, he'd removed some of the stigma from the disease. More people got tested. It could be that way for Paula. Much of her audience was in the Southeast, where diabetes was prevalent. If she could convince her viewers to go to the doctor and seek treatment, she could do a lot of good. If that treatment happened to be Novo's drug, Victoza (which cost around $300 per month), it would do the company a lot of good.

Novo offered Paula around $6 million, and in exchange, she would announce that she was suffering from diabetes, had started taking Victoza, and was changing her diet. People could find some of her new recipes on a Novo website.

Barry and Paula did not consult with Food Network about any of this. Novo wanted Paula to make her announcement with as big a splash as possible, and suggested that a slot on the top-rated *Today Show* would be best. In January 2012, Paula appeared with Al Roker and told him that she had started treatment after being diagnosed three years earlier. She referred viewers to a website she had set up with Novo Nordisk which would contain healthy recipes.

Al, a journalist, not a shill, pointed out that Deen was a paid spokesperson for Novo Nordisk.

"I have been compensated, just as you are for your work," said Deen defensively.

Al, undeterred, asked if there was something awry with her touting a diabetes drug after pushing fattening food on TV for years. Paula responded that she only tapes shows part of the year. "That's only thirty days out of three hundred and sixty-five, and it's for entertainment."

Her answers struck many as disingenuous, and the reaction was brutal. After all, she had gotten rich touting recipes like her sandwich consisting of a hamburger with a fried egg on top served between slices of a glazed doughnut. Now she was pushing Gingered Butternut Squash and Green Apple Mash? Among many critics, Tony Bourdain was the loudest, tweeting to his hundreds of thousands of followers, "Thinking of getting into the leg-breaking business, so I can profitably sell crutches later."

Food Network's media relations chief, Irika Slavin, a former Warner Brothers publicist in Hollywood, asked Jesse Derris to devise a strategy to distance the network from Paula. She was still an important star, but she had not consulted with the network before making the diabetes deal, so why should it be shackled to the resulting bad publicity? Food did not want the whole ship to be dragged down. Following Derris's advice, Irika called reporters and pointed out that Food Network had not been complicit in hiding Paula's diabetes. If the network had known of the diagnosis before the *Today* announcement, it might have suggested that the current season of Paula's cooking shows take a new, healthier approach, or at least acknowledge that one ought not to eat these treats every day. Perhaps they could have synchronized her show with her son Bobby's *Not My Mama's Meals.*

Instead, Irika said, the network had a season of unmitigated Paula in the can and felt blindsided.

Groundwork laid, Irika engaged in positive spin, announcing that the network had healthy programming debuting: *Fat Chef,* a weight-loss challenge show. Then, deflecting attention away from Food Network, she mentioned that Sam Talbot, a *Top Chef* contestant (and Sunshine Sachs client) who was diabetic, had a new cookbook out, and he could speak seriously about the disease.

The strategy seemed to blunt the blow. *People* magazine nicely roped Food's competitor into the problem: "Top Chef Sam Talbot: My Advice to Paula Deen" ran the headline of an article on Talbot in which he suggested she replace sugar with coconut and flaxseed.

At the SOBE festival a month later, Paula led a cooking demonstration with her husband and answered questions from a crowd of more than a thousand fans. She told them she had given up sweet tea and was walking thirty minutes a day.

"Miss Paula?" one fan asked. "Miss Paula, right here. Listen, we love you. So don't worry about the haters. Because there's so many of us that love you, it's like the haters don't even exist." The audience cheered wildly.

Barry Weiner, watching in the wings, noted how much affection was pouring her way.

"Paula's brand," he told me, "is not butter. Paula's brand, if anything, is hope."

Fortunately, by the time Tony Bourdain came onstage, she and her team had departed, driven by Lee Schrager's staff in golf carts toward the Loews Hotel, where she had a room with a smoking balcony.

In the audience of equal size to Paula's were many of the smartest writers, chefs, and publicists in food media, eager to hear what the outspoken and dangerous man might say this time.

"First question!" Tony opened, pointing to a friend he had planted in the audience, the chef Eddie Huang.

"Aren't you a hypocrite," Eddie asked, "smoking on your show and making fun of this nice old lady with diabetes?"

"I'm *glad* you asked," said Tony mockingly. "You're right. I did smoke cigarettes for a lot of years on my show. But I wasn't selling you motherfucking cigarettes!"

The crowd roared.

"I didn't sell 'Smoking Tony' dolls to your kids! You couldn't go to five or six casinos around the world to the Tony Bourdain smoking fucking section! And when I found a spot on my motherfucking lung, I didn't wait three years so I could get a deal selling you the patch!"

Tony had been attacking her for years, and Paula had long ago decided to laugh him off. In some ways, he and Paula were a lot more alike than they were different: food stars who can be gifted at expressing themselves, work hard, and were unafraid to be who they are. Paula, a gambler like so many TV cooking stars, once lost nearly $50,000 during a weekend binge in Las Vegas. "I don't think he has the ability to make or break my career," Paula had told me before the festival, "especially when he's going around eating unwashed anuses of wildebeests."

In the months following the diabetes announcement, the controversy gave Paula a whole new market to work. She was a celebrity guest playing for charity on *Who Wants to Be a Millionaire?*, endorsed a new line of Paula Deen mattresses, and sailed with four hundred fans on her annual "Party at Sea" on a cruise ship. She had a popular Paula Deen line of couches, tables, and love seats. She had turned it around like only the greatest steel magnolia can. Within a year, she and her two boys were on the cover of *People* magazine: "Paula Deen's Family Slim-down, Exclusive Diet Tips and Recipes. How the star chef dropped more weight and got her sons and husband fit. 'If the Deens can do it, anyone can!'"

Like her idol Martha Stewart, it seemed nothing could keep her down. Paula was money. "Now she's endorsing sugar-free chocolate," Barry Weiner boasted. "I doubled her brand."

The network introduced a new logo in January 2013, the first significant update since the logo Jeff Wayne's wife had approved in 1997, but as it approached its twentieth anniversary the viewer comments on the network's blog reflected a change, a sense that the network was a big corporation lagging far behind the vanguard of foodie culture. The new logo beefed up the font and added a thin metallic edge and a slight gradation of color, but the public's reaction to it indicated that the channel had lost some street cred.

"Work on your programming instead of logos! I'm so sick of *Chopped*, all the food wars, and *Iron Chef* everything!"

—A COMMENTER USING THE SCREEN NAME OKIE

"The new logo has no flavor. It looks hard, cold, and generic."

—GARNISH

"What a hunk of shit. Change that was clearly directed by someone in marketing."

—PENN

The network wasn't unaware of this changing attitude and Ken told investors the hope was that Cooking Channel would take a "deeper dive" into the food-obsessed cultural wave. But when Cooking went live on May 31, 2010, a critic for the *St. Petersburg Times* wrote, "*Foodography*, an hourlong bio-style report on a single topic hosted by TV personality Mo Rocca, repeated the same ice-cream episode so many times the first week I felt like I was trapped in the movie *Groundhog Day*."

No matter. Cooking's ratings were beyond all projections, doubling Fine Living's audience during parts of the day and up 70 percent total and 34 percent in prime time. Without having to staff an entire network from scratch, Brooke had delivered an impressive new source of income to Scripps.

A new generation discovered *Two Fat Ladies*. Bruce Seidel flew to England to meet with the surviving Fat Lady, Clarissa Dickson Wright, about creating a new version of the show by pairing her with another riding and cooking partner. Perhaps a gay man? But a deal did not come together.

Michael Smith had argued from the start that if there was room on cable for a variety of news channels—MSNBC, CNBC, CNN, Headline News, and Fox News—there would be room for more than one food channel. He was less interested in developing an audience slowly by finding a unique voice than in putting things on the air that attracted the biggest audience possible as fast as possible. This led to a disjointed schedule. In the late evening, Cooking Channel delivered the fresh and campy *Bitchin' Kitchen*, starring the Elvira of cooking, Nadia Giosia, a Canadian Slav with a macabre energy and a quick wit. But the daytime hours could see fare as regressive as *Drop 5 Pounds with Good Housekeeping*.

In the executive programming ranks at Food, only the most risk-averse seemed to thrive. Bob Tuschman, the head of programming, is a politically savvy fellow with some strong personal connections with the talent. As Susie was to Emeril, he is to Ina Garten; the executive she is closest to and can confide in. Eileen Opatut had tried to make it as an independent producer and landed a show on Cooking Channel, *Hungry Girl*, starring diet guru Lisa Lillien. When the series was canceled, Eileen became so disillusioned that she moved into the real estate business. Matt Stillman is an independent producer still dreaming up show ideas—one is a comedy based on TED Talks—but he has not set foot in the Food Network in a decade. Younger programming talent under Bob must run a gauntlet that over the years adopted the conservative ways of Knoxville and left behind the swashbuckling spirit of Reese.

Even what counts as a risk-taker at Food might be a reactionary at another network. Would *Feasts of Fury* really be such a bad idea? Imagine an over-the-top campy show where a kung fu fighter is shown being led around the world by a series of beautiful, ethnically diverse women who feed him, laugh at his jokes, and breathlessly watch him kickbox and fence, relaxing with a few too many Singhas on the banks of the Mekong when the fighting is done. Maybe too weird, but there was a time not so long ago when someone at Food might have authorized a pilot to find out. Nancy Dubuc, the president of entertainment and media at A&E Network, who took History Channel from the number 11 cable network to number 4 in six years, made the cover of *The Hollywood Reporter* at the end of 2012 for being a risk-taker who had brought a series of unlikely hits to air: *Pawn Stars, American Pickers, Hatfields & McCoys*, and *Duck Dynasty*, a reality series about a family who went from rags to riches by selling duck calls. Food had no Nancy Dubuc and did not seem capable of handling one. In 2013, Dubuc was named chairwoman of A&E Networks.

In January 2012, Bruce Seidel resigned. He was fed up with being told he needed to spend more time thinking about Food Network and less about Cooking Channel. He moved to Los Angeles and launched a YouTube cooking channel called Hungry, owned by Electus, an entertainment company formed by Ben Silverman, the former cochairman of NBC Entertainment. Some of Bruce's first shows showed the type of thing he'd hoped to land on Cooking Channel: *Brothers Green*, featuring a pair of Brooklynite musicians and underground caterers, and *Casserole Queens*, about two Austin woman obsessed with retro food.

In Bruce's wake, some of the programming on Cooking appeared to be more like Food Network 2 and was less that of an edgy alternative channel that, given time, might develop its own voice and attract a new audience. The schedule in mid-2012, two years after the launch, included regular helpings of Giada, Ina, and Tyler. There were old episodes of *Unwrapped* and *Good Eats*.

Meanwhile, the new shows appearing on Food's schedule seemed joined by themes of paranoia, ego, and conflict. *Restaurant Stakeout* was a reality series about spying on employees, as was *Mystery Diners*. Both thrived on finding dirt, lust, stupidity, and thievery. Rachael had stopped making new episodes of *30 Minute Meals*, focusing instead on her daytime syndicated talk show and, for Food, the prime-time reality conflict drama *Rachael vs. Guy*, in which they oversaw washed-up celebrities grasping for shards of broken fame. The most comforting show left in prime time was *Chopped*, which, despite its charms, did feature a tribunal of hypercritical judges. (There was talk of an anniversary episode featuring a ravenous Chihuahua, but to date, no dog.)

At a recent SOBE festival party thrown by William Morris Endeavor for its food clients, Guy, Bobby, Rachael, Brooke, Susie, Giada, Jon Rosen, and dozens of other industry players sipped champagne and grazed at a table spread with pink charcuterie.

At the end of the bar, Irika Slavin was threatening Bobby. His new series, *America's Next Great Restaurant*, produced by Magical Elves, the company that made *Top Chef*, was debuting on NBC in a few weeks. Food had tried to get the show, but Magical Elves went with NBC, the parent of Bravo, with whom they'd had so much success. Worse, from Food's perspective, Bobby's show was scheduled to run on Sunday nights opposite *Chopped All-Stars*, one of Food's tent poles. The talk around the network was that he was risking his standing as a big cable star by taking a gamble on broadcast network television. If his show failed, or if the ratings for *Throwdown* faltered because of viewer fatigue, he would rue the day he got too big for his britches.

"We're watching the stats," Irika muttered harshly to Bobby, implying that if his show did not do well in the ratings, it would illustrate that he wasn't as big a star as he thought. Irika knew enough to hire an outside crisis team to deal with straying talent, but not enough to give some respect to a star who had been reliable for nearly two decades. Bobby kept a cool silence. He was a survivor. He already had a plan to deal with any contingency. He was well aware that *Throwdown* was getting tired after seven seasons. He was working on a new show idea for Food. Or wherever. Bobby knew that Irika might stick around for years or she might be gone by the next festival. But the network needed proven stars like him more than ever, and it wasn't exactly minting Bobby Flays these days, was it?

In some ways, the network had perfected its programming recipe around 2003. Its greatest generation of In the Kitchen stars were in their first blush of success, including Ina, Rachael, Sandy, Giada, and Paula; *Emeril Live* was chugging in prime time; Tony Bourdain was delivering offbeat spice on *A Cook's Tour*; Bobby Flay was working with fire on *Boy Meets Grill*; the original *Iron Chef* was giving a mind-bending twist to weekend nights; Alton was hitting his stride on *Good Eats*; Tyler was traveling to southern Europe for the first year of the most fun show he ever made, *Tyler's Ultimate*; Marc Summers was churning out new episodes of *Unwrapped*, and Mario, Sara, and Jamie were still sizzling. No crisis management PR was needed. Most press was favorable and you could turn on the network almost any time of day for good-natured, interesting entertainment and images of tasty food.

The debut of *Top Chef*, the network's biggest challenger, was still years away. But, it did arrive, and in recent seasons, one of the most popular judges to join the cast has been a knowledgeable, award-winning, low-key chef named Emeril Lagasse.

In 1992, Tryg Myhren had told Joe that a food channel could expand someday into a magazine, cookbooks, and other properties, all generating profits. Scripps food websites, now including foodnetwork.com, cookingchanneltv.com, and food.com, attracted 435 million page views in November 2012 and more than 11.2 million video plays. Meanwhile, a paid smartphone app, In the Kitchen, was at the top of the culinary category on iTunes. Amazon announced a deal in February 2013 to deliver Food Network and other Scripps shows such as *Cupcake Wars*, *Diners, Drive-ins and Dives*, and *Chopped* on demand via the Web—no cable TV subscription required. The brand was thriving in print, too.

Food Network Magazine was miraculously still growing, the number one food magazine and the seventh best-selling magazine overall on the newsstand.

Reese Schonfeld had written to ProJo in 1992, "I am absolutely convinced that the Food Channel is a business that will be worth between $250,000,000 and $500,000,000 on the day that it is carried in 40,000,000 cable homes." Twenty years later it was in nearly 100 million American homes and worth roughly $3 billion. Cooking Channel had reached 59 million homes. Scripps Networks Interactive had a market capitalization of $8.7 billion—and investment brokers were speculating in the press that Disney might be considering buying SNI for $10 billion. Derek Baine, a respected industry consultant at SNL Kagan, said that the Fox Group, Rupert Murdoch's new entertainment company, disencumbered of its newspapers, could be a contender to buy SNI, as could Discovery. Those companies had the leverage of their successful channels to extract higher affiliate fees for Food Network and Scripps's other channels. Or with Tribune emerging finally from a long bankruptcy process, the Chicago company might be willing to sell its 30 percent of Food Network and Cooking Channel to Scripps. Scripps could then sell the whole shebang or come up with new avenues to capitalize. Anything could happen. Food Network was a big prize.

To some extent its success will remain tied to how interested the culture at large remains in food. Food Network has ridden the astounding food wave and even shaped it, both the network and the wave propelled by the simultaneous expansion of the public's interest in food, and cable and satellite television and the Internet. But waves that big are not controllable.

The head start Food Network had gained by having Joe Langhan get a recipe-rich website up in the mid-1990s before food media rivals did was no longer enough to ensure a market edge in the evolving digital world. Many media companies faced the issue of how to continue to make money amidst DVRs and cable-bill-weary consumers turning to streaming media. Scripps was aggressively trying to keep pace, signing the Amazon agreements and spreading its programming globally and, in April 2013, buying the Asian Food Channel. Turn on your TV in Ulan Bator, Sofia, Belgrade, or Nicosia and you might see Rachael Ray. For American viewers staying tethered to cable and satellite providers, the network invested so heavily in improving production values that it had an effect on corporate profits. SNI net income was down 3.7 percent in the first quarter of 2013 compared to a year earlier, even though revenues had increased 11 percent to $594 million—$208 million of which came from Food Network, now bringing in more cash than HGTV, and $26.3 million from Cooking Channel, a 33 percent improvement for the upstart.

At twenty years old and mature, whether Food Network's future will be as bright as its previous decade is more in its own hands now than before. It can no longer rely on riding the explosively growing waves it caught in its youth. Cable television and foodie culture are mature, too.

As the network announced its roster of new shows for the 2013–14 season, an overwhelming number of them were about how to open a restaurant and become a food professional. After two decades, this seemed to be the logical next step in the foodie fantasy. After watching so many cooking shows, vicariously traveling to so many locales in search of the tastiest morsels, what's left? Open a restaurant—or vent against those who have but who seem to know less than you about the industry. What's more, with the ratings success of *Restaurant: Impossible*, the network, concerned about soft prime-time ratings on other nights at the start of 2013, wanted to crowd out any competition. Copycatting was the rage in cable. The History Channel had *Pawn Stars* and its sister, A&E, had doubled down with the similar treasure hunt *Storage Wars*. TruTV volleyed with *Hardcore Pawn*, HGTV with *Flea Market Flip*, and even PBS had rushed in with its own junky treasure hunt, *Market Warriors*. Thus, the thinking went, if Food Network blew out the category of restaurant makeovers, there would be no room for a *Top Chef* or *Cake Boss* of copycat restaurant shows by rivals. And so, for Food's twentieth year, *Giving You the Business* awarded employees of food chains their own franchises, *Food Court Wars* had Tyler doling out mall outlets, *The Shed* (working title) portrayed a family that owns a chain of barbecue joints, *On the Rocks* featured the advice of a bar owner, *Bossover* (working title) schooled bad restaurant bosses, *Restaurant Divided* transformed family-owned spots, *Restaurant Express* had Robert Irvine taking aspiring owners on a bus trip and awarding one his own eatery, and *Undercover Critics* gave existing owners a chance to improve before reviews were published. Cooking Channel unveiled *The Freshman Class*, going back to Food Network's roots at Johnson & Wales by following four aspiring chefs through the Louisiana Culinary Institute, as well as *Restaurant Takeover* and *Ching's Menu Makeover*.

Also introduced at the April 2013 upfronts was a new show by Bobby Flay—he'd survived again, even though his attempt to sell a daytime talk show featuring himself and Giada to the broadcast networks failed—and, for Cooking Channel, it was *Pizza Cuz*, a cross-country exploration of all things pizza, a show Joe Langhan would have loved.

Figuring out one good idea and preparing it a dozen ways while trying to fluff up your proven commodities is not exactly a formula for the kind of groundbreaking television Food Network once delivered—and network executives knew it. To that end, a younger generation had been hired into the programming department under Bob, giving him the opportunity to hear new ideas but also signaling that his time to meet the crocodiles might be nearing—everyone in TV meets them eventually. The new hires who might one day succeed him included Lauren Wohl from Ryan Seacrest Productions and Andrew Schecter, formerly of Animal Planet, along with two new vice presidents of programming in March 2013, Todd Weiser, who had developed offbeat shows for Animal Planet, such as *Finding Bigfoot* and *Gator Boys*, and Mark Levine, who had been overseeing CookingChannelTV.com. The network had plans to double the number of shows in development—a move Eileen Opatut had begged for years earlier—and sent another programmer out to Los Angeles to engage with West Coast production companies who might pitch fresh ideas.

If the network was having trouble minting new stars, perhaps clever new formats would have to do for a while. Late one night after a charity party hosted by Sandra Lee in New York, the recently crowned winner of 2012's version of *Food Network Star*, Justin Warner, a whiz kid chef from Brooklyn, was walking in a not entirely straight line from the SoHo party space toward a downtown bar called Mother's Ruin.

Justin held up his hand to traffic while stepping into Centre Street, wanting to cross against the light. "Food Network star coming through!" he said.

The traffic didn't stop.

It took nearly a year for Food Network to produce a show starring Justin, *Rebel Eats*, a one-off budget road trip program. No future episodes were announced.

The changes the network was being forced to face came into extremely uncomfortable focus in June 2013, when a deposition transcript from a lawsuit involving Paula Deen became public. Lisa Jackson, a former restaurant employee of Deen and her brother, Earl "Bubba" Hiers, filed a racial- and sexual-harassment suit in the U.S. District Court for the Southern District of Georgia in March 2012, claiming she was subjected to "violent, sexist, and racist behavior."

Among the allegations in the original complaint was that Deen had once used the N-word when discussing the arrangements for a wedding. In a videotaped deposition in May 2013, Paula denied it. "I remember telling them about a restaurant that my husband and I had recently visited. . . . The whole entire waitstaff was middle-aged black men, and they had on beautiful white jackets with a black bow tie. I mean, it was really impressive. And I remember saying I would love to have servers like that, I said, but I would be afraid that somebody would misinterpret."

"Is there any possibility . . . you slipped and used the word . . . ?" she was asked.

"No," she answered, "because that's not what these men were. They were professional black men doing a fabulous job."

Later, the opposing lawyer asked, "Have you ever used the N-word yourself?"

"Yes, of course," she replied, explaining, "It was probably when a black man burst into the bank that I was working at and put a gun to my head."

Not good. *The National Enquirer* ran the first story about the deposition, headlined "Paula Deen's Racist Confessions Caught on Video!" With the transcript online for any reporter or fan to peruse, a media storm ensued on Wednesday, June 19. "Paula Deen on Her Dream 'Southern Plantation Wedding'" *Talking Points Memo* announced. Opinion pieces attacking her followed.

There was controlled panic among Paula's team. The timing was particularly awful for them because Paula's contract with Food Network was expiring that very month. The previous time her contract had neared its end—in 2010, two years before the diabetes announcement—Barry and his partner, Jonathan Russo, had played hardball, putting Paula on the open market and making Food Network bid for her against other suitors. Part of what they won was an agreement for the network to give her sons, Jamie and Bobby, each a season of their own shows.

The situation was different this time around, even before the revelations. After the diabetes announcement, Food Network executives were so upset at having been blindsided by it that *Paula's Best Dishes* was put on hiatus and no new episodes were shot for about a year. Meanwhile, Nielsen ratings were down 15 percent in total viewers and 22 percent in the key 18 to 49 demographic for the 2012–13 season, compared with the previous one.

Jonathan had been negotiating with Pat Guy at Food Network for months over a new contract for Paula to make more daytime cooking shows. Paula's team was so sure an agreement would be reached that Follow Productions, the producer of her shows, had already begun preparations to shoot new episodes.

But as with Emeril, she had become an increasingly expensive star who was no longer pulling audiences the way she used to, and it was taking a while to come to an agreement. She was not alone in losing viewers. The only shows seeming to hold their own in the ITK block were *Pioneer Woman* and *Trisha's Southern Kitchen*: new faces. And in prime time, the news was also dispiriting, with a 15 percent decline in total households for the 2012–13 season.

From Food Network's perspective, much of Paula's decline was her own fault—at least some fans had not forgiven her for the diabetes deal. Her shows were no longer comfort food. Even before the latest debacle, the two sides were talking about the need to "freshen" Paula's show, with proposals not unlike those that had been tried with *Emeril Live* years earlier: invite interesting guests to cook with her, move the show out of her kitchen and into interesting locales.

Now it was all in doubt. A decision was made by Deen's team, which included the California-based public relations duo of Jeffrey and Elana Rose, to offer Paula as a guest that Friday, June 21, on the *Today Show*, the broadcast outlet where she had made the diabetes revelation and other, more happy, and successful appearances. Their hope was that on the *Today Show* Paula could explain that she was not a racist, that she was simply honestly answering questions that had been put before her in a lawsuit brought by a disgruntled employee who saw the lawsuit as a way to take some of what Paula had earned. The racial slurs were not who she was.

But Barry Weiner, who was down in Savannah with Paula, was becoming concerned as he watched her grow more agitated. It was as if she had been told one of her children had been in a bad car accident. She could not believe that she was been pilloried like this.

To be on the *Today Show* requires getting out of bed at around 4:30 a.m. and being at the studio, all made up and composed, by 7 a.m. When Barry saw how sleepless and disheveled Paula, a sixty-six-year-old woman, was as the time approached to leave for Rockefeller Center, he advised her not to show up for the interview. He knew it would not be a softball interview and she might completely fall apart. You can't put someone in a position to be skewered like that. It might haunt her for the rest of her life, he thought, and she, having followed Barry's advice successfully for more than a decade, agreed.

As the *Today* broadcast started, Matt told viewers, "We just found out she's a no-show."

Rather than quelling the fires, this fed them. Paula's situation was now a mess playing out across all the points of mass media—TV, cable news, celebrity and food gossip websites, and social media. Exactly what Paula's team needed to do became clear when a call came to them from Cynthia Gibson, the chief legal officer for Scripps in Knoxville, a respected executive in the parent company. "What we need," she instructed, "is an unconditional statement of remorse and apology." There was no promise that if Paula made such a statement, all would be forgiven by her employer, but it offered hope.

Inside Food Network and Scripps, a frenzy had been growing. E-mails and phone calls were ripping back and forth. What should they do? Food Network had little stake in Paula's side businesses. Barry had resisted network efforts to get in on her action. Food did not get a cut of her clothing line or her new deal endorsing flavored "finishing butters." Not that they would have wanted it. What good was it that she was occasionally giving a nod to her new slimmer lifestyle by cutting down the fat in her recipes if she was endorsing a brand that showed you how to add it back? Didn't she get it? Brands need consistency. What did she stand for? For that matter, the message was undermining her own son's show. Bobby Deen's *Not My Mama's Meals* was predicated on avoiding heart attack ingredients.

Besides being a publicly traded company that complied with all equal-opportunity and anti-harassment laws, SNI maintained its stated core values, among them "compassion and support" and "diversity." A debate raged within the company about what to do and when to do it. Some wanted her gone immediately. Her contract was up. She had two major strikes against her. Why wait for the third strike? Others counseled patience. Even if they were going to let her go, why do it in the heat of the moment? Better to investigate for a few weeks, see how it played out, and do whatever they were going to do calmly, in their own time.

Consulting on this trouble again was Jesse Derris, who had left Sunshine Sachs and started his own crisis management PR firm. To Jesse, this was a moral question. And if that was the case, if Food Network had decided Paula was conclusively on the wrong side of the moral line here, she would have to be gotten rid of sooner or later. The time to do it was now, when she had taken all the hits and given no significant response. Do it and move on.

Even as this decision was nearing inevitability inside the network, Paula's team was scrambling to do what Cynthia had suggested, grasping at the idea that a complete apology would redeem her in the eyes of Scripps. The team set about preparing to record their own video apology, something they could control. After noon, a photo was tweeted of Paula preparing to record the video. When it was released soon after, it struck many as strange. Although the video was less than a minute long, there were three spliced-together segments that seemed repetitive and generic: "Please forgive me for the mistakes that I've made" was the final line. It almost seemed like a rehearsal—and it was. That video had been accidentally posted on a YouTube account, and then quickly pulled down. Nothing was going right.

Two more videos were then posted intentionally. They showed Paula apologizing more thoroughly and without edits. One was to her public: "The pain has been tremendous that I have caused to myself and to others, and so I am taking this opportunity, now that I've pulled myself together and am able to speak, to offer an apology to those that I have hurt. I want people to understand that my family and I are not the kind of people that the press is wanting to say we are. I've spent the best of twenty-four years to help myself and others. Your color of your skin, your religion, your sexual preference does not matter to me, but it's what in the heart."

And the other was to Matt for not showing up. "I'm a strong woman, but this morning, I was not."

Both were done very amateurishly. Paula was sitting on an office chair with what appeared to be a makeup tray, a can of Coke, and a partially unfurled roll of paper towel strewn haphazardly on tables behind her.

SNI was a multibillion-dollar publicly traded company. This would just not do. The company made its decision, and it was approved at the highest levels. Brooke called Barry and told him Food Network would not be signing another agreement with Paula.

Moments later, the network released a short statement and said it would not elaborate. "Food Network will not renew Paula Deen's contract when it expires at the end of this month."

Now the media fires exploded into an inferno. Paula retreated to her home in Savannah over the weekend with her sons and husband. Her career seemed to have fallen apart in a few days, all because of what she and her family saw as an extortionate lawsuit against her. On Monday, June 24, Smithfield Foods announced it was ending her endorsement deal. Other commercial partners issued statements saying they were considering what to do. Jeff and Elana Rose stopped returning reporters' calls.

Even as Paula was abandoned, a groundswell of her defenders was starting to grow. Carla Hall, one of the cohosts of *The Chew*, tweeted, "I love you and I support you @Paula_Deen!" Far more concerning for Food Network was a new Facebook page, "We Support Paula Deen," which by midweek was nearing half a million followers.

Tony Bourdain was keeping his powder dry. While shooting his CNN show in Italy, he tweeted, "I am 'continuing to monitor the situation.'" When *New York Times* columnist Frank Bruni wrote a piece attacking Paula's "obtuseness," Tony, still sore about Frank's 2011 column criticizing the "elitism" of Tony's attacks on Paula, simply tweeted about the newspaperman's "deft 180."

Inside Food Network, there was fretting. Had they acted too quickly? As legions of fans posted comments on QVC's website, demanding she be kept, Food Network worried it would lose swaths of female viewers, lowering ad rates. The network pulled back on its own social media—it was not the time to cheerfully tweet links to brownie recipes. Bobby Flay, making a regularly scheduled appearance on *Good Morning America*, sidestepped the issue expertly, saying, "You know, it's a real unfortunate situation, but I'm not going to comment on it. I'm here to talk about some ribeye . . ."

Lee Schrager, about to open up ticket sales for the fall Food Network

New York City Wine & Food Festival, faced the problem of whether or not to keep Paula's Gospel Brunch in the lineup. When tickets went on sale Monday, it had stayed.

Tiny victories, but Paula's future as a public figure was still at stake. Would any broadcaster or corporation ever want her again? Paula's camp, realizing it had not handled this well, finally brought in their own crisis management consultant, one of the heaviest hitters in the business, Judy Smith. She had helped Monica Lewinsky, Michael Vick, and Kobe Bryant. It was decided to try again with the *Today Show*, scheduling an interview for that following Wednesday, June 26. It was probably too late to get Paula back on Food Network, but maybe she could win back some fans and stem the perception that she was an irredeemable racist.

Well-coached and rested, but emotional, when she finally made her *Today* appearance on Wednesday morning, Paula sat for an thirteen-minute interview, a long segment for morning TV. Matt asked whether her apology was cynical, whether all she really wanted to do was protect her business interests. Paula said she did not want fans to boycott Food Network.

At the end of her *Today* interview, she looked at the camera tearfully and said no one was perfect: "If you have no sin, please pick up that stone and throw it so hard at my head that it kills me."

By the end of the interview, judging by chatter online and among food media people, there was a predictable split between those who thought she'd done a good job and those who thought she seemed to be desperately protecting her business empire, but there was a lot of agreement on the fact that it probably didn't matter either way. On NBC's Facebook page, 82 percent of people said the interview did not change their mind about Deen. Some of her other sponsors dropped her. The next day, Reverend Jesse Jackson announced he was helping her, likely a connection made by Judy Smith. "She should be reclaimed rather than destroyed," he told the Associated Press.

Paula might be back on TV somewhere or she might not. She might keep a few endorsement deals or, at sixty-six, just retreat to being the

well-to-do and sunny host of a Southern home-style restaurant in Savannah who had a dozen years of amazing adventures. What was clear
was that her moment as a key star on an explosively growing food network had ended. Both Paula and the network, if they had it in them,
were going to have to reinvent themselves if they wanted to rise
again.

It had certainly been a challenge for
Food Network. But they had had them
before, and they would have them again.
Reinventing themselves was something
they'd been doing ever since they began.
No matter who came or went, which
shows rose or fell, there was always something they could count on: Even as it faces
these challenges at the start of its third
decade, Food Network, ever-changing,

> "I'm sick that I never had the pleasure of meeting Julia Child. Because I think our style of cooking's a lot alike. She didn't hold back on the seasoning, she didn't apologize for the butter. She didn't apologize for the cream. She did not apologize."
>
> —PAULA DEEN

more profitable than ever, remains a source of pleasure to millions of
viewers who consider its stars members of their extended families. The
outside world can be rough, but the best of them are always there, serving something or lovingly teaching us how to serve.

I think that's why we tune in and will continue to do so in one medium or another: someone we feel comfortable with is in the kitchen
making something good, and it will be ready soon, soon, soon. The
cook can be a drill sergeant in a diner, a samurai warrior in silks, or a
mom who moved to a working ranch to find herself. We all need a little
warmth, and we all have our preferences among those from whom we
will accept it.

In the middle of 2012, Bob Tuschman went into the hospital for
minor surgery. He was in his room resting when Ina came to visit him.
She had brought him a cashmere blanket.

"It's always freezing in the hospital," she told him, "And you need something warm and soft."

She had not planned to stay, but Bob seemed fragile and alone.

"I'm going to sit by your bedside all day," she said, sinking into a chair and taking out her laptop to show she could busy herself. "Because you need someone to be there with you."

EPILOGUE

June 2013

I met Joe Langhan for lunch in New York City. He was visiting the city to meet with investors about a start-up he was leading called Media Program Network. The idea was to provide newspaper websites with lifestyle videos such as cooking segments. Newspapers got the videos for free and shared video advertising revenues with Joe's company.

Over Dan Dan Noodles with Minced Pork Chili Vinaigrette, Joe recalled that when he first started working in cable TV in the 1970s, his friends had ridiculed him.

"Joe," they snickered, "TV is free. Why would anyone pay for it?"

Joe had kept silent, admitting to himself, "I don't know."

A plate of sautéed spinach with garlic arrived. I had chosen the restaurant, a Szechuan place near Rockefeller Center.

As to his new business, Joe said it was still unclear how companies like his making on-demand videos would actually make money. "You start the thing and you adapt as you go," he said. That was how it was with Food Network. How it will evolve you can't say at the start. Aboard his company were a founder of Thomson Financial, a former RCN executive, and experienced video producers.

"Start-ups are fun," he added, "but really only if you succeed. It's not as much fun if you fail."

Apparently, though, so far, so good. The investors he'd met with at an office building in Midtown were glad to hear how things were going. He had more than six hundred videos up so far.

Before Joe left to start his trip home to Gloucester, Massachusetts, I asked him if he still ate a lot of pizza.

He did. A good thing had happened over the last two decades, he said. "It's not as hard as it used to be to find good pizza."

ACKNOWLEDGMENTS

It wasn't easy to resist food metaphors while writing this book! Events really did seem to come to a boil, situations required more seasoning, attitudes could be vinegary, and some hosts did not know their chèvre from their chinola. But the book came together thanks to an array of people who could be (but won't be, except this once) compared to dedicated sous chefs, maître d's, managers, investors, and everyone else it takes to make a restaurant run, including you, the customer, to whom I am grateful most of all. Thank you for buying, borrowing, or receiving this book and reading it. I and the following people worked hard on it and we are grateful for your patronage and hope you come back again. Deep gratitude to everyone who lent a hand:

My literary agent, Eric Lupfer, believed in and devotedly shepherded the book from its earliest stages. Original acquiring editor Marysue Rucci was a soothing voice of support and wisdom until she departed for a deserved promotion at another fine publishing house. Neil Nyren, the head wizard who inherited the book at G. P. Putnam's Sons, used a Coolidgeian efficiency and prestidigitation to bringing this baby home, along with associate editor Sara Minnich. Also top-notch at Putnam were president Ivan Held, Alexis Welby and Katie Grinch in publicity, and Kate Stark, Lydia Hirt, Chris Nelson, and all of the other great people in marketing and promotion.

Absolutely key was the brilliant crunch-time editing of Ruth Fecych— "examine the crystal."

I heartily recommend the services of Victoria C. Rowan, whose company Ideasmyth helped me and can help you give flesh to whatever creative idea you are carrying—basically can help you make your dream come true.

Marshall Poe, founder of the New Books Network, decorated scholar and so-so guitar player, heroically stepped in to help with a breakneck monthlong mission in late 2012 to help funnel the mass of raw material into manageable form.

I have employed a bevy of talented research assistants, none more dogged and long-lasting than Alex Carp. He transcribed many interviews from the start of the three-year process, remembered many things I didn't, and fact-checked as we went to publication. Also in this corner were Jamie Feldmar, a passionate and fun-to-read food writer in her own right; Andrea Feckzo, Casey Glynn; and, helping with photo rights and other art matters, Chloe Saint Etienne.

Some of those who read parts small and large, rough and smooth, and offered wisdom include the always effervescent Carolynn Carreno, Liz Rosenthal, Cassie Slane, Deborah Goldstein, Lara Pascali, Tracy Morgan, Sabrina Rotondi, Lara Rabinovich, whose scholarship on the history of pastrami is important work, Nora Isaacs, Jay Dixit, Carole Rowley, and Kathleen Collins, whose *Watching What We Eat: The Evolution of Television Cooking Shows* was a valuable resource, as was her encouragement.

Guidance with the book business came from Craig Young, Geoffrey Gray, Alyssa Shelasky, Susan Shapiro, Devan Sipher, David Feige, Jennifer Joel, and Laurel Touby.

The food and food media business is the friendliest business I have ever been a part of (beats selling rubber duckies and picking tomatoes!), probably because it involves so many eating and drinking pleasures in so many beautiful places. I am very fortunate that among those who offered counsel were Dana Cowin and Christina Grdovic of *Food & Wine*, Nilou Mohamed and Laura Begley of *Travel & Leisure*, "Restaurant Girl" Danyelle Freeman, Lockhart Steele, Ben Leventhal and Amanda Kludt of *Eater*, Diane Peterson of the *Press Democrat*, Elizabeth Minchilli and Katie Parla, Gabrielle Hamilton, Jordana Rothman, Josh Ozersky, Gail Simmons, Kat Odell, Susan Spungen, Caryl Chinn, Sarah Rosenberg, Rachel Wharton, Laren Spirer, Megan Murphy, Hedy Goldsmith, Heidi Ladell, and Dana Polan.

On the public relations side of that business are a group of unusually passionate people who helped set up interviews with their clients and shared meals and their years of perspective: Steve Haweeli, Philip Baltz, Kimberly Yorio, Sarah Abell, Jennifer Beck Baum, Jennifer Russo, Charlie Dougiello, Caroline Bubnis, Lois Najarian O'Neill, Becca Parrish, Helen Medvedovsky, Lauren Fonda, Alexis Altschuler, Jackie Sayet, Liz Errico, Jamie Siskin, Meghan Sherrill, Jay Strell, Melissa Sgaglione, Jesse Gerstein, Rebecca Brooks, Erika Martineau, Stephanie Jones, Vanessa Curtis, Jee Won Park, Rebecca Carlisle, Georgette Farkas, Karine Bakhoum, Stephen Hall, Sam Firer, Nora Lawlor, Allison Lane Simpson, Tom Fuller, Laura Millet, Ilana Alperstein, Susan Magrino, Paige Green, Lori Lefevre, Lauren Nowell, Diane Stefani, Juliette Daviron, Agatha Capacchione, Erika Pope, Pamela

Lewy, and especially Robin Insley, whose persistence in convincing me to meet Lee Schrager for the first time started me on the path leading to this book.

From the agenting world, Scott Feldman, Lisa Shotland, and Jonathan Russo helped with access to their clients and knowledge of who really does what. Those who offered me outlets to file stories while I researched this book include the editors of the now-defunct *Slashfood*: Colleen Curtis, Cheryl Brown, Sarah De Heer, and Michelle Boland; *Food Republic*'s Marcus Samuelsson, Richard Martin, and Matt Rodbard; *The Daily Meal*'s Colman Andrews; *Saveur*'s Helen Rosner; and the *New York and East End Edibles*' Brian Halweil and Gabrielle Langholtz.

At *The New York Times*, the storytelling wisdom of two editors who are now writers there was essential at early moments in this project, Trip Gabriel and Pete Wells, as was the moral support of my colleague Stephanie Rosenbloom, the photo-world acumen of Tiina Loite, food-world tips from Kim Severson, the cookies of Andrew Adam Newman, and a wise opinion from the esteemed James Stewart.

There are many at Food Network to thank—everyone, really, including those you read about here, interview subjects, and every person who has given their passion, their good years, and their sweat to producing content beloved the world over. They made you care enough to want to buy this book. Thank you all. Let me double down on the media and marketing department staff I bothered sometimes incessantly, where work (or worked) the dependable and professional Irika Slavin, Carrie Welch, Lauren Mueller, Erika Villalba, and Katie Ilch. The parent company, Scripps Networks Interactive, has in the director of its corporate communications group, Cindy McConkey, a true believer, whose memory and knowledge of "fruitlore" runs admirably deep.

There are many who are not named here because they requested anonymity, or because they are included in the narrative of the book. Thank you to everyone who gave me an interview and those who declined with class. Many of those interviewed sent photos, documents, memorabilia, videotapes, menus, hard hats, and other delightful detritus.

Locations to thank: The Bean cafés in New York City are some of the best creative business incubators I know: many power outlets, fairly priced drinks, solid Wi-Fi, and they let you sit at a table for fifteen hours straight without ever saying a word to roust you. Mark Hernandez, owner of Berkli Parc Cafe on the Lower East Side, is similarly friendly to those who need a nice place to work and a good salad. The staff of the Amagansett Public Library were cool on hot summer days, and Jack Mazzola of Jack's Stir Brew Coffee across the road sold stuff that warmed the winter. Back in NYC, the bar at the Roger Smith Hotel provided shelter during the "Superstorm," when everything downtown was blacked out.

Sheryl Hastalis kept my downward-facing dog downward and my smile upward, as did yoga teachers Jolie Parcher, Emily Liss, Leigh Anne Eberle, Jennifer Frasher, Leah Kinney, Marissa McNaughton, Kate Lalita Rabbinowitz, Kate Rossano, Jonathan Shoemaker, Emily Weitz at Mandala Yoga in Amagansett; Elena Brower, Allison Terracio, Dana Covello, Kevin Lamb, Laura Juell, and Susanna Harwood Rubin at Virayoga in Manhattan; and Alessandro Crocco at L'Albero e la Mano in Rome.

Ears and muse aided by provocations of Miles Davis and Adam Carolla. Curly inspiration by Lorraine Massey.

Kiri Tannenbaum's friendship and her knowledge of all levels of the food industry, along with her feedback on drafts of the book, were a constant and crucial morale boost. Friends who fed me when I was very hungry include Julyne Derrick, Gersh Kuntzman, Lisa Arbetter, Becky Wisdom, and Andy Erdman.

I am grateful for the hospitality of Jill Fink and Art Hohmann, Jessica Cunningham, Eric Payne, Cecilia Raffo, Dave Aquilina, and Lauren Burnham.

Meals, frustrations, and people to both grieve and celebrate with: Tamara Holt, Jonathan Bloom, Maria Damon, Joshua Neuman, Dustin Goodwin, Bill Hochhaus, Kris Pathirana, Steve Sherr, Francesco Isolani, Rachael Horovitz, Lauralee Kelly, Shay "Sheera" Lipshitz, Chris Bryson, Adam Park, and Glenn Goldstein.

My mother, Toby Salkin, gave endless encouragement and belief. My brother Doug, sister-in-law Jenny, nieces Alexandra and Lilly, and nephew Max kept me smiling, sane, and full of pumpkin pie.

My father, Jay Salkin, to whom this book is dedicated, passed away unexpectedly days after I handed in the manuscript. He had read a few excerpts, and I dearly wish he were still around to hold the book you are holding. He was a foodie before there was such a word. There wasn't great cooking in my childhood home, but there was serious exploring—BBQ ribs bought through bulletproof windows, Chinese food you'd drive hours for, seafood in the salt air. . . . Oh, how I wish I could have one more meal with him anywhere.

INDEX